PAGEMAKER FOR THE MACINTOSH

ROB KRUMM

ADVANCED COMPUTER BOOKS

MIS: PRESS

MANAGEMENT INFORMATION SOURCE, INC.

COPYRIGHT

Copyright © 1989 by Management Information Source, Inc.
P.O. Box 5277
Portland, Oregon 97208-5277
(503) 282-5215

First Printing

ISBN 0-943518-96-2

Library of Congress Catalog Card Number: 88-12945

All rights reserved. Reproduction or use, without express permission, of editorial or pictorial content, in any manner, is prohibited. No patent liability is assumed with respect to the use of the information contained herein. While every precaution has been taken in the preparation of this book, neither the publisher nor the author assumes responsibility for errors or omissions. Neither is any liability assumed for damage resulting from the use of the information contained herein.

PageMaker is a trademark of Aldus Corporation
Word and Excel are trademarks of the Microsoft Corporation
PostScript is a trademark of Adobe Corporation
Bitstream is a trademark of Bitstream Corporation
WordPerfect is a trademark of WordPerfect Corporation
Macintosh, MacPaint, and MacDraw are trademarks of Apple Computer

DEDICATION

To Morgan and Carolyn — they say the first year is the hardest. Lighten up!

ACKNOWLEDGMENTS

I would like to thank Qume Corporation for the use of their CrystalPrint Publisher Laser Printer in the preparation of this book.

The text of this book was written with Microsoft Word word processing software. All of the screens and illustrations in this book were printed with PageMaker 3.0, using the Qume CrystalPrint Publisher Laser Printer. Screen annotations were made using Superpaint from Silicon Beach Software.

The programs were run on a Macintosh SE computer under MultiFinder.

TABLE OF CONTENTS

Introduction v
   Conventions Used in This Book vi
      Key Notations vii
      Mouse Operations viii
   Special Notes on Word Processors viii
   Educational Video ix

Chapter 1: Basic Document Creation 1
   Creating a New Document 3
   Changing the Display Mode, or View 7
      Scrolling with the Mouse 12
      Showing the Entire Work Area 13
   Entering Text 14
      The Toolbox 16
   Applying Text Attributes 19
      Keyboard Selection 20
   Changing Alignment 27
   Adding Text to the Same Block 29
   Adding Special Symbols 31
      Bullets 33
   Cutting and Pasting Text 36
   Entering Paragraph Text 37
   Positioning a Block of Text 39
   Printing the Document 42
      ImageWriter Dialog Boxes 43
      Laser Printer Dialog Boxes 45
   Saving the Document 47
   Summary 49
      Answers to Exercises 51

Chapter 2: Multiple Text Blocks 53
   Text Blocks as Objects 54
   Creating the Document 55
      A Letterhead 55
      The Type Specifications Command 57
      Paragraph Attribute Menu 60
      Adding Another Text Block 62
         Kerning 64
      Positioning Text Blocks 66
      Copying Text into Blocks 68
   Adding More Text Blocks 72

    Text Blocks with Tabs 74
        Moving Tab Stops 80
        Deleting a Tab Stop 81
        Positioning the Table 83
    Adding Ruling Lines 84
    Adding Graphics 88
        Modifying a Graphic 89
        Multiple Graphic Objects 92
        Shaded Graphic Objects 95
        Drop Shadows 99
    Summary 103

Chapter 3: Styling Large Text Blocks 107
    Preparing the Document 108
    Placing Text into a Document 110
    Formatting with Styles 117
        Applying a Built-in Style 121
        Customized Style Settings 124
        Creating a New Style 126
        Editing an Existing Style 128
        Removing Styles 131
        Applying Styles 134
        Changes Based on Styles 135
        Indents 139
        Bullets 141
            Applying a Style to a Multiple-Line Selection 142
            First-Line Exceptions 143
    Ending a Page 145
    Continuing a Story 149
    Hanging Indents 152
    Styles with Tabs 155
    Numbering Pages 159
    Repeating Text 163
    Printing Thumbnails 165
    Summary 170

Chapter 4: Working with Columns 173
    Master Column Guides 174
    Copying Styles 177
    Automatic Text Flow 180
    Semi-Automatic Text Flow 183
    Temporary Automatic Text Placement 186
    Formatting the Text in Columns 186

Hyphenation Options...189
Spreading Text Across Columns...196
    Moving Multiple Text Blocks...197
    Moving a Multiple Selection..199
    Adding a Text Block to a Story...200
    Reshaping the Columns...203
Interrupting a Story..205
Big First Letters..213
Summary...221

Chapter 5: Newsletters...**223**
Text Documents and Styles...224
    Text with Style Symbols..225
    Adding Styles to a Text Document...229
The Column Layout...231
    Overriding the Unit of Measurement..233
Setting the Ruler..235
    Ruler Snap..237
        Choosing Different Ruler Units..238
Custom Guides...240
Creating a Masthead..243
Creating a Template..251
Placing the First Article...252
    Setting Styles...254
Placing a Second Article..259
Placing a Third Article..262
    Stretching a Title...262
Adding a New Page...265
Continuing a Story on Another Page..266
    A "Continued From" Style...268
    Continuing Another Article..271
Placing and Formatting a Sidebar..275
    Adjusting the Guides..279
Placing the Remaining Text...281
    Moving Text Blocks..284
    Removing Pages..291
        Compressing a File..292
Summary..293

Chapter 6: Adding Graphics to a Document...................................**295**
Image Basics...298
    Creating a Paint-type Image..198
    Sizing the Image..303

   Using Guides to Size a Picture 306
    Cropping 309
  Image Control 313
   Screened Images 318
   TIFF Images 323
  Combining Text and Images 330
   A Repeating Graphic 330
    Copying a Graphic 332
   Suppressing Master Page Items 334
   Displaying the Clipboard 334
   Flowing Text Around a Graphic 337
    Flow Around Master Page Items 343
   Spreading a Graphic Across Pages 345
   Framing a Graphic 347
  Text Flow Around Irregular Shapes 349
   Manual Adjustment of Graphic Frame 352
    Adding More Buttons 354
  Summary 358

Chapter 7: Spreadsheets and Charts **361**
   Converting a Spreadsheet to Text 362
   Charts 364
   Importing Spreadsheet Text 366
   Placing a Chart in a Document 370
   Summary 372

Appendix A: Additional Printing Options **373**
 Scaling 374
 Substitute Fonts 374
 PostScript Print Options 376
  PostScript Printer Files 377
 Preparing Files for Photo Typesetting 377
 Encapsulated PostScript (EPS) Graphics 378

Appendix B: Notes for Microsoft Word Version 4 Users **381**

Index **385**

The purpose of this book is simple and straightforward — to teach the reader how to prepare documents using PageMaker 3.0 on the Macintosh computer. The book is designed to be a detailed educational experience that allows readers to learn by working through a series of PageMaker projects on their own computer.

The projects are arranged in a logical educational sequence, which means that the book begins with the most fundamental PageMaker operations and concepts and builds upon each project in succeeding chapters.

Introduction

There are two primary advantages to the way this book is written.

- **Detail**. Every keyboard or mouse operation that is required to complete the projects is included in this book. In addition, the book contains over 200 screen illustrations that show how the document progresses through each stage of a particular operation. This type of detail is in contrast to manuals or books that simply discuss a feature or operation in general terms.

- **Context**. Every operation and technique discussed in this book takes place within the context of a specific example. This is a major advantage when you are trying to master a software application. It is not enough to know how isolated commands are supposed to work. Program mastery depends upon seeing how all of the elements work together to achieve the final result.

As you work through the projects in this book, you will learn more than how to use the commands in PageMaker. You will also learn the concepts that bind together all of the operations. It is these concepts that are the key to effectively using PageMaker.

While tips are valuable, it is important to remember that tips have no meaning unless you already understand the broader concepts on which an application is based.

It is my hope that you will find this book helpful to you in getting the most out of your PageMaker program and your Macintosh computer.

CONVENTIONS USED IN THIS BOOK

If you are an experienced Macintosh user, you already know the conventions of mouse and keyboard use. In this book, the following typographic conventions are used in referring to specific key and mouse operations.

Key Notations

The names of special keys are enclosed in square brackets. Following are a few examples:

[Return]

indicates that you should press the Return key.

list [Return]

or

**list
[Return]**

indicates that you should type in the word "list" and then press the Return key.

Parenthetical information to the right of commands is only for the reader's clarification and should not be entered. For example,

[Return] (3 times)

indicates that you should press the Return key three times.

You should also note that the Macintosh keyboard includes a key called the **Command** key. This key is not labeled "Command"; it is labeled with apple and cloverleaf symbols. This key appears as

[Command]

in this book.

PageMaker and most other Macintosh applications either require or allow the use of key combinations. PageMaker key combination shortcuts will be expressed as follows:

[Command + Shift + 7]

This notation represents holding down the Command and Shift keys and simultaneously pressing the number 7. Note that unless it is stated otherwise, the numbers you press will be those on the top row of your keyboard. Parenthetical notations will be made if you are to use the numeric keypad, as in the following:

3 (numeric keypad)

Mouse Operations

The following terms represent standard mouse operations:

- **Point** refers to moving the mouse so that the mouse pointer is positioned on a specific word, paragraph, or other item.

- **Drag** refers to moving the mouse while holding down the mouse button.

- **Click** refers to pressing the mouse button.

- **Double Click** refers to clicking the mouse button twice in rapid succession.

- **Scroll** usually refers to adjusting a menu listing or document display by clicking on a directional scroll bar arrow.

Instructions to perform mouse operations will appear as follows:

Point at Size
Drag to 36
Click on Bold
Click on OK

Introduction

SPECIAL NOTES ON WORD PROCESSORS

The Word processor assumed for the examples in this book is Word 3.01; however, other word processors, such as Full Write, Write Now, and WordPerfect for the Macintosh, can also be used to prepare the text for the example documents.

If you are using the latest release of Microsoft Word (i.e., version 4), see Appendix B for details on how to save your documents so they can be loaded by PageMaker.

EDUCATIONAL VIDEO

A 1.5 hour video based on the contents of this book is available from Rob Krumm Publications, 4830 Milano Way, Martinez, CA 94553 for $49.95 plus handling. Orders can be faxed to 415-372-5727.

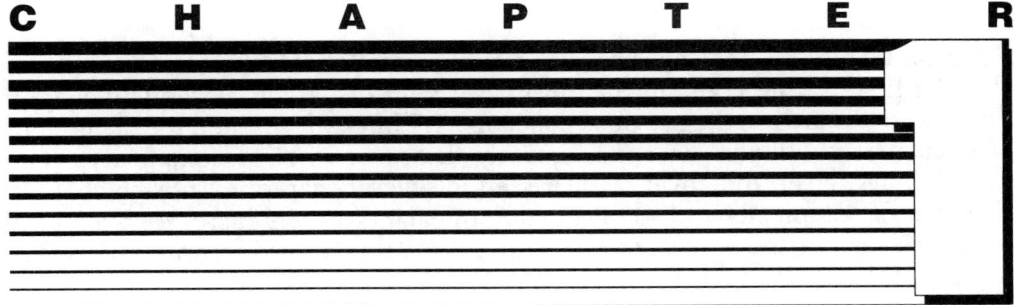

BASIC DOCUMENT CREATION

The purpose of this book is simple and straightforward—to teach the reader how to prepare documents using PageMaker 3.0 on the Macintosh computer. The book is designed to be a detailed educational experience that allows readers to learn by working through a series of PageMaker projects on their own computer.

The projects are arranged in a logical educational sequence, which means that the book begins with the most fundamental PageMaker operations and concepts and builds upon each project in succeeding chapters.

1 Basic Document Creation

The chapters in this book are organized in an **educational hierarchy**. This means that the first chapter contains the most basic concepts. Each subsequent chapter builds and expands on the previous concepts. Within each chapter, the documents created use techniques on approximately the same level of complexity. This means that a given topic will be discussed in several chapters. In each chapter, the level of complexity and sophistication of each topic will increase in a logical sequence. This is the best way to learn to use and understand an application such as PageMaker.

This type of organization is in contrast to a book that is in **topic sequence**. A topic oriented book will discuss all of the aspects of a given topic (e.g., graphics) in a single chapter. A topic organization sequence is better for reference after you have mastered the concepts of an application. To help referencing, a detailed index is provided at the end of this book.

Figure 1.1 shows the PageMaker logo that should appear when the program is loaded.

Figure 1.1   *PageMaker logo displayed when program is loaded.*

Basic Document Creation **1**

CREATING A NEW DOCUMENT

The first step in creating a document in PageMaker is to fill out the **Page setup** dialog box that defines the basic parameters of the document you want to create. This dialog box is displayed when you select the New command from the File menu.

> **Point** at File
> **Drag** to New

PageMaker displays the Page setup dialog box.

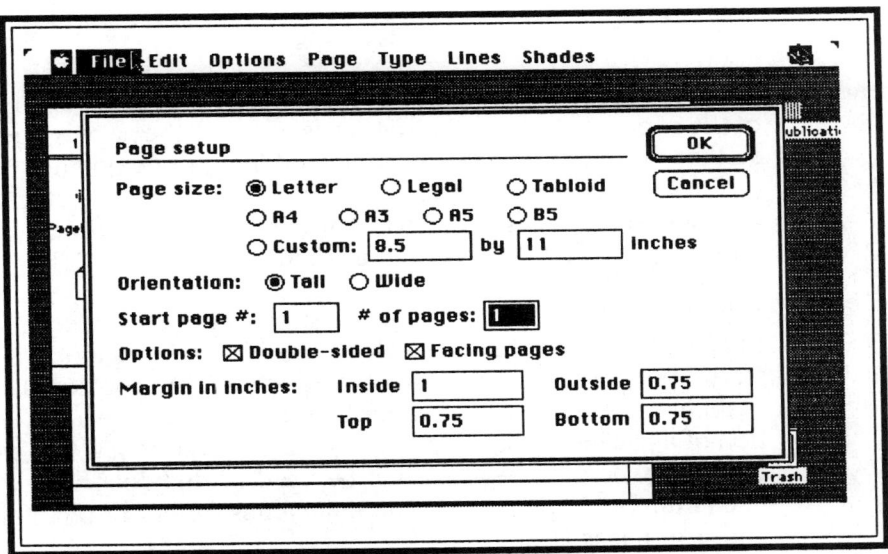

Figure 1.2   Page setup dialog box for new document.

3

1 Basic Document Creation

The menu consists of five sections:

Page size This option is used to select the size of the page you intend to print the information on. The size of the paper is displayed in the two boxes, width by length, in terms of inches. You can enter increments as small as .001".

You can select from seven pre-set standard paper sizes: **Letter** (8.5 × 11), **Legal** (8.5 × 14), **Tabloid** (11 × 17), **A4** (8.268 × 11.693), **A3** (11.693 × 16.535), **A5** (5.827 × 8.268), and **B5** (6.929 × 9.842). You also have the option of selecting **Custom** and entering your own width and length values.

The default setting is letter size paper.

Orientation Orientation refers to the relative position of the width and length of the paper. When the **Tall** setting is selected, the page is oriented so that the longest side is vertical. If **Wide** is selected, the page is oriented so that the longest side is horizontal. (Tall is referred to in other applications as "portrait" orientation, while Wide is called "landscape.") The default setting is Tall.

Start page # With this option you can enter the starting page number and the total number of pages that will be used in your document. The starting page number will usually be page #1, but you could enter a value other than 1 if you wanted this document to be a continuation of a previous document. The # of pages setting refers to the total number of pages that will be used in this document. The maximum is 128 pages. The default values for both **Start page #** and **# of pages** is 1.

Options The section contains two options. **Double-sided** documents make a distinction between left and right pages. This distinction is useful when your document will contain more than one page and the pages will eventually be reproduced by printing on both sides of the paper, as in books and magazines. The Double-sided option allows different settings for margins, page headers, footers, etc. for the left and right pages. If this option is not used, all pages are treated the same way.

Facing pages describes the way left and right pages are displayed on the screen. When selected, this option displays pages in left/right pairs. This allows you to create a layout that spans across two facing pages. This option is only available if you select Double-sided pages. If you select Double-sided pages but not Facing pages, only one page at a time is displayed for layout.

The default setting is for Double-sided and Facing pages.

Keep in mind that most documents begin with a right page (page 1) that is displayed by itself. The first pair of pages is 2 (left) and 3 (right).

Margin in inches

Margins are areas of blank space from the edge of the paper to the point at which information is placed on the page. All pages should have some sort of margins. The default settings are **Inside** = 1", **Outside** = .75", **Top** = .75" and **Bottom** = .75". Note that the usual terms for margins — "left" and "right" — are not used in Page-Maker because the meaning of left and right will change when you are working with left and right pages. The **inside margin** is the one closest to the binding seam. The inside margin is on the right on a left page and on the left on a right page. The **outside margin** is the one farthest away from the binding. (Note that when you work with laser printers, it is not possible to print to the exact edge of the paper even if you set the margins to zero because the paper-handling mechanism of the laser printer blocks off part of each page edge — about .25" — from printing.)

You might also wonder why PageMaker by default sets the inside margin larger than the others. The extra .25" allocated to the inside margin is assumed to be taken up by the page binding.

All of the settings entered into the Page setup dialog box can be revised after you begin the document through the Page setup command on the File menu; however, you will need to manually adjust the objects (e.g., text blocks and graphics) on the page if you want them to reflect these revised settings (e.g., text blocks won't automatically expand if you decrease the margins or contract if you increase the margins). These topics will be covered as you progress through the book.

1 Basic Document Creation

The first document you will create is a single-page flyer. This means that you can leave all of the settings with their default values, with one exception: the margin settings should be increased so that the page has 1" top margins and 1.25" inside and outside margins. Note that because this is a one-page document, you don't need to add extra space on the inside margin since the page will not be bound.

Create the new margins by entering

[Tab] (3 times)

The Tab key will move you among the entry boxes in the dialog box. However, the movement is not always in the direction you expect, i.e., sometimes it is straight up and down. In this case, the highlight moves up to the page width and length values and then down to the margin settings. Enter the new margin values.

1.25 [Tab]
1 [Tab]
1.25 [Tab]
1

Complete the page by entering

[Return]

PageMaker enters the page layout mode (see Figure 1.3), in which you can create the elements of your document and place them on the page.

The page appears in the center of the screen, reduced so that the entire page is visible.

The page display consists of two boxes. The outer box is the **page outline**, 8.5" by 11". The inner box, composed of a dashed line, shows the area of the page inside the margins. The lines that compose the inner box are called the **guides**. When you are typing text, PageMaker will wrap the lines according to the location of the guides. The guides also remind you of the margin locations you have selected.

Basic Document Creation 1

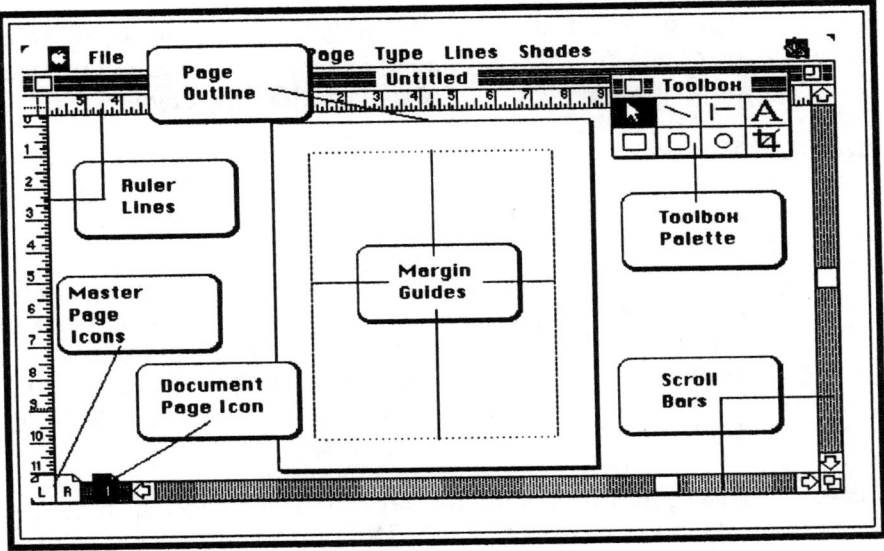

Figure 1.3   *Page layout mode display.*

On the top and left sides of the work area are the **ruler lines**. These lines indicate the actual size of items on the screen. As you move the mouse cursor, on both the horizontal and vertical ruler, dotted lines move to indicate the position of the cursor in terms of inches. Note that the zero point of the ruler lines is the upper left corner.

CHANGING THE DISPLAY MODE, OR VIEW

Because the standard Macintosh screen is smaller than the actual sheet of paper you will be printing on, you need a variety of ways of looking at the page. PageMaker supports five different views:

Actual size   This option causes the document to be displayed at the same size as it will appear on the printed page. The image has a **one-to-one correspondence** with the printed page. In this mode, the standard Macintosh Plus or SE screen will show 6.5" by 3.75" of the page, about 24 square inches of the page surface. If the printed page is 8.5" by 11", this view shows you about a quarter of the page on the screen at one time.

1 Basic Document Creation

75% size   This option displays the page at 75% of the actual size. If you were using an 8.5" by 11" page, this view would show you the entire width of the page and about 1/2 the length of the page.

50% size   This option shows the page at 50% of the actual size. The display area is a window that has a width of 13" and a height of 7.5", so you will see the entire page width and about 2/3 of the page length.

Fit to window   This option shrinks the page so that the entire page can be seen on the display at one time. The amount of reduction used by this option is relative to the size of the page being used and its orientation. (Because of the menu and title bars, the work area window is wider than it is tall. Wide-oriented pages fit into the display window with less wasted space.)

200% size   This option zooms the display so that it is twice as large as it will appear on the printed page. This magnified view reduces the page surface area displayed to 3.25" by 2", i.e., about 7% of the page.

You can change the display mode, or view, in two ways:

Page menu   The **Page** menu lists the view options. You can change the view by selecting one of the five view options just discussed from the menu. If you switch to a mode that magnifies the size of the page, e.g., from Fit to window to Actual, the section of document displayed will be approximately the center of the document.

Mouse   You can also use the mouse to change view modes. Holding down the Command and Option keys while clicking the mouse will toggle PageMaker from the Fit to window view to Actual view or from the Actual view to the Fit to window view. The advantage of the mouse technique is that when you are enlarging the view (e.g., going from Fit to window to Actual view), you can select which portion of the document you want to appear by pointing at that location with the mouse when you enter the **Command + Option + Click** command.

Basic Document Creation **1**

Use the menu method to change the view to Actual.

> **Point** at Page
> **Drag** to Actual size

The screen zooms in to show the page at actual size. While there is no text on the screen, you can see the distance between the guides and edge of the page, which is very close to the actual width of the outside margin, 1.25".

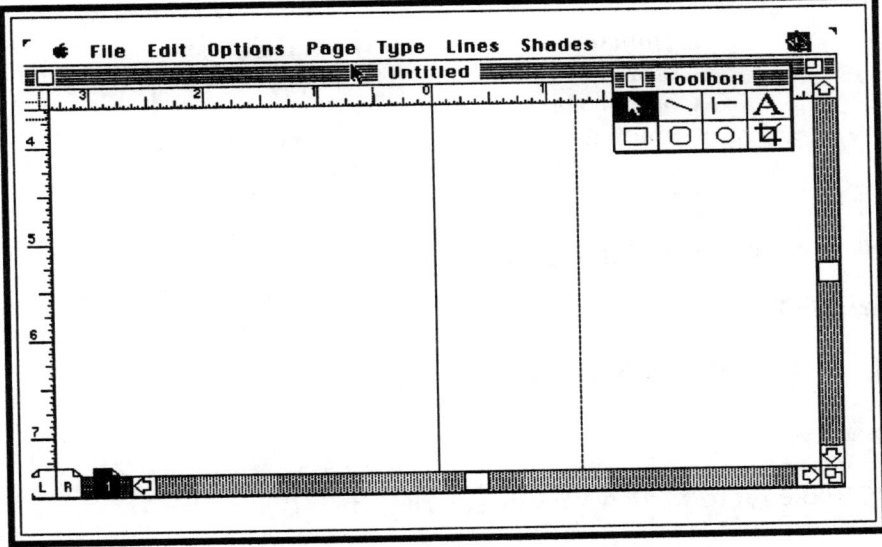

Figure 1.4   Screen displayed at actual size.

Change to the 75% view.

> **Point** at Page
> **Drag** to 75% size

1 Basic Document Creation

The view is reduced to show more of the page. Note that the page is still positioned in the center of the window. Return to the original display mode, Fit to window.

> **Point** at Page
> **Drag** to Fit to window

You can also execute the same commands by using Command key shortcuts.

Key Combination	Result
Command + 1	Actual size
Command + 7	75% size
Command + 5	50% size
Command + w	Fit to window
Command + 2	200% size

Change to Actual view by entering

Command + 1

Change to the 50% view by entering

Command + 5

Return to the Fit to window view by entering

Command + w

As mentioned previously, the advantage of the mouse method of changing views is that you can select which portion of the screen you want to see enlarged. For example, suppose you wanted to enlarge the upper left corner of the document.

> **Point** at the upper left corner of the guides
> **Command + Option + Click**

This time the upper left corner of the document is enlarged.

Basic Document Creation 1

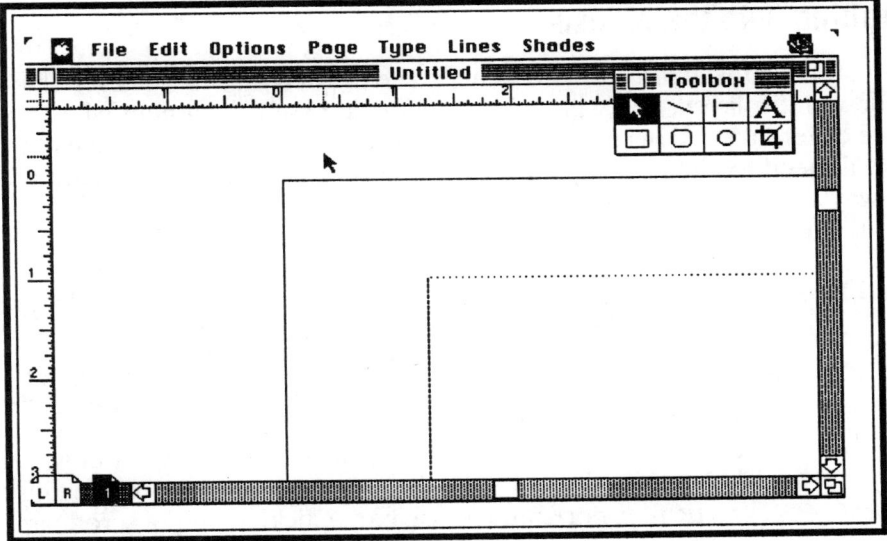

Figure 1.5   Command + Option + Click enlarges specific area.

You can use the same command to return to the Fit to window view. Note that when you move to the reduced view, the position of the cursor is not significant because the entire page will be displayed.

| Command + Option + Click |

Return to the Actual view one more time. Enter

Command + 1

1 Basic Document Creation

Scrolling with the Mouse

On a standard Macintosh SE or Plus screen, when any view larger than Fit to window is displayed, you will need to reposition your document when you want to see different portions of a page. Generally, the larger the view, the more often you will need to change the visible portion of the document. You can do this in two ways:

Scroll Bars You can move the window to another portion of the document by dragging the white box inside the horizontal or vertical scroll bars. This scroll bar works the same way as the bars that appear in the Macintosh operating system and in most other applications. (If you click on the gray area above or below the white scroll box, the display moves in 1/3-of-a-page increments—up or down, right or left, respectively, depending on whether you are clicking on the vertical or horizontal scroll bar. Clicking on the scroll bar arrows moves the display in smaller increments.)

Option + Mouse If you hold down the Option key while you drag the mouse, the display scrolls in the direction in which you drag.

Begin by pointing the mouse approximately in the center of the screen.

> **Option + Drag** upward

As you drag the mouse, the display scrolls upward, revealing more of the document. This method provides more direct control over which part of the screen you scroll to than using the scroll bar and scroll bar boxes does because you can drag the mouse in any direction, including diagonally, while the scroll bars will move in only one direction at a time—vertically or horizontally.

Basic Document Creation 1

Showing the Entire Work Area

The largest page size that can be displayed in PageMaker is 11" by 17". When your page size is smaller than that, PageMaker only reduces the display sufficiently for that size page to be viewed in full when you use the normal Fit to window option (i.e., it won't show the work area that surrounds the page, just the page itself). However, once you are already in the Fit to window view, you can display the entire work area by holding down the Shift key while you select Fit to window from the Page menu. Return to the Fit to window view by entering

Command+w

Display the entire work area.

> **Hold down** Shift
> **Point** at Page
> **Drag** to Fit to window

The page is shown in a reduced view that displays the entire work area. Page-Maker calls the entire work area the **pasteboard**, making an analogy to the way documents are pasted up without computers.

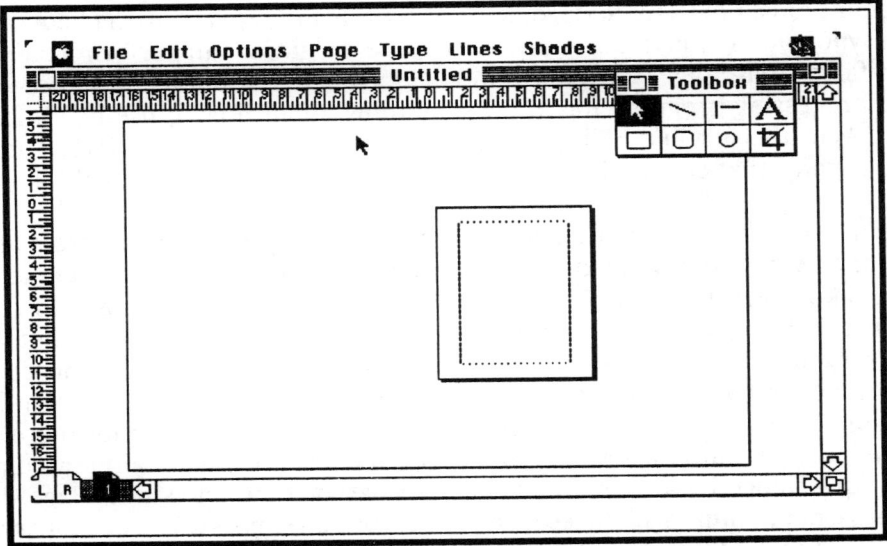

Figure 1.6   *Entire pasteboard work area displayed.*

13

1 Basic Document Creation

Return to the normal Fit to window display by entering

Command + w

ENTERING TEXT

There are two basic ways to place text into a PageMaker document.

Direct entry   Direct entry refers to text that is typed directly onto the Page-Maker page.

Importing   Imported text is text that is prepared in another application such as a word processing program.

If the total amount of text in the document is small, the direct entry method is acceptable. However, if the amount of text is more than a page or two, you should consider initially preparing the document in a word processing program so you can import it later.

The advantage of importing text is that word processing programs have much more powerful text editing features than PageMaker does. Word processing programs have powerful features such as search and replace, spell checkers, and even synonym dictionaries. In addition, these programs can perform text editing tasks faster than PageMaker. To import documents, you must have access to a word processing program and know something about how to use it. Microsoft Word, WordPerfect and Full Write are three popular, full-powered word processing programs that can easily be used to prepare documents for PageMaker.

Keep in mind that the text editing features of a word processing program are the only ones you actually need to learn how to use to prepare a document for PageMaker. Most word processing programs have commands that control line spacing, indents, and tab alignment; however, these features are not really necessary when preparing text for PageMaker. In most cases, you can use PageMaker to handle these types of text formatting. Note, however, that if you are using Microsoft Word style sheets to format complex documents, these styles can be imported into PageMaker along with the text. If you are already comfortable with advanced styling in Word, this can save you time when using PageMaker. If you are not familiar with these techniques, you can simply use Word for creating text and save the formatting for when you import it into PageMaker.

Basic Document Creation **1**

In this chapter's example, you will use the direct entry method. In later chapters, you will use the importing method.

The first step in entering text is to place PageMaker into a display mode in which you can view the text as you enter it. On the standard Macintosh screen, the Fit to window view reduces characters to a size that is not readable. You will need to change to an enlarged mode, in this case the Actual size view, to enter text.

In this example, you will begin entering text inside the upper left corner of the page guides. The exact location is not crucial because PageMaker will allow you to change the position of the text after it has been entered.

The **Command + Option + Click** method discussed in the previous section is the fastest and most direct way to change views and select the section of the screen you want to enlarge in a single operation.

> **Point** at the upper left corner of the guides
> **Command + Option + Click**

The upper left corner of the screen is enlarged and displayed in the center of the work area.

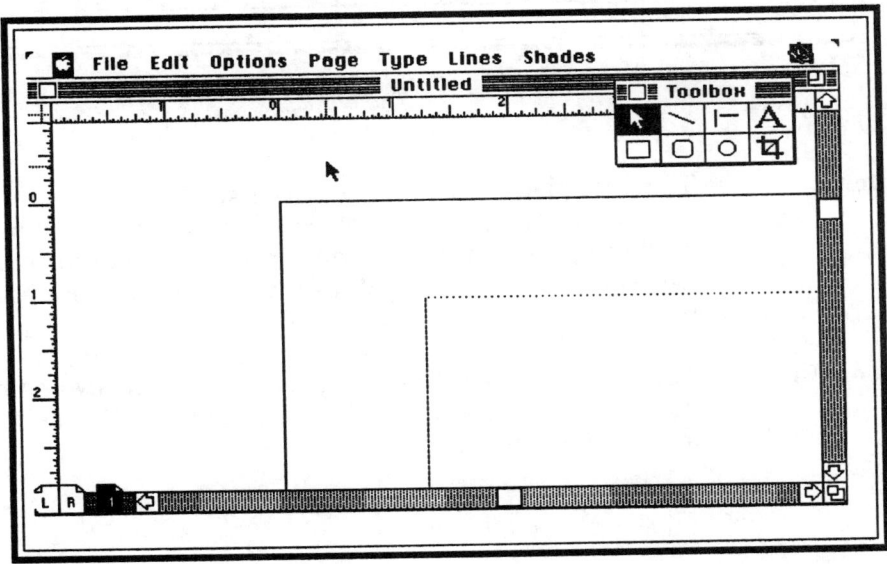

Figure 1.7   *Upper left corner enlarged and centered on screen.*

1 Basic Document Creation

The Toolbox

In the upper right corner of the screen is a small window labeled **Toolbox**. The Toolbox is used to help you select the **operational mode** you want to work in. There are eight icons in the window that stand for each of the operational modes used in PageMaker. They are discussed in the order in which they appear on the screen shown in Figure 1.8, from left to right, beginning with the top row.

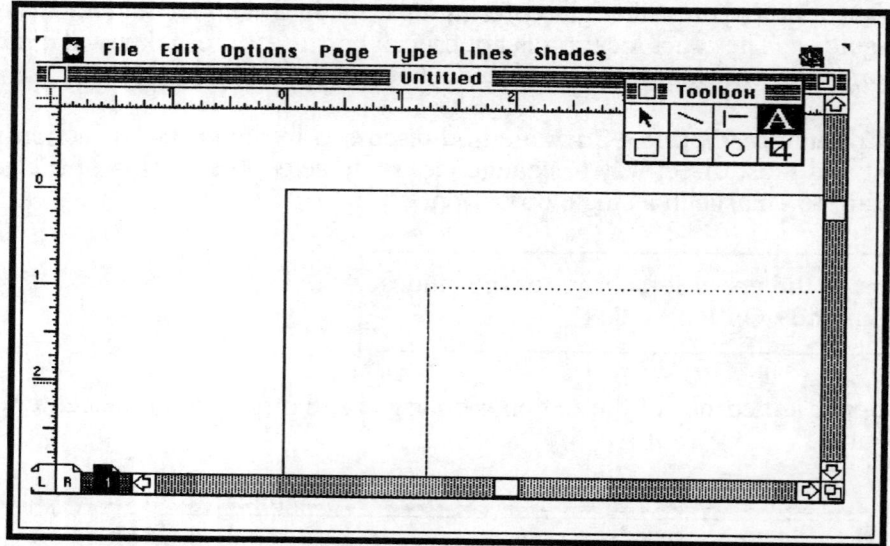

Figure 1.8   *Toolbox icons.*

Pointer   This tool places PageMaker into a **selection** mode in which you can select an object or objects. An **object** is a distinct part of the page that you want to perform some operation on. You will learn more about PageMaker objects as this book progresses.

Diagonal line   This tool allows you to draw lines between any two points on the page. The thickness of the line is controlled by the settings on the Lines menu.

Basic Document Creation 1

Perpendicular line This tool only allows you to draw lines that are parallel or perpendicular to the page edges, which is useful because it is sometimes difficult to move the mouse in an exactly straight line. When you are drawing in this mode, any wavering of the straight line is ignored.

Text When this tool (represented by the lettter "A") is selected, you can enter and edit text.

Rectangle Referred to as the "square-corner tool" in your PageMaker manual, this tool is selected when you want to draw a rectangle on the page. When this mode is active, you can draw a rectangle anywhere on the page by dragging the mouse. The line thickness and fill attributes of the rectangle are determined by the settings on the Lines and Shades menus. Note that the oval and rounded rectangle tools work the same way, except that the object drawn has a different shape.

Rounded rectangle This tool activates the rounded rectangle drawing mode.

Oval This tool activates the oval drawing mode.

Cropping This tool places PageMaker in the graphics cropping mode. **Cropping** is a procedure by which you select a portion of a graphic image to be displayed within a given space.

The default mode is the selection, or pointer, mode. When you want to enter or edit text, you must activate the text mode by selecting the text tool.

> **Point** at the text icon — the letter "A"
> **Click**
> **Point** at the upper left corner of the guides

17

1 Basic Document Creation

Note that when the text mode is activated the **mouse cursor** changes to an **I bar**. The I bar indicates that the text mode is active. To begin text entry, simply point the mouse cursor at the document location in which you want to enter the text, and click. In this case, the cursor should be pointed just inside the upper left corner of the margin guides.

> **Click**

When you click, PageMaker displays a flashing vertical line next to the left margin guide. This flashing line is the **text cursor**. When you are in the text entry mode, you will have both a text cursor and a mouse cursor on the screen. The text cursor will mark the actual location at which each character is entered. Like a cursor in a word processing program, the text cursor will advance as you enter each character.

You can now use the keyboard to enter text. The example you will prepare is a business announcement such as you might see in the *Wall Street Journal*. Enter

AMERICAN NATIONAL PRODUCTS, INC. [Return]
has acquired the assets of the [Return]
International Gear Fitting Products Division [Return]
of [Return]
UNITED MOGUL CORPORATION

The screen will resemble Figure 1.9:

Basic Document Creation **1**

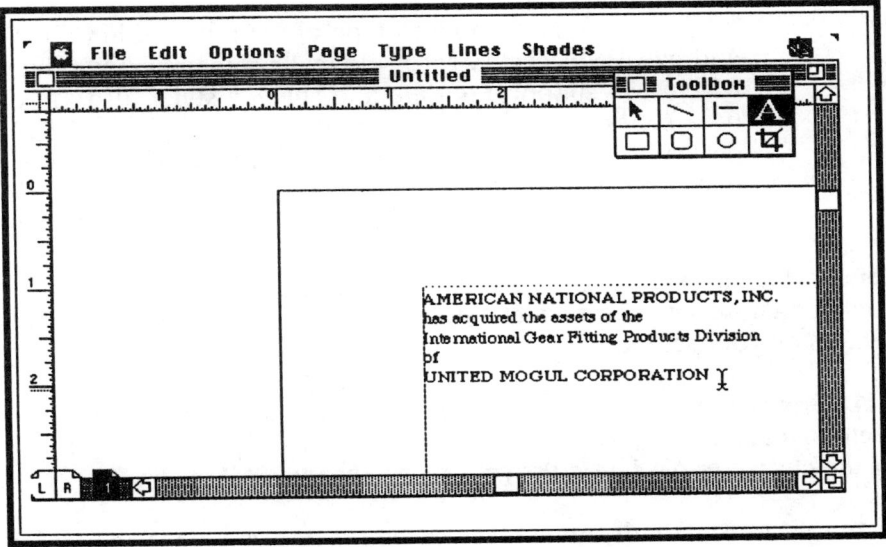

Figure 1.9   Text entered onto page

APPLYING TEXT ATTRIBUTES

One of the operations that you can carry out in the text mode is adding attributes to the text. Text attributes fall into three classifications:

Font "Font" refers to the refinements used in shaping the characters. For example, some types of lettering use lines that are always the same thickness while others use lines of varying thickness. Some fonts use all straight lines while others use curved lines. In PageMaker, the term "fonts" refers to the same concept as the term "typeface" used in the publishing business.

Size "Size" refers to the height of the characters in a given font. Height is measured in terms of **points**. A point is equal to 1/72". A 12-point character would have a height of 12/72" or 1/6". The smaller the point size, the smaller the character. (Note that while the use of the value 1/72 may seem odd today, when printing first developed, the use of numbers like 72 as a base simplified arithmetic because 72 could be evenly divided by many numbers, 2, 4, 6, 8, 9, 12, 18, 24, 36, etc.).

1 Basic Document Creation

Style "Style" refers to a standard type of variation within a given font and size. Typical styles are bold, italic, and underscored text. The Macintosh supports outline and shadow styles also. (Note that type styles are different from paragraph styles, which will be discussed later.) In printing, type styles are sometimes referred to as **weights**.

By default, PageMaker assigns text the Times font in 12-point size and a normal text style. These are the text attributes currently being used to display the characters on your screen.

Text attributes can be assigned to one character or to two or more consecutive characters. In order to change the text attributes of any part of the text, you must **select** the character or characters you want to change.

You can select text with the mouse, the keyboard, or a combination of mouse and keyboard operations. Mouse selection is performed by dragging the mouse cursor over the area of text you want to select.

Keyboard Selection

Suppose you want to change the attributes of the name **UNITED MOGUL CORPORATION**. You must first select the text. You can perform selection from the keyboard by using the arrow keys with the Shift key held down. Enter

Shift + left arrow

The first letter to the left of the current cursor position, **N**, is highlighted. You can increase the selection by one character each time you enter the **Shift + arrow** combination. Enter

Shift + left arrow

Now there are two characters highlighted. You can highlight in larger chunks by adding the Command key to the combination. The **Command + Shift + arrow** combination extends the highlight one full word at a time. Note that the term "word" refers to all of the text until the next space or period. Enter

Command + Shift + left arrow

Basic Document Creation **1**

The highlight now covers the entire word **CORPORATION.** You can move to the beginning of the line by using **Command + Shift + 7**. (The 7 you want is the on the numeric keypad, not the 7 on the top row of the main keyboard.) Enter

Command + Shift + 7 (numeric keypad)

You have now highlighted the phrase you want to change.

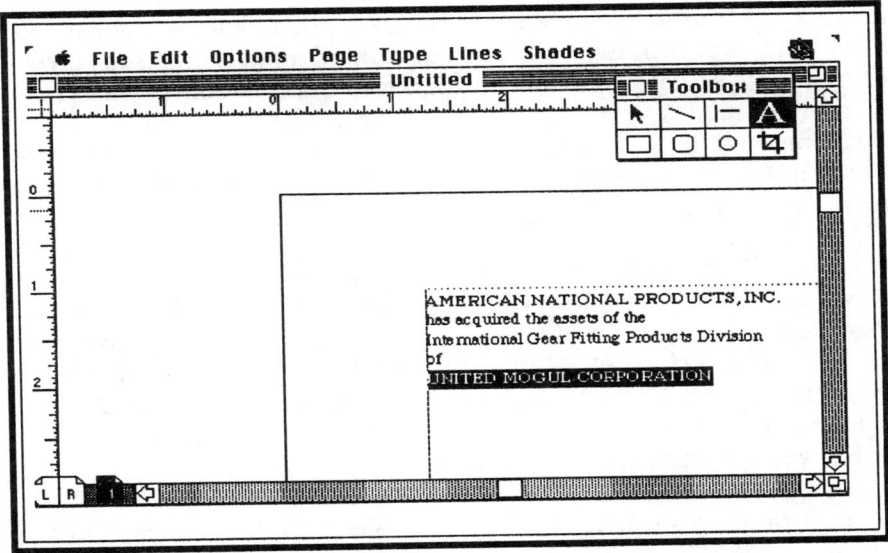

Figure 1.10   *Words selected in text mode.*

You can now select text attribute commands from the menus or use the keyboard shortcuts (where available) for style changes. Change the text to **Geneva** font.

> **Point** at Type
> **Drag** to Font
> **Drag** to Geneva

1 Basic Document Creation

Change the size to 24-point.

> **Point** at Type
> **Drag** to Size
> **Drag** to 24

Note that when you display the point sizes list, some of the numbers are shown in outline text. The outlined numbers indicate point sizes that are customized screen fonts installed as part of the Macintosh system. Other sizes are displayed on the screen by scaling existing point sizes up or down. The customized fonts will appear on the screen exactly as they will on the printer. The scaled fonts do not appear as well formed on the screen as they will appear on the printed page. The scaled fonts have a more "saw-toothed" edge than the custom installed fonts, which have a smooth appearance.

You can install screen fonts by using the **Font/DA Mover** Macintosh Utility program. When you first set up your Macintosh, the system contains a standard set of screen fonts, of which the largest point size is 24 point. Installing larger point sizes using Font/DA Mover reduces the amount of memory left for applications. Generally, if you are using a 1-megabyte Macintosh, 24-point fonts is the practical limit for screen font installation. If you add more memory to your computer, you can install more screen fonts.

Note that scaled fonts will print properly on PostScript-type printers even if the screen fonts appear "saw toothed."

Change the style to **bold**. This can be done by entering a keyboard shortcut. Following are keyboard shortcuts for assigning text attributes:

Key Combination	Result
Command+Shift+space	normal
Command+Shift+b	bold
Command+Shift+i	italic
Command+Shift+u	underline
Command+Shift+/	strike through
Command+Shift+d	outline
Command+Shift+w	shadow

Enter

Command + Shift + b

The text is now Geneva, 24-point, bold.

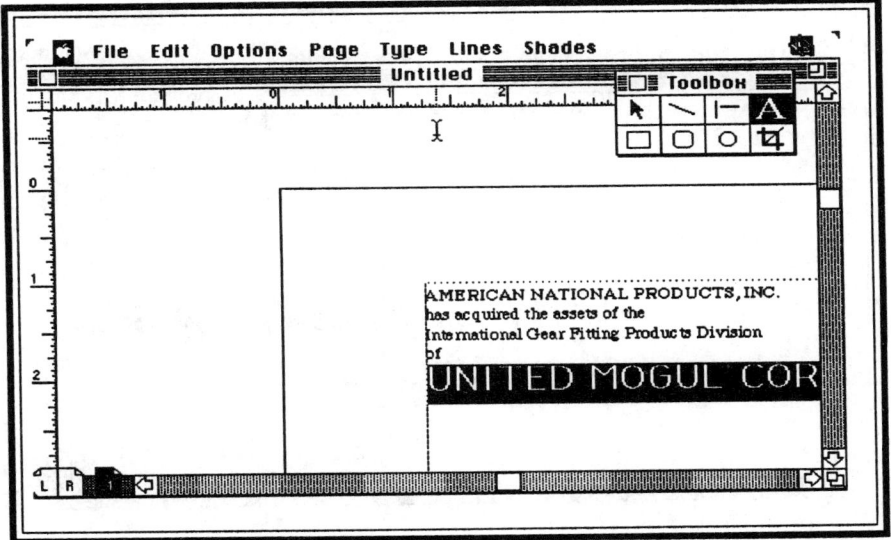

Figure 1.11   Font, size, and style changed to Geneva, 24-point, bold.

The next task will be to change the name **AMERICAN NATIONAL PRODUCTS, INC** to the same font, size, and style. To do this, you need to position the cursor at the beginning of the text by using the mouse or the **Command + 9** keyboard combination. Enter

Command + 9 (numeric keypad)

The cursor is now positioned at the first character in the text. Highlight the text on this line by entering

Command + Shift + 1 (numeric keypad)

1 Basic Document Creation

Exercise 1: Change the text to match the font, size, and style of the other company name. Try this on your own. The correct commands can be found under Ex-1 at the end of this chapter. When the change is completed, the screen will resemble Figure 1.12:

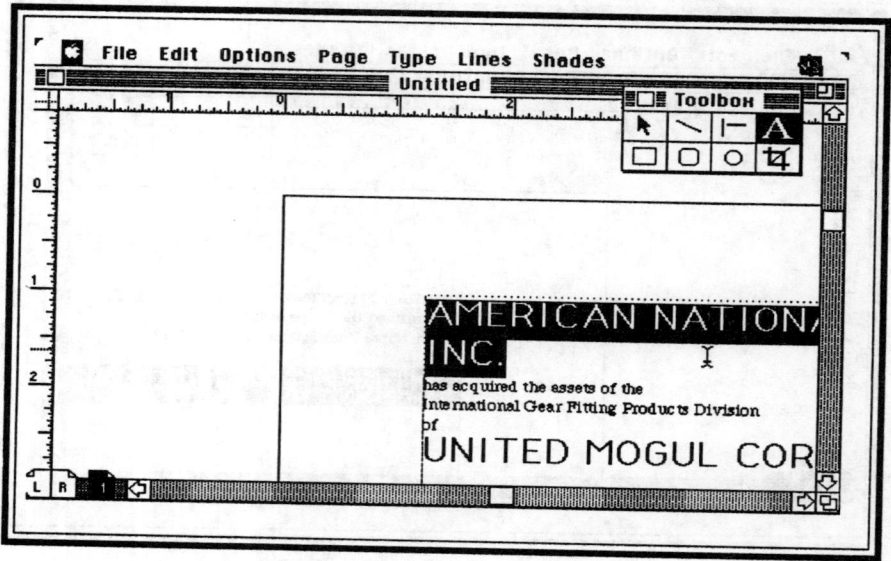

Figure 1.12   Font, size and style changed for first line.

In this case, you will notice that the word INC was placed on a line by itself as a result of the change in the font size. Always keep in mind that when you change the size of the characters the amount of space they take up increases both vertically and horizontally. At 24 points, the text extends to a second line because it is now too wide to fit within the page margins. Like a word processing program, PageMaker wrapped the line so that any text that did not fit on the first line was placed on another line.

However, the current screen view does not show the entire width of the page. Use the right arrow icon on the horizontal scroll bar to scroll the screen horizontally.

Click on the right arrow icon (4 times)

Basic Document Creation **1**

One solution to the problem would be to reduce the point size of the text to 18.

> **Point** at Type
> **Drag** to Size
> **Drag** to 18

The reduced point size now makes it possible for the text to fit on one line. However, this now makes the UNITED MOGUL CORPORATION line look more important than the AMERICAN NATIONAL PRODUCTS, INC. line. To keep the look uniform, you should change AMERICAN NATIONAL PRODUCTS, INC. to match the point size of the current selection. Move to the end of the text by using the **Command+3** keyboard shortcut. Enter

Command+3 (numeric keypad)

Highlight the line of text by entering

Command+Shift+7 (numeric keypad)

>   **Exercise 2:**   Set the size to 18 points. Try this on your own. The correct commands can be found under Ex-2 at the end of this chapter.

Note that when you change the size, PageMaker maintains the other settings for font and style and only changes the size of the characters.

Next, change the point size and style of the line that begins with "International Gear." Position the cursor by entering

up arrow (2 times)

Highlight this line by entering

Command+Shift+1 (numeric keypad)

25

1 Basic Document Creation

This time, change the point size to 14 but leave the font as it is.

> **Point** at Type
> **Drag** to Size
> **Drag** to 14

To make this text stand out, format it with an outline style. Enter

Command + Shift + d

The text should now resemble the text in Figure 1.13:

Figure 1.13   *Text attributes used to vary font, size, and style of characters.*

CHANGING ALIGNMENT

The lines that you entered into the document begin at the left guide. The placement of the text between the margins is called **alignment**. You can change the alignment of a line or group of lines by using the Alignment command on the Type menu. PageMaker uses four types of alignment.

Left The line begins flush with the left margin. Shortcut command: **Command + Shift + L.**

Center The line is centered between the margins. Shortcut command: **Command + Shift + c.**

Right The line is positioned so that the end of the line is flush with the right margin. Shortcut command: **Command + Shift + r.**

Justified This type of alignment adds space between the words on the line so that the left end of the line is flush with the left margin and the right end of the line is flush with the right margin. Because this alignment adds space between words, it is generally used with paragraph-type text that is set in character sizes of 12 points or smaller. If the text is entered in short lines (lines that do not extend all the way across the page) or if the text is larger than 12 points, justified alignment is not recommended. Shortcut command: **Command + Shift + j.**

The current text consists of a series of short lines. This text might look better if it were centered on the page. Center the currently highlighted line by entering

Command + Shift + c

You can change the alignment to right by entering

Command + Shift + r

1 Basic Document Creation

The text is now aligned flush with the right margin of the page. Suppose you wanted to center all of the lines. First select all of the text. PageMaker provides a special command that will automatically select all of the text. The command is the **Select All** command found on the Edit menu. You can also use the keyboard shortcut **Command + a**. Enter

Command + a

All of the text you have entered is now selected. Center all of the text by entering

Command + Shift + c

All of the text is now centered between the margins.

Figure 1.14   Text centered between margins.

ADDING TEXT TO THE SAME BLOCK

The text you have entered into the current document is called a **block** of text. The concept of a text block in PageMaker is different from the concept of a block in a word processing program. In a word processing program the term "block" refers to text that is physically grouped together. In PageMaker "block" refers to a group of text that is logically associated. PageMaker is designed to place sections of the same block of text at different physical locations within a document. PageMaker can also handle several blocks of text within one document. This is the primary difference between a desktop publisher like PageMaker and a word processing program. You will learn how to handle multiple blocks of text later in this book.

When you are adding text to your document, you need to keep in mind whether you want to add text to an existing block or begin a new block. Separate text blocks can be moved independently of each other to different places on the page.

In this document, all five lines of text are part of a single block, which is the simplest way to add text to a PageMaker document. In this case, you want to continue adding text to the same block. To add text anywhere within a block, you simply position the text cursor to the point where you want the text inserted and type the characters you want to insert.

In this example, you want to add the text to the end of the current block. Move to the end of the text block by entering

Command+Shift+3 (numeric keypad)

Add more text to the block by entering

[Return]
[Return]
Agent

PageMaker continues the text attributes of the previous line of text. In this case, that means that the new text will be Geneva, 18-point, bold text, center aligned on the page.

1 Basic Document Creation

That is probably not the style that would be appropriate for this text. Change the text back to the default text attributes — Times, 12-point, normal. Highlight the line of text by entering

Command + Shift + 1 (numeric keypad)

Change the text attributes.

> **Point** at Type
> **Drag** to Font
> **Drag** to Times
> **Point** at Type
> **Drag** to Size
> **Drag** to 12

Change to the normal type style by entering the shortcut key combination:

Command + Shift + space

The text attributes have now been changed back to the default settings. Move to the end of the line and continue entering text:

Command + 1 (numeric keypad)
[space]
for the purchase [Return]
[Return]

PageMaker formats the text you are entering as Times, 12-point, normal text. PageMaker will automatically format text that is inserted with the same text attributes as the surrounding text. In this example, changing the text to Times, 12-point, normal causes all text entered on that line to have the same quality.

Change the text attributes again so that the text line will be Geneva, 14-point, outline text.

> **Point** at Type
> **Drag** to Font
> **Drag** to Geneva
> **Point** at Type
> **Drag** to Size
> **Drag** to 14

Enter the command shortcut for outline text style.

Command + Shift + d

Enter

The First National Bank of Shrewsbury

This time you selected the text attributes before you typed the text. It makes very little difference which you do first because you can change the text attributes as many times as you like.

Note: You might wonder why there are no shortcut key combinations for the fonts and sizes. The exact fonts and sizes of text available are determined by the fonts added to the Macintosh system fonts list. This means that different users will have different lists of fonts and sizes, so it is not possible for PageMaker to build in shortcut keys for specific fonts and sizes; however, PageMaker does provide a facility called **user-defined styles** that can help you switch between sets of text attributes without having to define each section manually.

ADDING SPECIAL SYMBOLS

In addition to the characters that you can enter from the keyboard, PageMaker permits you to insert some frequently used typographical characters and symbols by using special command keys. Figure 1.15 shows the special characters that can be added by using characters combined with the Option and Shift keys. Note that in this case, the numbers shown refer to the numbers on the top row of the main keyboard, not the numbers on the numeric keypad.

1 Basic Document Creation

"	Option+[	®	Option+r	§	Option+6
»	Option+Shift+[	©	Option+g	¶	Option+7
'	Option+]	TM	Option+2		
'	Option+Shift+]				
•	Option+8				

Figure 1.15   Keyboard commands for special characters.

For example, suppose that you wanted to enter a trademark symbol next to the name that you have just typed. Enter

Option+2

The trademark symbol is inserted into the document.

Basic Document Creation 1

Figure 1.16   Special symbol added to document.

Bullets

Another character frequently added to the text of a document is a solid black dot called a **bullet**. The bullet character is used in front of items in a list. The next section of the current document will list the names of various banks. Begin by entering two blank lines. Enter

[Return] [Return]

Change the text style from outline to **bold**. This is not quite as simple as you might think. Style attributes can be combined. For example, if the text is currently outline and you enter **Command+Shift+b**, the text becomes both outline and bold. In this case, you want to change from outline to bold. This requires you to remove the outline before you add the bold, which is accomplished by first setting the style to normal (i.e., having no special attributes) and then setting it to bold. Enter

Command+Shift+space
Command+Shift+b

33

1 Basic Document Creation

To make this list, you will want to change the alignment from center to left. Enter the shortcut command for left alignment:

Command + Shift + L

The cursor jumps to the left margin. You can use the Tab key to indent the line. PageMaker is automatically set up to move .5" to the right each time the Tab key is entered into the text. Enter

[Tab]

Insert a bullet character using the **Option + 8** command. (Remember the 8 is the 8 on the top row of the main keyboard, not the 8 key on the numeric keypad.) Enter

Option + 8

Indent again. Enter

[Tab]

Now enter the text for this list.

The Chase Philadelphia Bank [Return]

Basic Document Creation 1

Figure 1.17   Bulleted line entered in document.

Enter more bulleted items for the list:

[Tab]
Option+8
[Tab]
The Mexican Imperial Bank of Commerce [Return]
[Tab]
Option+8
[Tab]
The Dominion National Bank [Return]
[Tab]
Option+8
[Tab]
The National Bank of Andorra [Return]

The document should now look like the following:

1 Basic Document Creation

Figure 1.18   *Bulleted list added to document.*

CUTTING AND PASTING TEXT

While extensive text editing is better done in a word processing program, PageMaker does have sufficient facilities for basic editing operations such as copying or moving text by using the cut and paste techniques. For example, suppose you decided that the bulleted list should place the items in a different order, e.g., that the Dominion Nation Bank should be placed first. PageMaker includes the standard cut, paste, and copy commands used in most Macintosh applications.

Key Combination	Result
Command+x	cut
Command+c	copy
Command+v	paste

To change the order of the items, highlight the item you want to move. Enter

up arrow (2 times)
Command+Shift+1 (numeric keypad)

Basic Document Creation **1**

With the line of text highlighted, cut it from its current position by entering

Command+x

Note that the text is removed, but the line, now blank, remains. Remove the blank line by entering

[Delete]

Position the cursor at the text location in which you want to insert the text you have just cut. Enter

7 (numeric keypad)
up arrow

Paste the text into the document at this position by entering

Command+v

The text is added to the current line. To place each item on a separate line, insert a return. Enter

[Return]

The text has been moved to a new location in the list.

ENTERING PARAGRAPH TEXT

All of the text lines entered into this document so far have been **short lines**. Short lines are lines of text that end with a return character before the text reaches the right margin. **Paragraph** text may contain one or more lines of text that end with a return only after the last line. PageMaker will automatically wrap lines of text that are two wide to fit inside the margins. In this sense, PageMaker operates exactly as a word processing program would operate.

Move the cursor to the end of the text.

Command+3 (numeric keypad)

1 Basic Document Creation

Add a blank line. Enter

[Return]

Note that PageMaker automatically scrolls the screen up so that you can see the line upon which the cursor is currently located.

Exercise 3: Change the size of the characters to 12 point, and make the type style normal. Try this on your own. The correct commands can be found under Ex-3 at the end of this chapter.

When you enter the following paragraph, do not be concerned about the line endings. PageMaker will insert them at the points where they belong automatically. They will not be the same as the line endings printed in the instructions in this book. Enter

This transaction will place

You can change text attributes in the middle of a line. In this case, switch to bold for the name of the company. Enter

[space]
Command + Shift + b
American National Products, Inc.

Return to the normal text style by entering

[space]
Command + Shift + space
in the leadership position within the world marketplace and achieve a large degree of hegemony in the production of vital structural components. **[Return]**

POSITIONING A BLOCK OF TEXT

You have now created a block of text on the page of your document. The position of the block of text on the page was simply determined by where you started typing and the consecutive lines that you typed. This is exactly how a word processing program would operate with text.

What makes PageMaker different from a word processor is that the blocks of text you create can be treated as **objects**. Objects in PageMaker, like objects in the real world, can be manipulated in various ways. Frequently you will want to move an object from one place to another.

In PageMaker, blocks of text can be moved around on the page surface. This ability to treat text as an object is one of the basic differences between word processing and desktop publishing (page layout) software.

Change to the Fit to window view by entering

Command + w

The view is reduced to show the entire page at one time (see Figure 1.19). Note that the text that is smaller than 18 point is too small to read. Instead of the actual characters, PageMaker displays blocks of gray, called **greeked text**. Greeked text graphically shows you the location of the text when the characters are too small to be formed in the current view.

When you want to work with objects, you need to activate the **selection**, or pointer, mode. You will recall the arrow shaped icon in the Toolbox is the pointer icon. Activate the selection mode by clicking on the pointer tool icon.

> **Point** at the pointer icon
> **Click**

When PageMaker is in the selection mode, you cannot enter text or operate on individual characters, words, lines, or paragraphs for such tasks as changing fonts, sizes or style attributes. What you can do is work with the entire block of text as a single object.

1 Basic Document Creation

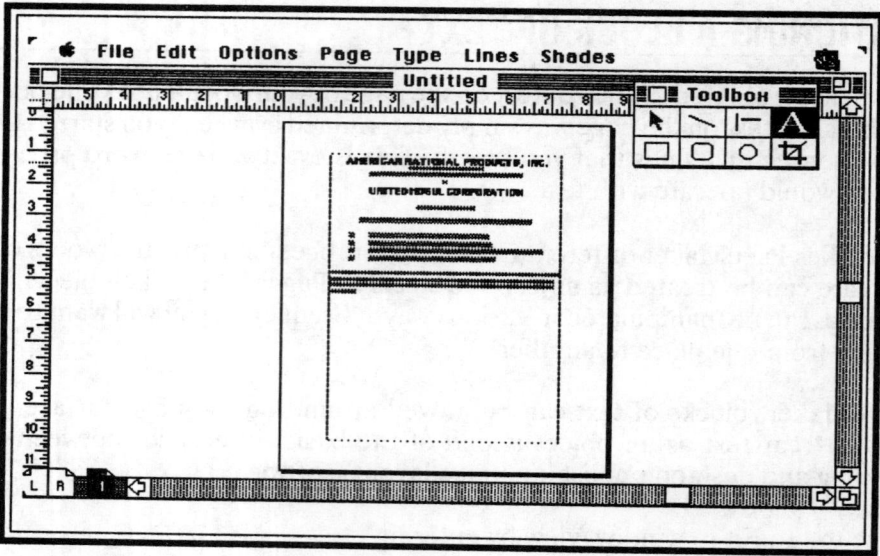

Figure 1.19   Document displayed with greeked text.

The first step is to select the object you want to work with by pointing at the object you want to select and clicking. In this case, the object is a block of text. You can point at any part of the block in order to select it.

> **Point** at the text
> **Click**

When you select the text, special markings appear at the top and at the bottom of the block. These markings are called **window shade handles**.

Basic Document Creation **1**

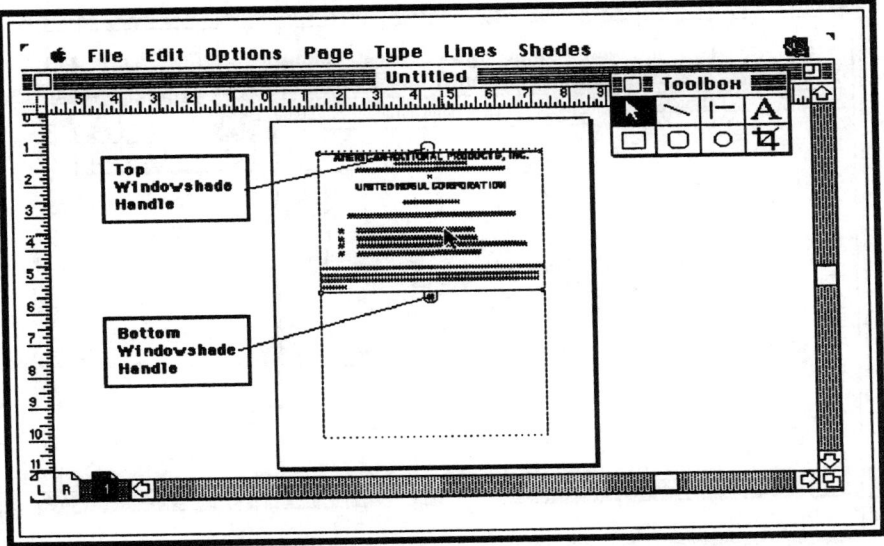

Figure 1.20   Window shade handles appear on a selected block of text.

The window shade handle is designed to help you perform special types of operations on the selected block. Each handle consists of several parts.

With the block of text selected, you can move it to some other location on the page. Note that the location does not need to be within the page margins. You can move a block by pointing the mouse cursor anywhere inside the block and dragging the block in the direction. In this example, you want to drag the block down so that it is centered on the page, as shown in Figure 1.21. Be sure not to move the block to the left or right of the margin guides.

Drag the block down

1 Basic Document Creation

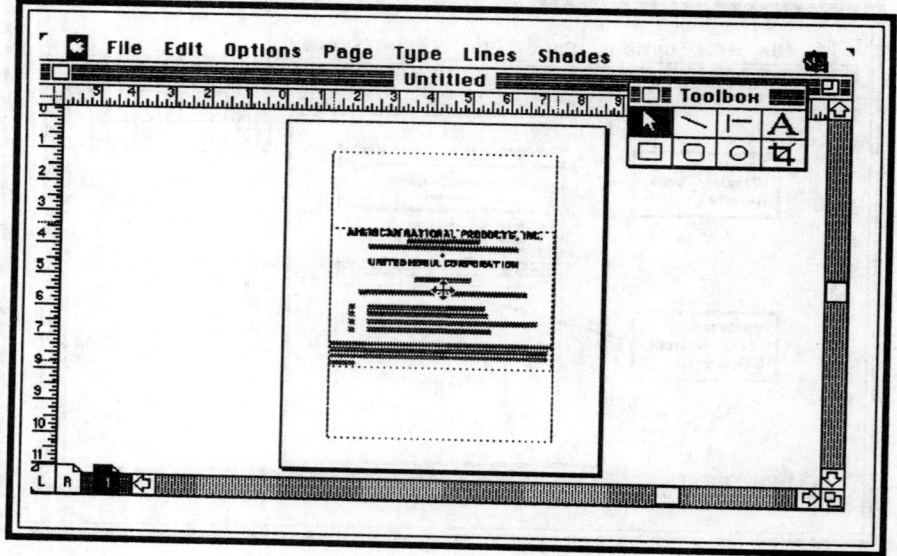

Figure 1.21   Block centered on the page.

PageMaker makes document layout quick and convenient by allowing you to easily position text on the page.

PRINTING THE DOCUMENT

This simple document is ready for printing. Note that it does not matter which display mode you are in when you print. The **Print** command can be found on the File menu or it can be executed with the shortcut command **Command+p**. Display the printing menu by entering

Command+p

The **Print options** dialog box is displayed.

Note that the contents of the dialog box will vary depending upon which printer you are using.

ImageWriter Dialog Boxes

If you are using an ImageWriter printer you will see a series of three dialog boxes. The first box contains options that PageMaker specifies. (Note these are similar to the options that appear for the LaserWriter.)

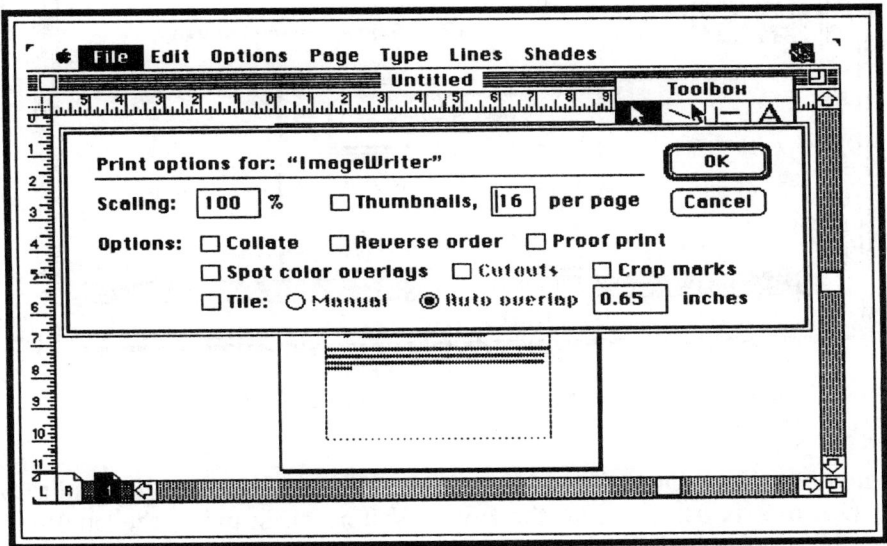

Figure 1.22   *Dialog box for ImageWriter.*

Details about printing options are covered in Appendix A. For now, accept the default settings by entering

[Return]

The next dialog box is specific to the ImageWriter and concerns paper handling and orientation. If you are using letter-size paper, you can simply accept the default settings by entering

[Return]

1 Basic Document Creation

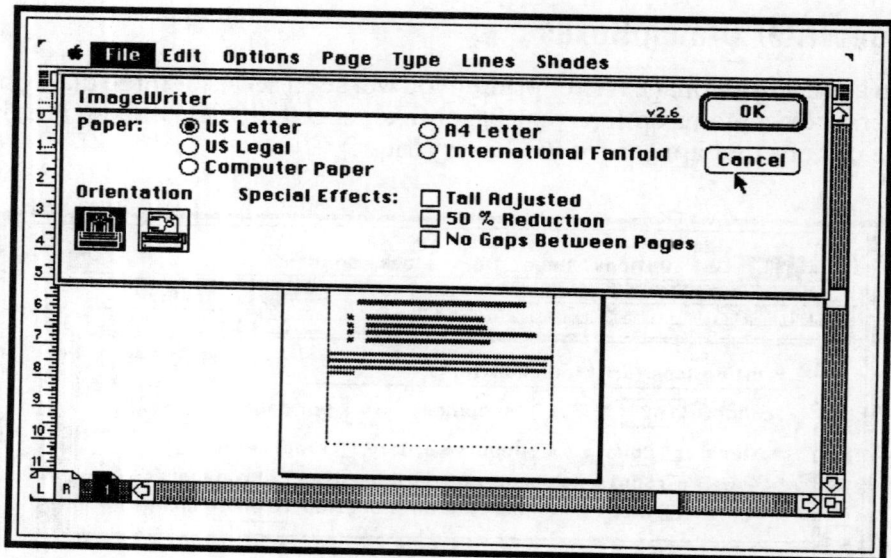

Figure 1.23   Paper-handling dialog box for ImageWriter.

The third and final dialog box for the ImageWriter concerns the quality of the print. Dot matrix printers like the ImageWriter can improve the quality of the printing by moving more slowly and printing several passes over the same area. You can speed up printing at the expense of quality by selecting either **Faster** or **Draft** printing.

You can also print a specific range of pages and multiple copies. The Paper Feed is set on **Automatic**, meaning continuous-form paper. If you are hand feeding letterhead, select **Hand Feed.** Accept the default settings, and initiate the print sequence by entering

[Return]

Note that you can cancel the printing by entering **Command+period**.

Basic Document Creation 1

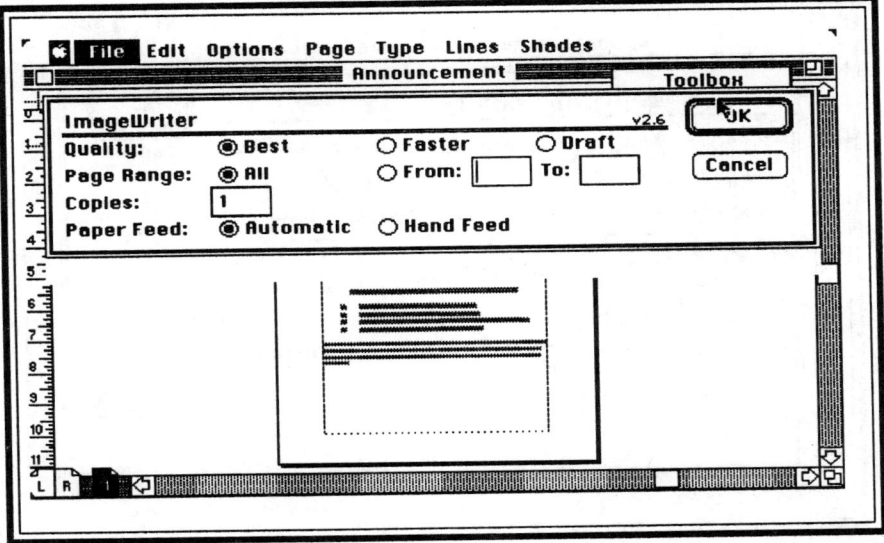

Figure 1.24   *Final ImageWriter Print dialog box.*

Laser Printer Dialog Boxes

If you are using an Apple LaserWriter or other PostScript laser printers, you will see a single dialog box as shown in Figure 1.25. The options on this menu will be covered as you progress through this book, and they are summarized in Appendix A.

1 Basic Document Creation

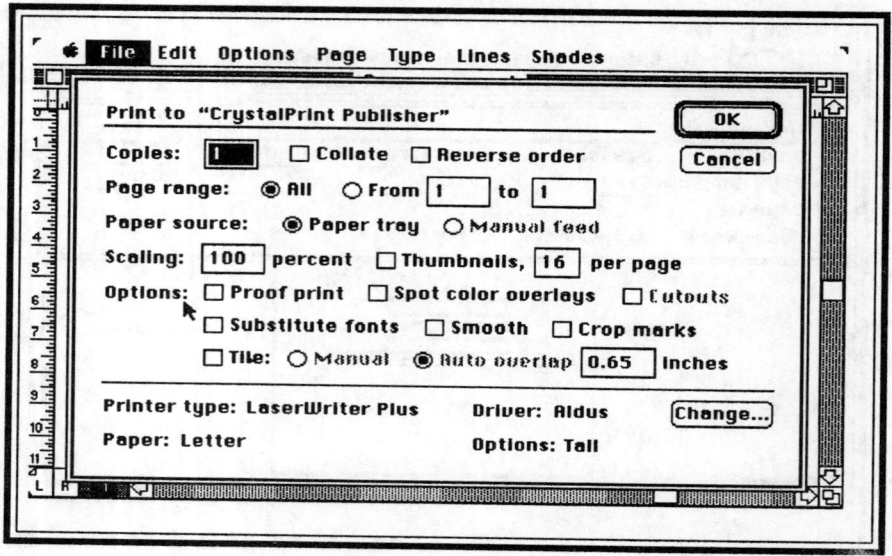

Figure 1.25   Dialog box for LaserWriter.

In this case, simply execute the default printing settings by entering

[Return]

PageMaker will take a few minutes to compose your document and the PostScript data will be sent to the printer. The document will then be printed. You can click the **Cancel** option to stop the printing.

The printed document will resemble Figure 1.26.

Basic Document Creation 1

> ## AMERICAN NATIONAL PRODUCTS, INC.
> has acquired the assets of the
> ### International Gear Fitting Products Division
> of
> ## UNITED MOGUL CORPORATION
>
> Agent for the purchase
>
> ### The First National Bank of Shrewsbury™
>
> - The Dominion National Bank
> - The Chase Philadelphia Bank
> - The Mexican Imperial Bank of Commerce
> - The National Bank of Andorra
>
> This transaction will place **American National Products, Inc.** in the leadership position within the world marketplace and achieve a large degree of hegemony in the production of vital structural components.

Figure 1.26   Printed document

SAVING THE DOCUMENT

When the document has printed, you will return to the normal PageMaker document display. The last step is to save the document you have created in a file so that you can print or revise the document at a later time.

1 Basic Document Creation

You can save a document by selecting the **Save** command from the File menu or by using the keyboard shortcut **Command+s**. Enter

Command+s

In this case, you will store the new document in the PageMaker folder. In this example, the document will be called **Announcement**. Enter

Announcement [Return]

Note that the document remains on the screen after you have saved it. To clear the work area for another document, you must close the current document.

> **Point** at File
> **Drag** to Close

You have now completed your first document. In this chapter, all of the text was created as a single text block. In Chapter 2, you will learn the advantages of creating documents with multiple text blocks.

Exit PageMaker.

> **Point** at File
> **Drag** to Quit

Basic Document Creation 1

SUMMARY

This chapter explains the basic operations used to add text to a PageMaker document by direct entry.

- **Page Setup.** PageMaker requires you to set page parameters when you create a new document. Unlike most word processing applications, PageMaker requires you to specify the number of pages the document will contain before you create it. Pages can be added or removed while you are editing the document. The page setup also includes specifications for the page margins.

- **View, or Display Mode.** PageMaker permits you to view a document from a number of different size perspectives. The two most commonly used views are **Actual**, in which the items on the screen appear the same size as they will when they are printed, and **Fit to window**, in which they are reduced to a size that allows the entire page to be displayed on the screen at one time. You can also select views that show the text reduced to 50% or 75% of the actual size or enlarged to 200% of the actual size. You can perform all PageMaker operations in any of the display views.

- **The Toolbox.** The **Toolbox** contains eight tool icons that represent the operational modes available in PageMaker—the selection (pointer), diagonal-line, perpendicular-line, text, rectangle (square-corner), rounded-rectangle, oval, and crop modes.

- **Text Attributes.** Text attributes are qualities that can be assigned to one or more characters in the text. The attributes fall into three classifications: **font** (the characteristic shape and form of the letters), **size** (the height of the characters measured in points), and **text style** (standard variations within a font such as bold, italic, outline, or shadow). The default text attributes are Times, 12-point, normal text.

- **Alignment.** Alignment refers to how the text is aligned horizontally between the margins. You can select left, center, or right alignment. Justified alignment causes the text to be flush with both the left and right margins by inserting spaces between words to ensure the correct alignment at the margins.

1 Basic Document Creation

- **Text Blocks.** A block of text in PageMaker is a logical, not physical, concept referring to a series of characters, words, and paragraphs. Blocks of text are treated as single objects for the purpose of positioning the text on the page. When selected as objects, text blocks display **window shade handles** that indicate the top and bottom of the block of text.

- **Moving Blocks.** A selected block fo text can be **dragged** anywhere on the page. You are not restricted to the area within the margins.

- **Printing.** PageMaker outputs a document to the current printer device. You can select the specific pages you want to print if the document contains more than one page. If you are using a printer such as an ImageWriter, you can select the print quality.

- **Saving a document.** Saving a document creates a file that contains all of the text, attributes, and page placement information you added to the PageMaker document. These files can be retrieved later for printing or revision.

Answers to Exercises

Ex-1: Change font, size and style.

```
Point at Type
Drag to Font
Drag to Geneva
Point at Type
Drag to Size
Drag to 24
```

Enter

Command + Shift + b

Basic Document Creation **1**

Ex-2: Change point size to 18.

> **Point** at Type
> **Drag** to Size
> **Drag** to 18

Ex-3: Change to 12-point normal.

> **Point** at Type
> **Drag** to Size
> **Drag** to 12

Enter

Command + Shift + space

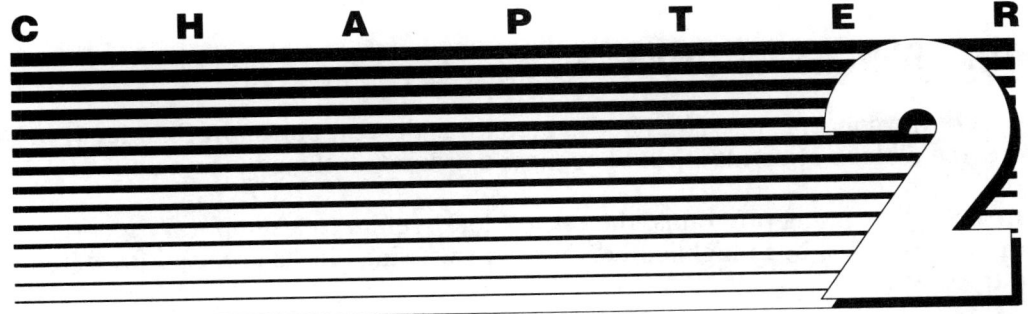

MULTIPLE TEXT BLOCKS

In Chapter 1 you learned the most basic method of document creation in PageMaker. In this chapter, you will learn how a document can be created by using multiple text blocks arranged on one or more pages. This type of layout provides a greater degree of flexibility than the methods shown in Chapter 1.

2 Multiple Text Blocks

TEXT BLOCKS AS OBJECTS

One of the concepts discussed in Chapter 1 was the **text block**. In Chapter 1, you created a block of text that could be moved around on the page as a unit.

In word processing programs, the term "block" refers to a temporary section of the text that has been highlighted. Word processing blocks are used for editing purposes.

A text block in PageMaker is quite different. As mentioned in Chapter 1, a PageMaker "text block" refers to a document **object**. The term "object" implies that the text block can be treated in a similar manner to the way you would treat a physical object on a desktop, i.e., it can be moved from place to place as a unit.

For example, suppose you wanted to create an advertising flyer with a coupon to mail to your customers. The finished flyer would actually consist of several distinct parts arranged on the same page. First, there would be a company logo of some type that would identify the source of the flyer, giving the company address and telephone number. Another part might be information about the product or service you offer. To encourage the customer to make an order, you might want to include a coupon that offers a discount or other incentives.

Viewed in this way, the flyer really consists of several separate sections. In PageMaker you can create individual text blocks for each section.

By creating a separate block for each distinct section of the document, you make it possible to move the various text blocks independently of each other. Take the coupon section of the flyer just discussed as an example. A coupon could be placed at the bottom or in the middle of the page. You might create four coupons and place each one in one of the corners of the page. If you attempt to do this with a single text block, you need to know the exact sequence and position the coupons will have on the page before you type the text. But if each coupon is a separate text block, you can move the blocks into a number of different arrangements until you arrive at the one you like best.

By dividing a page into a series of objects, you can create new layouts by moving the objects around on the page. This means that the sequence and placement of the text on the page need not be decided before you enter the text and can be changed as many times as necessary after the text has been created.

Multiple Text Blocks 2

By treating a document as a group of objects arranged on the page, PageMaker provides the ability to create layouts in a similar manner to the way a graphic artist would cut and paste sections of a layout. With PageMaker, you can perform the same type of manipulations but with greater ease, speed, and flexibility.

In this chapter, you will create a flyer that uses multiple text blocks for its final layout.

CREATING THE DOCUMENT

Again, you will create a document that needs to fit onto a single page. You can use the shortcut command for creating a new document, **Command+n**. Enter

Command+n

This is going to be a single-page flyer, so you can deselect the Double-sided option.

> **Point** at Double-sided
> **Click**

Create the one-page document by entering

[Return]

The default PageMaker display appears. This consists of the document page displayed in the Fit to window view with the ruler lines and the Toolbox palette displayed.

A Letterhead

Most documents produced by a business include the name, address, phone number, and company logo. These items are often grouped together into a **letterhead**. If you are creating a flyer, you will want to have one part of the document include this information.

Begin with the address information. The first step is to create a text block with the correct information. Place PageMaker in the Actual display mode.

2 Multiple Text Blocks

> **Point** at the upper left corner of the guides
> **Option + Shift + Click**

Enter the text entry mode.

> **Point** at the text icon in the Toolbox
> **Click**

When the text mode is active, you can create a text block by clicking the mouse cursor in any part of the document.

> **Point** at the upper left corner of the guides
> **Click**

The text cursor begins to flash next to the left margin guide line. You can now enter the text of the company name, address, and phone number.

Central Vacaville Pharmacy [Return]
1200 East Street [Return]
Vacaville, CA 94077 [Return]
415-999-0202 [Return]
Fax: 415-999-0205

The screen will resemble Figure 2.1.

Multiple Text Blocks 2

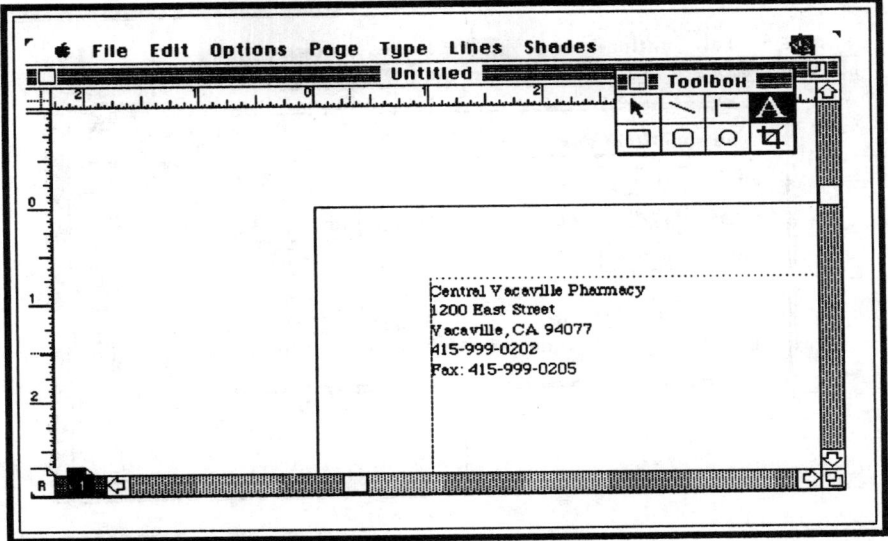

Figure 2.1   Text block entered into document.

The Type Specifications Command

In PageMaker, one of the advantages of creating small blocks of text, instead of placing all of the text into a single block as you did in Chapter 1, is that you can perform operations on the text blocks as individual units.

In this case, you will want to change the font attributes of the text. First, select all of the text in the current block by entering

Command + a

The entire text block is highlighted.

In Chapter 1, you were able to change the font, point size, and style by using the Type font, Type size, and Type style menus. However, there is another way to approach text attribute changes, using a single dialog box that allows you to select font, size, and type style. The dialog box can be activated by using the Type specs command on the Type menu or the **Command + t** shortcut command. Enter

Command + t

The Type specifications dialog box appears on the screen.

2 Multiple Text Blocks

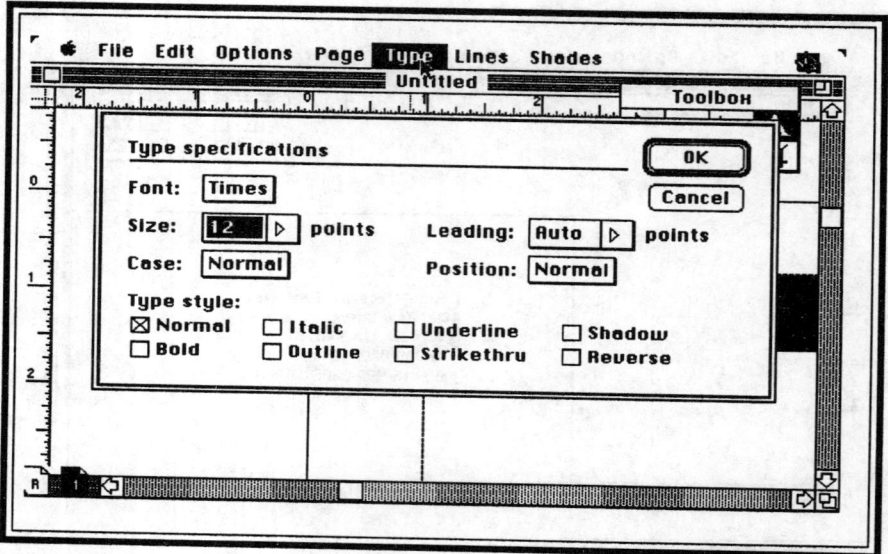

Figure 2.2   Type specifications dialog box.

This single dialog box combines the text attribute commands for font, point size, and type style along with three other text attribute options not mentioned so far:

Case   This option converts text from the case in which it was originally typed to either **All caps** or **Small caps**. The Small caps option converts any lowercase characters to uppercase but reduces their point size to only 70% of the size of normal uppercase letters. This option is used when you want uppercase letters but want to keep the sizing about the same as if the letters were lowercase. Note that the Small caps option does not affect characters that were entered in uppercase originally. Those characters remain normal uppercase characters.

Leading   Leading refers to vertical space PageMaker places between lines of text. By tradition, leading space should be 1.2 times the point size of the characters. If the text is 12 points, then the distance from the top of one line of text to the top of the next line would be 12 times 1.2 = 14.4 points high.

Multiple Text Blocks **2**

By using spacing that is taller than the characters, you leave a small amount of white space between lines. This white space is necessary in standard fonts to allow for characters that descend below the normal baseline of the text. For example, the characters "g" and "j" have tails that descend into the leading space above the next line. The standard setting for leading is **Auto**, in which PageMaker automatically calculates the leading necessary based on the largest point size characters in the text.

If you increase or decrease the size of the characters, PageMaker automatically adjusts the leading space. The alternative is to select a fixed value for the leading. The leading menu will display point size options for leading that range from 90% to 125% of the current point size. For example, if the current point size is 12, then the leading option ranges from 11 to 15 points. If the current point size is 18, then the leading options will range from 16 to 22 points.

Position Position refers to the placement of text on the line vertically. The options are **superscript** or **subscript** in addition to the default, **normal**.

In this case change the font to Venice, bold and the case to small caps.

Point at Font
Drag to Venice
Point at Case
Drag to Small caps
Click on Bold

Save all three changes by entering

[Return]

The text will now appear as shown in Figure 2.3. The advantage of the Type specs dialog box is that you can change several text attributes at the same time, which saves time when you are changing more than one text attribute.

59

2 Multiple Text Blocks

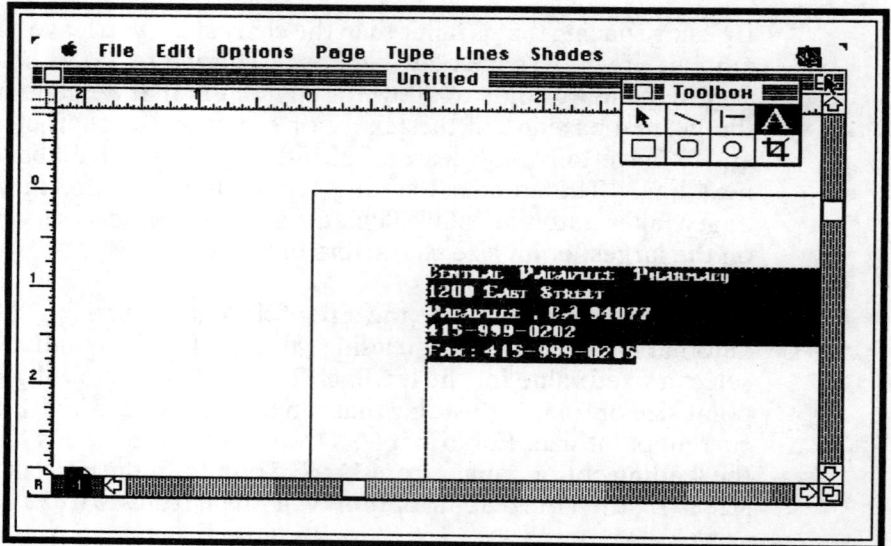

Figure 2.3   *Text attributes changed for text block.*

The Paragraph Attribute Menu

In Chapter 1, you learned that you could use shortcut commands to change the horizontal alignment of lines of text, e.g., **Command + Shift + c**, to center align text.

Alignment, along with other paragraph attributes, can be changed from a single menu that includes alignment with a number of other attributes. The Paragraph command on the Type menu will display a dialog box that contains the paragraph attribute settings. The dialog box can be displayed with the **Command + m** keyboard shortcut. Enter

Command + m

PageMaker displays the Paragraph specifications dialog box.

Multiple Text Blocks **2**

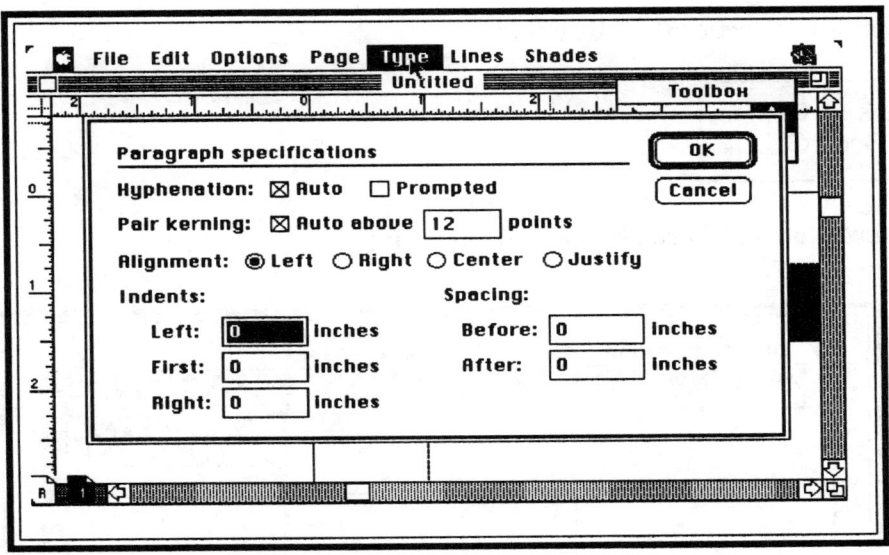

Figure 2.4   Paragraph specifications dialog box.

The box contains four settings in addition to alignment:

Hyphenation   When the **Auto** option is selected, PageMaker will insert hyphens into words when needed with wrap-around text. If **Prompted** is selected, you will be asked to confirm or skip the hyphenation.

Pair kerning   Kerning consists of adjustments made in the spacing between particular pairs of characters. Kerning is generally not needed with text that is 12 points or smaller. When large characters are used, kerning is sometimes necessary to narrow or widen gaps between characters. Kerning will be discussed in greater detail later in this chapter.

Indents   This setting allows you to set indents for the left or right margins or for the first line of a paragraph.

Spacing   This setting allows you to add extra lines of space before the first line or after the last line of a paragraph. Note that this spacing is different from the leading that is inserted for each line in the text.

2 Multiple Text Blocks

In this case, select center alignment.

> **Click** on Center
> **Click** on OK

The text is now centered between the margins.

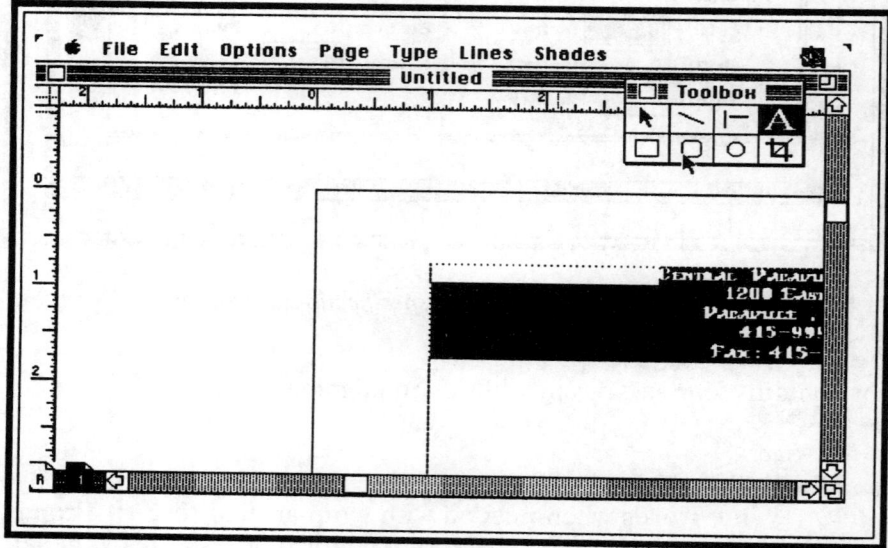

Figure 2.5   Text center aligned.

Adding Another Text Block

In addition to the address block, it is common for the letterhead to contain a **logo**. The logo of the document is a design that is used as a symbol for the company. Large companies spend a lot of time and money to have logos designed. In this chapter, you will create a simple logo design based on the name of the company.

Multiple Text Blocks 2

The logo will be placed into a different text block from the address. To start a new text block, simply click the mouse cursor anywhere on the document. In this case, point the cursor into the blank space below the address block:

> **Point** at the space below the address block
> **Click**

The text cursor is placed into the document below the address block. Note that the cursor is in the center of the document because the last text block created was set for center alignment. Change to left alignment by entering the shortcut command for left alignment:

Command + Shift + L

The cursor is now flush with the left margin guide of the page. The logo will be the first three letters of the name of the town. Enter

VAC

Change the text attributes to 24-point, bold, outline, and shadow. Enter

Command + a
Command + t

> **Point** at Size
> **Drag** to 24
> **Click** on Bold
> **Click** on Outline
> **Click** on Shadow
> **Click** on OK

The three characters are changed to the selected text attributes. Note that the commands used to select and change all of the text in one block have no effect on the text of the other block.

63

2 Multiple Text Blocks

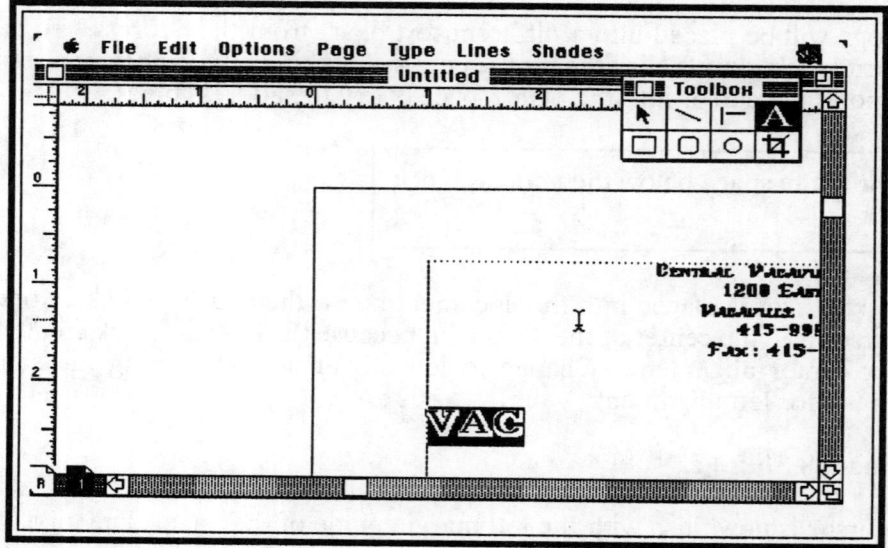

Figure 2.6   *Text changed in second block.*

Kerning

If you look closely at the three characters formatted as the company logo (see Figure 2.6) you will notice that the space between the first two characters "VA" appears to be greater than the space between the second and the third characters, "AC."

PageMaker doesn't actually vary the spacing. The amount of space left between the characters is exactly the same. However, characters such as "A" and "V" are composed of lines that slant. In this case, the right side of the "V" and the left side of the "A" slant in the same direction, creating an optical illusion that makes it appear as if the space between characters varies.

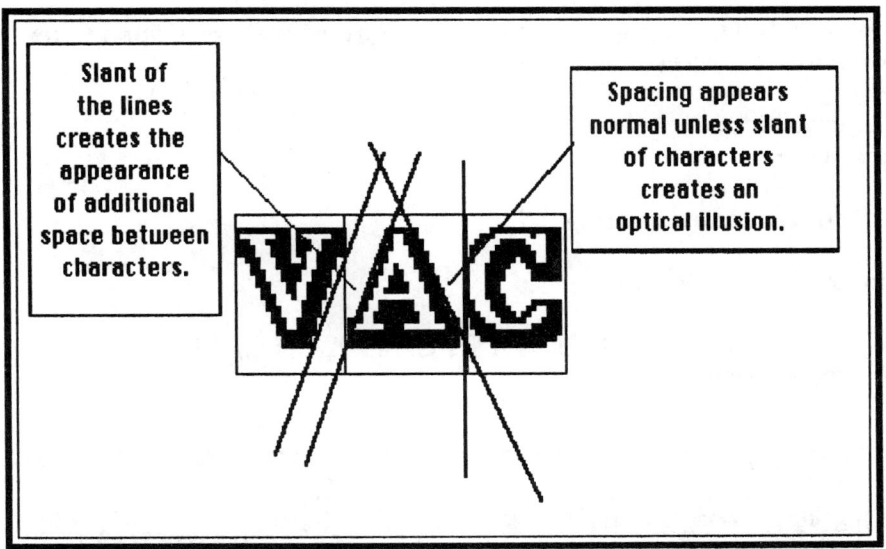

Figure 2.7   Space between characters appears greater because of slanting.

When the size of the characters is small — 12 points or smaller — this illusion is not very noticeable, but in larger point sizes you will notice this effect.

PageMaker allows you to make minute adjustments to the spacing between specific pairs of characters. This process is called **kerning**. You can use the kerning process to add more space between pairs, reduce the space between pairs, or some combination of both.

To kern the space between characters, you need to place the text cursor between the pair of characters you want to kern. Once the cursor is placed in the proper position, you can use the following special combinations to change the spacing.

Key Combination	Result
Command + Shift + Delete	add space
Command + Delete	remove space

2 Multiple Text Blocks

In this case, reduce the space between the letters "VA." Position the text cursor between the characters by entering

7 (numeric keypad)
[Right arrow]

Reduce the space by entering

Command + Delete (7 times)

The space between the letters "VA" is changed, causing the characters appear more evenly spaced.

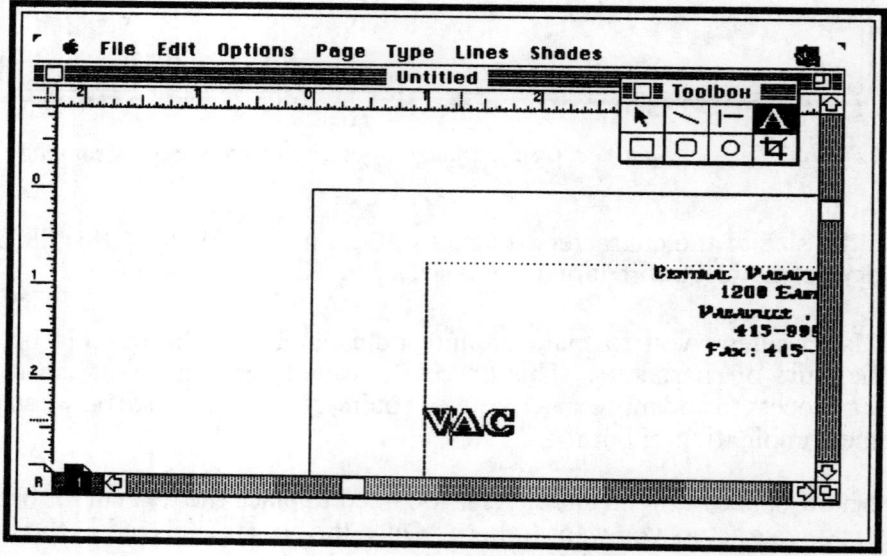

Figure 2.8   *Space between characters kerned.*

Positioning Text Blocks

The two text blocks that you have created can be moved to any place on the document. Suppose you wanted the logo text to be positioned beside the address block instead of below it.

In PageMaker this operation is simple. Just drag the text block to the location in which you want it to appear.

Multiple Text Blocks **2**

Place PageMaker into the selection mode. Recall that the pointer tool in the upper left corner of the Toolbox is the selection mode icon.

> **Click** on the pointer icon

Select the logo text block.

> **Click** on "VAC"

When you clicked on "VAC," PageMaker selected the text block that contains those characters. The window shade handles appear to indicate which object is currently selected.

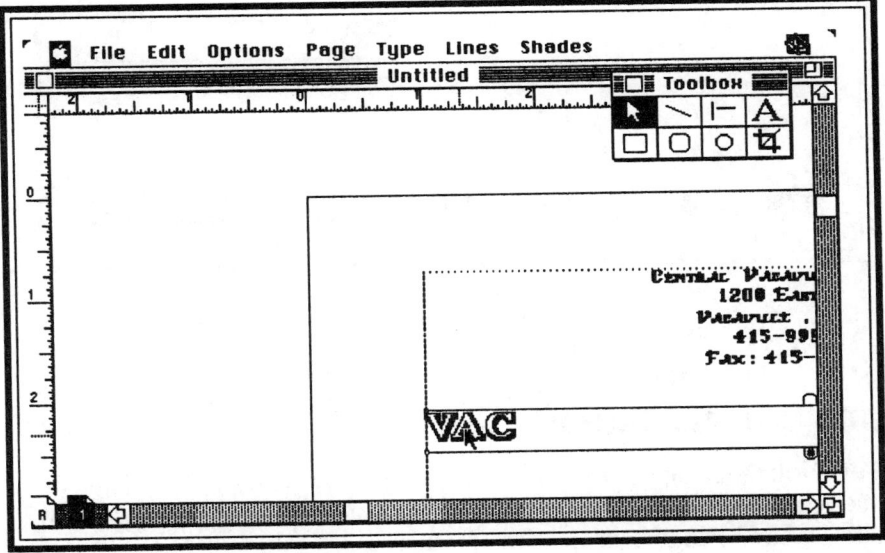

Figure 2.9   *Text block selected.*

67

2 Multiple Text Blocks

Note that the address block is not selected when you select the logo because you created the text in two different text blocks. You can now drag the text block so that it is positioned next to the address block.

> **Drag** the logo to new position (as shown in Figure 2.10)

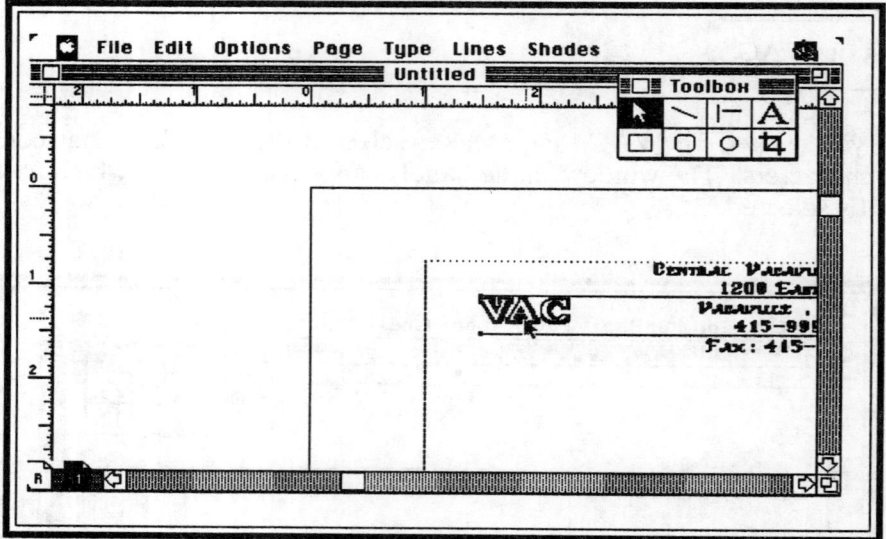

Figure 2.10   *Text block with logo positioned next to address.*

Copying Text into Blocks

In the previous section, you saw the advantage of creating text in separate blocks. Because each block can be positioned independently of the others, you were able to easily place the logo text next to the address block — an effect that could not have been achieved with a single block of text.

Positioning text blocks enables you to create a variety of special appearances. For example, suppose you wanted the letters of the logo to be stacked vertically, one underneath the other, in a column instead of simply spread out horizontally.

Multiple Text Blocks 2

This could be achieved by creating a separate text block for each letter and dragging the letters individually so that they form a column.

Given the way that text blocks are created in PageMaker, this is a rather straightforward procedure. Recall that a new text block can be created while the text mode is active by simply clicking the mouse cursor on any empty portion of the document.

To move or copy text from one text block into another, you can use the **copy**, **cut**, and **paste** commands. For example, if you cut the letter "C" from the logo, you could paste it into a new text block by creating the new block before you pasted the character back into the document.

The first step in this process is to activate the text mode.

> **Click** on the text icon

Select the letter that you want to cut and paste, in this case the letter "C" in the "VAC" logo.

> **Click** on "C"

When you click on a specific letter, PageMaker places the insertion point cursor just to the left of the character. You can select the character to the right of the insertion point by entering

Shift + Right arrow

Cut the letter from the document by entering

Command + x

Before you paste the letter back into the document, create a new text block by clicking in the blank area below the current text blocks.

> **Click** on the blank area below the current text blocks

69

2 Multiple Text Blocks

Note that the cursor is automatically positioned for center-aligned text. Do not be concerned because the character you are about to paste into this block will carry with it the paragraph and character attributes used in the block from which it was copied. Paste the character into the new block by entering

Command + v

The letter "C" is now placed into a text block of its own. Note that the exact position of the "C" depends on where you created the new block.

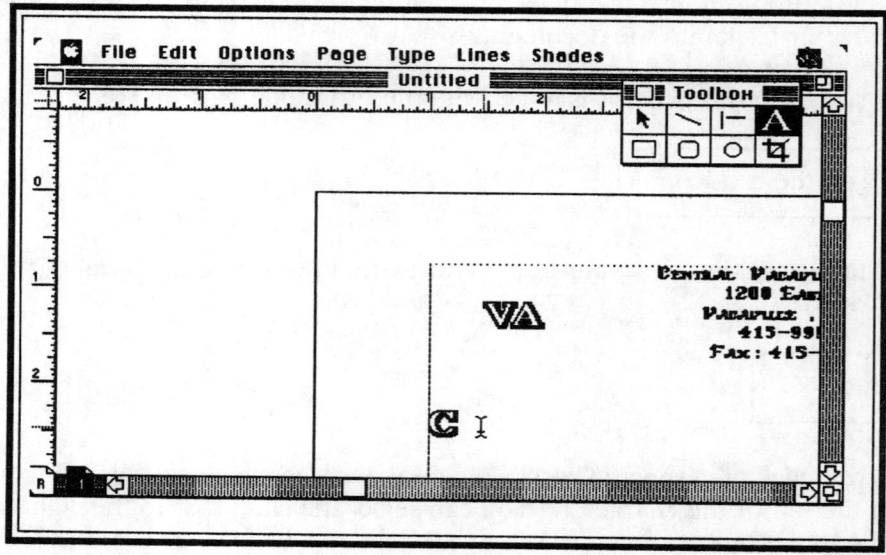

Figure 2.11   *Character moved into a separate text block.*

Repeat the process with the letter "A."

| **Click** on "A" |

Enter

Shift + Right arrow
Command + x

Multiple Text Blocks 2

Create a new text block and paste the character into the new block.

> **Click** on a blank area

Enter

Command + v

Now that each character in the logo has been placed into a separate text block, you can use the mouse to position each character independently. In this case, you will align the characters in a column. Place PageMaker into the selection mode.

> **Click** on the pointer icon
> **Click** on "V"

The window shade handles appear for the text block. Note that only the letter "V" is included in this text block. Now position this character as shown in Figure 2.12.

> **Drag** "V" to new position (as in Figure 2.12)

Repeat the process for the other two characters in the logo.

> **Drag** "A" to new position (as in Figure 2.12)
> **Drag** "C" to new position (as in Figure 2.12)

2 Multiple Text Blocks

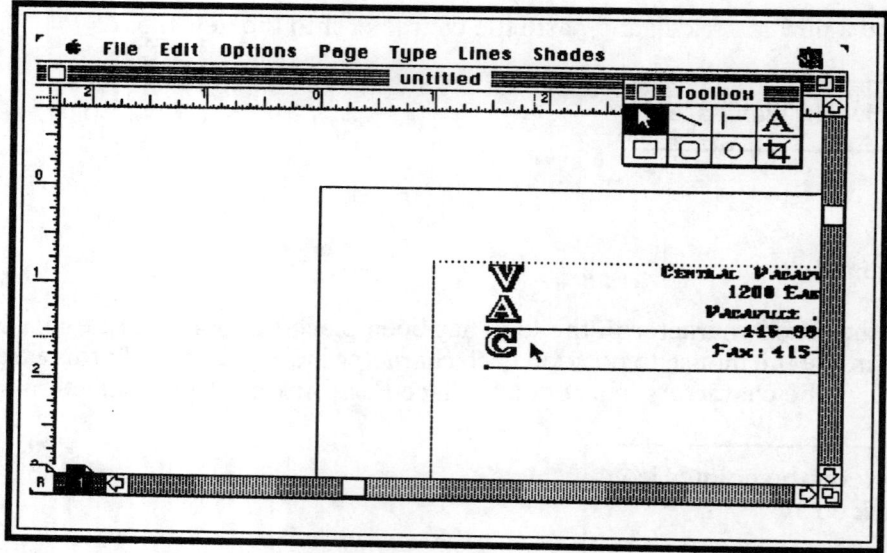

Figure 2.12   Text blocks aligned to form a column.

Adding More Text Blocks

The next part of the flyer will be the text that explains what product you are advertising. In this case, it will be a special offer on photo finishing.

Scroll the screen display down and to the right so that the center of the page is displayed in the window.

> **Click** on the right scroll bar arrow (4 times)
> **Click** on the down scroll bar arrow (4 times)

Enter the text entry mode.

> **Click** on the text icon

Multiple Text Blocks 2

Create a new text block approximately in the center of the screen.

> **Click** on a blank area

Enter the following text:

Now! [Return]
By Popular Demand! [Return]
Express Photo Finishing [Return]
for LESS!!!

Note that this text is center aligned. In this case, center alignment is fine. However, for this example you will want to enlarge the point size to 24. First, select the text. Enter

Command + a

Again, the Select all command (**Command + a**) highlights only the text within the current text block, which is an advantage of working with several small blocks of text rather than one large block. Change the point size to 24.

> **Point** at Type
> **Drag** to Size
> **Drag** to 24

The screen now resembles Figure 2.13.

73

2 Multiple Text Blocks

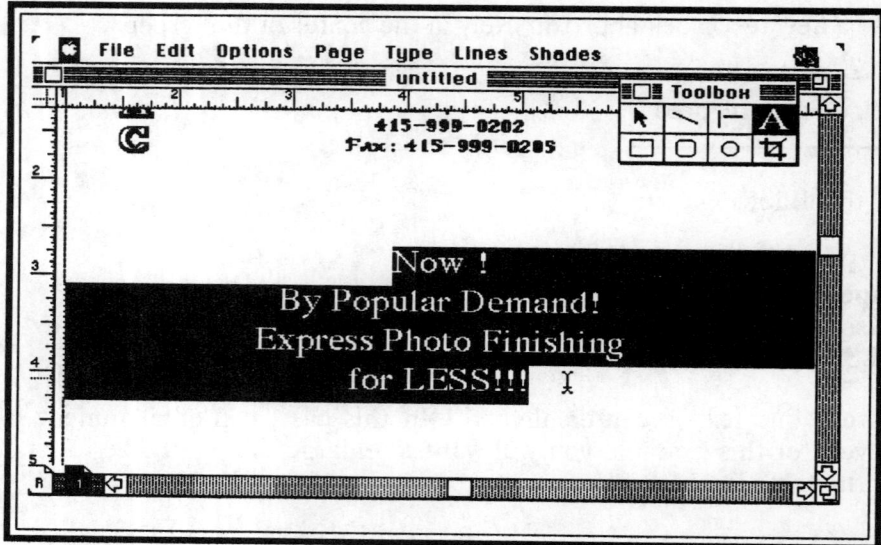

Figure 2.13   Text block enlarged to 24-point.

TEXT BLOCKS WITH TABS

In the next section of the document, you will create a text block that lists the specifics of the offer, including prices. This information takes the form of a table. As with word processing, you can create tables by creating tab stops that can be used to align text at specific horizontal locations.

Create a new text block below the current block.

> **Click** on the blank area below current block

Multiple Text Blocks 2

The text is set to the attributes used in the first text block you created, i.e., center alignment. Change the alignment to left by entering

Command + Shift + L

In this block of text, you will want to have four columns of information:

1) Roll Size
2) Print Size
3) Copies
4) Price

In order to space the text in columns, you need to create tab stops. Many people who are used to typing or word processing feel they must set tabs before entering text. In fact, this is not the case. It is probably simpler to type the text you want to include in the table and then designate the tab stops. It is easier because when you set the tabs you can immediately see their effect on the text. If you set the tabs before you enter text, then you must imagine what their effect on the text would be. There is no reason why you should work at this disadvantage.

Enter the following text. Note that each time the symbol **[Tab]** appears, you should press the Tab key. Enter

[Tab]
Roll Size [Tab]
Print Size [Tab]
Copies [Tab]
Price [Return]

Note that the effect of the tabs is uneven because PageMaker automatically sets tabs every .5" across the page. Each time you enter a tab, the text is aligned to the next tab stop. In creating a table such as this, it is unlikely that the preset .5" tabs will correctly align the text. However, that is not important when you are simply creating the text for the table. What is important is that each item in the table should be separated by a tab character. Later, you can change the location of the tabs. Enter three more lines for this table:

2 Multiple Text Blocks

[Tab]
24 [Tab]
3 x 5 [Tab]
1 [Tab]
10.99 [Return]

[Tab]
36 [Tab]
3 x 5 [Tab]
1 [Tab]
13.99 [Return]

[Tab]
36 [Tab]
3 x 5 [Tab]
2 [Tab]
15.99

Select all of the text in this block. Enter

Command+a

You can set or revise tab stops by using the Indent/Tabs command found on the Type menu. The shortcut key combination **Command+i** performs the same function. Enter

Command+i

PageMaker displays the Indents/Tabs dialog box (see Figure 2.14).

The dialog box contains a ruler line that shows the position of all of the tabs currently set. The display shows that there is a tab set every .5" across the page. Before you can set individual tabs, you must clear the existing tabs.

Click on Clear

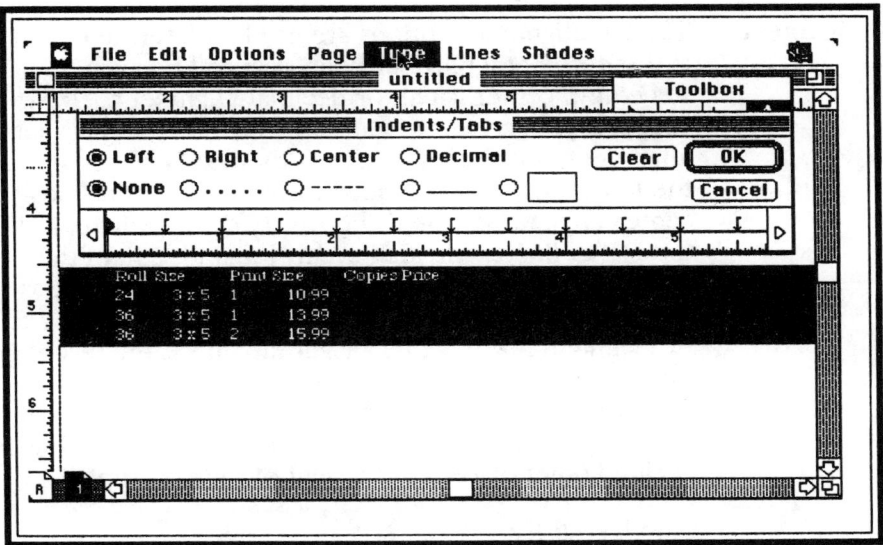

Figure 2.14   Indents/Tabs dialog box.

All of the tab markers are removed from the ruler line in the dialog box. You can set a tab by clicking the mouse on the ruler line at the position where you want the tab set. You can also enter a value in inches into the box to set a tab at an exact location. The location of the tabs is measured from the current left margin, not from the edge of the page. (If you divide the page into columns, the tabs are measured from each column boundary.)

There are two settings that determine the type of tab created: tab alignment and tab leader.

2 Multiple Text Blocks

Tab Alignment The tab alignment options are used to determine the way the text entered at a particular tab stop will be aligned. You can select left, center, right, or decimal alignment. For example, suppose you create at tab stop at 1.5". If you select left alignment, the *first* character in the text is placed at 1.5", and the rest of the text is placed to the right of that position. A center-aligned tab would align the *middle* character at 1.5" with the rest of the text divided evenly left and right of the tab stop. A right tab would place the *last* character in the text at 1.5" with the other characters spread out to the left of the 1.5" mark. A decimal tab works like a right tab unless the text aligned at that tab contains a period. If a period is entered, such as the decimal point in a number, a decimal-aligned tab would align the *decimal* at 1.5", with all the characters following the decimal point placed to the right of the tab stop.

The default is **left** alignment.

Note that when you enter numbers that always have the same number of decimal places, such as dollar and cent amounts, you would usually use a right-aligned tab, not a decimal tab to align them. When all of the numbers you will enter have the same number of decimal places (e.g., dollar and cent amounts always have two decimal places), then there is no practical difference between a decimal and a right-aligned tab. Also, there is one reason to prefer a right tab over a decimal tab in this circumstance. When you enter the headings for a column of numbers, the heading is composed of text, not numbers. A right-aligned tab will align the right end of the heading with the right-most digit of the numbers. If you choose a decimal tab, the right end of the heading will line up with the ones column digit, with the decimal point and decimal places extending to the right, past the end of the heading. This is a small detail, but it usually makes your document look better if a right tab is used instead of a decimal tab in these situations.

The **decimal** tab is used if the number of decimal places in the numbers varies as they are entered in the column, e.g. 10%, 10.5%, 10.75%, etc. With values such as these, a decimal tab ensures that the digits line up according to their place value.

Multiple Text Blocks 2

Tab Leader	In most cases, the text aligned at each tab stop will fill only part of the space between the tabs. Normally this space is left blank. However, you can set a tab so that any space not filled by text is filled with a series of periods, dashes, or underlines. These characters are called tab leaders and are used to create a table of contents appearance. The default is None, i.e., the space between tabs appears blank.

Note that you can choose your own character to use as a tab leader. The box with the flashing cursor allows you to enter a character, e.g., a bullet dot, **Option+8**.

In this example, the first tab will be set at 1" from the margin and will be a right tab. Before you set the tab, you must set the alignment type.

> **Click** on Right
> **Click** at 1" on the ruler

Note that when you click, PageMaker displays the tab location to the left of the Cancel option. When you click on the ruler, the value that appears may differ slightly from the location you intended, e.g., 1.016" instead of 1". This is because it is hard to point the cursor at exactly the position you want. In most cases, these small differences are not significant, but if you have missed your target by a small amount, you can change the position of the tab by dragging left or right on the ruler.

Note that the tab icon inserted onto the ruler line has a tail that points to the right, indicating that this is a right-aligned tab. Create a left-aligned tab at 2".

> **Click** on Left
> **Click** at 2" on the ruler

This tab stop icon has a tail that points to the left, indicating that this is a left-aligned tab. Add two more right-aligned tabs at 3" and 4".

2 Multiple Text Blocks

> **Click** on Right
> **Click** at 3" on the ruler
> **Click** at 4" on the ruler

Save the tab settings by entering

[Return]

The text in the table aligns to the new tab stops.

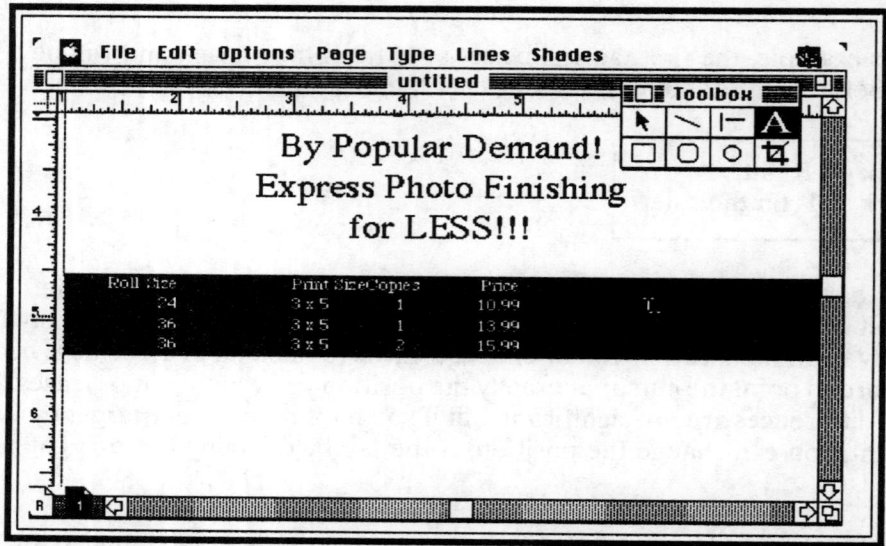

Figure 2.15   Text aligned at new tabs.

Moving Tab Stops

The positions you selected for the tabs were simply an estimate of where the text ought to be positioned. As you look at the results of this selection, you may very well feel that your choices were not ideal. This is no real problem. In fact this is probably what will frequently happen when you create a table on your own.

Multiple Text Blocks **2**

PageMaker makes it simple to change the tab locations. Display the Indents/Tabs dialog box again. Enter

Command + i

Tabs can be moved by dragging the tab stop icons to new locations. For example, drag the tab at 4" to 5".

> **Point** at the tab at 4"
> **Drag** to 5"

Now, drag the tab at 3" to 3.5".

> **Point** at the tab at 3"
> **Drag** to 3.5"

Deleting a Tab Stop

Suppose you want to change the alignment characteristic of a tab stop. For example, the text aligned at the 2" tab is left aligned, but it might look better if it were center aligned.

You cannot change the alignment of a tab stop directly. You must first delete the existing tab and replace it with a new tab. You can delete a tab stop by dragging the tab icon down below the ruler line.

> **Drag** the 2" tab icon down below the ruler line

When you drag the tab icon down below the ruler line, it disappears. When you release the mouse button, the tab stop is deleted.

2 Multiple Text Blocks

Create the tab to replace it by selecting Center and then placing the tab on the ruler line.

> **Click** on Center
> **Click** on 2"

Note that a center tab icon has no tail, left or right. Save the new tab setting by entering

[Return]

The text in the table is realigned at the revised tab stops.

Remember, tab stops are based on the location of the tabs, not the size of the text, so even if you change the point size of the text, it will still be aligned at the same locations. Change the text to Geneva, 14-point, bold. Enter

Command + t

> **Point** at Font
> **Drag** to Geneva
> **Point** at Size
> **Drag** to 14
> **Click** on Bold
> **Click** on OK

The table should now look like the one in Figure 2.16.

Multiple Text Blocks **2**

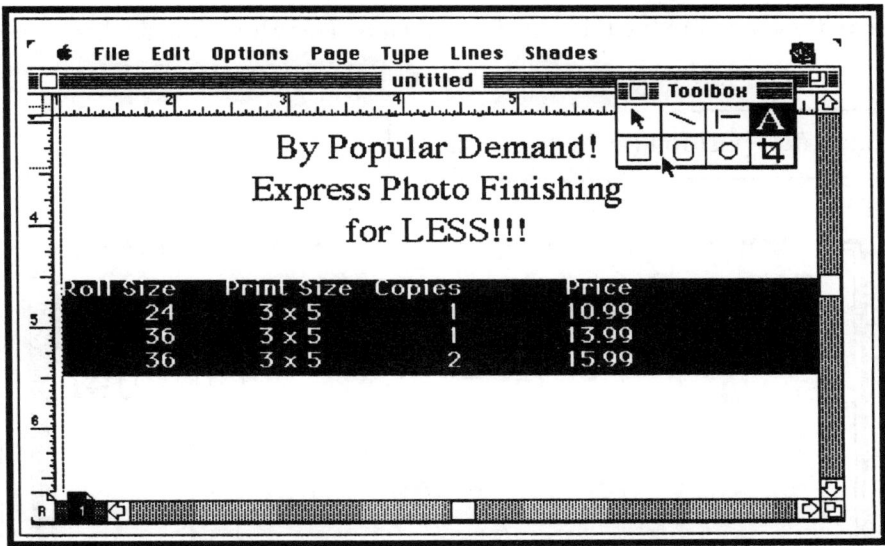

Figure 2.16   Table realigned to revised tabs.

Positioning the Table

Now that you have created a tab-formatted table, you can position the table on any part of the page as a single text block. Reduce the view to 50% of actual size to make it easier to position items on the page. Enter

Command + 5

Place PageMaker into the selection icon.

> **Click** on pointer icon

Select the text block by clicking on any part of the table.

> **Click** on "Copies"

2 Multiple Text Blocks

You can now position the table by dragging it to a new location, as shown in Figure 2.17.

> **Drag** to new position (as in Figure 2.17)

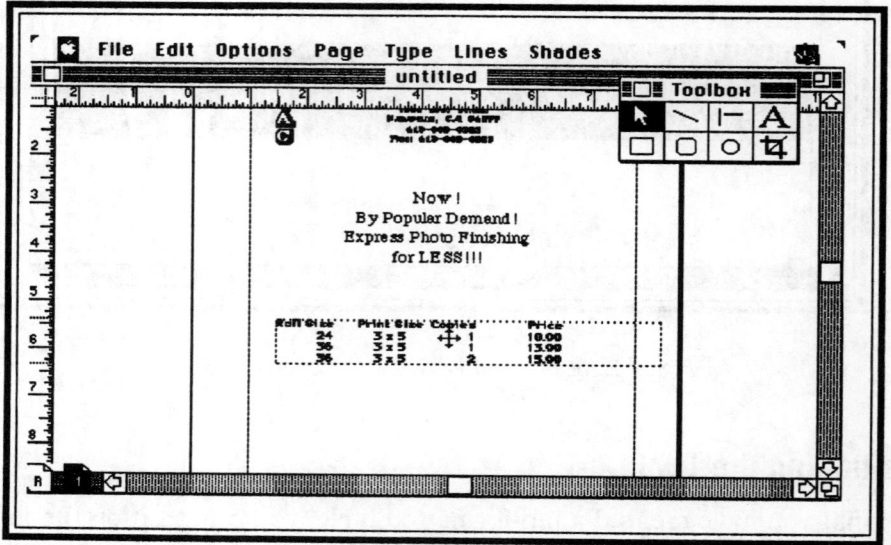

Figure 2.17   Table repositioned on the page.

ADDING RULING LINES

The document you have created contains several blocks of text formatted with different text attributes and tab stops. Another way to enhance a layout such as this is to add **ruling lines** to the document. Traditionally, ruling lines are drawn horizontally or vertically on the page, although with PageMaker you can draw diagonal lines as well.

Ruling lines can be added to any part of the document by activating the perpendicular line icon in the Toolbox palette. Dragging the mouse in this mode causes PageMaker to draw a vertical or horizontal line or a 45-degree diagonal line.

Multiple Text Blocks 2

The thickness of the line is determined by the settings on the **Lines** menu. With this menu, you can set the thickness of the line from .5 points (.007") to 12 points (.167"). You can also select a **hairline** (.25 points, or .0035").

In addition to the solid lines, you can choose nine different patterned lines. The pattern lines are composed of solid lines with white space in between. The thicknesses of these patterned lines cannot be changed and are as follows:

1. **Double Line, 4 points thick**
   .5 point line
   3 point space
   .5 point line

2. **Double Line, 5 points thick**
   2.5 point line
   2 point space
   .5 point line

3. **Double Line, 5 points thick**
   .5 point line
   2 point space
   2.5 point line

4. **Triple Line, 6-points thick**
   .5 point line
   1.5 point space
   2 point line
   1.5 point space
   .5 point line

5. **Dashed line, 1 point high**
   each dash 10 points wide
   each space 3 points wide

6. **Dashed line, 3 points high**
   each dash 10 points wide
   each space 3 points wide

7. **Dashed line, 6 points high**
   each dash 10 points wide
   each space 3 points wide

8. **Dashed line, 4 points high**
   each dash 4 points wide
   each space 4 points wide

9. **Dotted line, 4 points high**
   each dot 4 points wide
   each space 4 points wide

Enter the perpendicular-line mode.

> **Click** on the perpendicular-line icon

Select a 6-point line.

> **Point** at Line
> **Drag** to 6 pt

2 Multiple Text Blocks

Once you have selected the thickness of the line, you can draw by dragging the mouse between any two points on the page. Note that once you begin to draw horizontally or vertically, PageMaker locks you into that direction. For example, if you begin by dragging to the left or right, you automatically activate horizontal drawing. The vertical position of the line is fixed, allowing you to move only left or right.

If you attempt to drag the mouse up or down, the line will snap to a 45-degree diagonal and then to a vertical line and to a 45-degree diagonal again. By restricting your movement when drawing, PageMaker helps you draw straight lines. Note that PageMaker has a separate diagonal-line mode (which you can enter by clicking on the diagonal line icon in the Toolbox) that will permit a line of any angle — not just 45 degrees — to be drawn.

Begin drawing the line at a point 2.5" down on the left page guide. You can use the vertical ruler line to estimate 2.5" down.

> **Point** at left page guide, 2.5" down

Draw a line across the page, starting about 2.5" down, between the left and right page guides, as shown in Figure 2.18.

> **Drag** to the right page guide

Repeat the operation by drawing another line across the page, below the text block at 4.5" down.

> **Drag** across page guide at 4.5" down

Your page should now resemble Figure 2.19.

Multiple Text Blocks 2

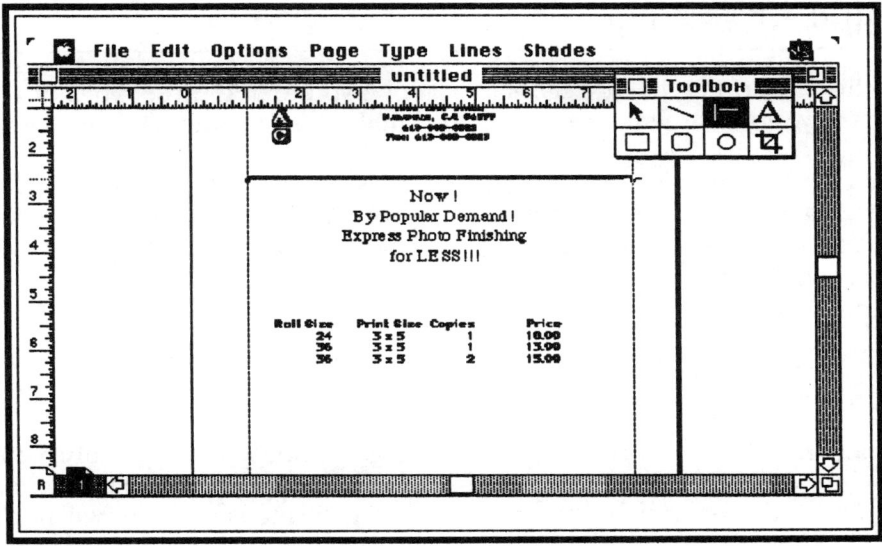

Figure 2.18   Line drawn across the page.

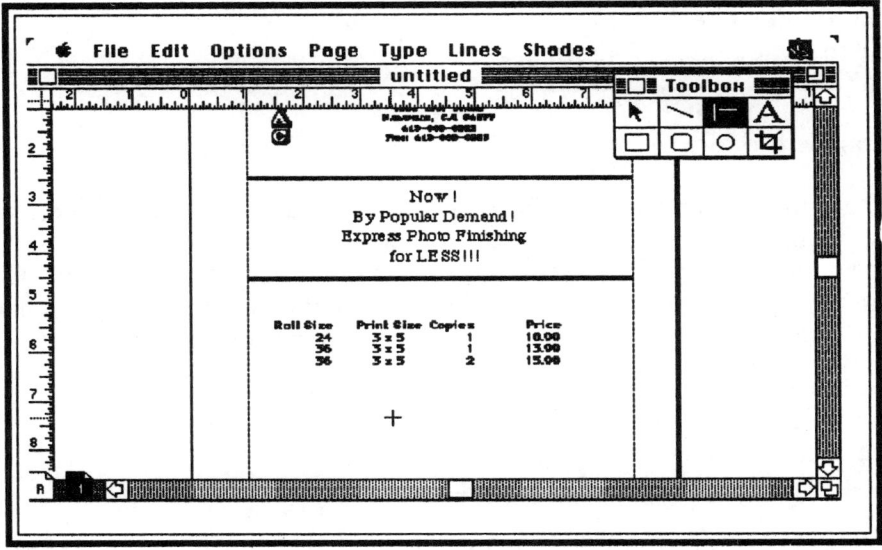

Figure 2.19   Ruling lines above and below text block.

2 Multiple Text Blocks

ADDING GRAPHICS

In addition to ruling lines, PageMaker allows you to add three types of graphic objects to your document: rectangles, rectangles with rounded corners, and ovals.

These graphic objects can be used to create designs or enhance text. For example, the pricing chart you created might draw more attention if it were enclosed in a box. You could use either a rectangular box or a rectangular box with rounded corners. In this case, use a rounded rectangular box.

> **Click** on the rounded rectangle icon

You can draw a rounded rectangle by pointing the mouse at the position you want for the upper left corner of the rectangle and dragging the mouse to the position you want for the lower right corner. As you drag the mouse, the box will be drawn.

In this case, you will want to surround the pricing table with the box, which you can do by pointing at the left page guide about 5" down the page and dragging to the right page guide about 6.5" down the page.

> **Point** at left guide 5" down
> **Drag** to right guide 6.5" down

A rectangle is drawn around the pricing table (see Figure 2.20).

Note that the line thickness of the rectangle is the same as the thickness for the last ruling lines you drew — 6 points. You can change the thickness or pattern of the rectangle's outline by selecting a different line from the Lines menu. Change the line to a double line pattern — in this case the double line with a thin line first and a thicker line second. This is the 12th option on the Lines menu.

> **Point** at Lines
> **Drag** to Double line (12th item on menu)

The rectangle is now drawn as a double line around the text.

Multiple Text Blocks **2**

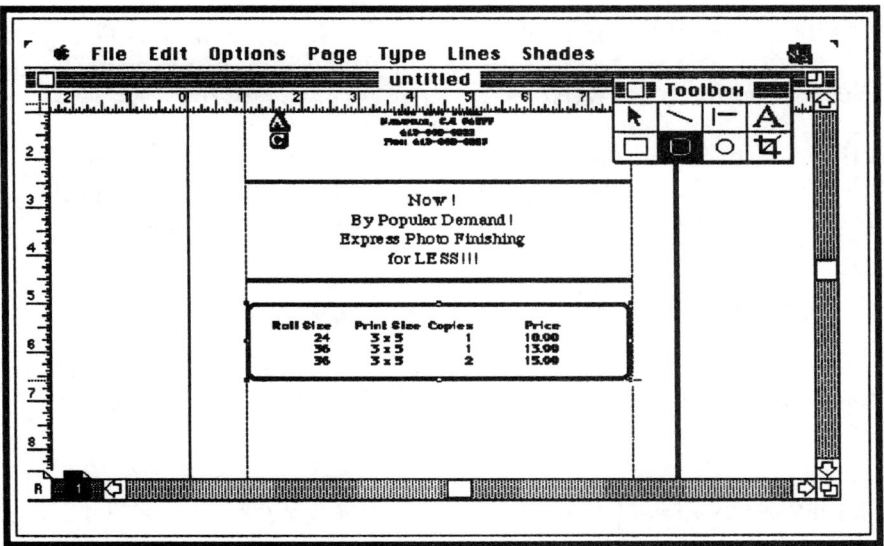

Figure 2.20   Rounded rectangle added to document.

Modifying a Graphic

Note that there are eight small squares that appear at the corners and in the middle of each line of the rectangle you have just drawn. These are the **selection buttons** that appear on a selected graphic object. You can change the size and shape of the object by dragging these buttons.

Button	Changes
Upper left	Move left and top
Center left	Move left side
Bottom left	Move left and bottom
Center top	Move top
Center bottom	Move bottom
Upper right	Move top and right
Center right	Move right
Bottom right	Move right and bottom

Suppose you wanted to move the sides of the box in .5" from the guides. You could make this change by dragging the left center and right center buttons.

2 Multiple Text Blocks

You can also move the graphic object to another location on the page by dragging the entire object. You can drag the entire object by pointing at any part of it except the selection buttons.

Note that these operations must be carried out from the selection (pointer) mode—*not* from the drawing mode. If you drag in the drawing mode, you will simply create another rectangle. Change to the selection mode.

> **Click** on the pointer icon

As soon as you change modes, the rectangle is no longer selected. To select the rectangle, you can click on any part of the rectangle's outline.

> **Click** on the rectangle

Move the left side of the rectangle in by .5"

> **Drag** the left center button to 1.5"

When you drag the mouse, the mouse cursor changes to a left/right arrow, indicating that you can move the left side of the selected object to the left or the right but not up or down. Use the right center button to move the right side of the rectangle to about 7", i.e., in about .5".

> **Drag** the right center button to 7"

Multiple Text Blocks 2

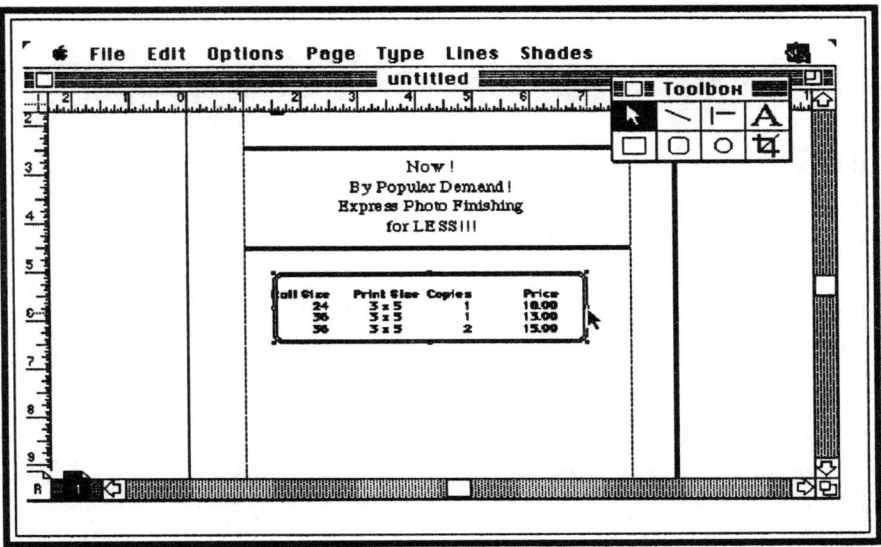

Figure 2.21   Rectangle's size modified.

The reduced rectangle will probably not be positioned correctly in terms of the text within it. In PageMaker, you can move either the rectangle or the text block. In this case, the rectangle is centered correctly on the page, so it would be better to position the text to match the rectangle.

> **Click** on "Copies"

PageMaker displays the window shade handles, indicating that the text block is selected. Position the text block so that it is centered inside the rectangle, as in Figure 2.22.

> **Drag** text block to center of rectangle

2   Multiple Text Blocks

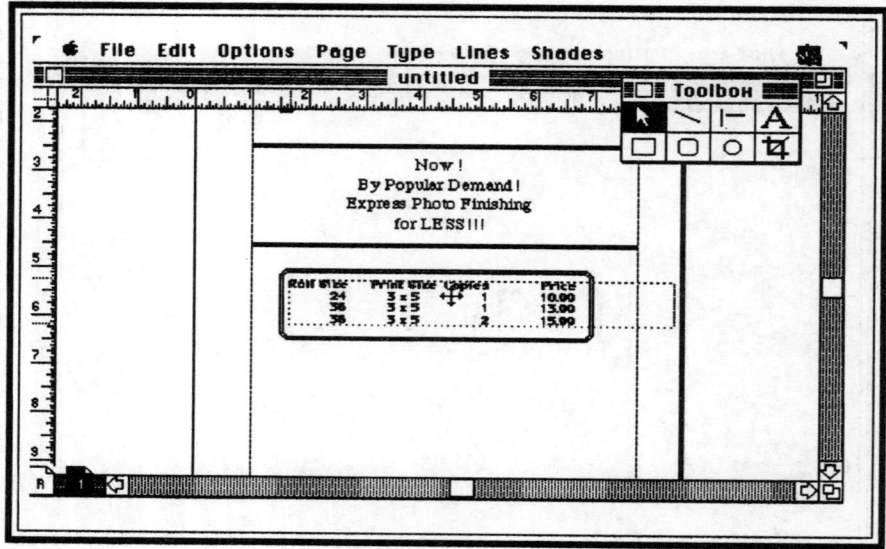

Figure 2.22   Text centered inside of rectangle.

Multiple Graphic Objects

The previous examples of adding graphics to a document use a single shape — a line or a rectangle — to outline or set off a section of text. In this section, you will use text along with several graphic objects to create the visual effect you want.

The last part of this document is a coupon with a special offer. You might add this type of coupon to the flyer to motivate the reader to use your service. Scroll the display so that you can see the bottom of the page.

> **Click** on the scroll bar down arrow (2 times)

Create a new text block in the center of the blank area at the bottom of the page.

> **Click** on the text icon
> **Click** in the blank area at the bottom of the page

Multiple Text Blocks 2

Change to 18-point, Geneva, outline text.

Command+t

> **Point** at Font
> **Drag** to Geneva
> **Point** at Size
> **Drag** to 18
> **Click** on Outline
> **Click** on OK

Enter the following text.

Special Offer with this Coupon [Return]
[Return]

Change to 24-point, shadow text. Enter

Command+t

> **Point** at Size
> **Drag** to 24
> **Click** on Shadow
> **Click** on OK

Enter

1 EXTRA SET [Return]
of COLOR PRINTS [Return]

Change to a smaller font. Enter

Command+t

> **Point** at Size
> **Drag** to 12
> **Click** on Normal
> **Click** on OK

2 Multiple Text Blocks

Enter

with the purchase of any of our [Return]
regular low priced photo finishing services [Return]
Offer expires May 1, 1989

The text will look like Figure 2.23. If your text block is not in the same position, place PageMaker into the selection mode and move the text block by selecting and dragging it.

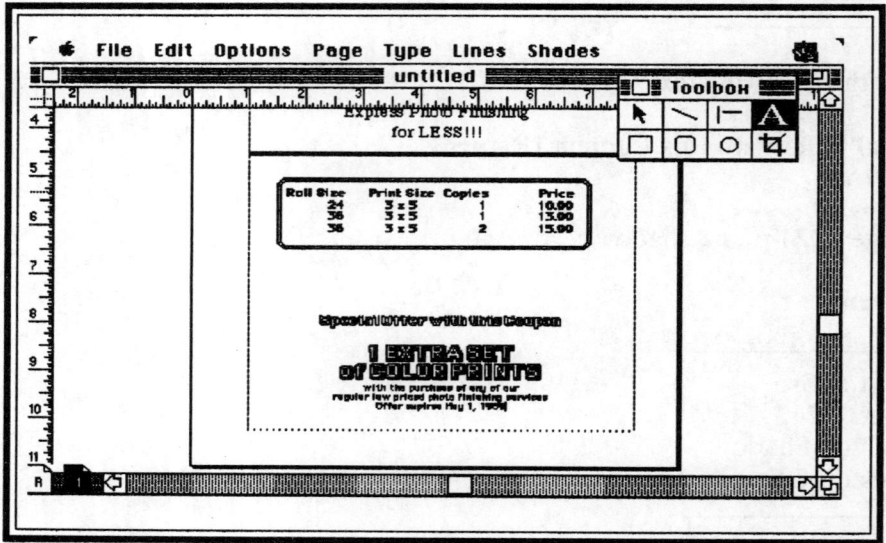

Figure 2.23   *Text block added to bottom of document.*

To make the coupon portion of the document appear detachable, you can draw a dashed line across the page. Place PageMaker into the perpendicular line drawing mode.

> **Click** on the perpendicular-line icon

Select a 3-point, dashed line, the 15th item on the Lines menu.

> **Point** at Lines
> **Drag** to the 3-point, dashed line

Draw a line across the page, from the left to the right guides, approximately 7.5" down the page, which should place the line above the coupon text.

> **Drag** a line across the page at 7.5"

The dashed line creates a separation between the coupon and the rest of the document, showing the reader which part should be torn off.

Shaded Graphic Objects

When you draw a rectangle or oval on a PageMaker document, it consists of two parts: the outline and the enclosed area.

Outline The outline is the line that marks the edges of the rectangle or oval. The thickness or pattern of the line is controlled by the currently selected option on the Lines menu. You can change the outline by selecting the graphic object and choosing a different pattern from the Lines menu.

Enclosed area The enclosed area is the space inside the outline of the rectangle or oval. By default, this area is empty, which means that the graphic object is treated as a transparent shape in which any other objects (such as text blocks) that are enclosed by the outline appear inside the enclosed area with a white background. However, the options on the Shades menu can be used to fill the enclosed area with a shade of gray or a hatching pattern of vertical, horizontal, or diagonal lines.

2 Multiple Text Blocks

To enhance the appearance of the coupon, you can draw a rectangle around the text. Place PageMaker into the rectangle drawing mode.

> **Click** on the rectangle icon

Select a 2-point thickness for the rectangle's line.

> **Point** at Lines
> **Drag** to 2 pt

Draw a rectangle around the text at the bottom of the page, as shown in Figure 2.24.

> **Drag** rectangle around text (as in Figure 2.24)

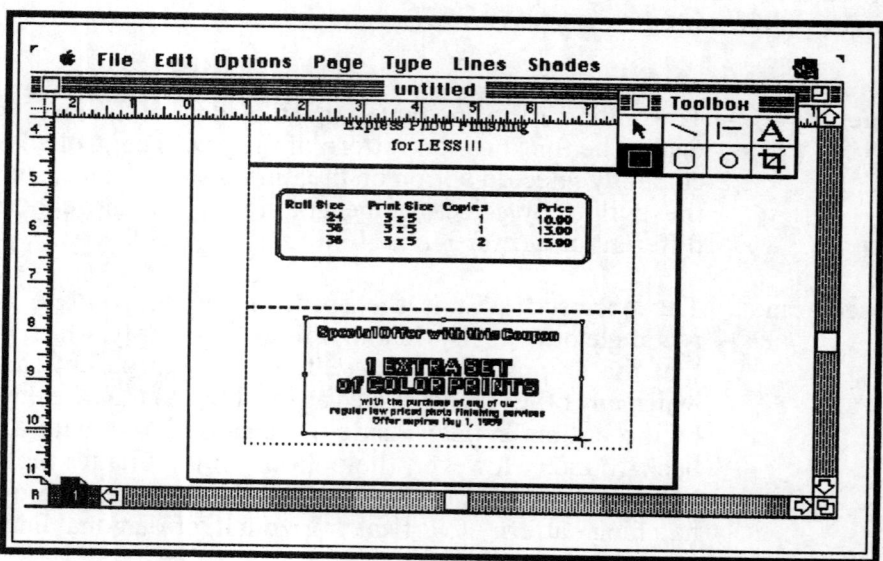

Figure 2.24   *Rectangle drawn around text.*

The rectangle you drew is simply a box, i.e., an outline of a rectangle with an empty center. PageMaker permits you to fill the rectangle with a shade or pattern. The Shades menu lists **shades** (from solid to 10% through 80% shading) and **patterns** composed of lines with which the object can be filled.

The default setting on the Shades menu is None, which creates the empty rectangles that you have been drawing so far. Change the current rectangle to a 10% shaded rectangle.

> **Point** at Shades
> **Drag** to 10%

The rectangle is filled with a 10% shade, but this filled rectangle covers the text that had been visible inside the empty rectangle. When more than one object is placed onto the same part of the document, PageMaker **layers** the objects on top of each other. The newest objects are stacked on top while the objects created earlier are stacked below.

In this case, the text block was the first object created in this area of the document, so when you added the rectangle, it was placed on top of the text block. As long as the rectangle was empty, it didn't make any difference which object was on top because the text could be seen through the empty space inside the rectangle, but when the 10% shading was used to fill the rectangle, the text underneath it was obscured.

The layering of objects is a concept that is consistent with PageMaker's method of manipulating the images on the screen as if they were real objects. PageMaker allows you to change the order in which objects are layered so you can display the objects in the order that best suits your purpose.

PageMaker provides two commands, on the Edit menu, for this purpose: Bring to front and Send to back.

Bring to front   Places the selected object at the top layer.
Shortcut: **Command+f**

Send to back   Places the select object at the bottom of the layers.
Shortcut: **Command+b**

2 Multiple Text Blocks

You can use these commands to shuffle the objects stacked upon each other until you get the correct arrangement. If there are only two objects, the procedure is straightforward; one is the foreground object and the other the background. When there are three or more objects, shuffling the layers can be a bit tricky. By repeated selections and movements to the top or the bottom, you can eventually restack any group of objects in the order you want.

In this case, you have two objects. Currently, the rectangle is the foreground object while the text is in the background. The shaded rectangle should logically be the background, allowing the text to be read on top of the background shading.

You can restack the two objects by using the Send to back command. Enter

Command + b

The shaded rectangle is now sent to the bottom of the object stack, allowing the text to appear on top of the background.

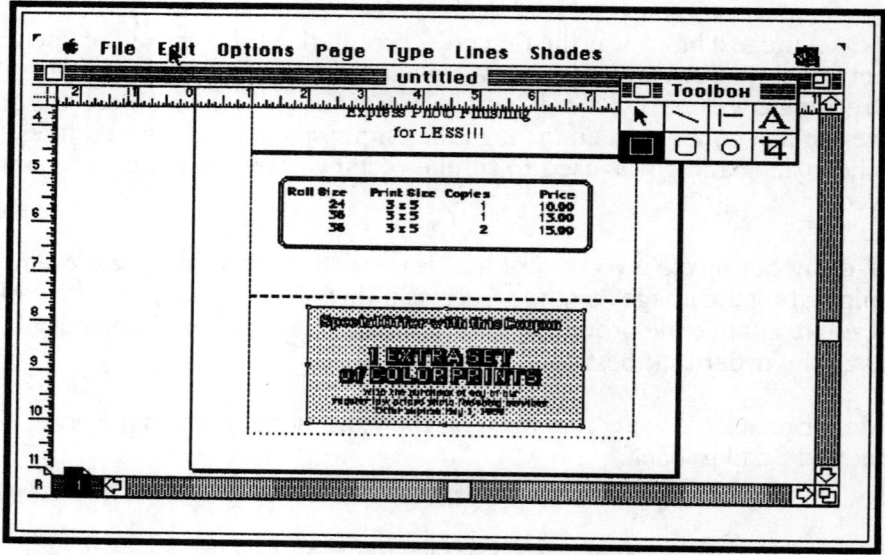

Figure 2.25   Shaded rectangle placed at the bottom of the object stack.

The screen display makes it appear that the text is very hard to read when placed on the 10% background. Keep in mind that the contrast between the shaded background and the text as displayed is not as clear as it will be when the document is printed. If you are using a laser printer, the 10% shading will be a smooth, light gray tone over which the printed text will be clearly readable. The problem is caused by the difference in resolution between the screen display and the printer. Printers typically have a much higher dot resolution than screen displays. The Macintosh has a display density of about 75 dots per inch. A laser printer will have a resolution of 300 dots per inch.

Once you have printed shades of various percentages, the true effect of the shading on the printed document will be clearer to you.

Drop Shadows

One common effect that can be achieved by stacking objects is called a **drop shadow**. A drop shadow effect can be added to text by selecting the shadow style. A three-dimensional look is created when a dark outline is placed around the right side and bottom of the lines that make up an object or character. On a rectangle, you would place the drop shadow on the right side and the bottom line.

One easy way to create the appearance of a drop shadow for a rectangle is to place a dark rectangle at the bottom of a stack — slightly below and to the right of a lighter colored rectangle stacked above it. The dark rectangle would be at the bottom of the stack, so only a small portion of it would show because the rest would be obscured by the lighter shaded rectangle stacked above it, giving the appearance of a drop shadow.

The effect is easily achieved by copying the shaded rectangle and then changing the shading to a darker shade or even to solid black. Copying the rectangle ensures that both rectangles are exactly the same size and shape.

Graphic objects can be cut, copied, and pasted just like text or text blocks. The object that is currently selected is the 10% shaded rectangle. Create a copy of the currently selected object by entering

Command + c
Command + v

2 Multiple Text Blocks

The rectangle is placed back into the document at a slightly different position from the original rectangle it was copied from. Change the shading to a solid black rectangle.

> **Point** at Shades
> **Drag** to Solid

To use this rectangle as a drop shadow, drag it to a position about .25" below and .25" to the right of the shaded rectangle at the bottom of the page, as shown in Figure 2.26.

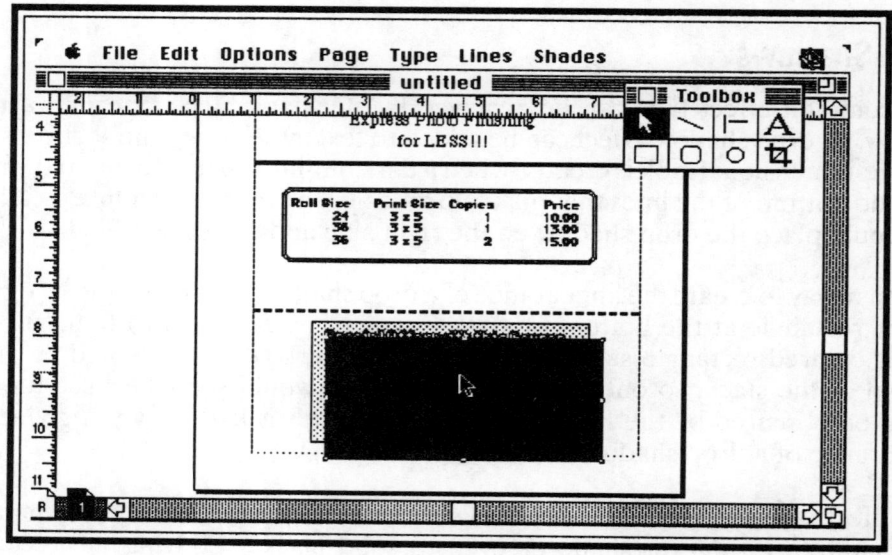

Figure 2.26   Solid rectangle moved into position.

Once you have positioned the rectangle, create the drop shadow effect by moving the rectangle to the bottom of the object stack. Enter

Command + b

The solid rectangle is now positioned underneath the text block and the shaded rectangle. Only the right and bottom edges of the solid rectangle are visible, creating the drop shadow effect.

Multiple Text Blocks 2

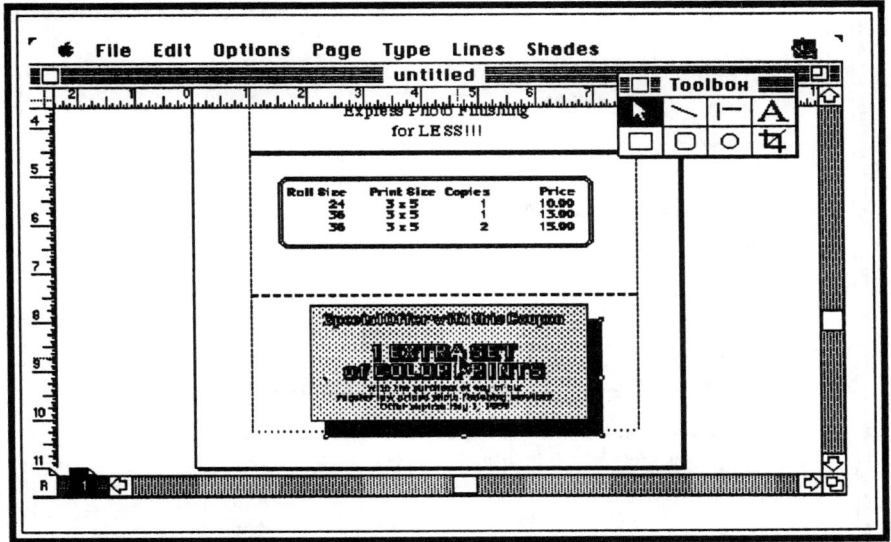

Figure 2.27   *Drop shadow effect created by layering graphics.*

Print the document by entering

Command + p
[Return] (3 times if your printer is an ImageWriter)

The document should resemble Figure 2.28.

2 Multiple Text Blocks

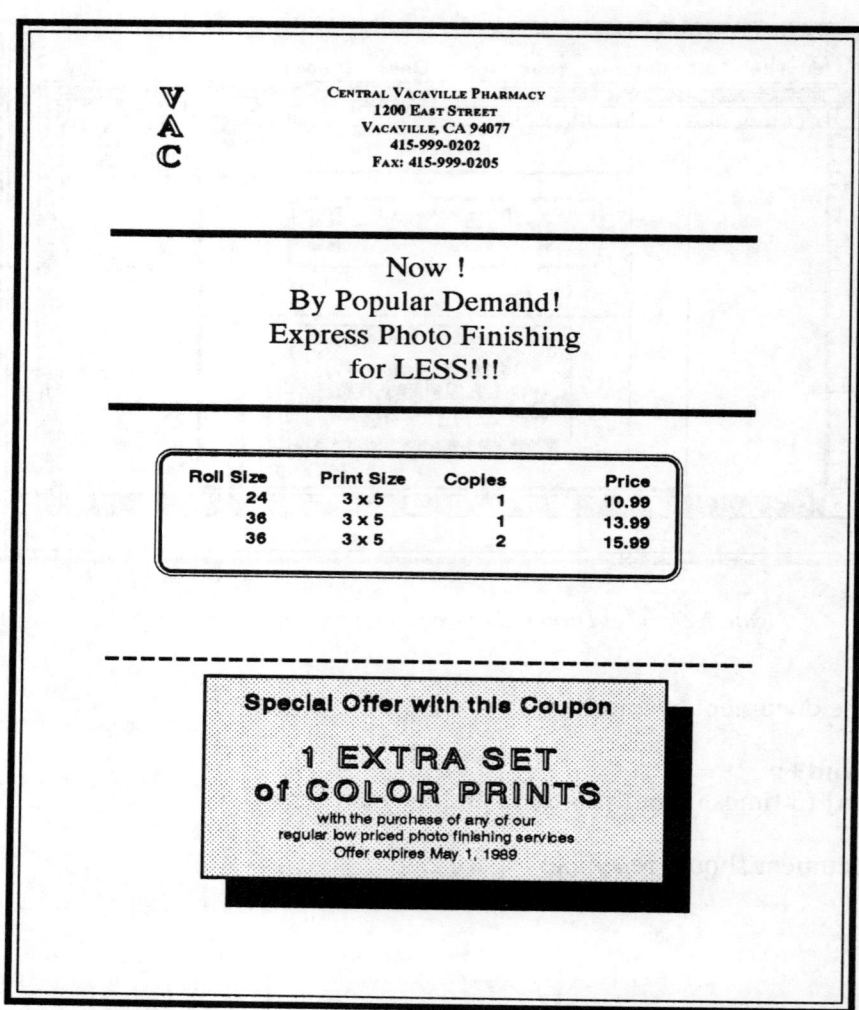

Figure 2.28   Printed document.

When the document is printed, save it by entering

Command + s
Photo Special [Return]

Close the document window.

Point to File
Drag to Close

SUMMARY

In this chapter you learned how a document can be assembled by creating a series of objects that can be moved and arranged on the document page independently of each other. The objects can be text blocks or drawn graphics such as lines, ovals, or rectangles.

PageMaker documents are compositions of many individual parts — not just a single item.

- **Text Blocks.** The text in a document can be divided into a number of text blocks. Text blocks can contain as little as one character. The blocks can be positioned independently of each other, which enables you to position text in ways that are not possible when you enter text in just lines and paragraphs.

- **Arranging Blocks.** You can change the location of a text block from the **selection** mode by selecting the block and dragging it to its new location. By default, text blocks are transparent and can be positioned over one another to create effects by superimposing characters over blank space left in another text block.

- **Kerning.** Kerning is a process by which the horizontal space between individual characters can be adjusted. While PageMaker automatically spaces characters based on their font, point size, and style, certain pairs of characters create the appearance of having either too much or too little space between them because of their shape or way that they slant. The keyboard shortcut **Command + Shift + Delete** adds space between characters while **Command + Delete** removes space between characters.

2 Multiple Text Blocks

- **Type Specifications.** The Type specifications dialog box, **Command+t**, allows you to change the font, size, style, leading, case, or position of text in a single menu. Recall that PageMaker provides individual commands for font, size, and type style. If you intend to change more than one type specification at a time, using the dialog box is faster than using a sequence of individual commands.

- **Tabs.** By default, PageMaker sets tabs every .5" for each line of text. You can use the Indents/Tabs dialog box (**Control+i**) to remove, set, and adjust tabs in order to lay out tables of information aligned at tab locations. You can select left, right, center, and decimal tabs. You can also select a lead character with which any blank space left in front of a tab will be automatically filled.

- **Ruling Lines.** Ruling lines are straight lines drawn across or down the page to mark off sections of text. PageMaker allows you to draw lines on any part of the page. The Lines menu lists thicknesses and patterns for the ruling lines you draw.

- **Rectangles and Ovals.** PageMaker allows you to draw ovals and rectangles with square or rounded corners on any part of the document. A rectangle or oval consists of two parts: the outline and the enclosed area. The outline of the rectangle or oval can be controlled by choosing a thickness or pattern from the Lines menu. The enclosed area is left empty by default, which means that any graphic or text objects that are enclosed by the rectangle or oval will appear in the enclosed area.

- **Line Thickness.** The Lines menu lists options for the thickness or pattern of ruling lines or the outlines of rectangles or ovals. Note that line thicknesses or patterns are described in terms of points, with each point equal to 1/72".

- **Shading.** The enclosed area of a rectangle can be filled with shading or line-hatching patterns. When a shade or pattern is selected for the enclosed area, the area is filled with that selection. Note that selecting this type of shading or pattern will cause the rectangle to become an opaque object that covers any graphic or text objects underneath it.

- **Layering Objects.** Objects placed onto the same area of the document are layered or stacked one on top of the other. The top objects may cover some or all of the objects underneath. PageMaker allows you to place an object on the top or the bottom of the stack or somewhere in between. You can create a variety of visual effects by placing objects on top of one another in special sequences.

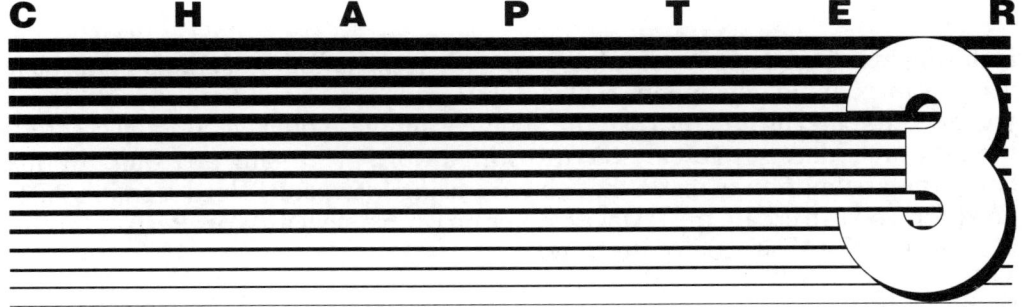

STYLING
LARGE TEXT BLOCKS

PageMaker is capable of creating almost any type of document. Chapters 1 and 2 explained the basic operations in PageMaker by using examples that contained a small amount of text entered directly in PageMaker. In this chapter, you will create a document that contains more text than the previous examples. You will learn how to import this text into PageMaker from your word processor and learn how PageMaker can be used to format imported text.

3 Styling Large Text Blocks

Entering text directly in PageMaker is fine when the amount of text is small, as it was in the example documents in Chapters 1 and 2, but when the amount of text you need to enter is greater than the simple examples you have already created, the best procedure is to create the text with a word processing program. In this book, the assumption is made that you are using Microsoft Word Version 3.01; however, you can create the text with other programs such as WordPerfect for the Macintosh, Full Write, or Write Now.

Preparing text with a word processing program has many advantages. With word processing programs, you can edit text more quickly than in PageMaker because you have available search and replace functions, spell checkers, and other aids to document preparation.

PREPARING THE DOCUMENT

As mentioned, the assumption is that you have available Microsoft Word Version 3.01 or a comparable word processing program for preparing a text document. The entire text of the document you will prepare in this chapter is shown in Figure 3.1.

Note that the text in the document is not formatted, i.e., no effort was made to add lines between paragraphs; change font, size, or type style; or create tab stops or paragraph indents. When you create a document that will be imported into PageMaker, you are simply concerned with the raw text. The formatting will be handled within PageMaker.

The text of the document shown in Figure 3.1 includes special characters that indicate where you need to Press the Tab key (**[tab]**) and Return key (**¶**). If no symbol appears at the end of a line, then that line was simply wrapped by the line-wrap feature of the word processor. Just make sure you enter the tabs in the correct places and enter returns at the end of each short line or paragraph as shown in the figure. These special symbols are guides for your entry and should not appear as text in your final document.

The bullet (•) characters can be entered with the **Option + 8** key combination.

When you have created the document, save it with the name **CORPORATIONS**.

Setting Up Your Own Corporation¶
Before you can decide whether or not you want to incorporate your business, you need to understand the advantages and disadvantages of incorporation.¶
Kinds of Corporations¶
The state of California recognizes four basic types of corporations.¶
1.[tab]Nonprofit Corporations¶
A nonprofit corporation is founded for the benefit of the public, the mutual benefit of its members or for religious purposes. The main reasons for forming this type of corporation are certain tax benefits extended to nonprofit corporations. In most cases distribution of the profits to the members of the corporation is prohibited.¶
2.[tab]Professional Corporations¶
Members of professions that license their members may form a professional corporation. Note that many professions are not subject to the requirement to form a professional corporation but can form a regular profit corporation. Professions that fall into the professional corporation classification are:¶
•[tab]Accountant¶
•[tab]Attorney¶
•[tab]Nurse¶
•[tab]Veterinarian¶
3.[tab]Close Corporation¶
If there are 35 or less members in the corporation it is considered a "close corporation."¶
4.[tab]Privately-Held Profit Corporation¶
This is the most common type of corporation and the one that most individuals would consider for their business.¶
Who Runs a Corporation?¶
Members of a corporation are classified in three ways:¶
•[tab]Incorporator¶
•[tab]Officer¶
•[tab]Shareholder¶
A corporation needs money as well as people to operate. The value of the money or other tangible assets used to create the corporation is called "capital."¶
Capital can be acquired by a corporation by selling stock or borrowing money.¶
Debt to Equity Ratio¶
A.[tab]When creating a corporation out of an existing business it is a mistake to transfer all of the assets of the unincorporated business to the corporation in exchange for a note.¶
B.[tab]The general rule of thumb is that the debt to equity ratio should be no more than 3 to 1.¶
C.[tab]Example:¶
Book Value of Business[tab]$200,000¶
Debt[tab]$150,000¶
Equity[tab]$50,000¶
Dividends¶
A.[tab]Dividends can be paid to the members of a corporation only if the amount of earning in the corporation equals or exceeds the total amount of the dividends to be paid. In other words you cannot incur debt to pay a dividend.¶
B.[tab]In addition the following condition must also be met:¶
Corporate assets following the dividend must be 1.25 times the liabilities.

Figure 3.1   *Text document.*

3 Styling Large Text Blocks

When you have created and saved the document, you can exit your word processing program.

Open your PageMaker folder and load PageMaker.

PLACING TEXT INTO A DOCUMENT

When PageMaker is loaded, you are ready to create a new PageMaker document.

> **Point** at File
> **Drag** to New

In this example, create a two-page document. Enter

2

Also, change the margins to 1" for Top and Bottom and 1.25" for Left and Right.

[Tab] (3 times)
1.25 [Tab]
1 [Tab]
1.25 [Tab]
1

Deselect the Double-sided option. In this example, the assumption is being made that this document will be printed on one side of the page only, i.e., it will be produced on your printer, but it will not be reproduced later by a commercial printer with text on both sides of the page. In that case, it is not necessary to make a distinction between left and right pages.

> **Click** on Double-sided (to deselect it)

Create the new document by entering

[Return]

Styling Large Text Blocks 3

The new, empty document appears on the screen. On the left side of the bar at the bottom of the screen, there are two page icons, labeled **1** and **2**. These icons stand for the pages in the document. Keep in mind that if the number of pages you select at the beginning is not correct, you can add or delete pages as needed.

In Chapters 1 and 2, your first task was to place PageMaker into the text mode so you could create some text for the document. But in this case, because the text has already been created and stored in a word processing file, your first task is to **import** the text into PageMaker instead of entering it.

PageMaker calls this process **placing** text into a document. The term "place" reflects the concept that you must select a text block location in order to place text into a PageMaker document. Because you are not actually typing the text but drawing it from a stored disk file, the process of entering and choosing a location is compressed into a single operation called **Place**.

The Place command is found on the File menu. You can also execute the command with the shortcut key combination **Command + d**.

> **Point** at File
> **Drag** to Place

PageMaker displays the Place document dialog box (see Figure 3.2). The main part of the display is the file selector scroll box in the left side of the dialog box. In addition, there are two sections: Place and Options. These options are only available when you have positioned the selection highlight on a text or graphic file.

You need to highlight the name of the text file you created — **CORPORATIONS**. This file is probably *not* in the current folder, i.e., not in the PageMaker folder. You will need to use the folder selection box, at the top of the scroll box, to activate the folder in which the word processing document is stored. For example, if you created the document with Microsoft Word, you would change to the Word folder by first accessing your hard disk from the folder selection box at the top of the scroll box and then selecting Word from the new list of folders that appears in the scroll box.

3 Styling Large Text Blocks

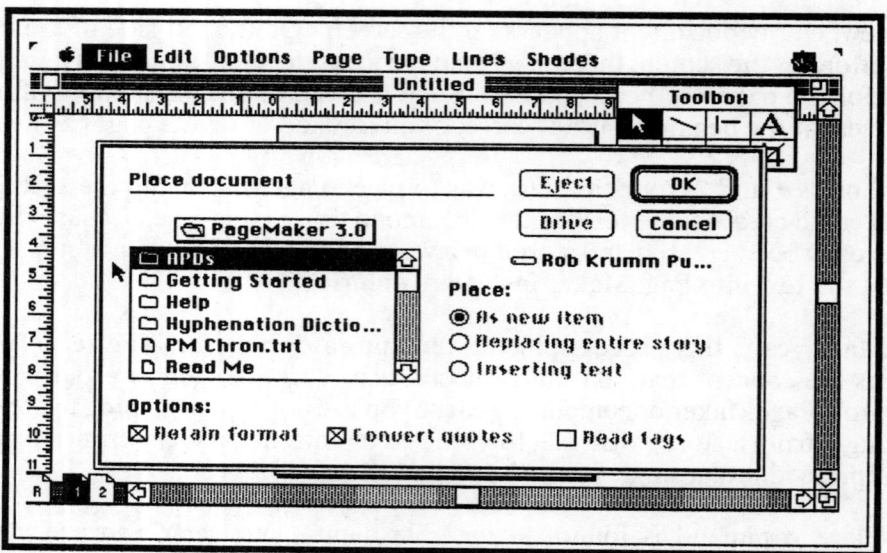

Figure 3.2   Place document dialog box.

Once you have accessed the correct folder, you can select the document you created for this chapter.

> **Click** on CORPORATIONS

When you select a text file such as CORPORATIONS, PageMaker automatically activates the options in the dialog box that are relevant to text documents. PageMaker knows the type of document you selected because the Macintosh operating system stores information about how the file was created. PageMaker reads this information when you select the file name and displays default settings appropriate for a text document created with Microsoft Word. If the file was a graphic file, such as one created with MacPaint, the options in the dialog box would be different.

The Place options are as follows:

As new story The As new story option is selected because you have not entered any text into PageMaker yet. The menu item introduces a new term, **story**. The concept of a story is related to the fact that the text in this document is being drawn from a file created with a program other than PageMaker. A story is all of the text "stored" in the file you are about to place into the PageMaker document.

It is important to realize that the text stored in the file could potentially fill one or more PageMaker pages. This raises a significant problem. When you were entering text directly into PageMaker, you created text blocks as you entered the text. If you are importing a large amount of text, it may be necessary to break the text into more than one text block . For example, the text you are importing from the CORPORATIONS document is probably too long to fit on one page. You may place some of it in a text block on page 1 and the remainder in a text block on page 2. It may turn out that blocks on additional pages are necessary. No matter how many blocks are used, they all have one thing in common: they all come from the text stored in the original text file. A story in PageMaker refers to all of the text blocks that draw their text from the same text file.

Replacing entire story This option is available when the text cursor is placed in a text block that is part of an existing story. If that is the case, this option will replace the current story with the text in the selected document.

Inserting text If you have selected a section of text, this option can be used to delete only the selected text from the PageMaker text block and replace it with the text stored in the file. This operation will blend the remainder of the text block with the imported text.

3 Styling Large Text Blocks

The Options section of the Place dialog box shows two options selected: Retain format and Convert quotes.

Retain format   The Retain format option will carry over any formatting options and styles used in the original document. This option is useful when you want to import a document that was already structured using Microsoft Word format or style commands. PageMaker will attempt to format the text in exactly the same way as it appeared in Word if this option is selected. If this option is not selected, formatting created in Word will be ignored. This is useful when you want to create a totally new format in PageMaker and don't want to have the Word options carried into the PageMaker document.

Convert quotes   This option is specifically aimed at the use of quotation marks with the text file. Word processing programs use the same character (") for both opening and closing quotation marks. In PageMaker, unique characters for beginning and ending quotes are provided. For example, when manually entering text, the command **Option + [** inserts opening quotation marks (") and **Option + Shift + [** inserts closing quotation marks ("). When the Convert quotes option is active, PageMaker automatically substitutes these characters for the quote characters used in the word processing program. You will recall that there are two pairs of quotation marks used in the example text file. Note that if the character in front of the quotation mark is an Arabic number (0-9), PageMaker assumes that the marks are abbreviations for feet or inches and does not convert the marks.

The Read tags option is also available.

Read tags   This option enables you to import styled text if you use a word processor, such as WordPerfect, that does not support styles. (For more about this option, see Chapter 5).

You can begin placing the text into a PageMaker document.

> **Click on OK**

Styling Large Text Blocks 3

(**Note**: Error message 7605:5312 will appear if the fonts installed in the word processing program are different from the font set used by PageMaker. This happens if you have modified your font list in between the time you installed the word processor and the time you installed PageMaker. This message is not significant. If this message appears, simply click on Continue.)

The PageMaker document screen appears. The mouse cursor has changed to a rectangle. The icon indicates that you are placing text into a document.

When the manual place mode is active, you create a text block for the imported text by drawing text block rectangles. Dragging the mouse will create these text blocks. In this case begin the text block in the upper left corner of the page guides.

> **Point** at the upper left corner of the guides
> **Drag** to the right guide
> **Drag** down to about 4"
> **Release** the mouse button

When you release the mouse button, PageMaker creates a text block within the area in which you dragged the placement cursor. The block is filled with text that appears greeked in the Fit to window display mode.

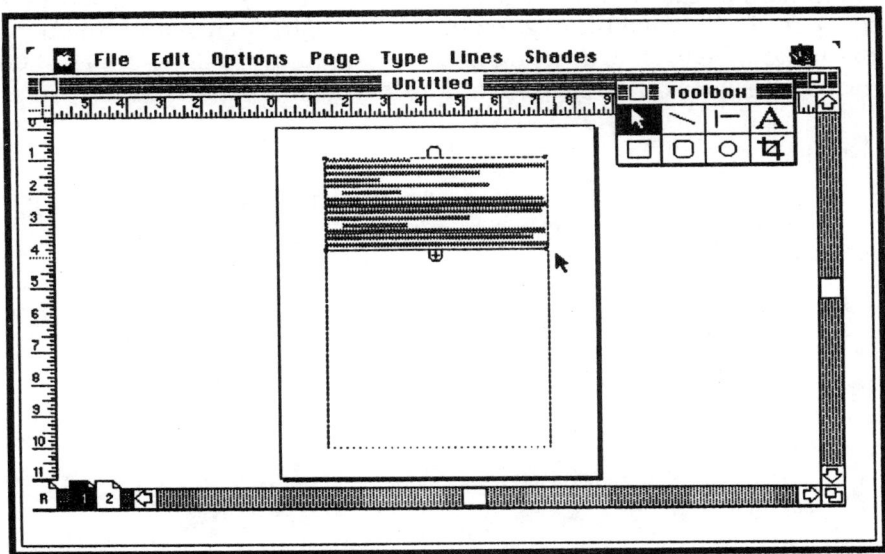

Figure 3.3   *Text block created by placement.*

115

3 Styling Large Text Blocks

The text block is bracketed by window shade handles. It is important to note exactly which handles you should use. The top handle is empty, which indicates that it is the first text block for that story. The window shade handle at the bottom of the block shows a +. The + means there is more to the story than is currently displayed.

You can expand the area of the text block to display more text from the story by dragging this bottom handle.

> **Point** at the +
> **Drag** down to 7"

The text block is extended to cover more of the page. As the block expands, PageMaker fills the area with more text from the story file. The + in the bottom handle indicates there is still more text in the story that is not displayed.

> **Point** at the +
> **Drag** down to bottom guide

The handle jumps back to a position about 9" down the page. The character in the bottom handle has changed from a + to a #. The # indicates that you have now exposed all of the text that was entered into the file. The handle jumped back from the bottom because you didn't need to extend the text block to the bottom of the page to display all of the text in the story file.

Styling Large Text Blocks **3**

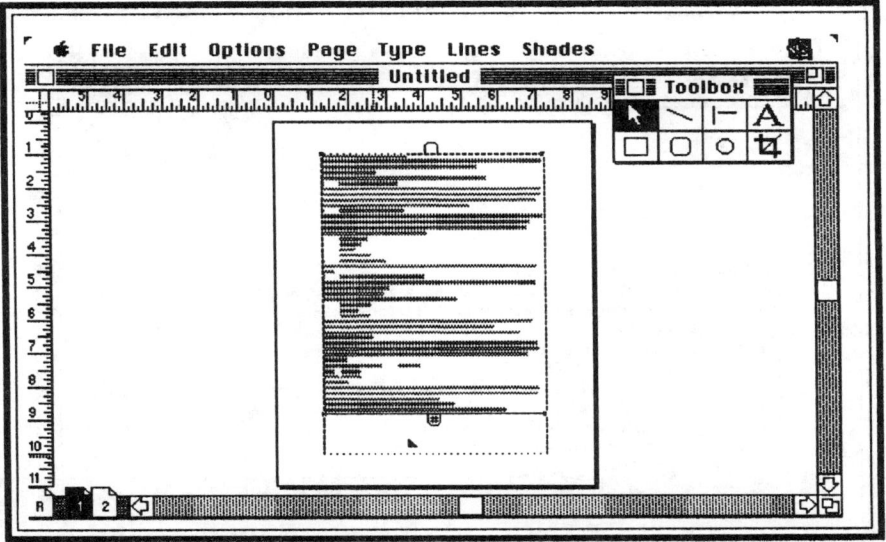

Figure 3.4   Text block displays all of the text from the file.

FORMATTING WITH STYLES

The text imported from the text file is **unformatted** text. The term "unformatted" refers to the fact that none of the text is enhanced with special fonts, sizes, or text styles and that none of the paragraphs is spaced, indented, or tabbed.

Enlarge the view so you can actually read the text within the text block.

> **Point** at the top window shade handle
> **Option + Command + Click**

The top portion of the text block is enlarged to actual size.

3 Styling Large Text Blocks

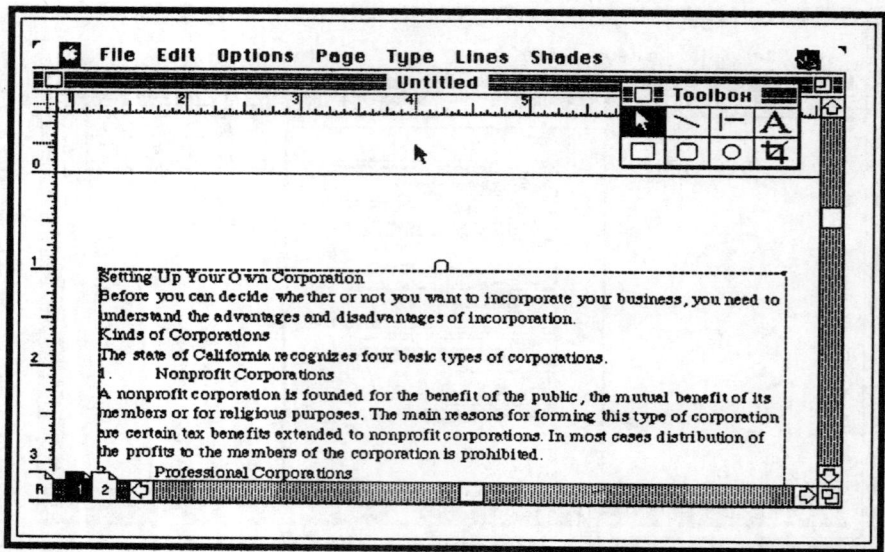

Figure 3.5   *Top portion of text block enlarged to actual size.*

Logically, the text in the current text block is not meant to be simply listed as text, all with the same type size, indents, and spacing. The text is really composed of lines and paragraphs that all serve a different purpose. For example, the first line in the document, "Setting Up Your Own Corporation," is a major heading in the text. In addition, there are subheadings, numbered headings, normal paragraphs, and lists of items.

The purpose of formatting is to provide visual clues and subtext so readers can clearly identify the various parts of the document. Formatting makes a document easier to read and comprehend because it matches the appearance of the text with its function and meaning; it matches form with content.

In Chapters 1 and 2, you encountered the main formatting options in PageMaker: Type specifications, Paragraph specifications, and Indents/Tabs. Every short line or paragraph in a document has a complete set of specifications on these three menus. If you do not make any selections from these menus, the text is still formatted because PageMaker provides default values for all of the settings in the Type specifications, Paragraph specifications, and Indents/Tabs dialog boxes. Formatting text by using these options is called **manual formatting**.

Styling Large Text Blocks 3

Manual formatting assigns a unique set of specifications to the selected text. The advantage of manual formatting is that you can change the format of any section of the text. This section can be an entire text block, a paragraph, a sentence, a group of words, a single word, or a single character. Together, the Type specifications, Paragraph specifications, and Indents/Tabs dialog boxes include 15 manual formatting settings:

1. Font
2. Size
3. Leading
4. Case
5. Position
6. Type Style
7. Hyphenation
8. Pair Kerning
9. Left indent
10. Right indent
11. First line indent
12. Spacing before
13. Spacing after
14. Tabs
15. Color

However, manual formatting does have its disadvantages. For example, you have several major headings in the document you just imported. It makes sense for each major heading to have the same set of formatting specifications because this makes it easier for the reader to see the logical structure of the document.

If you were restricted to manual formatting, you would have to re-enter all of the Type specifications, Paragraph specifications, and Indents/Tabs settings each time you encountered a major heading. If the formatting is complex, this method is quite time-consuming and tedious. In addition, it is often difficult to remember all the specifications exactly so you can re-enter them each time you need to format a major heading. If you forget to enter a setting, the document will be inconsistent in its format.

PageMaker provides an alternative method for formatting more than one paragraph with the same set of attributes. The method is called **Styles**.

3 Styling Large Text Blocks

When you consider all of the fifteen settings that make up a particular paragraph's format, you are discussing the paragraph's **style**. Keep in mind that "style" refers to a concept different from *type* style, which refers to options such as bold, underline, or italic style lettering. In PageMaker, a *paragraph's* style refers to the complete set of options that are used to format the paragraph as a unit. To allow you to refer to all fifteen settings easily, PageMaker allows you to assign a name to all of the settings for a particular type of paragraph. For example, you might assign the name "Major Heading" to the set of specifications you want to use for your major heading paragraph.

Styles are created in four ways.

Import	Word Processing programs such as Microsoft Word use styles in a manner similar to the way PageMaker uses styles. Word documents carry their style names and settings into the PageMaker text block. It is important to remember that paragraphs created in a Word document are automatically assigned what is called the **Normal** style. When these documents are imported into a PageMaker text block, each paragraph is assigned the Normal style as it is copied from the Word document. Styles created by importing appear with an * following their name in the style listing.
Use built-in style	PageMaker has five built-in styles: **Body text, Caption, Headline, Subhead 1**, and **Subhead 2**. You can select any one of these styles, which will automatically format the selected paragraph or paragraphs to the specifications assigned to each style.

Body text	Times 12-point, normal, auto leading, first-line indent .333"
Caption	Times, 10-point italic, auto leading
Headline	Times, 30-point, bold, auto leading
Subhead 1	Same as Headline, except point size 18
Subhead 2	Same as Subhead 1, except point size 12

Styling Large Text Blocks **3**

Create a style   You can create a new style from scratch or by copying an existing style.

Edit a style   You can create a new style by editing one of the existing styles.

Applying a Built-in Style

The simplest way to use a style is to select one of the built-in styles. Styles are applied to paragraphs in the text mode. Activate the text mode.

| **Click** on the text icon |

Select the first paragraph in the document for formatting.

| **Click** on "Setting" |

You need not highlight the entire paragraph to apply a style. The style will affect the paragraph if the insertion point is located anywhere in that paragraph.

The Style command is the last one on the Type menu. When you select the Style option, PageMaker displays a list of the current styles. A check mark appears next to the style that is currently in use (if there is one).

Another way to display the list of styles is with the **Style palette**. The Style palette is a small window that lists the available styles and can be displayed on the PageMaker document window at any time or all the time. The Style palette command on the Options menu will activate the Style palette display. The shortcut combination **Command+e** can also be used for this purpose. Enter

Command+e

The Styles palette appears on the right side of the display.

3 Styling Large Text Blocks

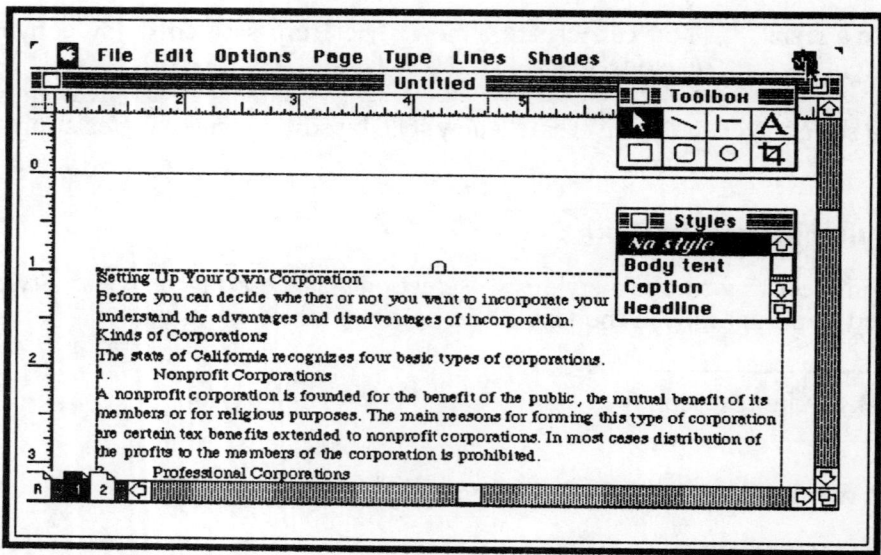

Figure 3.6   Style palette displayed.

The highlight in the Style palette is placed on the normal style. All of the paragraphs in the text imported from Word will automatically be formatted to the normal style. The * next to the name indicates that this style was imported along with the text from the word processing program used to create the text file. The + indicates that the current paragraph contains a **style override**. For example, even in a styled paragraph, you might use the type style commands to make one word bold or italic so that it would stand out from the rest of the text. However, in this case, the override marker (the + sign) is caused by the importing process from a Microsoft Word file. For now, you can ignore it.

You can change the style of the current paragraph by selecting one of the other styles listed on the palette display.

Click on Headline

Styling Large Text Blocks 3

The style of the paragraph is changed to the Headline style.

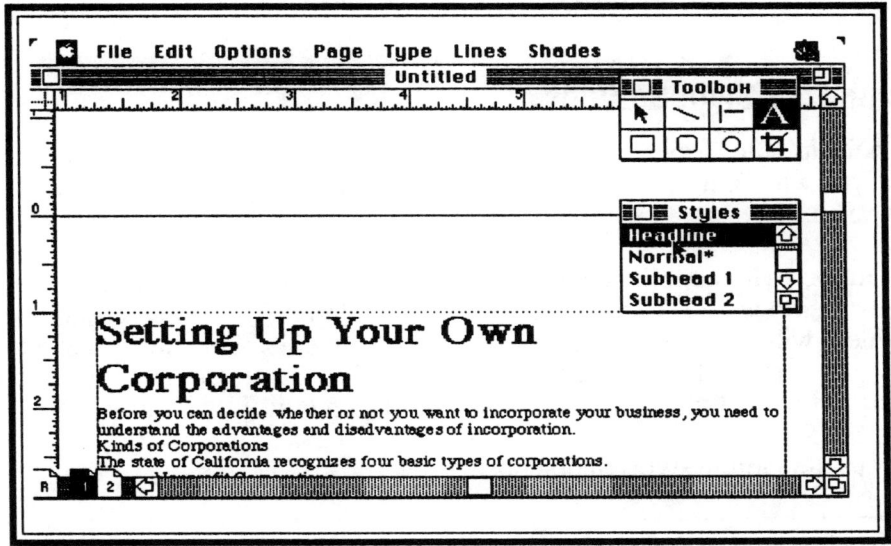

Figure 3.7   *Paragraph changed to Headline style.*

The headline style is pre-set by PageMaker for 30-point, Times, bold characters with auto leading and left alignment.

You can change to another style to see how it would look by selecting another name from the palette display.

> **Click** on Subhead 1

The text changes to the Subhead 1 style, which is predefined by PageMaker as 18-point, Times, bold characters with auto leading and left alignment.

You can even return to the original style, which would format the text exactly as it was before you began to experiment with different styles.

> **Click** on Normal

3 Styling Large Text Blocks

The text returns to the **Normal** style. Note that the + (the override marker) no longer appears in the style palette. Once you begin to style imported text, the + is removed from the name of that paragraph's style.

Customized Style Settings

The built-in styles provided by PageMaker are simple examples of styles. In most cases, you will want to create additional styles or modify the built-in styles to suit your purposes.

The Define styles command located on the Type menu allows you to create, copy, edit, or remove styles from the document palette. The styles created in this document will not affect the styles in other documents. For example, even if you modify or remove the Headline style in this document, the Headline style will appear in the next new document you create with built-in defaults.

Activate the Define styles dialog box.

> **Point** at Type
> **Drag** to Define styles

PageMaker displays the Define styles dialog box (see Figure 3.8).

Style · This scroll box contains the list of styles displayed in the Style palette. The first name in the box is always **Selection**, which refers to the style of the currently selected paragraph. If you look below the scroll box, the name of the style used by the current paragraph is displayed, in this case, Normal.

New This option allows you to add a new style to the list of styles in this document. It is important to understand that a new style is not created from scratch. It is always based on an existing style. PageMaker creates a new style by copying an existing style and assigning it a new name. When a new style is first created, the new style and the style from which it was copied have exactly the same settings. You can make the new style unique by using the Edit options to alter the settings. New styles are always based on an existing style, so you can save time by basing the new style on the style that is the closest in format to the new style you have in mind.

Styling Large Text Blocks 3

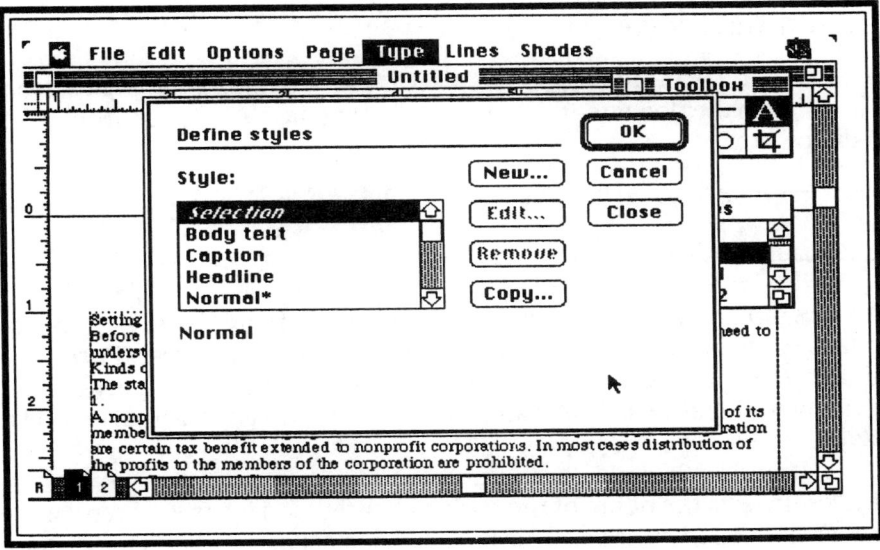

Figure 3.8   *Define styles dialog box.*

Edit   This option allows you to change the settings, type specifications, paragraph specifications, indents and tabs, or colors of a style. It is this option that actually assigns the formatting settings to each style.

Remove   This option allows you to remove a style from the current list of styles. Any paragraphs that are currently formatted with the style you are removing will automatically be formatted with the style upon which the style you are removing was based. If the style was an imported or built-in style, the text reverts to the Body text style.

Copy   This option is used when you want to copy styles that you defined in another PageMaker document into the current document. When you select this option, a dialog box with a file selector box will appear. When you select a PageMaker file, all of the styles defined in that file are added to the current list of styles in the current document.

If an incoming style has the same name as an existing style but different settings, PageMaker will prompt you to skip the incoming style or replace the existing style with the incoming style copied from the other document.

3 Styling Large Text Blocks

Creating a New Style

Suppose that you want to create a new style called Major Heading to use for the main heading in the document. Begin by selecting the New option from the Define styles dialog box.

> **Click** on New

The New command leads you to the Edit style dialog box. Note that the name of the style is blank because you are creating a new style. The Type, Para, Tabs, and Colors options display the Type specifications, Paragraph specifications, Indents/Tabs, and Define colors dialog boxes for defining the actual settings of the new style.

PageMaker inserts the name of the style currently used for the current paragraph, normal, as the Based on style. This means that the basic settings for the new style will be the same as the normal style. Enter the name of the new style:

Major Heading

Before you leave this menu, you should use the options to define the characteristics of this style.

> **Click** on Type

The Type specifications dialog box appears. Choose Helvetica, 18-point, bold, italic type.

> **Point** at Font
> **Drag** to Helvetica
> **Point** at Size
> **Drag** to 18
> **Click** on Bold
> **Click** on Italic
> **Click** on OK

Styling Large Text Blocks 3

In addition, you want to specify that the Major Heading style should be centered between the margins.

> **Click** on Para
> **Click** on Center
> **Click** on OK

The bottom of the Edit dialog box lists a description of the settings that make up the Major Heading style. The description begins with the name of the style on which the current style is based, **Normal**. The **+** indicates that Normal has been enhanced with a new typeface, **face:Helvetica + bold + italic**, a new point size, **size: 18**, and a new alignment, **centered**.

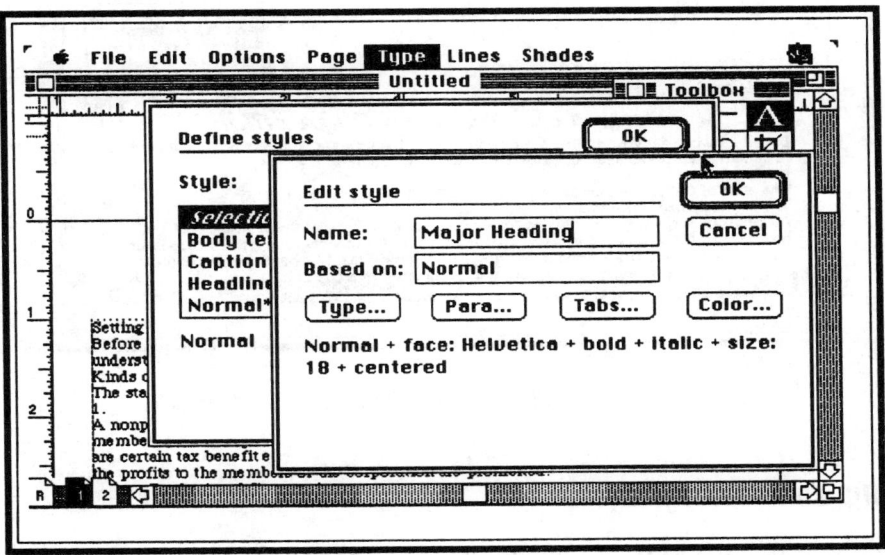

Figure 3.9   *Settings listed in Edit style dialog box.*

Save the new style.

> **Click** on OK

127

3 Styling Large Text Blocks

The name **Major Heading** is added to the list of styles. Return to the document by entering

[Return]

When you return to the document, PageMaker processes the new style settings and formats the text accordingly.

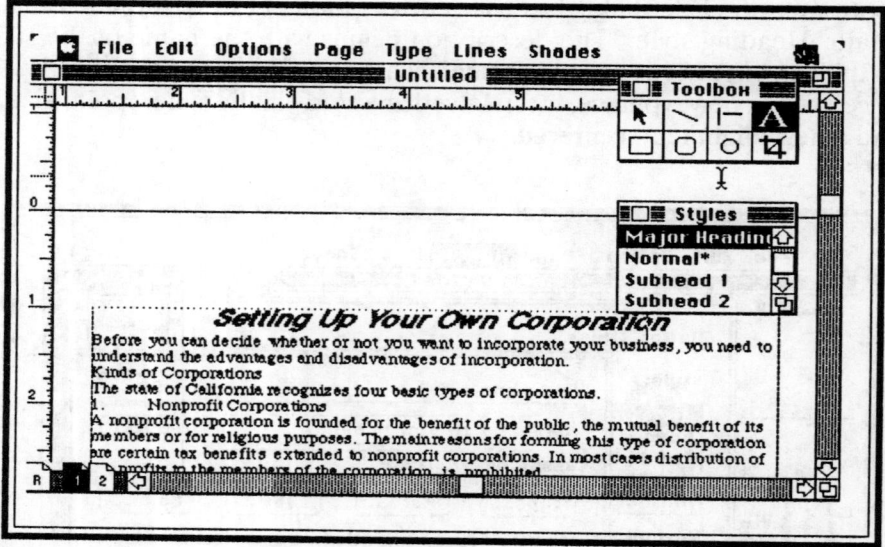

Figure 3.10   First line set with Major Heading style.

Editing an Existing Style

One of the problems with the current document is that all of the paragraphs below the major heading are displayed without any space between them. Because all of the paragraphs are formatted as the Normal style, you could add space between them by editing the specifications used for the Normal style.

> **Point** at Type
> **Drag** to Define styles

Select the Normal style. You will need to scroll the list in the box in order to see the Normal style.

> **Scroll** the list down
> **Click** on Normal

PageMaker displays the settings for the Normal style in the bottom of the dialog box. Display the editing dialog box.

> **Click** on Edit

In this case, you want to add space before each paragraph. In word processing programs, many people create space between paragraphs by entering extra returns between paragraphs. In PageMaker, the extra space can be automatically inserted before or after a paragraph as part of the paragraph's formatting. Display the Paragraph specifications dialog box.

> **Click** on Para

The space before or after a paragraph is entered in terms of inches. Suppose you wanted to leave the amount of space equivalent to a single line of text; however, the height of a single line of text will vary with the point size of the text you are talking about. In this case the Normal style is set for 12-point text. When leading space is included, each line is 14.5 points in height. But you need to enter the value for spacing in inches, not points. A little arithmetic is required.

Recall that each point is 1/72" in height. If you divide 1" by 72, you get a decimal number of approximately .014". 14.5 points multiplied by .014" for each point yields .203" for the height of each line. Therefore, in this case, the height of a single line of blank space is approximately .2".

> **Double Click** on the Before: box

Enter

.2 [Return]

3 Styling Large Text Blocks

"**space before: 0.2**" is added to the style description. Return to the document display.

> **Click** on OK
> **Click** on OK

The text of the document is changed so that space appears between the paragraphs. As a by-product of this process, PageMaker reassigned the Normal format to the current paragraph. However, this is not much of a problem because the correct style, Major Heading, is still part of the style list.

> **Click** on Major Heading

The first paragraph is returned to the Major Heading style.

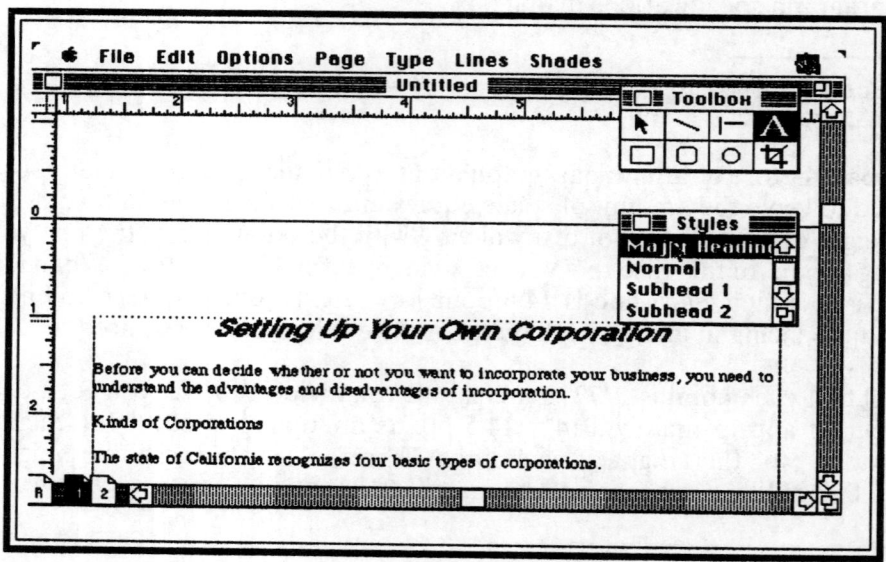

Figure 3.11   Normal style modified by adding space before.

Removing Styles

The document you are working on has several levels of subheadings. You should create styles for these headings. You may have noticed that there are already styles called **Subhead 1** and **Subhead 2**. To simplify the process, it might be useful to remove styles that you don't need for this document. The Subhead 1 and Subhead 2 styles are related to the Headline style. You can remove all of these styles.

> **Point** at Type
> **Drag** to Define styles

Remove the built-in styles from the style list. Remove Body text, Caption, and Headline. Note that as you remove a style, the name of the style under it is highlighted.

> **Click** on Body text
> **Click** on Remove
> **Click** on Remove
> **Click** on Remove

Remove the subheading styles.

> **Click** on Subhead 1
> **Click** on Remove
> **Click** on Remove

Create two new styles called Level 2 and Level 3 for the second- and third-level headings in the document. It is probably a good idea to base these headings on the Major Heading style.

> **Click** on Major Heading
> **Click** on New

Enter the name of the first new style:

3 Styling Large Text Blocks

Level 2

Change the type to 14-point, Times, bold, italic.

> **Click** on Type
> **Point** at Font
> **Drag** to Times
> **Point** at Size
> **Drag** to 14
> **Click** on Italic
> **Click** on OK

Change the alignment to left.

> **Click** on Para
> **Click** on Left
> **Click** on OK
> **Click** on OK

You have now added a Level 2 subheading style to the style list for this document. You can create the next style based on the Level 2 style you just created. Note that PageMaker automatically places the highlight on the style name that you just created.

> **Click** on New

Enter the name of the new style, which will be based on the Level 2 style:

Level 3

Change the point size to 12.

Styling Large Text Blocks **3**

> **Click** on Type
> **Point** at Size
> **Drag** to 12
> **Click** on OK
> **Click** on OK

You now have four styles listed for this document. Return to the document display by entering

[Return]

Because you have not moved your cursor from the first paragraph, that paragraph was assigned the Level 3 style when you exited the menu. Again, set this paragraph to the Major Heading style.

> **Click** on Major Heading

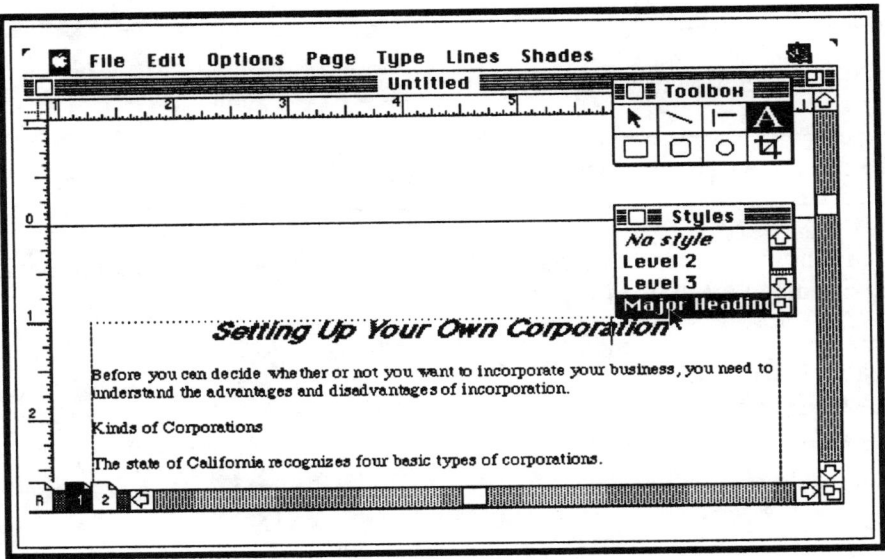

Figure 3.12   Style palette list.

133

3 Styling Large Text Blocks

Applying Styles

Once you have created the styles that you need, you can format a document by selecting the paragraphs and applying the styles from the Style palette.

> **Click** on "Kinds of"
> **Click** on Level 2

The line is formatted as a Level 2 heading.

To see more of the text, change the view mode to the 75% view. Enter

Command + 7

Apply a Level 3 style to the paragraph that begins "1. Nonprofit."

> **Click** on "Nonprofit"
> **Click** on Level 3

Scroll the screen down.

> **Click** on the scroll bar down arrow (5 times)

You can now see more of the text block. Change the line that begins "2. Professional" to a Level 3 heading.

> **Click** on "Professional"
> **Click** on Level 3

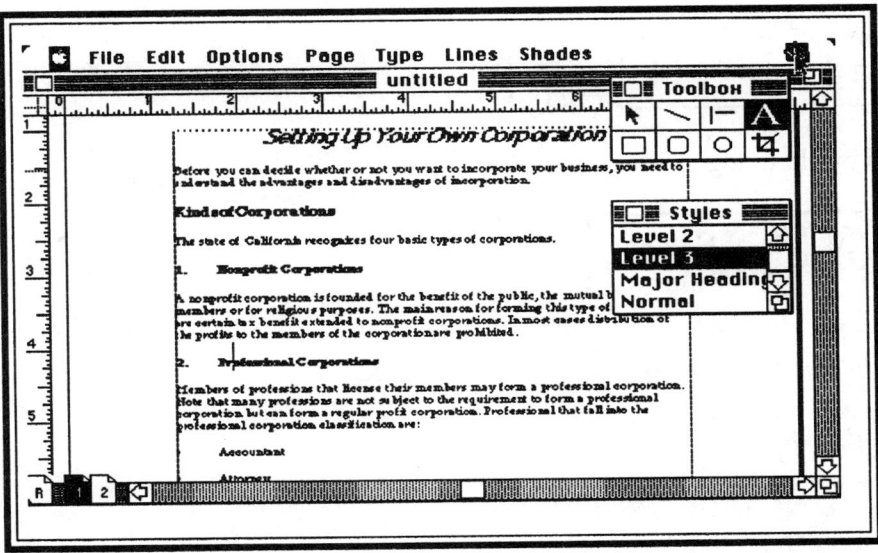

Figure 3.13   *Styles used to format text headings.*

Changes Based on Styles

Using styles to format a document has an additional benefit that may not be obvious at first. When you assign styles to the paragraphs, you are creating a logical structure to your document. When you enter text without styles, the only way to carry out an operation is to specifically select the character, paragraph, or area of the text that you want to affect.

Styles provide another way to affect the text. This method is **indirect formatting**. The term "indirect" implies that the text affected by this type of operation is not selected directly by manually highlighting the text but indirectly by changing the style settings.

For example, suppose that you wanted to change all Level 3 headings to 14-point characters with an underline. Because the Level 3 headings are marked with the Level 3 style, you can change all of the headings throughout the document by changing the style settings. PageMaker will then update the entire document so that all paragraphs assigned the Level 3 style are formatted to the latest settings.

In this case, you will make changes to all three headings. Display the Define styles menu.

3 Styling Large Text Blocks

> **Point** at Type
> **Drag** to Define styles

Begin by changing the Major Heading style.

> **Click** on Major Heading
> **Click** on Edit

Add outline and shadow attributes to the style.

> **Click** on Type
> **Click** on Outline
> **Click** on Shadow
> **Click** on OK

Note that the outline and shadow attributes are now listed as part of the Major Heading style. Return to the document.

> **Click** on OK

The Major Heading paragraphs, such as the first paragraph in the document, are formatted in the way that you would have expected (see Figure 3.14). The outline and shadow attributes were added to the Major Heading style so that all paragraphs assigned the style should be updated to reflect the new settings.

But PageMaker did not stop there. In addition to changing the Major Heading, PageMaker also changed the Level 2 and Level 3 paragraphs to outline and shadow printing.

Styling Large Text Blocks 3

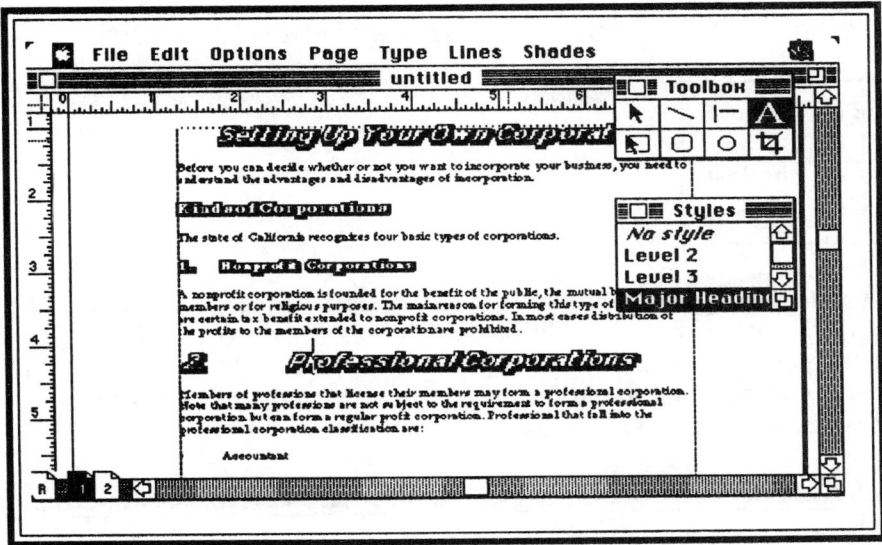

Figure 3.14   Document altered by modifying style settings.

The reason for this involves the concept of a **base style**. A base style is used as the "basis" for creating a new style. You will recall that the Level 2 and Level 3 styles were based on the Major Heading style. The description of the styles began with Major Heading+. PageMaker flows changes made in the base style into all of the styles built from it unless these changes are specifically overridden, so when you added the outline and shadow attributes to the base style, Major Heading, PageMaker flowed them though to styles Level 2 and Level 3 as well.

If you do not want a characteristic added to the base style to appear in the dependent styles, you must specifically reset those styles. For example, if you want the Level 3 headings to be bold only, you must now use the Define styles command to remove the outline and shadow attributes from the style.

> **Point** at Type
> **Drag** to Define styles
> **Click** on Level 3
> **Click** on Edit

3 Styling Large Text Blocks

Use the Type option to remove the attributes from the Level 3 style only.

> **Click** on Type
> **Click** on Outline
> **Click** on Shadow
> **Click** on OK

Look at the description of the style in the bottom of the dialog box. In addition to the + signs used to show additional attributes, the description includes - signs. These indicate that certain qualities have been removed from the base style. In this case, **- outline - shadow** indicates that these are qualities contained in the base style that shouldn't be part of the current style.

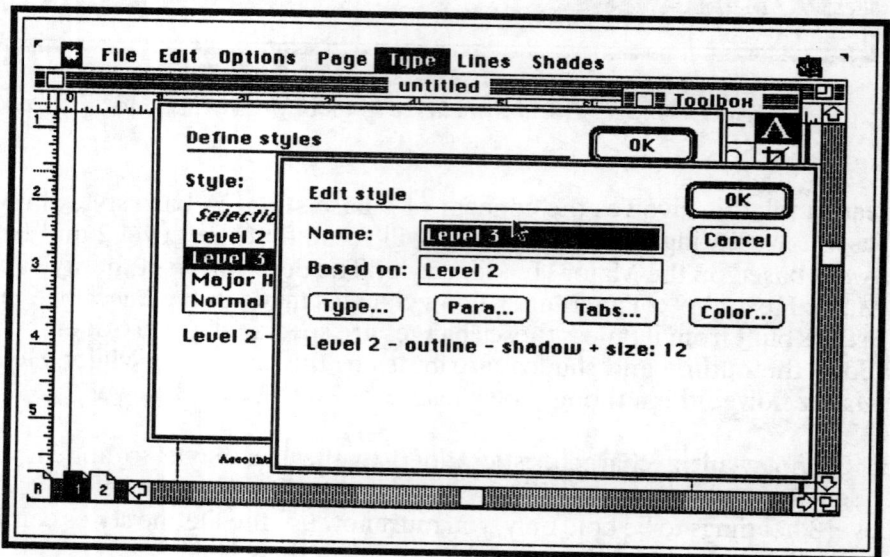

Figure 3.15   Minus signs show qualities removed from style.

Styling Large Text Blocks **3**

Return to the document.

> **Click** on OK
> **Click** on OK

The outline and shadow elements are removed from the Level 3 headings.

Indents

Another type of formatting implemented with styles is the use of indents to format paragraphs of text. For example, you might want to indent the text under the Level 3 headings so that they are more clearly defined as text under those heading topics. Begin by placing the text cursor in the paragraph below the Level 3 heading "Nonprofit Corporation."

> **Click** on "A nonprofit..."

With the cursor positioned in one of the paragraphs you want to format, display the Define styles dialog box and create a new style called **Topic**.

> **Point** at Type
> **Drag** to Define styles
> **Click** on New

Enter the name of the new style:

Topic

Select Paragraph specifications:

> **Click** on Para

In this case, you want the text below a Level 3 heading to be indented 1" from the left and right margins. Enter

139

3 Styling Large Text Blocks

1 [Tab] [Tab]
1 [Return]

Return to the document.

Click on OK
Click on OK

The text is indented below the heading to which it is related. This improves the appearance of the document by reflecting the logical organization of the text in the visual layout of paragraphs.

Apply the Topic style to the text below the next Level 3 heading.

Click on "Member"
Click on Topic

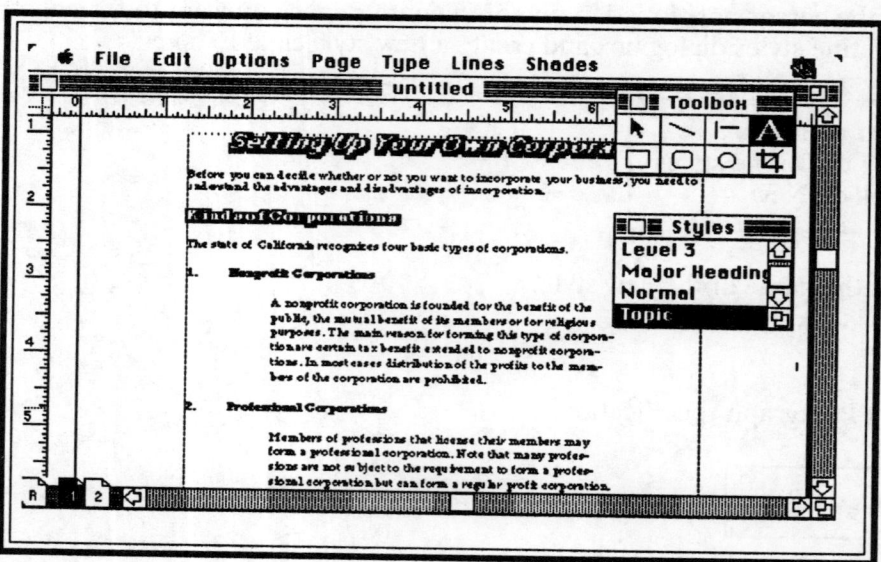

Figure 3.16   *Paragraphs indented below headings.*

Bullets

The next section of the document to be formatted is the series of lines that list the professions. At this point that list is not visible on the screen. Scroll the display down to reveal the bottom of the page.

> **Click** on the scroll bar down arrow (8 times)

Each of the four lines begins with a bullet character. Lists that are formatted like this are referred to as **bulleted lists**.

The bulleted list poses slightly different formatting problems. You will recall that you originally modified the Normal style so that a .2" space would be automatically inserted above each paragraph. However, in the case of a list, such as the list of professions, the additional space inserted above each line is not the correct format. The list consists of a series of short lines. Technically each line is a complete paragraph because it ends with a return character.

This type of list ought to be formatted so that the spacing between each line in the list is the same as the spacing between lines within the same paragraph.

The solution is to create a style for the bullet lines that does not insert the additional spacing. Select the first bullet.

> **Click** on "Accountant"

Display the Define styles dialog box and create a new style called **Bullet**.

> **Point** at Type
> **Drag** to Define styles
> **Click** on New

Enter the name of the new style:

Bullet

3 Styling Large Text Blocks

Display the Paragraph specifications dialog box.

> **Click** on Para

Indent the bullet lines 1.5" from the left margin but remove the .2" space above each paragraph. Enter

1.5
[Tab] (3 times)
0

Return to the document

> **Click** on OK
> **Click** on OK
> **Click** on OK

The Bullet style eliminates the space between the bulleted line and the previous line.

Applying a Style to a Multiple-Line Selection

Because the Bullet style needs to be applied to more than one line in a row, you can apply the style to all four bullet lines by selecting all four before you apply it.

> **Point** at "Accountant"
> **Drag** to "Veterinarian"

Note that it is not necessary to select the entire beginning or ending paragraph. If any part of a paragraph is selected, the style will be applied to the entire paragraph. Select the Bullet style.

> **Click** on Bullet

All four lines are now formatted as a list.

3 Styling Large Text Blocks

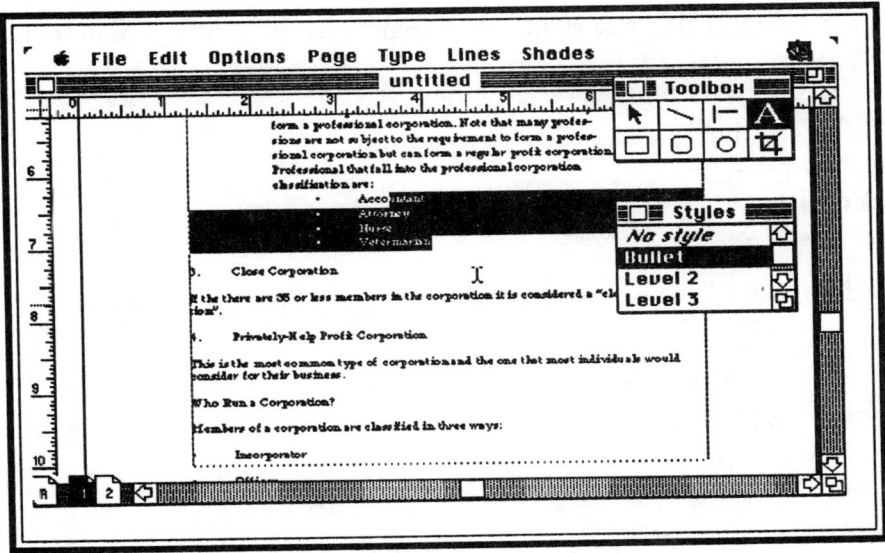

Figure 3.17   Bulleted lines grouped closely together.

First Line Exceptions

In looking at the Bullet style, you might realize that this solution exhibits one flaw. While you did want to reduce the space between the bulleted lines, you probably would have liked to retain the space before the first bullet. In a series of formatted lines or paragraphs, you will frequently want to create the first paragraph or line differently from the rest of the list.

In this case, you need to create a different style for the first line that will insert some additional space before the bulleted lines begin. Select the first line in the bullet series.

> **Click** on "Accountant"

Create a new style called **1st Bullet**.

> **Point** at Type
> **Drag** to Define styles
> **Click** on New

143

3 Styling Large Text Blocks

Enter the name of the new style. Note that this new style will be based on the Bullet style. Enter

1st Bullet

> **Click** on Para

In this case, you will want to add some space before the paragraph, .1".

> **Double Click** on Before:

Enter

.1 [Return]

Return to the document.

> **Click** on OK
> **Click** on OK

The first line of the bullet series is now formatted to insert a small amount of space before the series of bullets.

You can now use the styles you have created to format more of the document.

> **Click** on "Close"
> **Click** on Level 3

> **Click** on "35"
> **Click** on Topic

> **Click** on "Privately"
> **Click** on Level 3

> **Click** on "most common"
> **Click** on Topic

The document should now resemble Figure 3.18.

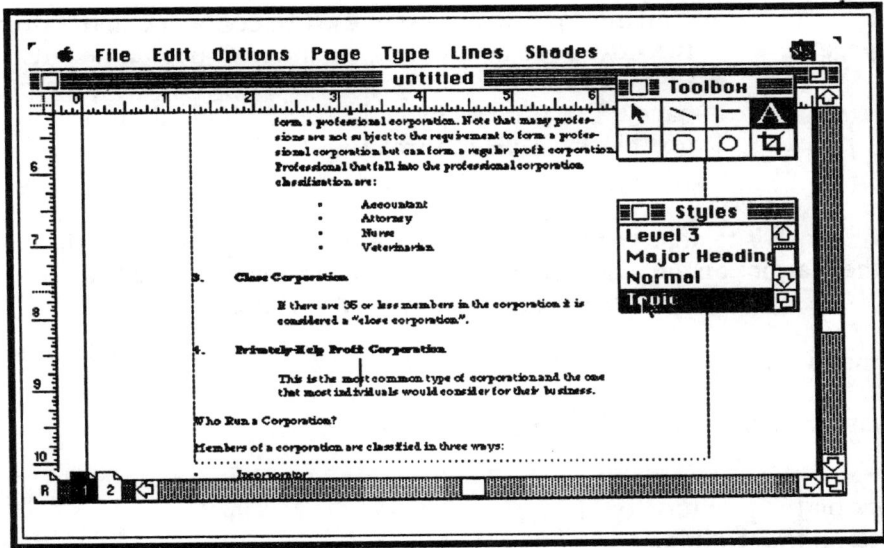

Figure 3.18   First page of the document formatted.

ENDING A PAGE

When you initially placed the text from the word processing document into the PageMaker document, all of the text was able to fit onto a single page. However, the formatting process has caused the text to increase in length. It is now no longer possible to fit the formatted text onto a single page.

To continue you must now do two things: end the current page and start a new page.

3 Styling Large Text Blocks

End the page Not only has the formatting process increased the length of the text, but PageMaker has extended the text block in which that text was contained. In Chapters 1 and 2, where the text blocks were small, this automatic expansion seemed natural and was convenient; however, in this case, the text block has extended below the bottom margin of the page.

Start new page You must place the rest of the text contained in the story onto the next page by creating on the next page a new text block that continues the story from the text block on the previous page. The process by which a story is laid out in a series of text blocks is called **threading**.

The first task is to adjust the text block on the current page so that it fits correctly into the margins on the page. To perform this operation you need to see the entire page. Change to the Fit to window display mode. Enter

Command+w

Activate the selection mode and select the text block.

> **Click** on the pointer icon
> **Click** on the text block

The bottom window shade handle shows that the formatting process has caused the text block to fill the remainder of the page. Note that the symbol in the bottom handle has changed from a # to a +. This means that even though the block has extended to the bottom of the page, there is still more text in this "story" than can be displayed. The + tells you that another page or more will be needed to display the rest of the story.

Styling Large Text Blocks 3

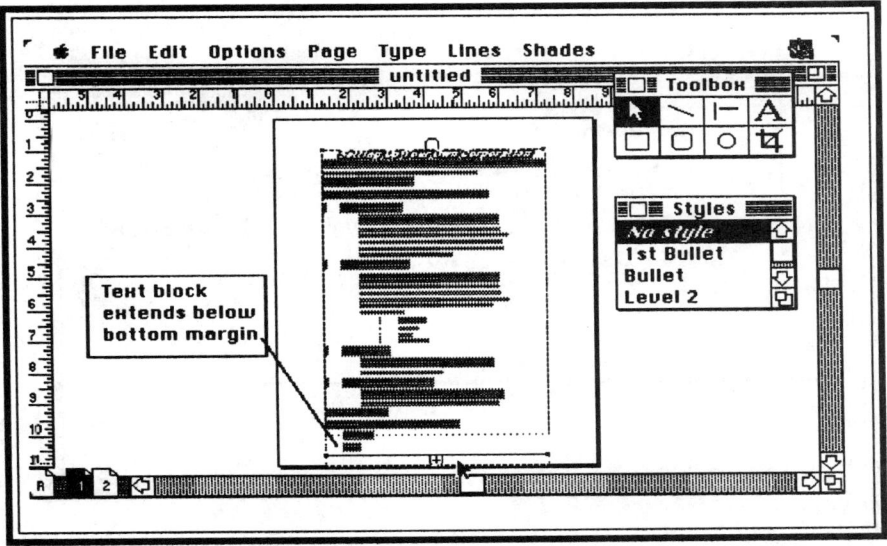

Figure 3.19   *Text block extends past page end.*

The text block has automatically expanded past the end of the page, which means that there is text placed into the margin area of the page. You can use the handle to reduce the size of the text block so that it fits inside the margin.

> **Point** at the + in the window shade handle
> **Drag** the handle up to the margin guide

To see exactly where in the story the block ends, return to the Actual size mode.

> **Point** at the + in the handle
> **Option + Command + Click**

You can see that the text block ends just above the bottom margin.

3 Styling Large Text Blocks

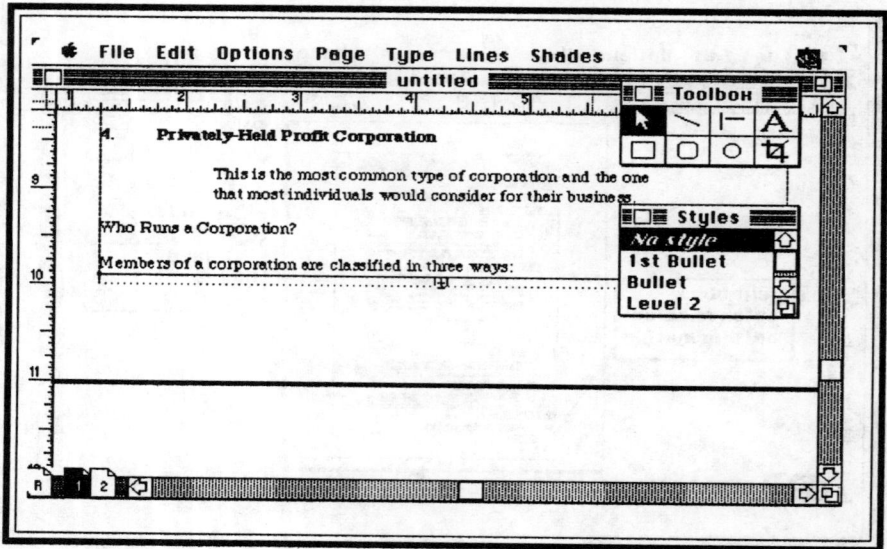

Figure 3.20   Text block just above bottom margin.

In most cases, you would simply leave the block as it is and go on to the next page. But in this case, you might want to consider the exact text that appears at the bottom of the page. In this example, the line "Who Runs a Corporation" is a major heading. It might be better to end the page before this line and begin the next page with the major heading at the top.

You can accomplish this task by reducing the text block farther so that the last line that appears is the paragraph that ends with "their business."

> **Point** at the + in the window shade handle
> **Drag** up past "Who Runs a Corporation"

The text on the first page now ends with a regular paragraph. The next text block for this story will begin with the major heading.

CONTINUING A STORY

The first page is now filled with text. To display more of the story you need to add a text block to the next page.

As mentioned earlier, the process by which you start a new text block that continues the text from a story placed in a previous text block is called **threading a story**. The concept of threading is familiar to most people from reading newspapers and magazines in which one story appears in blocks on several different pages.

In this case, you have only one story, but you still need to thread its text onto another page. New text blocks are normally created in the text mode. However, when you want to create a *threaded* text block, you do so in the selection mode. Clicking on the + in the bottom handle activates the place mode. The story to be placed is based on the story contained in the text block whose handle you select. For example, if you click the + handle of a block that contains the CORPORATIONS story, the new text block will continue the CORPORATIONS story from the point at which the text stopped in the previous block.

> **Click** on the + in the window shade handle

The mouse cursor changes to the square placement icon. Move to page #2. Movement from page to page is accomplished by clicking on the page icon of the page you want to activate.

> **Click** on the Page 2 icon

PageMaker displays the second page of the document. Note that the program automatically switches to the Fit to window display mode.

You can now place more of the story text on this page.

> **Point** at the upper left corner of the guides

3 Styling Large Text Blocks

You can place the remainder of the story on the page by clicking when the placement icon is pointed at the upper left corner of the page. Pointing shows PageMaker where to begin the block. The program will extend the block until all of the text is placed or the end of this page is reached.

> **Click**

PageMaker automatically generates a text block with the remainder of the document. Note that the top handle shows a +, indicating that it is a continuation of a story. The bottom handle shows a #, indicating the end of the story.

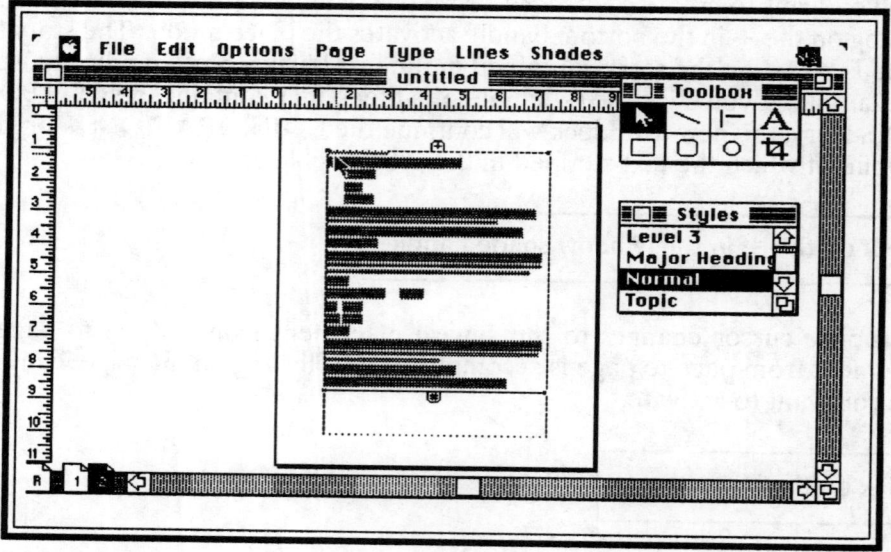

Figure 3.21   Text block placed on second page.

Enlarge the view of the top of the page.

> **Point** at the + in the top handle
> **Option + Command + Click**

The major heading **Who Runs a Corporation?** is the first line in this text block. This is the line you wanted to start page #2 with.

Place PageMaker into the text mode so that you can begin formatting the text with the styles you created.

> **Click** on the text icon

Create another major heading.

> **Click** on "Who"
> **Click** on Major Heading

The list under members is a bulleted list. Recall that you have a special style for the first line in a bulleted list. Note that the style palette must be scrolled up to display the 1st Bullet and Bullet style names.

> **Click** on "Incorporator"
> **Scroll** Style palette up
> **Click** on 1st Bullet

Format the rest of the items in the list.

> **Point** at "Officer"
> **Drag** to "Shareholder"
> **Scroll** Style palette up
> **Click** on Bullet

You can see that once created, the styles can help you quickly format a document.

3 Styling Large Text Blocks

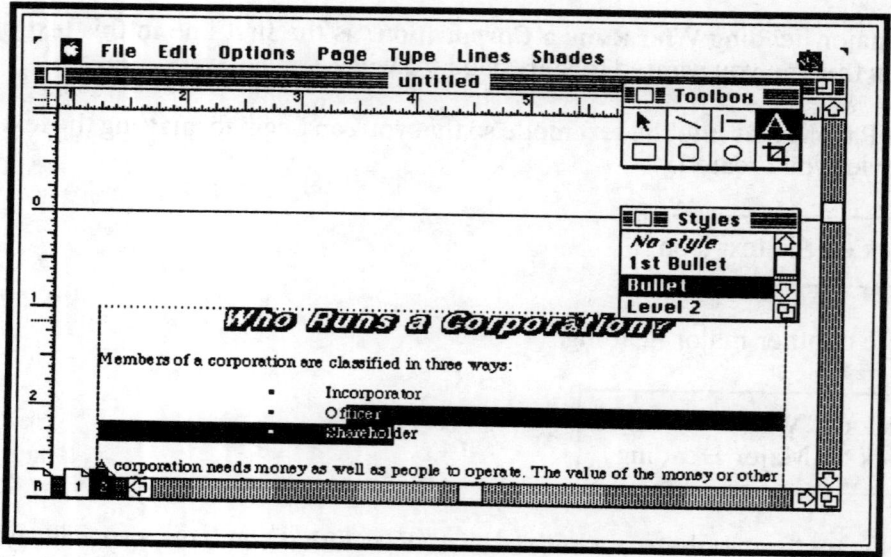

Figure 3.22   Text on second page formatted by styles.

Scroll down one screenful by entering

3 (numeric keypad)

> **Click** on "at Debt to"
> **Scroll** style palette up
> **Click** on Level 2

HANGING INDENTS

The next section of text presents paragraphs that pose a slightly different type of indenting problem. These are paragraphs that begin with a letter, number, topic name, or bullet, but unlike the paragraphs in the previous bulleted list, these paragraphs contain more than a single line of text each. As a result, the second, third, etc., lines of the paragraph wrap around to the left margin.

Styling Large Text Blocks 3

For numbered paragraphs such as this, you may want to create a hanging indent. This type of indent allows the number on the first line to hang out from the rest of the paragraph. Hanging indents allow the paragraph number, letter, topic name, or bullet to stand out because the other lines of the paragraph are indented farther than the first line.

In the current document, you could set the indent for the paragraph text at 1" on the left and the same as the Topic style on the right. The difference is in the way the first line is indented. PageMaker has a special setting that affects only the indent of the first line of a paragraph. Unlike normal indents, the first line indent can use either positive or negative values.

Positive   If the first line indent value is a positive number, the amount of space specified is added to the left indent value, if there is one. For example, suppose you set the left indent value at 1" and the first line indent value at .5". This would mean that the first line would be indented 1.5" while the second, third, and any following lines would be indented only 1".

Negative   If the first line indent value is a negative number, the amount of space specified is subtracted from the left indent value. For example, suppose you set the left indent value at 1" and the first line indent value at -.5". That would mean that the first line would be indented 1" - .5" — that is, .5". The rest of the paragraph would be formatted with the full 1" indent. The effect would be that the first line would hang out from the rest of the paragraph.

Create a new style called **Hangout** that will create a hanging indent paragraph format.

> **Click** on "A."
> **Point** at Type
> **Drag** to Define styles
> **Click** on New

Enter the name of the new style:

Hangout

153

3 Styling Large Text Blocks

To set the indents, select the paragraph specifications dialog box.

> **Click** on Para

In this example, create a left indent of 1", a first line indent of -.5", and a right indent of 1". Enter

1 [Tab]
-.5 [Tab]
1 [Return]

Return to the document.

> **Click** on OK
> **Click** on OK

The paragraph is formatted as a hanging indent with the **A.** standing out clearly from the text of the paragraph.

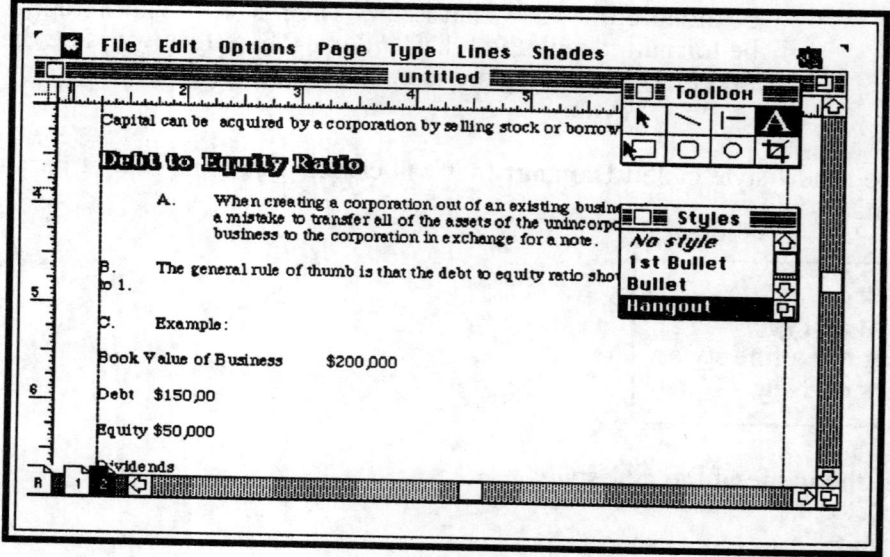

Figure 3.23   Hanging indent style created.

You might have noticed that all the indent settings have been made using .5" increments. This is done to take advantage of the fact that PageMaker automatically reestablishes tab stops every .5". In the case of the hanging indent paragraph, this was particularly useful. Recall that the **A.** is separated from the text of the paragraphs by a tab. This means that the first character following the **A.** will be placed at the first tab stop, i.e., at .5" in from the left margin. The existence of a tab stop .5" from the margin was the reason for using the value of -.5" for the first line indent.

As a rule, a hanging indent should be set in conjunction with a tab stop. If you wanted to create a smaller hanging indent, .25" for example, you would have to set a tab at the location .25" inches in from the first line indent.

Format the next two paragraphs with the Hangout style.

> **Point** at "A."
> **Drag** to "C."
> **Click** on Hangout

STYLES WITH TABS

The next section of the document consists of a simple numeric table similar to the numeric table used in Chapter 2. In this example, you will create a style that will be used to format the lines of this numeric table.

In this case, you can select the lines that need to be formatted before you create the style.

> **Point** at "Book Value"
> **Drag** to "Equity"

Create a new style called **Table**.

> **Point** at Type
> **Drag** to Define styles
> **Click** on New

3 Styling Large Text Blocks

Enter the name of the new style:

Table

In this case, you will change the style of text as well as the indents and tabs. Numeric tables are often set in Helvetica or other Swiss typefaces because these are **sans serif** typefaces. The term "serif" refers to a small tail or foot added to the end of the straight lines used in letters. Most paragraph text, such as the text in this book, is printed in a serif font. Sans serif fonts do not have these extra lines (i.e., "sans" means "without") and present a cleaner appearance. Numeric tables, catalogs, and directories often use sans serif fonts. In this case, change the font to Helvetica.

> **Click** on Type
> **Point** at Font
> **Drag** to Helvetica
> **Click** on OK

Display the Indents/Tabs dialog box.

> **Click** on Indents/Tabs

It might seem odd that PageMaker calls this dialog box "Indents/Tabs" when the Paragraph specification dialog box contains settings for the left, first line, and right indents. PageMaker allows you to set indents in this dialog box as well as in the Paragraph specification dialog box. The primary difference is that in this dialog box the indents are set by dragging icons on the ruler line rather than by entering values.

If you look at the left side of the ruler, you will notice two triangular icons. The top icon represents the position of the first line indent. The bottom icon represents the position of the left indent. Currently, they are both positioned at zero. The white arrows at either end of the ruler line will scroll the ruler display to the left or right. If you scroll to the right, you will see a dark triangle pointing left. This is the right indent marker, which can be dragged to set a right indent.

Styling Large Text Blocks 3

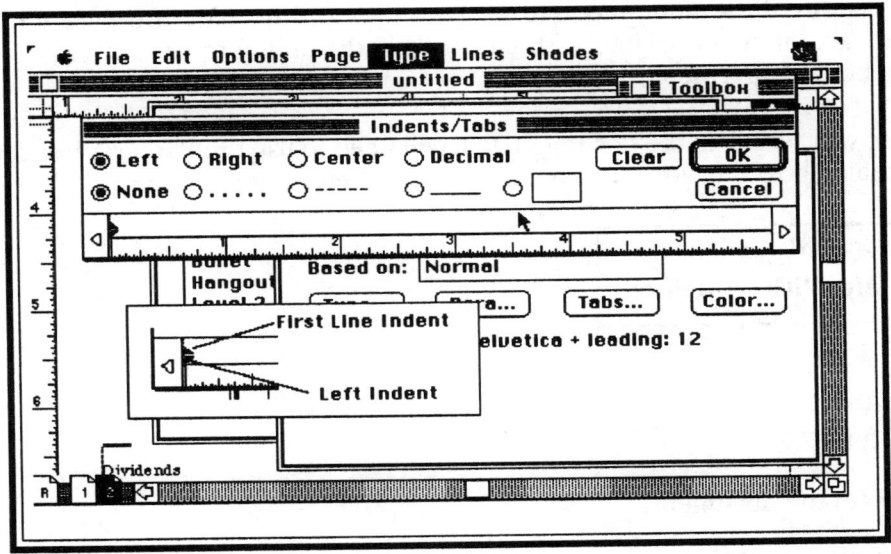

Figure 3.24   *Tab dialog box shows indent markers.*

You can set the left or first line indent by dragging the icons across the ruler line to the position you want. If you point at the top icon (first line indent), it will move independently of the bottom icon. However, if you point at the bottom icon (left indent), both icons will move together.

Set the left indent at 2".

> **Drag** the left margin icon to 2"

You also need to set a tab on which to align the numbers in the table. Make this a right tab with a dot leader at 5".

> **Click** on Right
> **Click** on the dot leader
> **Click** on 5"
> **Click** on OK

157

3 Styling Large Text Blocks

You have used the same menu to set both tabs and indents. Because tabs and indents are often associated with each other, the ability to set both in a single dialog box is convenient.

Before you return to the document, you will need to use the Paragraph specification dialog box to reduce the amount of space before each line to .1".

> **Click** on Para
> **Double Click** on Before:

Enter

.1 [Return]

Return to the document.

> **Click** on OK
> **Click** on OK

The text is formatted into a tab-aligned table (see Figure 3.25).

Scroll down to the next screenful of text. Enter

3 (numeric keypad)

Format the last section of the document, using the styles you have created.

> **Click** on "Dividends"
> **Scroll** Style palette up
> **Click** on Level 2

> **Click** on "A."
> **Drag** to "B."
> **Scroll** Style palette up
> **Click** on Hangout

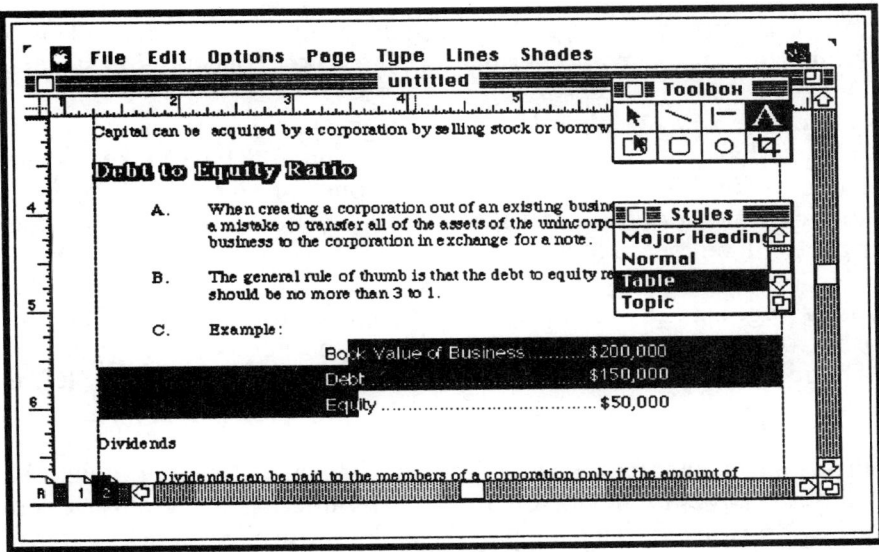

Figure 3.25   Style formats text into tabbed table.

You have now formatted all of the text drawn from the CORPORATIONS word processing file.

NUMBERING PAGES

Now that you have created a document that consists of more than one page, you might want to include page numbers on each page. PageMaker will automatically number the pages in your document in two different ways.

Repeating Placement	If you want to print the page number in the same place on each page of the document, you can create a single master page number symbol that will number all of the pages.
Manual Placement	If you want the page number to appear only on selected pages or if you want to change the location of the page number from page to page (e.g., for left- and right-sided pages), you can manually insert the page number on the specific pages and specific locations you want.

3 Styling Large Text Blocks

The most common type of page numbering is repeating placement. This type of page numbering brings up another major PageMaker concept — **master pages**.

When you create a PageMaker document, PageMaker creates one or two master pages. If you have selected a double-sided document, PageMaker creates two master pages — one for left-sided pages and one for right-sided pages. If you create a single-sided document, as you did in this example, only a right-sided master page will be created.

The master pages are presented by master page icons that appear in the bottom left corner of the PageMaker display, next to the numbered page icons. The master page icons are labeled **R** for "right master page" and **L** for "left master page."

The purpose of master pages is to provide a means of creating items that will affect all of the pages in the document. Page numbering is one of the operations that can be performed on a master page. By adding the page number to the master page, you create automatic page numbering that will flow through to each page in the document.

To create an automatic page number, activate the master page by selecting the master page icon. Note that because this document is a single-sided document, there is only one master page icon, the R(ight) master page.

> **Click** on the R page icon

PageMaker displays the master page for this document. The page appears just as a normal document page would appear (see Figure 3.26).

In fact, the master page behaves exactly like any other page in the document except that anything added to the master page is repeated on each page of the document (for single-sided documents). If you are working on a double-sided document, the repeating would be specific to all left or right pages.

Adding a page number is accomplished by inserting a text block on the master page in the position where you want the page number to appear on each of the document pages. The most common place to put a page number is in the center of the bottom margin.

Styling Large Text Blocks 3

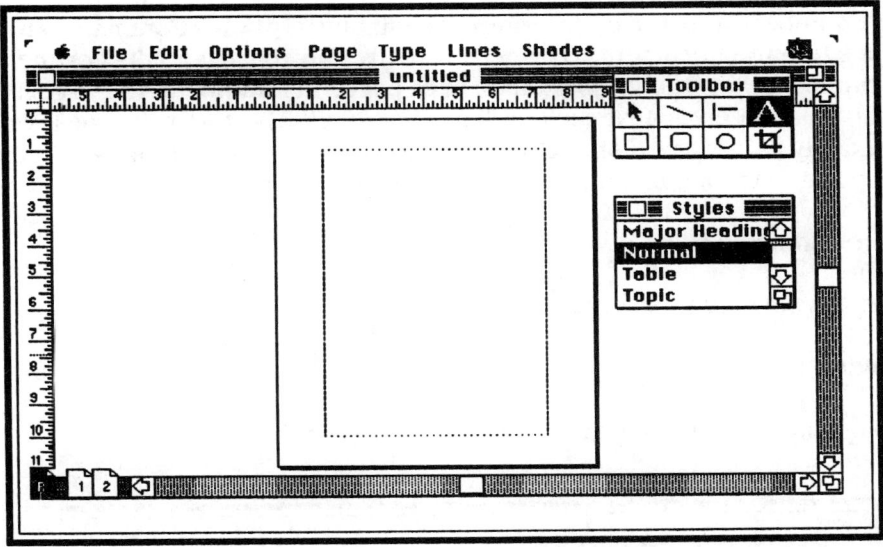

Figure 3.26   *Master page displayed.*

Enlarge the view of the bottom of the page.

Point at the center of the bottom margin
Option + Command + Click

Create a text block by clicking the mouse in the bottom margin about .5" from the bottom of the page. Align the cursor as closely as possible with the left margin guide.

Click in the bottom margin .5" from bottom of page

---

3 Styling Large Text Blocks

A page number is created by entering the command **Option + Command + p**, which inserts a 0 in the document. The zero is really only a place holder for the actual page numbers that will be inserted on each page. In addition to the page number symbol, you can enter text such as "Page" or "Pg." The text will repeat on each page exactly as it is typed on the master page, but the page number will change to correspond to the actual page number of the page. Enter

Option + Command + p

Center the page number horizontally by entering

Command + Shift + c

The page number text is centered between the margins.

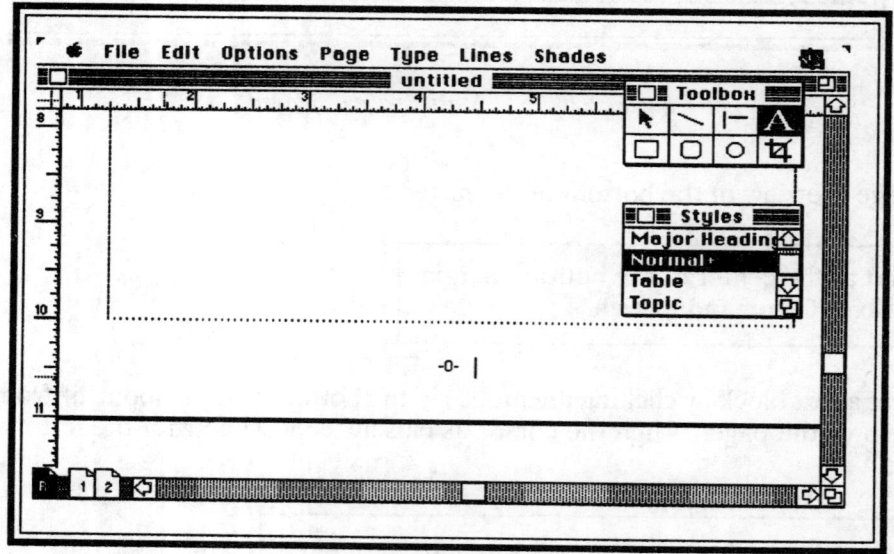

Figure 3.27   *Page number inserted into master page.*

You can format the page number text block exactly as you would another text block. For example, you might want to print the page number in a smaller point size than the text (e.g., 10 points), or you might want it to be italicized. As an example, change the text to 10-point italic. Enter

> **Command + a**
> **Command + t**

> **Point** at Size:
> **Drag** to 10
> **Click** on Italic
> **Click** on OK

REPEATING TEXT

The master page can be used to repeat any type of text on all pages of that type (right or left) throughout the document. In word processing, this type of text is often called **header** or **footer** text. The PageMaker master page broadens this concept to include any type of text or graphic that you want to repeat on each page. Note that this means you could repeat an object (text or graphics) at the top, bottom, left, or right margin of each page. You could even repeat the item in the document area within the margins.

A simple example would be text that repeats at the top of every page. Suppose you wanted to print a copyright notice on the top of every page. Display the top of the master page.

> **Option + Command + Click**
> **Point** at the center of the top margin
> **Option + Command + Click**

Create a text block about .5" from the top of the page and aligned with the left margin guide.

> **Click** on top margin .5" from top

3 Styling Large Text Blocks

Enter the copyright notice. The **Option+g** combination inserts a copyright symbol into the text. Enter

Copyright
Option+g
[space]
Smalltime Press

Center the text by entering

Command+Shift+c

The copyright notice will appear at the top of each page.

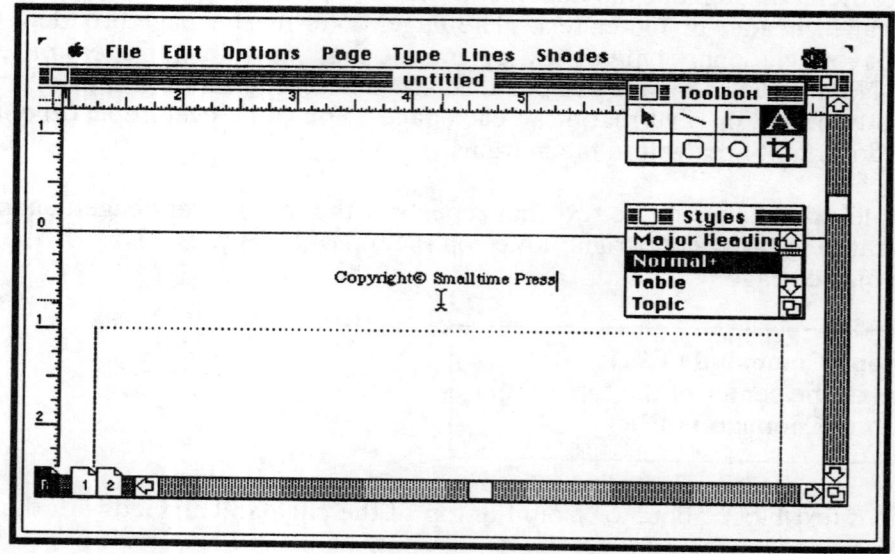

Figure 3.28   *Copyright notice will be repeated on each page.*

Styling Large Text Blocks 3

Activate the first page of the document.

> **Click** on the page 1 icon

Note that when PageMaker returns to a page, the view and position of the view on the page are the same as when you left the page. In this case, you left the page when the view was positioned on the bottom of the page. You can see the effect of the page number entry on the master page. The page number appears with the dashes—just as it was entered on the master page, with the exception that the number corresponds to the page number in the document.

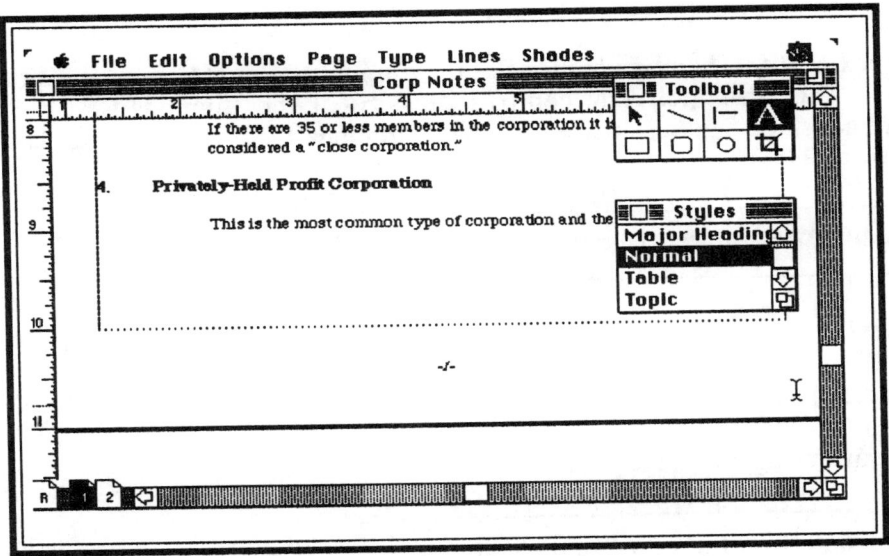

Figure 3.29   Page number appears at bottom of first page.

PRINTING THUMBNAILS

When you have created and formatted a document with a number of pages, PageMaker provides a fast way to scan the printed pages to see if you have made any gross mistakes. The method is called a **thumbnail print**. In this type of printing, PageMaker reduces the size of each page so that you can print 2 to 16 small pages on one printed page. The more thumbnails you select (up to 16), the smaller each one prints on the page.

3 Styling Large Text Blocks

Even the smallest thumbnail print provides you with sufficient detail to see gross errors such as missing page numbers or misaligned text blocks. In many cases, this is easier than trying to view all of the pages in the document and faster than printing the entire document.

To print thumbnails for a document, display the Print dialog box. Enter

Command + p

Select the Thumbnails option.

> **Click** on Thumbnails

The box next to Thumbnails specifies the number of thumbnails to print on each page. This also indirectly controls the size of the thumbnails. The more thumbnails, the smaller in size each page thumbnail is printed. In this case, you can enter 2.

> **Double Click** on Per page box

Enter

2 [Return]

If you are using an ImageWriter,

> **Click** on OK in the next two dialog boxes

The thumbnails that print give you a good idea of the formatting used in the document.

When you are satisfied with the document, you can print at the normal page size. Enter

Command + p

Note that the Thumbnails option remains selected until you specifically deselect it and return printing to its normal size.

> **Click** on Thumbnails

Print the document at normal size.

> **Click** on OK

The pages should look like Figures 3.30 and 3.31, respectively.

Save the document as **Corp Notes** by entering

Command + s
Corp Notes [Return]

Close the document window.

> **Point** at File
> **Drag** to Close

3 Styling Large Text Blocks

Copyright© Smalltime Press

Setting Up Your Own Corporation

Before you can decide whether or not you want to incorporate your business, you need to understand the advantages and disadvantages of incorporation.

Kinds of Corporations

The state of California recognizes four basic types of corporations.

1. **Nonprofit Corporations**

    A nonprofit corporation is founded for the benefit of the public, the mutual benefit of its members or for religious purposes. The main reasons for forming this type of corporation are certain tax benefits extended to nonprofit corporations. In most cases distribution of the profits to the members of the corporation is prohibited.

2. **Professional Corporations**

    Members of professions that license their members may form a professional corporation. Note that many professions are not subject to the requirement to form a professional corporation but can form a regular profit corporation. Professions that fall into the professional corporation classification are:

    - Accountant
    - Attorney
    - Nurse
    - Veterinarian

3. **Close Corporation**

    If there are 35 or less members in the corporation it is considered a "close corporation."

4. **Privately-Held Profit Corporation**

    This is the most common type of corporation and the one

-1-

Figure 3.30 Page 1 printed.

Styling Large Text Blocks 3

Copyright © Smalltime Press

that most individuals would consider for their business.

Who Runs a Corporation?

Members of a corporation are classified in three ways:

- Incorporator
- Officer
- Shareholder

A corporation needs money as well as people to operate. The value of the money or other tangible assets used to create the corporation is called "capital."

Capital can be acquired by a corporation by selling stock or borrowing money.

Debt to Equity Ratio

A. When creating a corporation out of an existing business it is a mistake to transfer all of the assets of the unincorporated business to the corporation in exchange for a note.

B. The general rule of thumb is that the debt to equity ratio should be no more than 3 to 1.

C. Example:

Book Value of Business	$200,000
Debt	$150,000
Equity	$50,000

Dividends

A. Dividends can be paid to the members of a corporation only if the amount of earning in the corporation equals or exceeds the total amount of the dividends to be paid. In other words you cannot incur debt to pay a dividend.

B. In addition the following condition must also be met:

Corporate assets following the dividend must be 1.25 times the liabilities.

-2-

Figure 3.31   Page 2 printed.

3 Styling Large Text Blocks

SUMMARY

This chapter discusses how a document prepared in a word processing program can be imported into PageMaker and formatted using the PageMaker Styles feature.

- **Placing text.** Text prepared in other applications such as word processing programs can be imported into a PageMaker document, using the **Place** command. The Place command allows you to select a file on the disk whose text or graphics will be added to the PageMaker document. If the data imported is text, the Place command creates a text block large enough to hold all of the text or to fill the page, whichever comes first.

- **Stories.** The text from an imported document can be distributed in a document in one or more **text blocks**. A **story** refers to all of the text contained in all of the text blocks drawn from the same text file.

- **Threading text.** When text from a file is distributed through a series of text blocks, the process is called **threading**. The text flows dynamically between text blocks as the size of the blocks is increased or decreased. The text block that begins a story has a blank top handle while the block that ends the story has a # in the bottom handle. Blocks that are not the beginning or the end have + symbols in both handles.

- **Styles.** The format of every paragraph is determined by the settings entered for the 15 options that make up a paragraph format. A **style** is a set of paragraph formatting options that is given a special name. The entire set of options can be applied to a paragraph by selecting the name of the style from the Styles menu or from the Styles palette, if it is displayed. PageMaker is supplied with a set of built-in styles. You can apply those styles, modify them, or create styles of your own. If you import text from a word processing program that supports styles, e.g., Microsoft Word, PageMaker will attempt to integrate the styles set for that document into the PageMaker styles. Word styles are compatible with PageMaker styles. You can also copy styles from the existing PageMaker document to new documents.

- **Style-structured documents.** When a document has been formatted using styles, the document is structured so that any changes in the style definitions will cause all of the paragraphs in the document associated with the modified style to reflect the formatting changes. This saves time and creates a more consistently formatted document.

Styling Large Text Blocks 3

- **Define styles.** The Define styles menu allows you to create, edit, remove, or copy styles from another document. You can change the type, paragraph, or tab specifications for styles you are creating or editing. Each new style is related to one or more of the existing styles.

- **Hanging indents.** PageMaker allows you to create special paragraph formats in which the first line of the paragraph is treated differently from the other lines. The first-line indent value affects only the first line of the paragraph. The left and right indents affect all of the lines. The value used for the first-line indent will be added to the left indent if positive or subtracted from the left indent if negative. A negative first-line indent is used to create a hangout-type paragraph.

- **Master pages.** PageMaker creates a master page for each left or right page used in the document. Single-sided documents have only a right master page. The master page is used for adding special items that are meant to appear on each page—right or left—of the document. Text blocks added to the master page will repeat on all subsequent pages, creating effects such as automatic page numbers, headers, footers, or marginal repeating text.

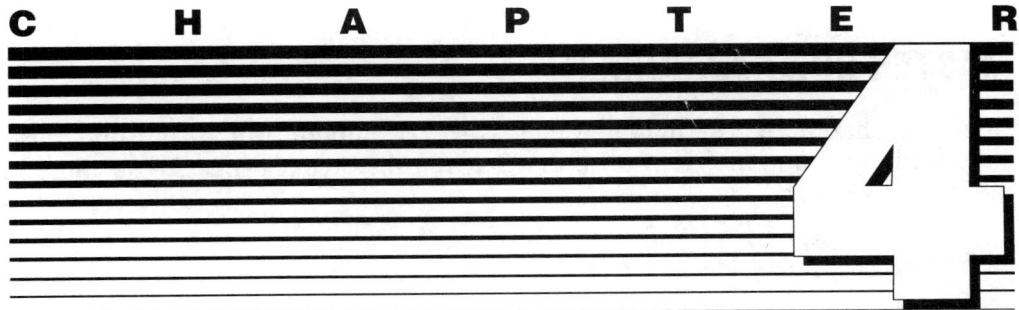

CHAPTER 4

WORKING WITH COLUMNS

The documents you have created so far have been formatted so that the text flows across the entire width of the page — from the left margin to the right margin. In this chapter and in Chapter 5, you will learn how text can be formatted into vertical columns. Column formats are commonly used in many types of documents, including newsletters and other publications.

In this chapter, you will use the same text file, CORPORATIONS, that you used in Chapter 3, but this time you will create a multiple-column layout. When you format text into more than one column per page, a number of issues arise that are not as crucial when you are placing text in the margin-to-margin format used in Chapter 3. While multiple-column documents are a bit more complicated to create, they do offer a more sophisticated and professional appearance.

4 Working with Columns

MASTER COLUMN GUIDES

Begin this chapter by creating a new PageMaker document. Make this a one-page, single-sided document. If you fill that page in the layout process, you can add more later. Enter

Command + n

> **Click** on Double-sided (to deselect it)
> **Click** on OK

Column layout in PageMaker can be created in two ways: page-by-page or with master columns.

Page-by-Page — The Page-by-Page option allows you to set the number of columns and the widths of the columns on each page of the document. This method allows you to use different column setups on different pages. For example, you might want a three-column layout on page 1, a two-column layout on page 2, and a four-column layout on page 3.

Master columns — An alternative to creating column layout on a page-by-page basis is to create a column layout on the master page (or master pages for doubled-sided documents) that will flow through to all of the pages of the document. This method is much faster than setting a column layout for each individual page and is the preferred method for columns. The master column method will create the same column layout on each page of the document.

You can see that the primary difference between the two methods is the amount of control retained by the user versus the amount of control given over to the computer. The master column method is the preferred method because it allows the computer program to automatically set the column layout for each page in the document. In cases where the column layout will vary from page to page, e.g., in a complicated newsletter layout, you can avoid a master layout and handle each page individually.

Working with Columns 4

In this example, you will use the master columns method. Activate the master page for this document.

> **Click** on the R page icon

Column layouts are created by using the Column guides command found on the Options menu. This command will evenly divide the horizontal space on the page into columns based on the number you enter. You can also specify the amount of space to leave between each pair of columns. Activate the Column guides dialog box.

> **Point** at Options
> **Drag** to Column guides

The dialog box uses two values: the number of columns and the amount of space, in inches, to be left between the columns.

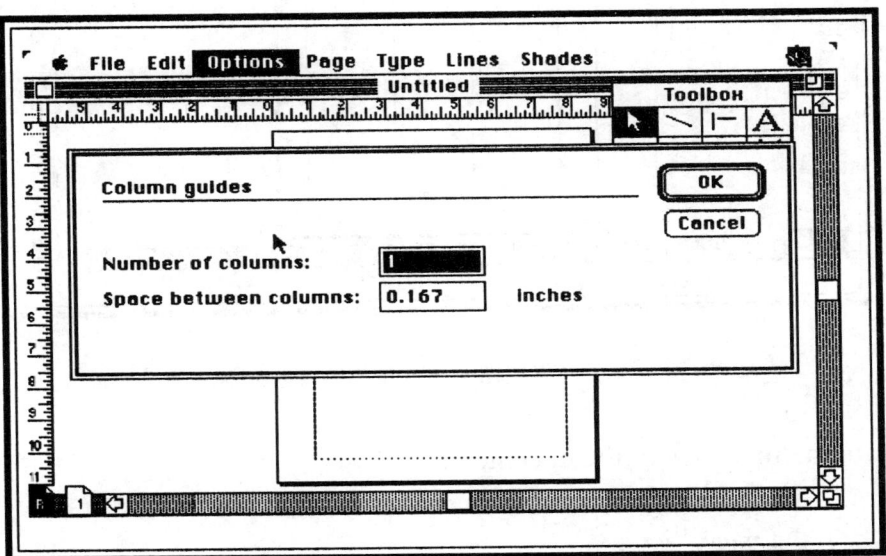

Figure 4.1   Column guides dialog box.

4 Working with Columns

In this case, create 3 columns with .25" space between them. Enter

3 [Tab]
.25 [Return]

The master page now displays additional guide lines, indicating the location of the columns. Note that these column lines are only guide lines. You can still place text on any part of the page or spread across any or all of the columns if you want. The column guides simply act as a guide to the automatic PageMaker operations or a point of reference for you when you are making manual modifications to the page.

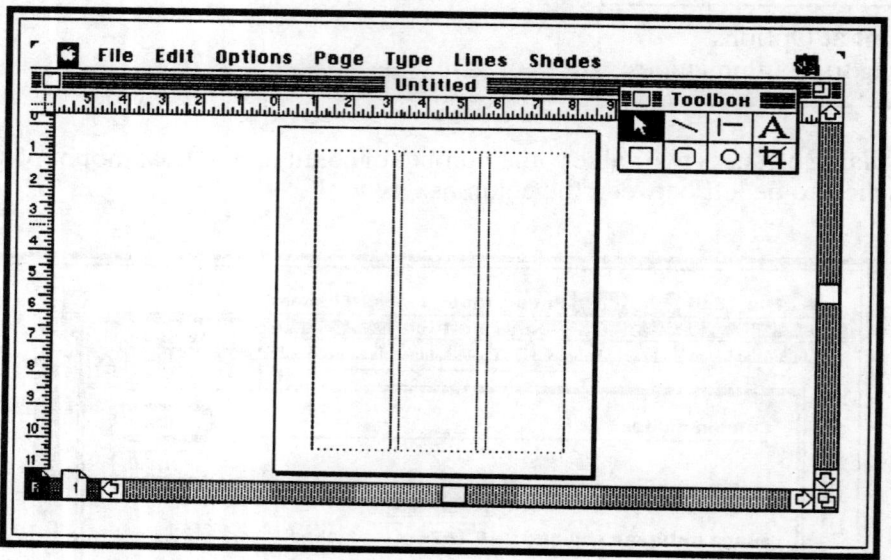

Figure 4.2   *Column guides displayed on the master page.*

Activate the first page of the document.

Click on the page 1 icon

Because you have created column guides on the master page of the document, the guides automatically appear on each normal page of the document.

COPYING STYLES

In the document created in Chapter 3, you developed a list of styles that you used for formatting the various parts of the text: Major Heading, Level 2, Level 3, etc. Because you are using the same text in this document as you did in the previous one, you might want to begin by copying the paragraph styles from the previous document into the current document. If you produce a number of documents, you will find that they frequently have much in common, including the way they should be formatted. Once you have worked out a set of styles that meet your needs, you can save a lot of time and effort by copying styles from one document to another rather than starting from scratch each time. Copying styles also makes your document formatting consistent from document to document. Even if you expect that you will need to make adjustments to the styles for this particular document, it is usually easier to modify existing styles than create them from scratch each time.

In this case, you can copy the styles that you created for the Corp Notes PageMaker document into the current PageMaker document. The copying process is executed from the Define styles dialog box.

> **Point** at Type
> **Drag** to Define styles

The styles listed on this menu are the built-in set of styles that PageMaker creates for each new document. The styles you copy from another document will be merged with any existing styles. If one of the styles that you are copying has the same name as an existing style, PageMaker will prompt you to decide which style, the old one or the new one, should be retained.

You might want to remove the built-in styles whenever you are sure that you will not use them in a document. In this example, you can use the Remove command to eliminate the built-in styles from the list.

> **Click** on Body text
> **Click** on Remove

4 Working with Columns

Remove the next four styles as well.

> **Click** on Remove (4 times)

Select the Copy command to copy styles from an existing PageMaker file.

> **Click** on Copy

PageMaker displays a file selector dialog box called Copy styles. In this case, you want to select the PageMaker document Corp Notes. When you were working on the Corp Notes document in Chapter 3, PageMaker assumed that you wanted to store the PageMaker file in the last selected folder. In Chapter 3, the last selected folder was the same one in which the CORPORATIONS document was stored. You selected that folder in order to place the text from the CORPORATIONS file into the PageMaker document.

Use the folder selector box to select the same folder in which you stored the CORPORATIONS file, e.g., Word 3.01. The name Corp Notes will appear in the file selector scroll box (see Figure 4.3). Keep in mind that only PageMaker files will appear in the scroll box when you are using the Copy styles command because you can only copy styles from other PageMaker documents.

Load the styles from Corp Notes into the current document.

> **Click** on Corp Notes
> **Click** on OK

The style selector box is now filled with the styles that were used in the Corp Notes document (see Figure 4.4).

Return to the document by entering

[Return]

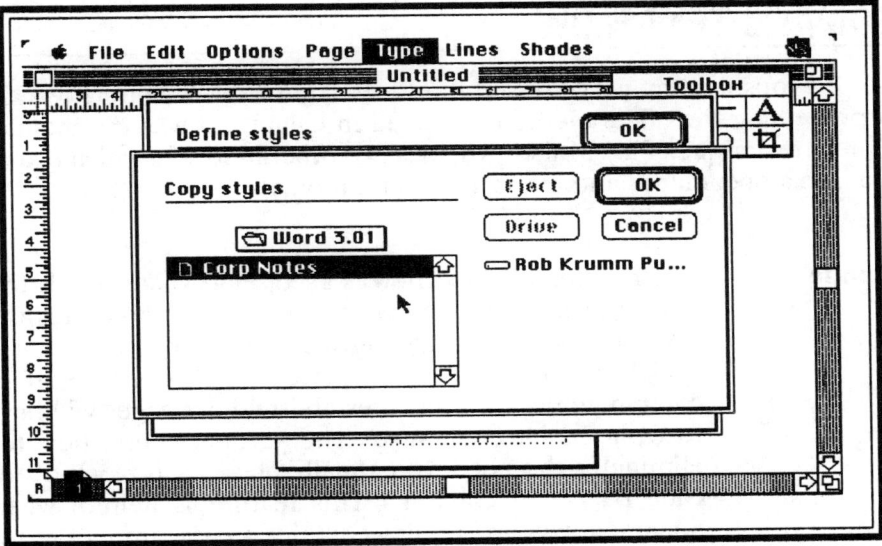

Figure 4.3   PageMaker file appears in selector box.

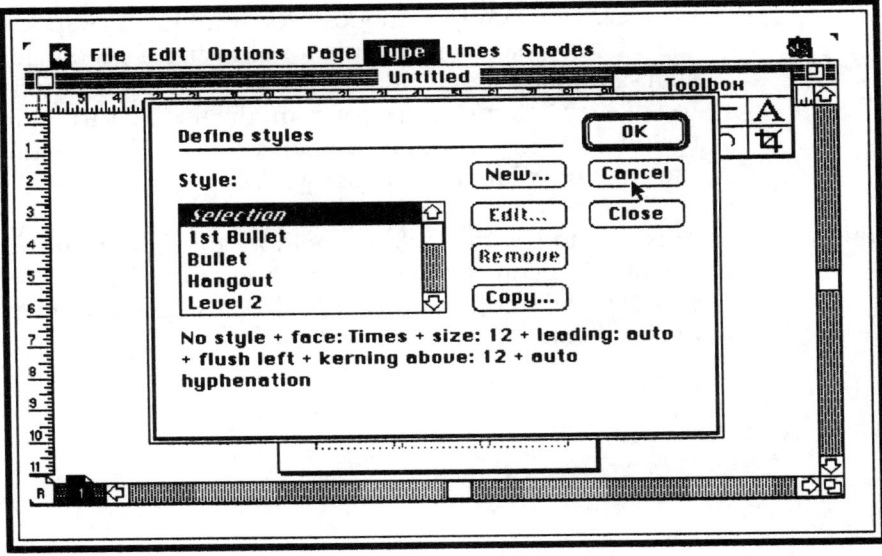

Figure 4.4   Copied styles appear in the selector box.

4 Working with Columns

AUTOMATIC TEXT FLOW

In the previous document, you used the Place command to import text from a word processing file. The method you used in Chapter 3 was the manual text placement technique. PageMaker provides two other modes in which text can be placed into a document: automatic and semi-automatic.

Automatic When automatic text flow is used, PageMaker loads the text from the selected document and automatically creates as many text blocks on as many pages as necessary (up to the Page-Maker limit of 128 pages) to place the entire text file. If master column guides have been established, all pages will have the text placed into columns. The automatic text flow feature eliminates the need to manually place each block of text on each page and column. This feature is helpful when the document you are loading contains a large amount of text.

Semi-Automatic The semi-automatic mode fills one page or column of text and then pauses. You can then select a starting location for the next section of text. The semi-automatic mode assumes you want to exercise some manual control over the text placement process. For example, suppose you want to leave space at the top of each page or column for drawing a rectangle. The semi-automatic mode allows you to select the location at the top of each column where you want the text flow to begin. The text, if a sufficient amount remains, will fill the remainder of the page or column and pause again.

Manual This method is the default method and is the one used in Chapter 3. You can use this method to create text blocks of specific sizes and locations or to flow a single column or page worth of text.

Working with Columns 4

Keep in mind that when text from a text file is placed into a PageMaker document, the text is a copy of the text stored in the file you selected. Once the text has been copied into PageMaker, there is no correspondence between the original text file and the PageMaker document. Once you load a word processing document into PageMaker and save it, you have created two separate documents — the original word processing document and the new PageMaker document. If you make editing changes in the original word processing text file after a copy of it has been placed into a PageMaker document, none of those changes will appear in the PageMaker document. On the other hand, if you make changes to the text once it has been placed into the PageMaker document, the original word processing text file is unaffected.

Suppose you find that you have placed text into PageMaker without having performed a spelling check on the text in your word processing program. If you want to place the correct, spell-checked text into PageMaker, you must replace the text in the current PageMaker document with a new, spell-checked copy of the text file. Once you have returned to your word processor and spell checked the text file, load the PageMaker document again and select the text block that contains the story you want to update. Enter the place mode, **Command + d**, and select the file name of the new, spell-checked text file. Before you click OK, select the Replace existing story option to cause the new story to replace the old version.

To understand how these options work, experiment with flowing text from the CORPORATIONS document into the current page layout. To use automatic flow, you must select the Autoflow option on the Options menu.

> **Point** at Options
> **Drag** to Autoflow

Select a document for placement.

Command + d

Because you have already selected the folder you used in Chapter 3, the text file CORPORATIONS should appear in the file selector box.

> **Click** on CORPORATIONS
> **Click** on OK

4 Working with Columns

The program returns to the document mode. Note that the icon used for the place mode shows a snaking arrow instead of the paragraph icon used in the manual placement mode. To flow the text into the document from the beginning to wherever it ends, select the upper left corner of the first column.

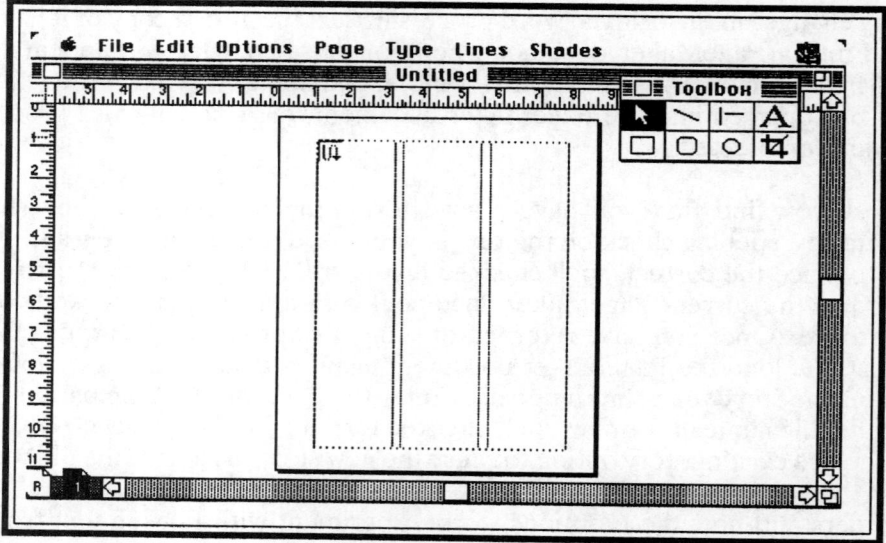

Figure 4.5   Placement icon changed when Autoflow is active.

> **Click** on the upper left corner of first column

PageMaker automatically creates three text blocks — one in each column on the page. The last block shows a # in its window shade handle, indicating that all of the text from the document has been placed. If necessary, PageMaker would have automatically created additional pages and filled their columns with text until the entire text was placed.

Working with Columns **4**

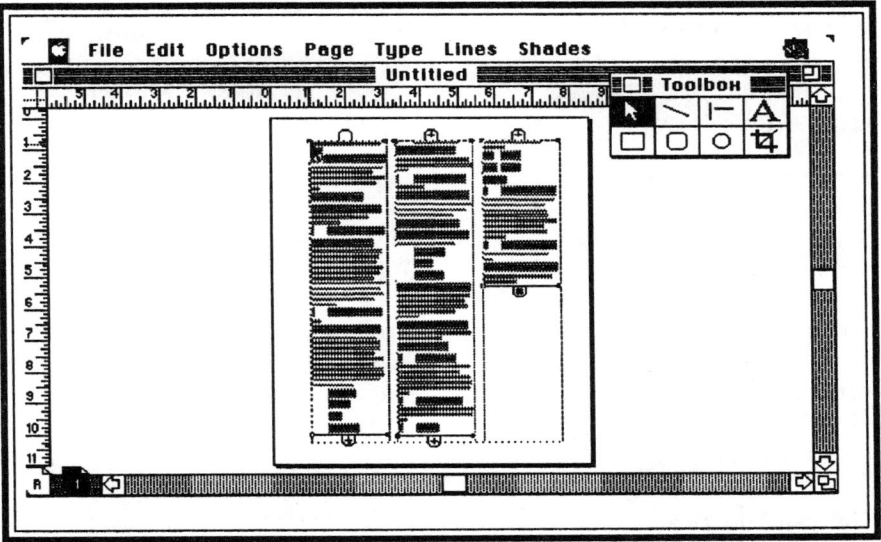

Figure 4.6   Text automatically flowed into columns.

SEMI-AUTOMATIC TEXT FLOW

To get a feel for the difference between automatic and semi-automatic text placement, delete the current text and reload the document, using the semi-automatic method.

Note that when PageMaker finished the automatic text placement, all of the text blocks on the page were selected. You could tell they were all selected because all of the blocks displayed window shade handles. Remove all of the text you just placed by entering

[Delete]

The text is cleared from the document. Turn off the automatic text flow option.

> **Point** at Options
> **Drag** to Autoflow

183

4 Working with Columns

Load the text from the document again. Keep in mind that Autoflow is turned off. Enter

Command+d

> **Click** on CORPORATIONS
> **Click** on OK

The normal placement icon appears. This means that you are currently in the manual placement mode. To change to the semi-automatic placement mode, you must press and hold down the Shift key. Press

Shift (hold down)

With the Shift key pressed and held down, PageMaker changes the icon to a snaking arrow with a dotted tail. This indicates you are in the semi-automatic placement mode. Note that you don't need to keep the Shift key pressed down once PageMaker is in the semi-automatic placement mode. You just need to **Shift+Click** initially to place PageMaker into the semi-automatic placement mode.

> **Shift+Click** on the upper left corner of first column

PageMaker flows the text into the first column only. This is exactly the way the manual placement mode would operate, with one exception. In the manual mode, PageMaker exits the placement mode after a block, page, or column has been filled. In the semi-automatic mode, PageMaker remains in the text placement mode. The text placement icon reappears to indicate that the program is still in the text placement mode.

The advantage of the semi-automatic mode is that it pauses between column or page placements to allow you to select a new starting position for the next column or page. Suppose you wanted to leave the top half of the second column empty so you could insert a text block that is not part of the current story. You could accomplish this by Shift+Clicking the icon in the middle instead of at the top of the second column.

> **Shift+Click** in the middle of the second column

The text flows into the second column, starting at the position you clicked on instead of at the top of the column as would have been the case with fully automatic text placement.

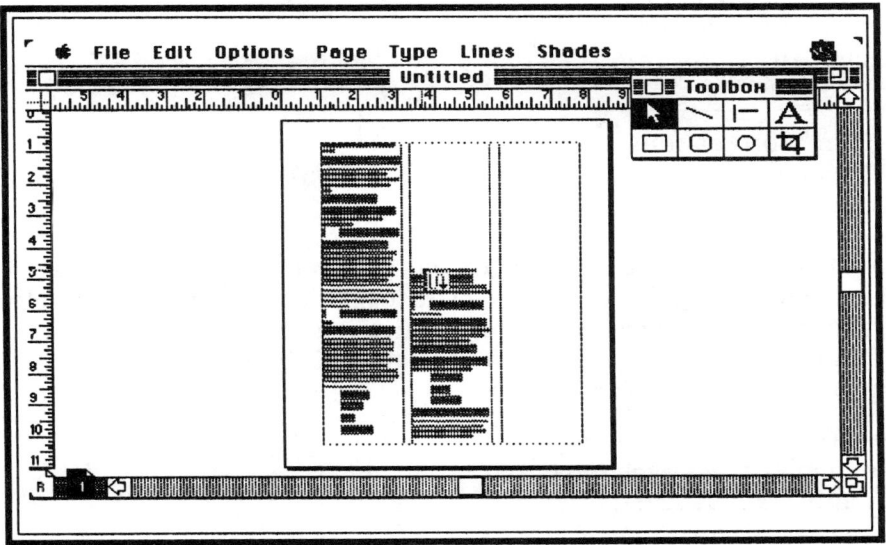

Figure 4.7   Semi-automatic placement pauses between columns.

Note that the mouse cursor's shape indicates that the place mode is still active and that you can place more text onto the page.

Shift + Click on the top of the third column

The semi-automatic mode has flowed the text into the columns but has allowed you the flexibility of choosing the starting points in each column.

Remove the text blocks you created by semi-automatic placement. The Select all command, **Command + a**, will select all of the text blocks on the page when you are in the selection mode. Enter

Command + a
[Delete]

TEMPORARY AUTOMATIC TEXT PLACEMENT

Suppose you began to place the text from a text document into a PageMaker document layout without thinking about whether or not you have turned on the automatic placement mode. Enter

Command + d

> **Click** on "Corporations"
> **Click** on OK

The placement icon indicates that you have forgotten to turn on the automatic placement mode. PageMaker allows you to toggle between manual and automatic placement modes by using a **Command + Click** combination with the mouse icon. If you are in the manual mode, as you are in this example, using **Command + Click** will cause the text to be placed as if it were in the automatic mode.

> **Command + Click** on the top of the 1st column

Pressing the Command key causes PageMaker to change the icon to the automatic text flow icon. The text is then automatically placed into the available columns.

FORMATTING THE TEXT IN COLUMNS

You can format text placed into columns just as you would text placed onto a page with only left and right margin guides. Display the text of the document in the Actual size mode.

> **Point** at the top of the second column
> **Option + Command + Click**
> **Click** on the scroll bar down arrow (4 times)

The lines of the text are formatted inside of the page columns instead of the page margins. Each column operates as if its column guides were its own individual left and right margins.

Working with Columns 4

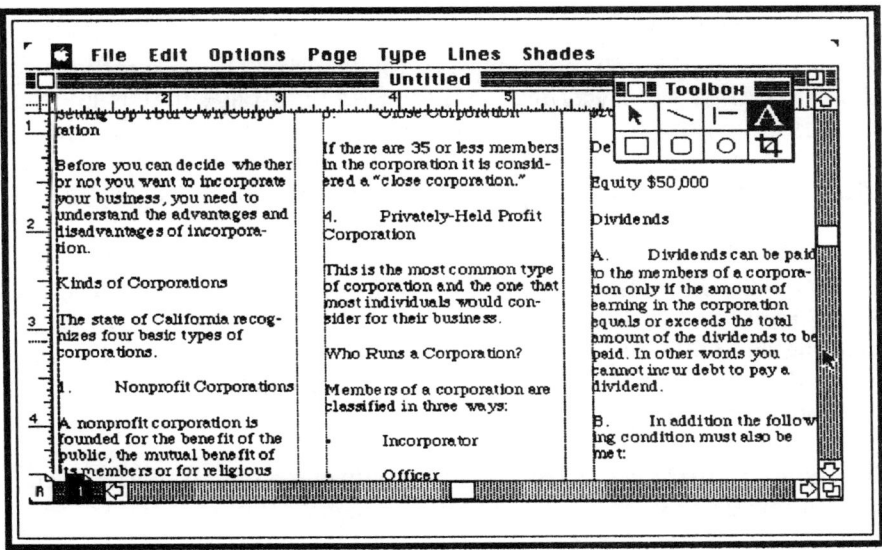

Figure 4.8   Text formatted within each column on the page.

You can apply the styles that you copied from the Corp Notes document. Place PageMaker into the text mode and format the first paragraph with the Major Heading style.

> **Click** on the text mode icon
> **Click** on "Setting Up"

Display the Style palette.

Command + e

> **Click** on Major Heading

There are two significant results of applying this style. The most obvious is that the text in the first paragraph is formatted as a major heading, i.e., a different, larger type, with centered alignment. However, the centering now has the effect of centering the text within the column rather than centering it across the page width.

4 Working with Columns

The second change is that when the text in the first column increased in size, all of the other text in the columns began to move also. This is another aspect of threading that affects the way text is formatted on a page that is laid out with columns. Because the text does not yet fill all three columns, PageMaker will extend the last column on the page as the amount of space occupied by the text expands. If the amount of space used by the text contracts, PageMaker will shorten the last text block.

This process will automatically update each time a change in the text causes the space occupied by the text to expand or contract. If the expansion forces the last column to the end of the page, the text will have to be continued by adding another page to the document. Note that PageMaker will not automatically create a new text block on the next page.

You can demonstrate how this dynamic flow between columns works by changing to Fit to window display mode and making changes to the text that will change its distribution.

> **Click** on "Before you"
> **Option + Command + Click**

Note that the current paragraph is formatted as Normal style text. If you changed the style to Major Heading, you would cause PageMaker to expand the area occupied by the text.

> **Click** on Major Heading

PageMaker changes the text in the paragraph to the larger font used in the Major Heading style. This change causes the text to use more space. PageMaker ripples the changes through the columns, moving the text to make room for the enlarged characters. You will see that the end of the text in the third column is moved down the page, toward the bottom margin.

If you return to the Normal style, PageMaker will contract the text, moving the end of the text in column #3 up toward the top margin.

> **Click** on Normal

The ripple effect causes the text in column #3 to end in a different place.

Change to the 75% view by entering

Command + 7

HYPHENATION OPTIONS

The next task is to apply the styles to the paragraphs in the document. The next paragraph that needs a style selection is the one that reads "Kinds of Corporations." In the previous document, this heading was a Level 2 style.

> **Click** on "Kinds of"
> **Scroll** the Style palette up
> **Click** on Level 2

When you selected the Level 2 style for this paragraph, the area occupied by the text expanded because the type style used in the Level 2 style was larger than the Normal style. In this case, the word "Corporations" could not fit on the first line. PageMaker inserted a hyphen into the word so that part of it appears on the first line while the rest is wrapped to the second line (see Figure 4.9).

When you were formatting the document in Chapter 3, it was usually obvious which lines were short and which ones would be wrapped by the right margin; however, when you create multiple columns on a page, the chances that lines will be wrapped and hyphens inserted is much greater.

In the case of paragraph text, the insertion of hyphens would cause little problem. However, when headings such as the current line are hyphenated, it detracts from the appearance of the document. In most cases, you will want to eliminate or control the use of hyphens in heading lines.

4 Working with Columns

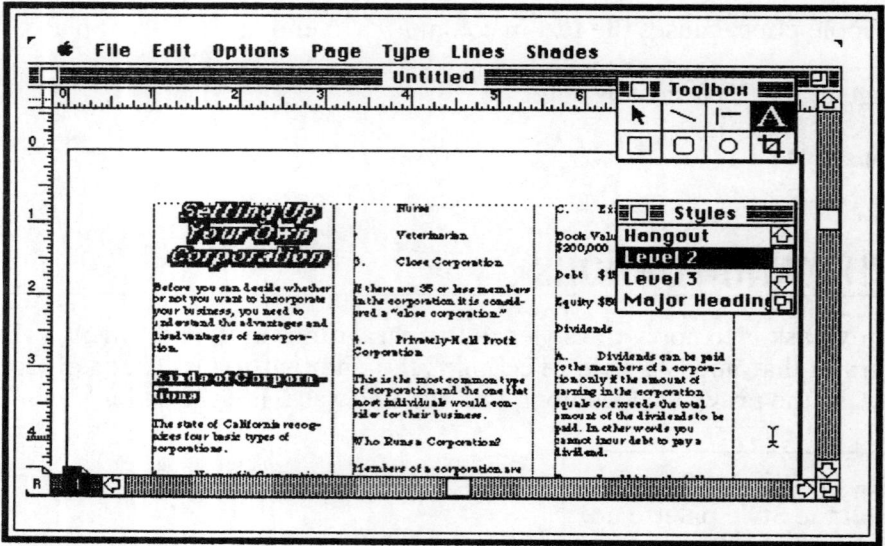

Figure 4.9   Hyphen inserted into Level 2 heading.

Before you deal with that option, format a line as a Level 3 heading. Note that you may need to scroll the display down a bit in order to see the paragraph.

Click on the scroll bar down arrow (2 times)
Click on "1. Nonprofit"
Scroll the Style palette up
Click on Level 3

The same problem occurs in the Level 3 heading. To solve the problem, you would need to modify the settings in the Major Heading. Because the Level 2 and Level 3 styles are based on the Major Heading style, you can stop the hyphenation for all headings by changing the base style — Major Heading.

Point at Type
Drag to Define styles

Select the Major Heading style.

> **Scroll** the style list down
> **Click** on Major Heading
> **Click** on Edit

Hyphenation is controlled by the settings in the Paragraph specification dialog box.

> **Click** on Para

The first item in the dialog box is Hyphenation. The box shows two options: Auto and Prompted.

Auto This setting is the default setting for PageMaker text and causes PageMaker to automatically insert hyphens when needed. PageMaker is supplied with a dictionary file of 110,000 words that is used to determine hyphenation points. In addition to the dictionary, you can add your own words to a text file called **PMUSUSER.TXT**. PageMaker also checks the words in this file when performing hyphenation.

Prompted If this option is selected, PageMaker will prompt you to accept or skip hyphenation when necessary.

If you deselect both options, lines will be broken only between words, with no hyphens inserted. Turn off the hyphenation.

> **Click** on Auto (to deselect it)
> **Click** on OK (2 times)

Before you return to the document, recall that you are working on a paragraph that should be styled as Level 3.

4 Working with Columns

> **Click** on Level 3
> **Click** on OK

The hyphens are removed from all of the paragraphs formatted with any of the styles based on the Major Heading style.

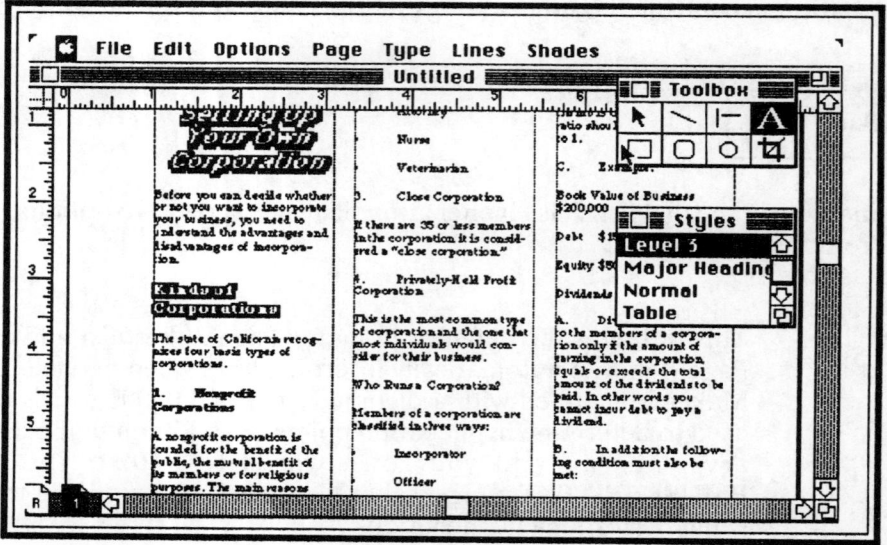

Figure 4.10   *Hyphens removed from headings.*

Scroll the display one screen down. Enter

3 (numeric keypad)

Format the paragraph that begins "2. Professional" as a Level 3 heading.

> **Click** on "2. Professional"
> **Click** on Level 3

Working with Columns **4**

In looking at the format used for the Level 3 headings, you can see that what was an effective format in a full-page width document may look odd in a column format in which the length of the lines is considerably reduced. For example, in the Level 3 headings, the .5" space left by the tab following the number seems too large when compared to the narrow width of the column. You might want to reduce the size of the tab stop, which might also make it possible to fit all the text on a single line.

> **Point** at Type
> **Drag** to Define styles
> **Scroll** the list down
> **Click** on Level 3
> **Click** on Edit
> **Click** on Tabs

The Indents/Tabs dialog box is displayed. In this case you want to change the Level 3 style to a hangout-type format. The left indent should be set at .25". You should also create a tab at that location. To create the hangout, place the first line indent back at zero. This can all be accomplished by dragging the icons on the ruler line.

First, set the left indent at .25". Remember that the bottom triangle is the left indent icon.

> **Drag** the left indent icon to .25"

Next, create a first-line indent of -.25" by dragging the first line indent icon to the left .25".

> **Drag** the first-line indent icon to -.25"

Finally, set a tab at .25"

> **Click** on .25"

193

4 Working with Columns

Keep in mind that if the location of your click is not exactly .25", you can move the tab to that exact location by dragging the tab icon. Return to the document by entering

[Return] (3 times)

The blank space between the number and the text in the Level 3 headings has been reduced to .25". Also, Level 3 headings are now formatted as hangouts if the text requires more than one line.

There are two more paragraphs labeled **3.** and **4.** that should also be formatted as Level 3 headings. Move to the top of the page so you can see the top of the middle column. Enter

9 (numeric keypad)
9 (numeric keypad)

> **Click** on "Close"
> **Click** on Level 3
> **Click** on "Privately Held"
> **Click** on Level 3

You can also use the 1st Bullet and Bullet styles. Enter

3 (numeric keypad)
3 (numeric keypad)

> **Click** on "Accountant"
> **Scroll** the Style palette up
> **Click** on 1st Bullet

Enter

9 (numeric keypad)
9 (numeric keypad)

> **Point** at "Attorney"
> **Drag** to "Veterinarian"
> **Scroll** the Style palette up
> **Click** on Bullet

Again you can see that the spacing used in the previous document does not fit well with a column layout.

You can adjust both the Bullet and 1st Bullet styles in one modification because 1st Bullet is based on Bullet.

> **Point** at Type
> **Drag** to Define styles
> **Click** on Bullet
> **Click** on Edit
> **Click** on Tabs

First, change the left indent to 0" on the ruler by dragging the left indent icon, the bottom triangle, to the left.

> **Drag** the left indent icon to 0"

Set a tab at .25".

> **Click** on the ruler at .25"

Save the modifications to the Bullet style by entering

[Return] (2 times)

The change you have just made to the Bullet style will also flow through to the 1st Bullet style because it is based on the Bullet style. Return to the document by entering

[Return]

4 Working with Columns

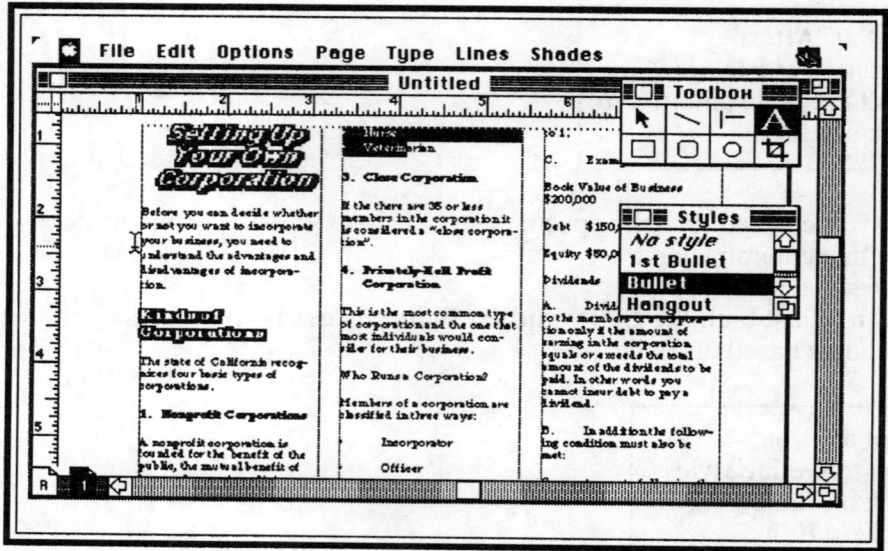

Figure 4.11   Bullets adjusted for column formatting.

In a normal situation, you would continue formatting the text until you have placed all of the paragraphs into suitable paragraph styles. In this example, you will leave the formatting as is and go on to other issues raised by multiple-column layouts.

SPREADING TEXT ACROSS COLUMNS

The Major Heading of this document is currently formatted so that it fits into the top of the first column on the page. Frequently, this type of heading stretches across all of the columns at the top of a page. Creating this type of effect illustrates how three major concepts in PageMaker are related: text blocks, the flow of stories, and column layouts.

The basic solution to the problem is to change the width of the text block so that the text flows across all three columns. Of course, before you can do that, you must move the other text blocks to make room for the expanded text of the heading. To achieve this effect, you will use a number of procedures that illustrate how text block operations work when the blocks are part of the same story.

Working with Columns **4**

Moving Multiple Text Blocks

The column guides you created for this document are guides for the layout of the text blocks, but once you flow the text into text blocks, the columns act as series of text blocks. You can perform operations such as size and location changes with these text blocks just as you did with the small text blocks you created in Chapters 1 and 2.

However, often you will want to move a number of individual blocks as if they were a unit. In this example, you will move all three column text blocks down the page to make room for the major heading you want to place at the top of the page.

One way to perform this operation is to select and move each column individually. However, you can select more than one item on a page by using the **Shift + Click** technique.

Change to the selection mode.

> **Click** on the pointer icon

Remove the Style palette from the screen by entering

Command + e

Select the text block in the first column.

> **Click** on "Setting"

The window shade handles appear at the top of the block, indicating that it is selected.

> **Click** on "Nurse"

When you click on "Nurse," the text block in the middle column is selected and the selection is removed from the block in the left column. This is the way selection normally works. But suppose that you want both the left and middle column text blocks selected?

197

4 Working with Columns

> **Shift + Click** on "Setting"

This time PageMaker operates differently. The use of Shift+Click causes the program to add the text block in the first column to the previous selection. Now both columns are selected at the same time. This technique is called **multiple selection**.

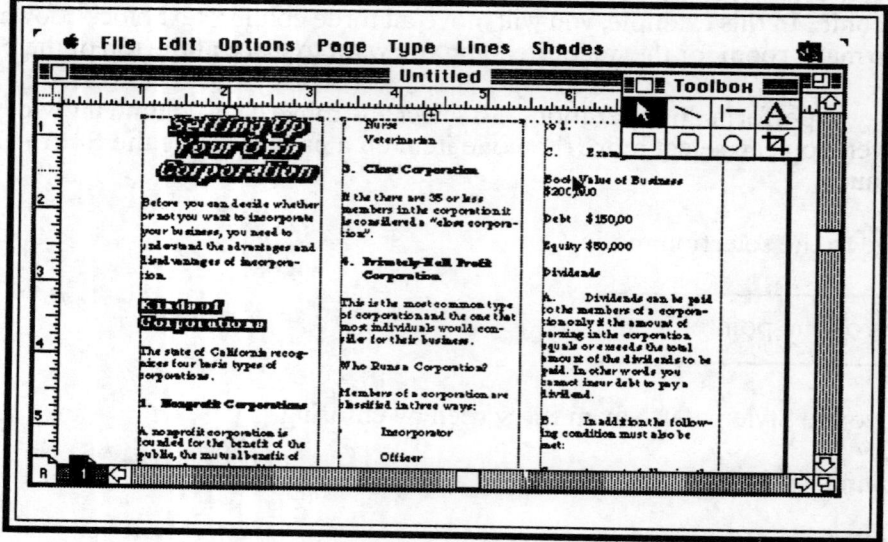

Figure 4.12   Two columns selected at the same time.

The advantage of this technique is that all of the selected items can be moved as if they were a single item. In this case, all three columns can be moved down the page with a single command. This also ensures that all of the columns are repositioned at the same location relative to each other, which might be difficult to achieve if all three were moved individually.

Add the right text block to the selection.

> **Shift + Click** on "Example:"

Moving a Multiple Selection

You can move a multiple selection of text blocks by pointing inside of any of the text blocks and dragging them in the direction you want.

In this case, you want to move the text down the page so that you have room to place the major heading at the top of the page. It is probably convenient to point at a place in the middle of the selection when you want to move a large segment of text.

> **Point** at "Close Corporation"
> **Drag** down to 1.5" on the vertical ruler (as in Figure 4.13)

Be sure not to drag the columns to the right or left so that they are no longer aligned with the column guides. If this happens, simply drag the blocks back so that they align with the column guides again.

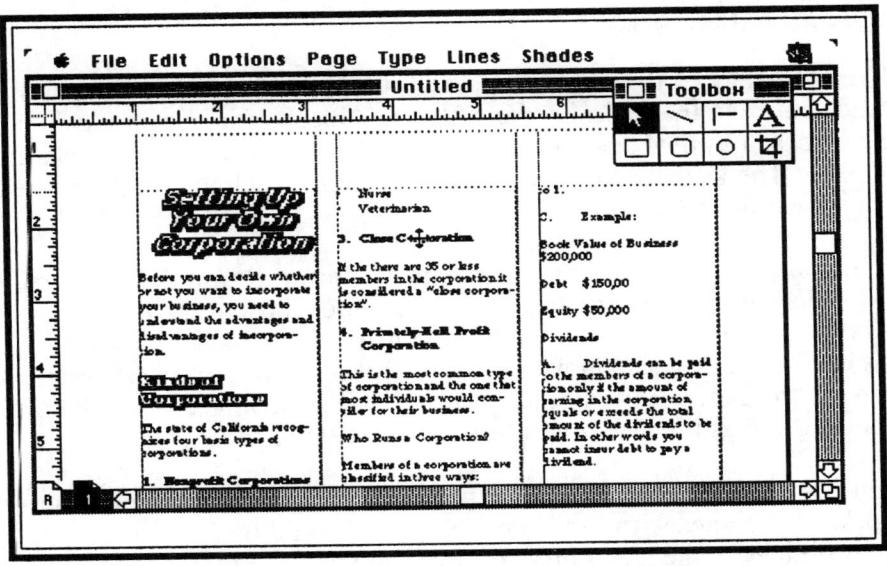

Figure 4.13   Columns moved down the page.

4 Working with Columns

Adding a Text Block to a Story

You have now created an area at the top of the document in which you can insert a text block that will contain the major heading for the document. However, the text block you are about to add is not an ordinary text block such as the ones you created in Chapters 1 and 2. Those blocks contained text that was not related to a specific story.

The type of text block you want to insert in this document is one that is related to the flow of the story from the CORPORATIONS document file. In this case, you want to create a new text block that will contain the first paragraph of the document. Ideally, you would want the text to be rearranged so that all of the text following the first paragraph of the story would be flowed into the three column-wide text blocks.

PageMaker allows you to achieve this type of arrangement by using a special form of the Place command. The command is issued by clicking on one of the window shade handles of a selected text block. If the handle is empty, indicating that this block is the first text block for a story, the new text block is logically inserted at the beginning of the story.

In adding new blocks to an existing story, it is important to keep in mind the difference between the logical order of the text blocks and the physical order of the text blocks. **Physical order** refers to the order in which the text blocks appear on the page. The **logical order** refers to the order in which the text from the story is arranged within the blocks.

When you allowed PageMaker to automatically flow text into the three columns, the text blocks were created starting in the upper left corner of the page and moving down one column and then the next in a snaking pattern. This automatic process created text blocks in which the logical order and physical order of the blocks were the same. Put another way, the text as arranged in the blocks is in the exact order that the text was entered into the word processing file.

This will not always be the case. It is possible to have the physical order of the text blocks at variance with the logical order. It would be easy to drag the right column text block to the left column position and the left column text block to the right column. The major heading "Setting Up Your Own Corporation" would appear at the top of the right column on the page even though it is the first text block in the story. This type of arrangement will occur in complicated documents, such as newsletters or magazine layouts in which several articles and advertisements appear on the same page.

When you add a text block to a story, you must to consider how the text block will affect the logical and physical arrangement of the story in text blocks.

In this case, your goal is to insert a text block at the top of the document and retain the current physical and logical order. Because the new text block will appear at the top of the document, the first line of the text should flow backward from its current location in the first column into the new text block. All of the other text should flow backward to refill the space at the top of the left-most column.

This concept is much easier to understand when you examine how it works. To tell PageMaker that you want to add a text block to the beginning of the story, you must click on the handle at the beginning of the story. Note that this handle will always be the empty handle.

> **Click** on the empty window shade handle

This action places PageMaker into the placement mode again. Note that the mouse cursor has changed to the manual placement icon.

Drag the mouse to draw a text block that covers the blank area from the top margin guide to the tops of the column text blocks, covering the page from the left to the right margin guides.

> **Point** at the upper left corner of the margins
> **Drag** to the right margin 1" down vertically (as in Figure 4.14)

When you release the mouse button, PageMaker flows the text into the newly created text block and rearranges the rest of the story in the column text blocks. Remember, because you selected the handle at the beginning of the story, PageMaker assigned the new text block as the first logical text block for the story. Therefore, the first paragraph in the document was moved to that block. The column text blocks that were formerly the first, second, and third blocks became the second, third, and fourth blocks, respectively (see Figure 4.15).

4 Working with Columns

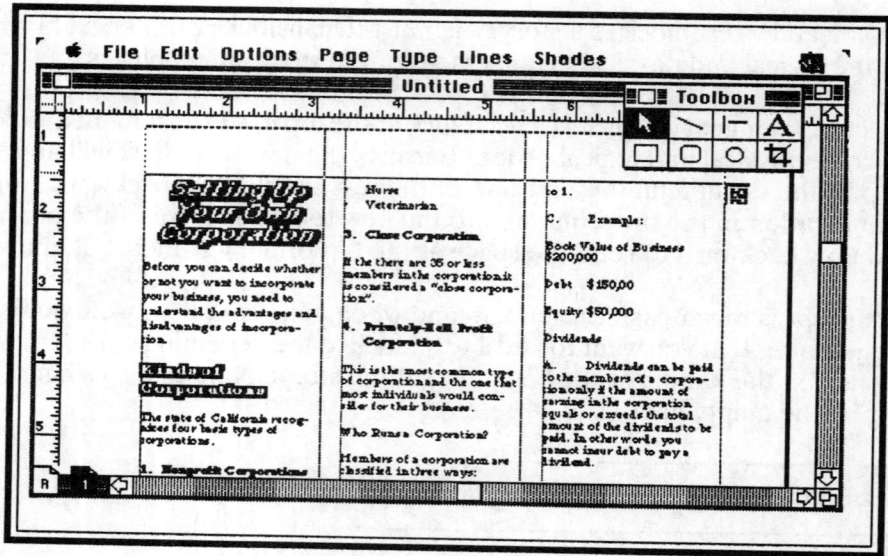

Figure 4.14   *Drawing new text block at top of page.*

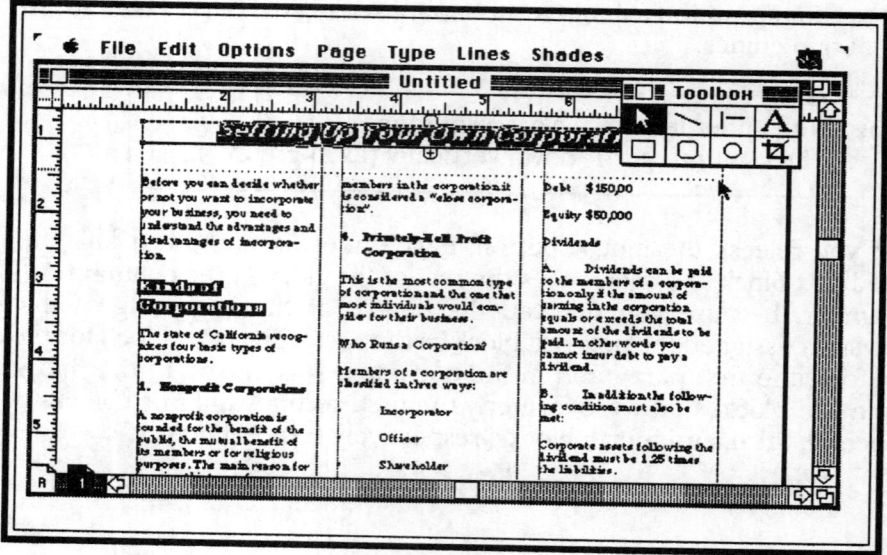

Figure 4.15   *Text rearranged into text blocks.*

The relationship between the physical order of the text blocks and the logical order in which text from the story flows into the blocks is very important. Note that PageMaker does not display or directly indicate the logical sequence of the text in the blocks. If you were not familiar with the contents of the document and the document did not contain obvious major headings, you might find it difficult to determine whether the text on the page was placed in the correct order. It is therefore important that you keep track of the logical order of the text blocks for each story because PageMaker can't do that for you.

Reshaping the Columns

To examine the overall layout of the page, change to the Fit to window view. Enter

Command+w

When you moved the text columns down the page to make room for the heading across the top, the text blocks retained their original length. The left and middle text blocks now extend past the bottom margin guide.

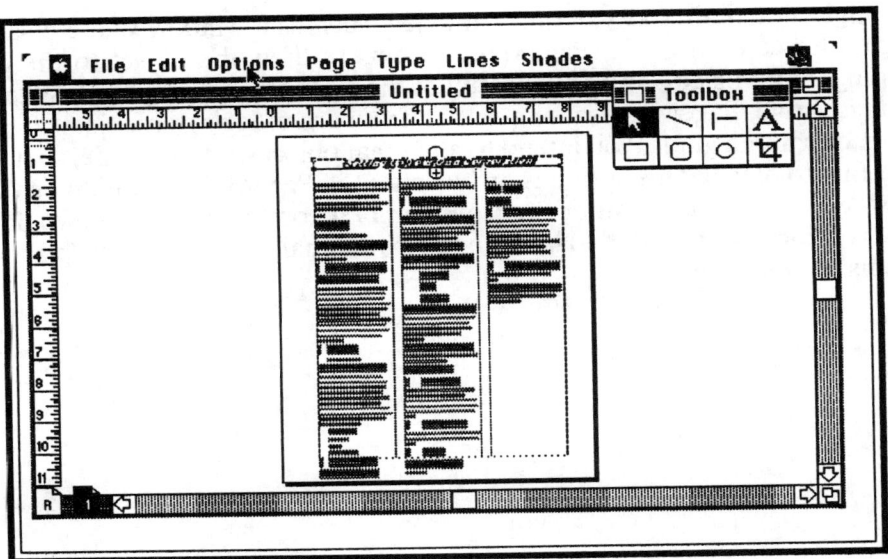

Figure 4.16   *Moved columns exceed bottom margin.*

4 Working with Columns

You must now manually adjust the length of the columns to fit into the page margins.

> **Click** on the left column

This selects the left column and causes PageMaker to display its window shade handles. Adjust the column length by dragging the bottom window shade handle up to the bottom margin guide.

> **Drag** the bottom + window shade handle up to the bottom margin

Perform the same operation on the middle column.

> **Click** on the middle column
> **Drag** the bottom + window shade handle up to the bottom margin

You might notice that as you drag an object such as a window shade close to a margin of a column guide, PageMaker seems to draw the object to the guide, snapping it into place. This is the result of the Snap to guides option. When this option is active, PageMaker assumes that if you are dragging an object close to a margin or column guide, you intend to align that object with the guide, so it snaps the item into place. This option is on by default in PageMaker and can be turned off using the Options menu or the **Command+u** combination. You would turn off this option if you wanted to have complete manual control over the placement of items on the page.

INTERRUPTING A STORY

The current document consists of a single story formatted in four different text blocks. Suppose you want to insert an object into the document that was not part of the story text. The object could be a graphic or some text block that is related to but not part of the story. In this case, suppose you wanted to create a **lift** text block. A lift is a text block that is inserted into a column layout — usually in headline-size print — to gain the reader's interest by presenting an idea or quotation contained within the text. Lifts are commonly used in magazines and newsletters to give readers a sense of the article's contents by displaying a phrase out of context. The term "lift" refers to the fact that the phrase is lifted out of the text and displayed in a manner similar to a heading.

Creating a lift is an interesting task because it involves placing an unrelated text block into the middle of an existing story. It requires you to understand the difference between text blocks that are linked together as parts of a story and text blocks that are independent of stories.

The first step is to select a phrase that you want to use as the lifted text.

> **Point** at the middle of the left-most column, 5" down
> **Option + Command + Click**

The text you want is under the heading "Nonprofit Corporation." In this example, you will want to create a lift out of the second sentence in the paragraph, the one that begins "The main reason. . . ."

To create a lift of the text, you must copy the text into memory. Later, when you have created a text block for the lift, you will paste this text back into the document. Change to the text mode.

> **Click** on the text icon

Select the text that you want to copy.

> **Point** at the "T" in "The main. . . ."
> **Drag** to the period following "corporations"

4 Working with Columns

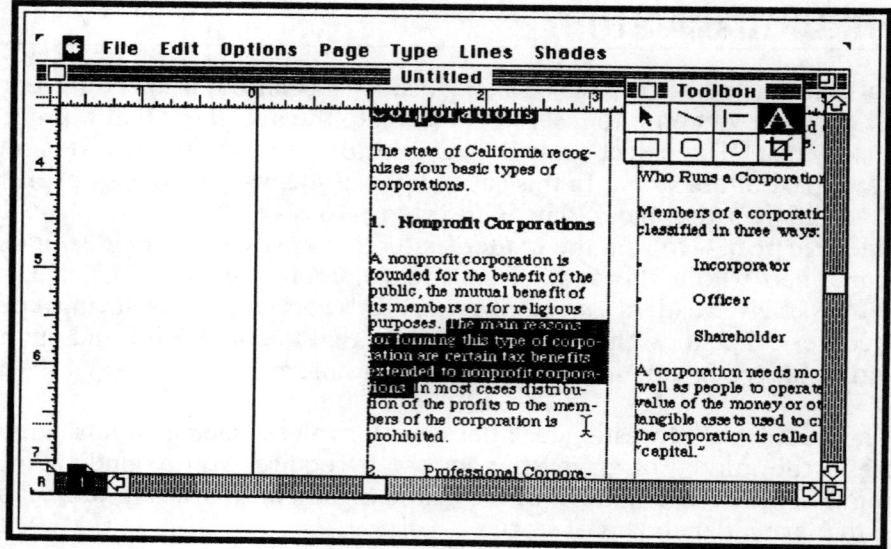

Figure 4.17   *Text from which the lift will be created is selected.*

Copy the text into the memory clipboard. Enter

Command + c

The next step is to create a place on the document for the lift text block to be inserted. Return to the Fit to window display. Enter

Command + w

Activate the selection mode so that you can move and size text blocks.

> **Click** on the pointer icon

In this case, you will want to place the lift in the center of the middle column. The problem is that currently that space is occupied by a text block, so you must shorten the text block that is currently in the middle column. You can then place the lift below the shortened column. When you are done you can fill whatever space is left at the bottom of the column with another text block of the story.

Working with Columns 4

The first step is to shorten the text block in the center column.

> **Click** on the middle column

The window shade handles appear on the middle column, indicating that it is selected. You can use the bottom window shade handle to shorten the block. In this case, you will want to drag the bottom of the window shade up to the 5" vertical mark on the ruler.

> **Drag** the bottom handle up to 5"

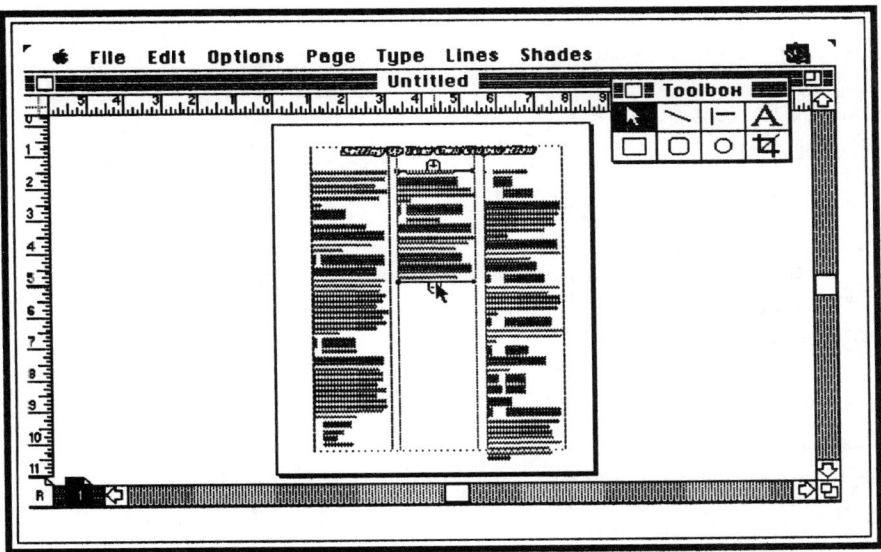

Figure 4.18   *Text block shortened to 5" vertical.*

You now have space below the shortened block in which you can insert a text block. Note that this block is a **free-form** text block, such as the ones you created in Chapters 1 and 2, not a linked text block like the ones you have used so far in this chapter. A free-form text block is not related to a story file. You create these free-form text blocks in the text mode by clicking on an empty area of the page. Activate the text mode.

4 Working with Columns

> **Click** on the text icon

Create the new free-form text block just below the shortened text block in the middle column.

> **Click** in the middle column below the text block

PageMaker displays a text cursor on the left edge of the middle column, just below the text from the story text block. Here you want to insert the phrase you copied from the document. Enter

Command+v

The text is inserted into the new text block.

Because the lift text ought to stand out from the rest of the document, change the type to 24-point, bold, italic. Select the text by entering

Command+a

Note that the Select all command, **Command+a**, selects all of the text in the free-form block but ignores the text in the other linked blocks. Change the type specifications. Enter

Command+t

> **Point** at Size
> **Drag** to 24
> **Click** on Bold
> **Click** on Italic

If the text has been imported from a document such as Word, the leading is set for 12-point text because when you cut a section of text, the paragraph style is not carried with it unless you take the entire paragraph. In this case, the text reverts to the format it would have if no style was applied to it. Text imported from Word will use the Word default settings and apply a fixed leading value to the text. This is fine when the text is 12 points, but if you enlarge the type size you must choose a larger leading or set the leading to automatic.

> **Point** at Leading
> **Drag** to Auto

Return to the document view.

> **Click** on OK

The lift text expands to fill more of the middle column.

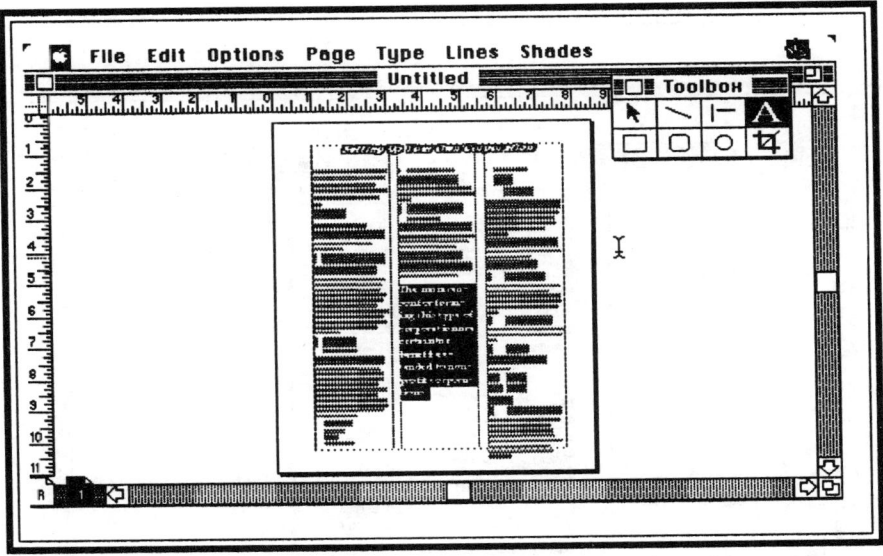

Figure 4.19   Text in block expands when type size enlarged.

4 Working with Columns

In addition to the change in type size and style, you can draw lines above and below the lift to indicate that this block is separate from the logical flow of the article.

Place PageMaker into the perpendicular-line mode.

> **Click** on the perpendicular-line icon

Set the line drawing at 8 points.

> **Point** at Line
> **Drag** to 8 pt

Draw a horizontal line above and below the lifted text, as shown in Figure 4.20.

> **Draw** line above text
> **Draw** line below text (as in Figure 4.20)

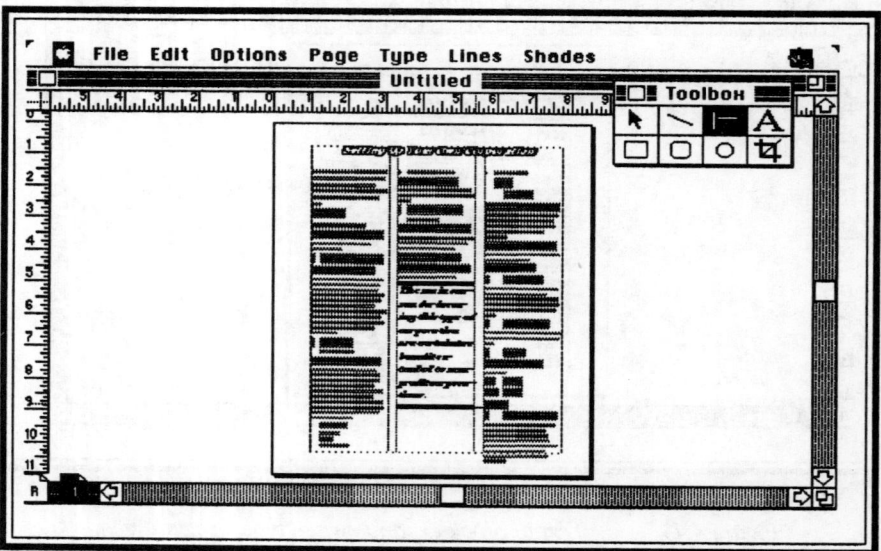

Figure 4.20 *Lines drawn above and below lift text.*

The last step is to fill any portion of the column that was not used for the lift with a text block linked to the story. The text block should be linked specifically to the story block at the top of the column. By doing that you will cause PageMaker to continue the story from the point at which it stopped in the first block in the column.

To create a linked block, you must be in the selection mode.

> **Click** on the pointer icon

Activate the text block at the top of the middle column.

> **Click** on the text block (top of middle column)

The window shade handles on the top and bottom of this block both contain + signs, which indicate that the block is in the middle of a story. To continue the story, select the bottom handle of the story block.

> **Click** on the bottom + handle

Clicking on the handle places PageMaker into the manual text placement mode. You can fill the space at the bottom of the column by clicking with the placement icon just below the line at the bottom of the lifted paragraph, as in Figure 4.21.

> **Point** just below the lift text in the middle column (as in Figure 4.21)

4 Working with Columns

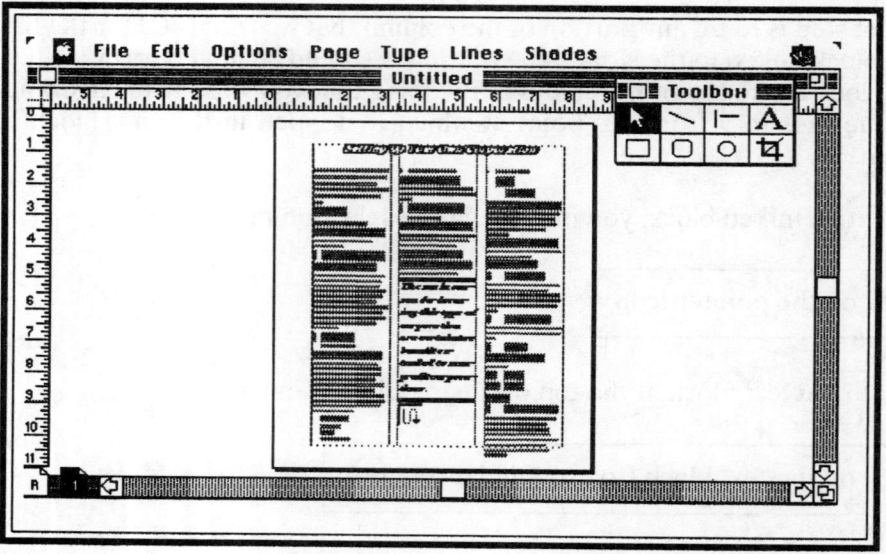

Figure 4.21   *Placement icon positioned to fill remainder of column.*

Insert the text by clicking with the icon in this location.

> **Click** below the lift text

The lift text that you created is independent of the text blocks linked to the story. This means that while the text in the story blocks will flow through the linked blocks, the text in the free-form text block will remain exactly where it is on the page until it is manually repositioned.

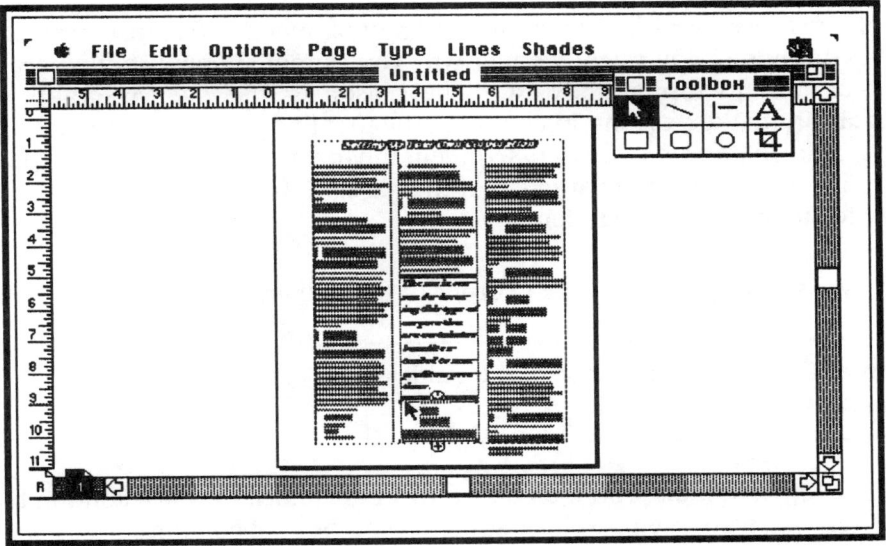

Figure 4.22   *PageMaker flows text into the remainder of the column.*

BIG FIRST LETTERS

Another enhancement frequently used in column layout is the use of a **big first letter** (also known as a dropped capital). "Big first letter" refers to enlarging the first character in the first paragraph of the text. It has been a traditional way to indicate the start of a document or section since the middle ages and is frequently used in publications today.

The big first letter effect is created by using both free-form and linked text blocks. In PageMaker a big first letter is created by placing the first character of the document in a free-form text block. The character's size and type is typically changed so that its point size is double the point size of the rest of the text in the paragraph.

The enlarged first character creates an interesting formatting problem. Because it is at least twice as high as the other characters on the first line, it is necessary to create an indent for the second, or in some cases the third, line of the paragraph so the big first letter can fit without overlapping text in the paragraph.

This effect is accomplished by manipulating text blocks. Because the problem involves an indent, you might wonder why you cannot simply use the paragraph indent options to format the text. The reason is that the paragraph indent specifications make a distinction between the first line and all subsequent lines of a paragraph. In this case, you want to indent the first two or three lines (depending on the size of the big first character) of the paragraph. PageMaker has no direct facility for making such an indent.

Begin by displaying the upper left corner of the document.

> **Point** at the upper left corner of the guides
> **Option + Command + Click**

The first step is to make room on a free-form text block that will contain the big first letter. Activate the text block at the top of the first column.

> **Click** on "Before"

The window shade handle appears on the text block. Shorten the block by dragging the handle down to 2" vertical.

> **Drag** the window shade handle to 2"

You can now create a free-form text block that will contain the enlarged first letter of the paragraph. Recall that free-form text blocks are created in the text mode.

> **Click** on the text mode icon

Create a text block on the left margin guide about 1.5" down vertically on the page.

> **Click** on left guide 1.5" down

Working with Columns **4**

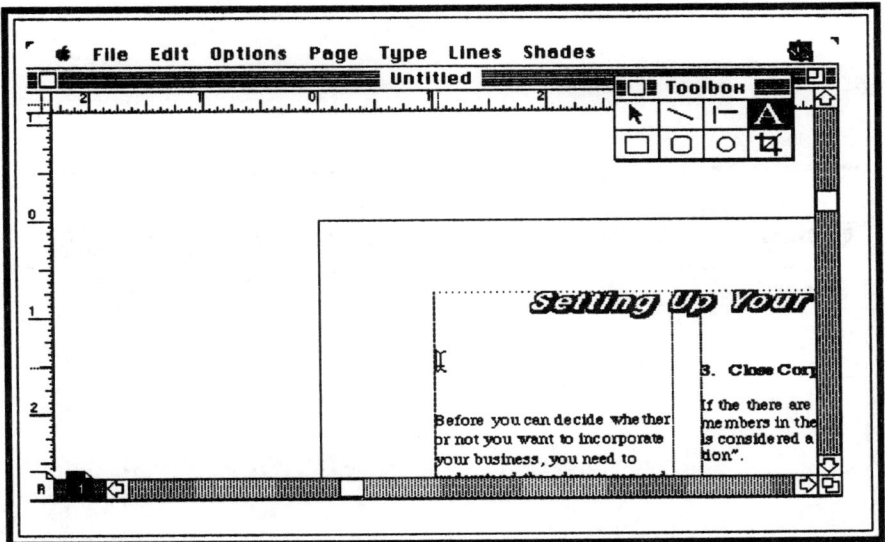

Figure 4.23   Text block inserted in first column

Note that the type specifications are picked up from the major heading style, i.e., outline, italic, and shadow. Change the type specification to 24-point, outline, bold, shadow. Enter

Command+t

Point at Size
Drag to 24
Click Bold
Click on Italic (to deselect it)
Click on OK

Enter the first character.

B

Now that you have added the first letter block to the document, you want to delete the letter "B" from the story block.

Click between "B" and "e" in the word "Before"

215

4 Working with Columns

Enter

[Delete]

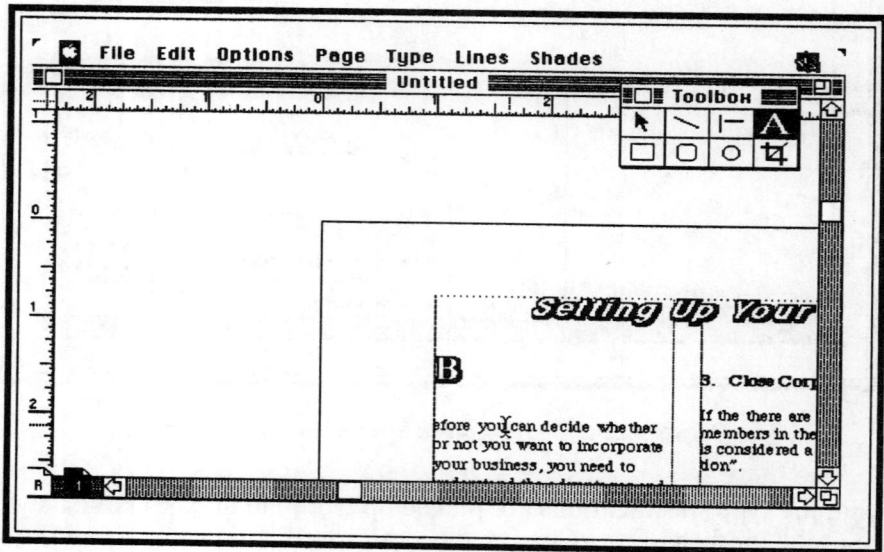

Figure 4.24 Big first letter placed into document.

With the character added, your next step is to flow the text from the beginning of the story into a text block that will be positioned next to the big first letter. This will be a linked block, so change to the selection mode.

Click on the pointer icon

Activate the linked text block at the top of the first column.

Click on "decide"

The window shade handle appears at the top of the text block. Activate the placement mode.

Working with Columns **4**

> **Click** on the + in the handle

The mouse changes to the manual placement icon. Your task is to create a new text block linked to the story. In this case, you will not draw the block starting at the left column guide; you will begin it next to the big first letter. Draw a block as shown in Figure 4.25.

> **Point** the icon next to the big "B"
> **Draw** a text block (as in Figure 4.25)

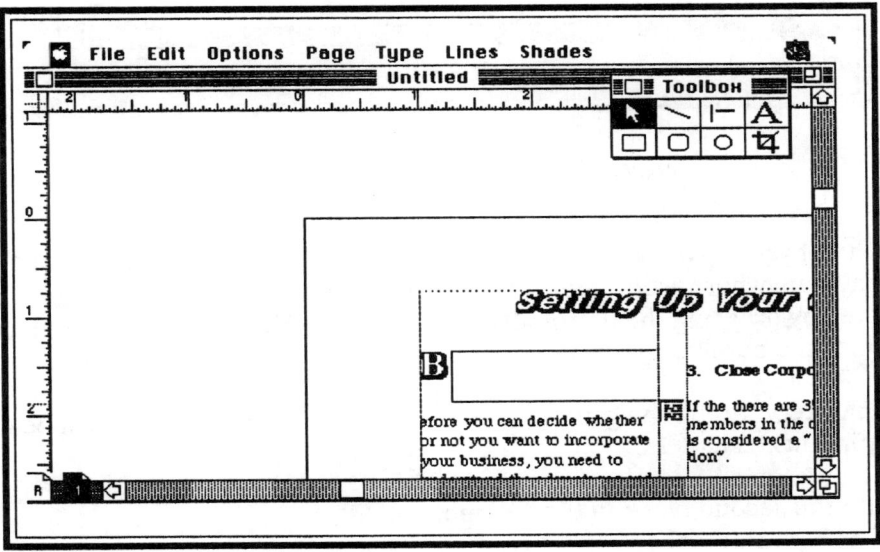

Figure 4.25   Linked text block drawn next to big first letter.

When you release the mouse button, PageMaker will flow the first two lines of the text into the linked block.

4 Working with Columns

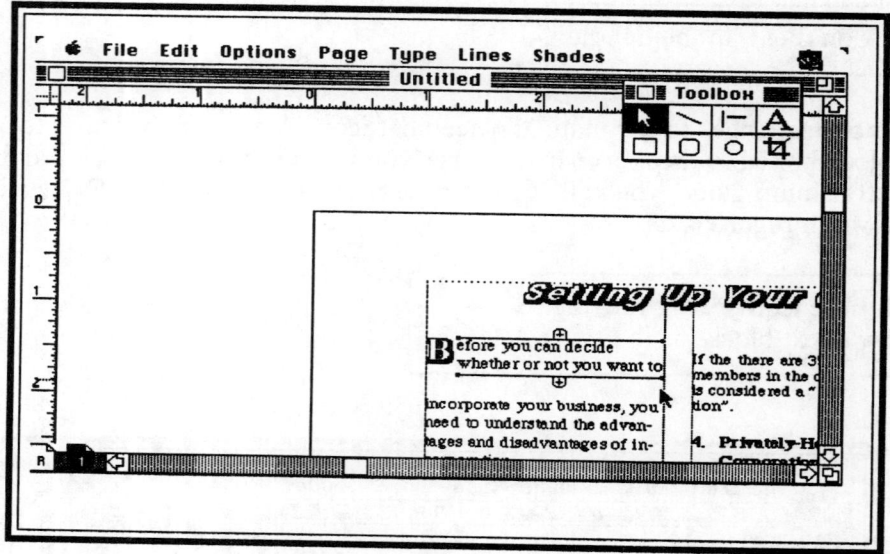

Figure 4.26   Text flowed into new block.

Note that if you drew your block a bit differently from the one in Figure 4.25, you may have anywhere from one to three lines of text in the block. This is easily corrected by dragging the bottom handle of the new block up or down to increase or reduce the number of lines in it.

The final step is to fill the gap between the two text blocks to give the appearance of continuous text.

Activate the second block in the column.

> **Click** on "Business"
> **Drag** the + handle up to 2.75" vertical

The text block moves back up to fill the gap.

Working with Columns 4

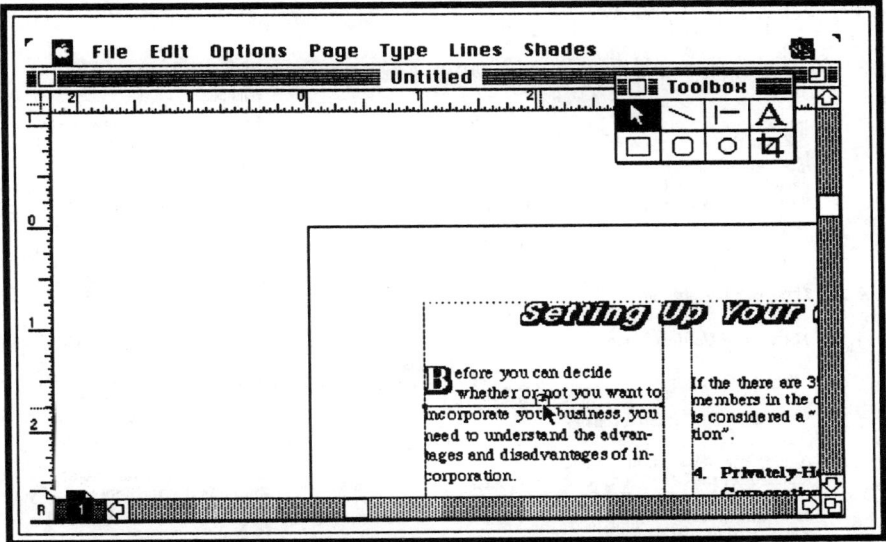

Figure 4.27   Blocks converge to create continuous appearance.

Print the document. Enter

Command + p
[Return]

If you are using an ImageWriter, press Return when the additional dialog boxes appear.

The finished document will resemble the one in Figure 4.28:

Save the document by entering

Command + s
columns [Return]

Close the document window.

> **Point** at File
> **Drag** to Close

4 Working with Columns

Setting Up Your Own Corporation

Before you can decide whether or not you want to incorporate your business, you need to understand the advantages and disadvantages of incorporation.

Kinds of Corporations

The state of California recognizes four basic types of corporations.

1. Nonprofit Corporations

A nonprofit corporation is founded for the benefit of the public, the mutual benefit of its members or for religious purposes. The main reasons for forming this type of corporation are certain tax benefits extended to nonprofit corporations. In most cases distribution of the profits to the members of the corporation is prohibited.

2. Professional Corporations

Members of professions that license their members may form a professional corporation. Note that many professions are not subject to the requirement to form a professional corporation but can form a regular profit corporation. Professions that fall into the professional corporation classification are:

- Accountant
- Attorney
- Nurse
- Veterinarian

3. Close Corporation

If there are 35 or less members in the corporation it is considered a "close corporation."

4. Privately-Held Profit Corporation

This is the most common type of corporation and the one that most individuals would consider for their business.

Who Runs a Corporation?

Members of a corporation are classified in three ways:

- Incorporator

> *The main reasons for forming this type of corporation are certain tax benefits extended to nonprofit corporations.*

- Officer
- Shareholder

A corporation needs money as well as people to operate. The value of the money or other tangible assets used to create the corporation is called "capital."

Capital can be acquired by a corporation by selling stock or borrowing money.

Debt to Equity Ratio

A. When creating a corporation out of an existing business it is a mistake to transfer all of the assets of the unincorporated business to the corporation in exchange for a note.

B. The general rule of thumb is that the debt to equity ratio should be no more than 3 to 1.

C. Example:

Book Value of Business $200,000

Debt $150,000

Equity $50,000

Dividends

A. Dividends can be paid to the members of a corporation only if the amount of earning in the corporation equals or exceeds the total amount of the dividends to be paid. In other words you cannot incur debt to pay a dividend.

B. In addition the following condition must also be met:

Corporate assets following the dividend must be 1.25 times the liabilities.

Figure 4.28   Reduced image of final document.

Working with Columns 4

SUMMARY

This chapter examined how a document can be formatted into vertical text columns.

- **Column Guides.** PageMaker allows you to set a series of vertical column guides on any of the pages of the document. If you set the guides on the master pages, then the guides will appear on all pages of the document. The column guides are used to place text into columns within a page. Column guides will be automatically recognized by the flow process used with the Place command.

- **Copying Styles.** You can copy a set of styles from an existing PageMaker document or template file into the current document. The styles will be added to the current list of styles in the current document. If the incoming styles have the same name as an existing style, you will be asked if you want to retain or replace the existing style. Note that you cannot have two styles with the same name in a PageMaker document.

- **Stories.** A story is all of the text contained in a file placed into a PageMaker document. A story can be placed into a single text block or into a series of text blocks.

- **Text Flow.** Depending on the placement mode you use, PageMaker can automatically or semi-automatically place text into blocks within a PageMaker document. PageMaker can automatically fill a column or page, creating the text blocks as they are needed. This process is faster than drawing each individual text block.

- **Manual Text Flow.** The manual method of text flow is the default method. Manual Text Flow is initiated by clicking with the placement icon at the point where you want the text block to begin on the page — or column if the page contains more than one column. PageMaker automatically creates the text block and fills the entire column with text, stopping when all of the text has been placed or the bottom margin is reached. When the text flow stops, the placement mode is terminated.

4 Working with Columns

- **Automatic Text Flow.** Automatic text flow will fill an entire page with text even when the page contains multiple columns. Automatic placement is useful when you want to flow text through a series of columns without having to select each column's starting point. Following the first column, in which the cursor position determines the starting point of the first text block, PageMaker assumes that you want to start flowing text from the top margin to the bottom margin or until no more text is available. Automatic text flow can be selected from the Options menu or by holding down the Option key when the placement mode is active.

- **Semi-Automatic Text Flow.** Semi-automatic is the same as automatic except that PageMaker pauses after each column is filled, which allows you to change the starting position of the next column of text. During the pause, PageMaker remains in the place mode.

- **Multiple Block Selections.** When more than one text block is placed on a page, you can move more than one block at a time by creating a multiple selection. After you select a text block, if you select another text block with a **Shift+Click** instead of the normal click, PageMaker adds the selected item to the current selection instead of switching the selection to the newly selected block. You can add as many blocks as are present on a given page (or two pages if you are in the facing pages display mode).

- **Linked Blocks.** Linked text blocks are blocks that share the same story. Linked blocks have a dynamic relation when it comes to flowing text. If one block in a linked block series is expanded or contracted in size, the text in all of the linked blocks is adjusted to the new size. The last block in the story will be lengthened or shortened by changes made to the other blocks.

- **Non-Linked Blocks.** A non-linked block is created manually without using the place mode. Such blocks are not linked to a specific story and do not flow text dynamically when changes are made that affect size or shape.

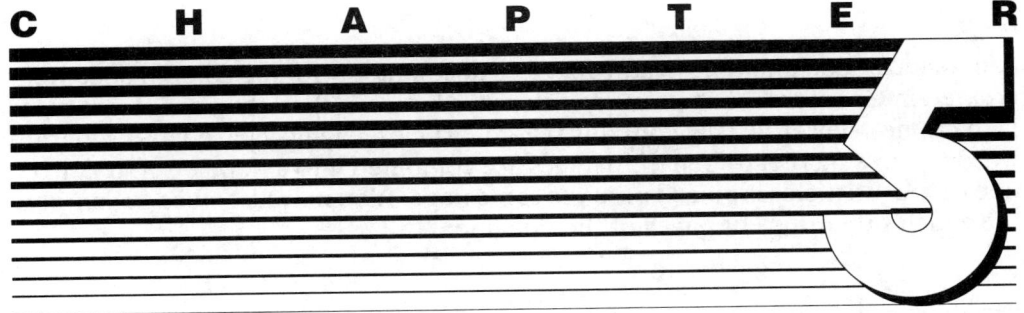

NEWSLETTERS

In Chapter 4, you learned how PageMaker formats text into vertical columns. You also learned how PageMaker imports text prepared in word processing programs into a PageMaker document. The skills you learned in Chapter 4 are essential to creating more complicated documents, such as newsletters. In this chapter, you will learn the additional techniques and concepts needed to create multiple-article newsletters in PageMaker.

5 Newsletters

A newsletter document has many features in common with the column document created in Chapter 4. The primary difference between these two document types is that a newsletter usually contains several articles, each prepared as a separate word processing file. When the articles are combined into a newsletter, text from one or more articles is placed onto the same page. You may also need to continue the articles on different pages of the document.

TEXT DOCUMENTS AND STYLES

In Chapter 4, you imported text from a word processor text file. Once the text was placed into the PageMaker document, you assigned styles to the paragraphs by selecting each paragraph and assigning the style you wanted.

In many cases, you know at the time you are preparing the document what style you want to assign to various parts of the text. PageMaker allows you to include style designations as part of the text of the document so that the style names are automatically assigned to the paragraphs when the text is placed into the PageMaker document. Placing the paragraph style names in the text is a much faster process than manually selecting and assigning styles to paragraphs once the paragraphs have been placed in a PageMaker document.

To assign a style name to a paragraph, you simply type the name of the style at the beginning of the paragraph to which you want to assign that style. When you type the name, be sure to enclose it in angle brackets so PageMaker can distinguish the style name from the actual text. For example, to style a paragraph as a Headline style, you would enter <headline> at the beginning of the paragraph. Note that capitalization is not significant when you enter a style name.

Once PageMaker encounters a style name in a document, it assigns that style to all following paragraphs until it encounters another style name. This means if there are five consecutive paragraphs with the same style, only the first paragraph requires a style name designation.

Keep in mind that it is not necessary or even desirable to decide the specifications of each style while you are creating the text file. All you need or actually want to do is decide which paragraphs belong to a particular classification and make up the appropriate style name for that classification.

For example, the title of each article in the newsletter should be assigned the same style title. You can be sure of this even though you are not sure of the font, point size, or style of the characters. When you add style names to a text file, you are creating groups of paragraphs that should have the same formatting specifications. You are not yet choosing what those specifications are.

If you are using Microsoft Word 3.01, you can also import Microsoft Word styles into PageMaker as an alternative to writing the style name symbols into the text. However, in some ways it is probably better to simply use the style name symbols because if you intend to import the text into a layout scheme, e.g., multiple columns, you may find the formatting choices you made in the word document are not appropriate to the PageMaker layout.

The newsletter that you will create will be an extension of the do-it-yourself corporation article created in Chapter 4. In this case, you will use three different documents to create a newsletter with three different articles, and you will use additional text to create a sidebar. You will need to create two new articles and modify the CORPORATIONS document made for the previous chapters.

All the documents used in this chapter will be used in the following chapters as well. There is a total of approximately 1,000 words in the text files you will use for the newsletter. If you want to save time by using other text documents you have already created, you can do so, keeping in mind that the exact spacing characteristics of your newsletter may vary from the figures shown in this book.

Text with Style Symbols

The first text document to prepare is one that will be called "Formalities." This document discusses some of the final formalities required when you set up a corporation. The article will be one of several on the topic to be included in the newsletter.

5 Newsletters

In Figure 5.1, the text of the document is displayed. Note that in this document many of the paragraphs are preceded by special text symbols indicating the names of the styles that should be used to format the text. In this document and other articles appearing in the newsletter, there are seven style name symbols used:

- <1st list>
- <list>
- <sub title>
- <topic title>
- <hangout>
- <standard>
- <title>

The documents shown as text illustrations contain some items used to make the illustrations more readable that should not actually be entered into your text documents. The style names are shown in bold, e.g., **<title>**, in Figure 5.1 and the other word processing document figures to make it easier to distinguish the style names from the actual text; however, style names should be entered as plain text. Adding bold to style names will cause PageMaker to misread the style names when the text is loaded. Also note the paragraph symbols (¶) that are displayed at the end of each paragraph to indicate where you should press the Return key. These characters will not appear in your document but are added to the figures to show which lines were actually ended with returns.

The figures also show the symbol [tab] in each position where you should press the Tab key. "[tab]" should not appear in your document. Instead, the word processor will create a blank space where you insert the tabs.

Create the document shown in Figure 5.1. When the text has been entered, save it under the name **Formalities**. This document contains 308 words. If you are using the latest release of Microsoft Word, version 4, see Appendix A for details on how to save your documents so they can be loaded by PageMaker.

```
<title>FINAL FORMALITIES
<sub title>What You Need to Do After You Set Up A Corporation
<standard>Once you have officially set up your corporation there are still a number of important
tasks that you need to carry out.
<topic title>Domestic Stock Statement
<standard>You must file an Annual Domestic Stock statement with the state of California within
90 days of the date on which you filed the Articles of incorporation.
Each year you will be sent another statement which must be filled out and sent in on or before the
date indicated on the form.
<topic title>Fictitious Name Statement
<standard>If your corporation will do business under any name other than the official corporation
name then you must file a Fictitious Name Statement with the county in which you plan to operate.
This statement must be filed no later than 40 days following the first date upon which you carry out
a transaction under the fictitious name.
<topic title>Notify Creditors
<standard>If you have transferred assets from an existing business to the new corporation you are
required to notify all creditors in writing of the change in ownership.
You are also required to carry out the following:
<hangout>a.[tab]Obtain two copies of the Notice of Dissolution of a Partnership from a legal
newspaper.
b.[tab]Fill out the notice following instructions.
c.[tab]Send the notice to a legal newspaper within 30 days.
d.[tab]Notify creditors by mail.
<sub title>Tax Forms - Federal
<standard>You will need to file some or all of the following forms:
<1st list>S Corporation Tax Election
<list>Federal Employer Identification Number
Employee's Withholding Certificates
Income and Social Security Tax Withholding
Quarterly Withholding Returns and Deposits
Annual Wage and Tax Statement
Federal Unemployment Tax
Corporate Income Tax
S Corporation Income Tax Return
Corporation Employee and Shareholder Returns
Estimated Corporation Income Tax Payments
```

Figure 5.1   *Formalities document.*

5 Newsletters

The second document you will use in the newsletter is called "Business," shown in Figure 5.2. This document is a general introduction to the topic of incorporation, which is the overall theme of the newsletter. Create the document as shown in Figure 5.2, and save it with the file name **Business**. This document also includes style names from the list of style names used in the Formalities document. The Business document contains 262 words.

\<title>DIFFERENT WAYS TO DO BUSINESS¶
\<sub title>Advantages and Disadvantages of Forming A Small Corporation¶
\<standard>As business owners you know that almost every business, in particular a small business, develops its own style of operating. But to the law all business operations fall into three major categories:¶
\<1st list>Sole Proprietorships¶
\<list>Partnerships¶
\<list>Corporations¶
\<standard>This month's Small Business Newsletter is devoted to the topic of incorporation for small business. Sole proprietorships and partnerships can be entered into with a minimum of legal complications. Incorporation is a major decision for a small business and you should carefully weigh all of the positive and negative features before you decide to take the step.¶
\<topic title>Why Incorporate?¶
\<standard>The primary difference between a corporation and other forms of doing business is that the corporation is viewed by the law as a separate entity. The corporation is treated as a fictional person who can be taxed separately from the owners of the corporation.¶
\<standard>When you incorporate you now become an employee of the fictional person who is the corporation. You are then eligible for tax deductible fringe benefits.¶
\<standard>Another attractive feature of incorporation is the limit of liability. Any liability against the corporation can reach only the assets of the corporation not the assets of the owner or owners of the corporation.¶
\<standard>On the other hand creating a corporation is not always a tax benefit. Changing corporate and personal tax rates requires that you make specific calculations to determine the tax implications of incorporation since they vary with each individual owner and business.¶

Figure 5.2   Business document.

The third new document used in the newsletter is called "Sidebar" (see Figure 5.3). This document is shorter than the full article documents and will be formatted in a special way. **Sidebars** are used in newsletter or magazine layouts to display additional information related to but not included in the actual articles. Editors frequently add sidebars to articles to fill in background information not supplied by the main article. Sidebars can be skipped by readers who are familiar with the background material without interrupting or changing the flow of the main article.

Create the text document shown in Figure 5.3 and save it under the file name **Sidebar**. The document contains 93 words.

```
<title>CORPORATE TAX DEDUCTIONS¶
<standard>Salaries paid to employees of the corporation are deductible from corporate taxes. Note
that if a shareholder is paid a salary it must be a reasonable salary for services actually performed. If
not, the IRS may consider these payments as nondeductible dividends.¶
As with salaries, payments made for employee benefits are deductible from corporate income.
Medical benefits, accident, health, life and disability insurance can all be paid by the corporation for
their employees.¶
In contrast, sole proprietorships and partnerships can deduct only 25% of health and accident insur-
ance.¶
```

Figure 5.3   Sidebar document.

Adding Styles to a Text Document

The fourth document for the newsletter is not a new document at all. You will use the text from the CORPORATIONS document. However, you will modify the document to include the style names for the paragraphs. You will also make some changes so that the text will conform to the seven styles used in the Business document.

By adding these styles to the CORPORATIONS document, you will avoid the need to manually style each paragraph, which can be a slow and tedious process in PageMaker, as demonstrated in Chapter 4.

Modify the CORPORATIONS document as shown in Figure 5.4. Instead of using the Save command to save the file, use the Save as command with a new name, **Setup Corp**. The revised document will contain 411 words.

<title>Setting Up Your Own Corporation¶

<standard>Before you can decide whether or not you want to incorporate your business, you need to understand the advantages and disadvantages of incorporation.¶

<sub title>Kinds of Corporations¶

<standard>The state of California recognizes four basic types of corporations.¶

<topic title>Nonprofit Corporations¶

<standard>A nonprofit corporation is founded for the benefit of the public, the mutual benefit of its members or for religious purposes. The main reasons for forming this type of corporation are certain tax benefits extended to nonprofit corporations. In most cases distribution of the profits to the members of the corporation is prohibited.¶

<topic title>Professional Corporations¶

<standard>Members of professions that license their members may form a professional corporation. Note that many professions are not subject to the requirement to form a professional corporation but can form a regular profit corporation. Professions that fall into the professional corporation classification are:¶

<1st list>Accountant¶

<list>Attorney¶

<list>Nurse¶

<list>Veterinarian¶

<topic title>Close Corporation¶

<standard>If the there are 35 or less members in the corporation it is considered a "close corporation."¶

<topic title>Privately-Held Profit Corporation¶

<standard>This is the most common type of corporation and the one that most individuals would consider for their business.¶

<sub title>Who Runs a Corporation?¶

<standard>Members of a corporation are classified in three ways:¶

<1st list>Incorporator¶

<list>Officer¶

<topic title>Shareholder¶

<standard>A corporation needs money as well as people to operate. The value of the money or other tangible assets used to create the corporation is called "capital."¶

<standard>Capital can be acquired by a corporation by selling stock or borrowing money.¶

<topic title>Debt to Equity Ratio¶

<hangout>A. [tab] When creating a corporation out of an existing business it is a mistake to transfer all of the assets of the unincorporated business to the corporation in exchange for a note.¶

B. [tab] The general rule of thumb is that the debt to equity ratio should be no more than 3 to 1.¶

C. [tab] Example:¶

Book Value of Business [tab] $200,000¶

Debt [tab] $150,00¶

Equity [tab] $50,000¶

Dividends¶

A. [tab] Dividends can be paid to the members of a corporation only if the amount of earning in the corporation equals or exceeds the total amount of the dividends to be paid. In other words you cannot incur debt to pay a dividend.¶

B. [tab] In addition the following condition must also be met:¶

Corporate assets following the dividend must be 1.25 times the liabilities.¶

Figure 5.4   Setup Corp document.

When you have saved the four documents required for the newsletter, change to the PageMaker folder and load the PageMaker program. You are now ready to create the newsletter layout.

THE COLUMN LAYOUT

The newsletter document you are about to create has much in common with the multiple-column layout you created in Chapter 4. The primary difference is that text placed into the newsletter will consist of text drawn from several text files, which means the columns on a given page will contain text from one or more documents. When you place text into these columns, you will need to take into consideration how far down the columns the text should flow.

In newsletter layouts, it is common practice to restrict the amount of information from any one article to a predetermined section of the page. If the article contains more text than can be displayed on the page, the article will continue on to another section of a different page. This layout is different from a standard document that flows the text from beginning to end in the order in which it was first entered in the word processor. Therefore, you will need to maintain more precise control over the flow of text into columns than you used in Chapter 4, where PageMaker was allowed to automatically fill as many columns as necessary to display all the text.

Create a new PageMaker document. Enter

Command + n

Accept the default settings, except for margins, to maintain a double-sided, facing pages layout. This layout makes sense because it is likely that a newsletter will be reproduced by a professional printer who will print on both sides of the page. Change the margins to 1" on all sides.

> **Double Click** on Top

Enter

1 [Tab]
1 [Tab]
1 [Return]

5 Newsletters

Note that the double-sided, facing pages layout includes two master page icons, L and R, shown on the bottom scroll bar (as in Figure 5.5).

Activate the master pages.

> **Click** on the L master page icon

PageMaker produces a dual-page display, showing the left and right master pages.

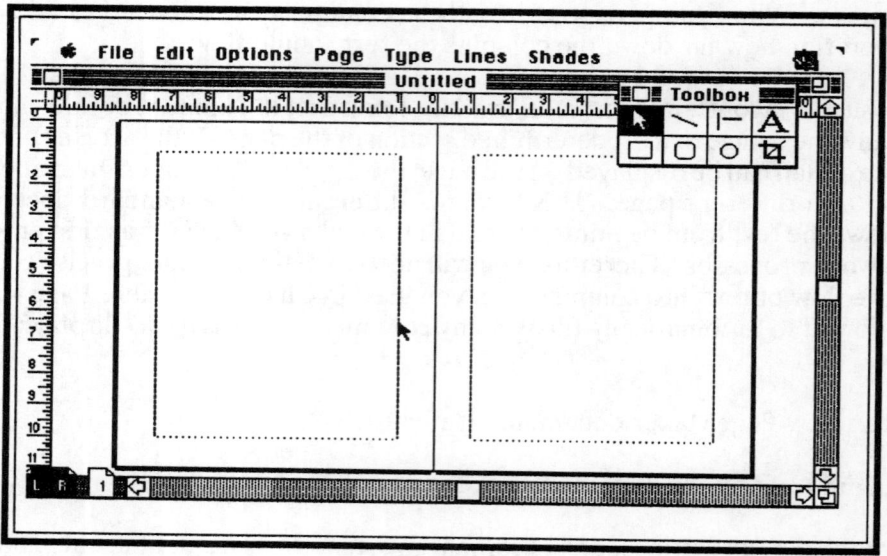

Figure 5.5   Dual-page display.

The advantage of this display is that you can add items to both left and right pages at the same time. For example, the newsletter will be formatted into four columns on each page. In this respect, the column guides for the left and right pages will be the same. With the dual-page display active, the Column guides command will place guides on both master pages at the same time.

> **Point** at Options
> **Drag** to Column guides

The dialog box shows the word **Both** above the value boxes as a result of using this command with a dual-page display. Note that the dialog box contains an option, Set left and right pages separately, in case you want to override the effect of the dual-page display. In this example, though, you do want to set both the left and right pages with the same column guides.

Enter the number of columns.

4 [Tab]

Overriding the Unit of Measurement

The next value required is the amount of space between the columns on the page. The default value is 0.167". PageMaker uses different units of measurement, depending upon the item or dialog box. For example, when you select a line thickness, PageMaker expresses the thickness in terms of points. For space between columns, the value is entered as inches. These units of measurement change according to what the designers of PageMaker thought was the most appropriate way to measure a specific feature.

PageMaker allows you to override the unit of measurement used on the dialog box by entering the value plus a letter that indicates the unit of measurement you want to use. For example, you might find it easier to relate column spacing to points because you select text in terms of point size, not inches. By now you are familiar with the size of a 12-point character because that is the default size for characters printed in PageMaker. You could set the distance using the 12-point characters as a reference point (e.g., 12 points between columns, or 6 points — half the height of a standard character).

You can enter a value in the unit of measurement you prefer by preceding the value with the letter **p**, e.g., p6 stands for 6 points.

In addition to p for points, PageMaker recognizes other letters for different units of measurement.

5 Newsletters

Letter	Example	Value
i	6i	6 inches
m	6m	6 millimeters
p	6p	6 picas
p	p6	6 points
p	6p6	6 picas & 6 points
c	6c	6 ciceros
c	c6	6 points
c	6c6	6 ciceros & 6 points

Recall that a **point** is 1/72". A **cicero** is a measurement used in countries that use the metric system. One cicero is equal to 4.55 millimeters. You might wonder how many points are equal to the default value of 0.167". You can calculate the points by multiplying .167 by 72, which gives you 12.024 points.

Picas are typically used as a measurement of space. One pica is equal to 12 points. If you want to reduce the blank space between columns by half the default value, you would enter .5p, which is 1/2 pica. Note that when you enter the letter "p" before a number, it is interpreted as "points," and when you enter it after a number it is interpreted as "picas." In this case, set the distance between columns at 1/2 pica by entering

.5p [Return]

Both pages are now formatted into four vertical columns.

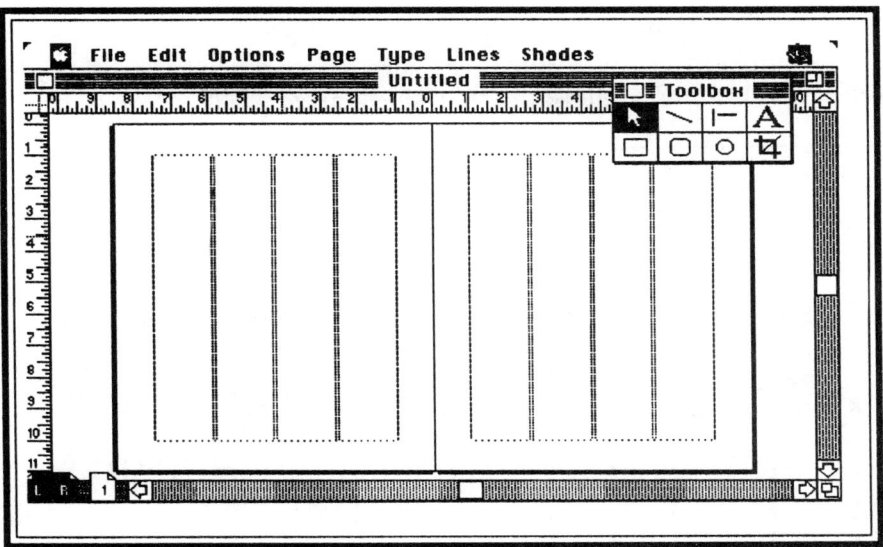

Figure 5.6   *Master page column guides displayed.*

SETTING THE RULER

The ruler line is very useful in a layout such as a newsletter because it provides a way to divide the page into sections for article placement. In most cases, you can rely on column guides to determine the width of the article text. However, you will also need to determine the vertical location in which the article text should start or stop.

PageMaker automatically displays vertical and horizontal rulers at the top and left side of the work window; however, the zero point is usually placed at the upper left corner of the page, not at the page margins. The **zero point** is the place on the ruler where the horizontal and vertical rulers meet.

In a dual-page display, you are working with the zero point at the top of the page where the upper right corner of the left page meets the upper left corner of the right page.

In many cases, it is more useful to place the zero point at the upper left corner of the text guides rather than at the page edges.

5 Newsletters

You can change the position of the zero point of the rulers by dragging the zero point icon to the location you want. The zero point icon is located in the upper left corner of the window where the ruler lines meet.

> **Drag** the zero point icon to the upper left corner of the margin guides (as in Figure 5.7)

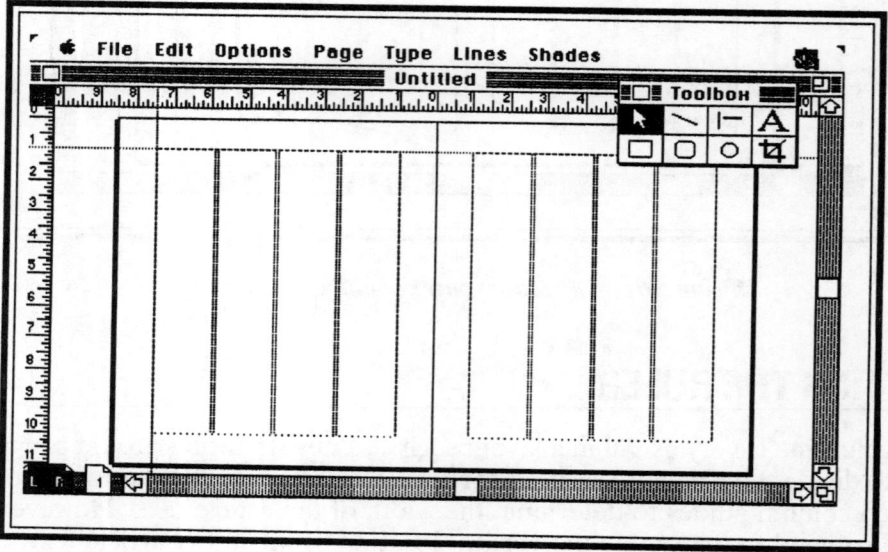

Figure 5.7   Ruler zero point dragged to margin corner.

When you release the mouse button, PageMaker adjusts the scale on both rulers to begin measuring from the selected location, rather than from the edge of the page. In most cases, it is more useful to measure the area used for text than it is to measure the entire page, including margins.

Newsletters **5**

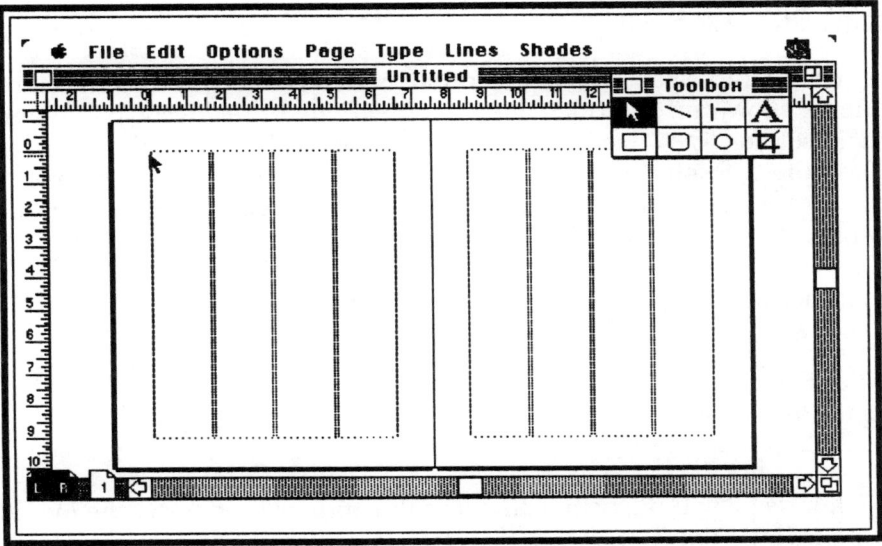

Figure 5.8   *Rulers zero set at margins.*

Ruler Snap

One of the advantages of creating guides on a page is that you can use the Snap to guides feature to ensure items are placed at precise locations. PageMaker also has a feature called Snap to rulers that operates in a similar manner to Snap to guides.

When Snap to rulers is activated, dragging operations move in increments according to the marks on the ruler lines. The rulers, by default, display marks every 1/8", which means the Snap to rulers option will cause dragging to move in 1/8" increments.

Turn on the Snap to rulers option.

> **Point** at Options
> **Drag** to Snap to rulers

The shortcut key combination **Command+y** will toggle the Snap to rulers option on or off.

5 Newsletters

Choosing Different Ruler Units

The effect of the Snap to rulers option is determined by the measurement increments shown on the ruler line. As mentioned previously, by default, this option is set for 1/8" increments for both the horizontal and vertical rulers. However, the 1/8" marking may not be the best choice for all situations. PageMaker allows you to change the ruler markings and thereby create different page locations to which items can be snapped.

The units are set from the Preferences dialog box.

> **Point** at Edit
> **Drag** to Preferences

PageMaker displays a dialog box that lists the options used to set the increments on the ruler line. The increments shown on the ruler line will change, depending on which view is active.

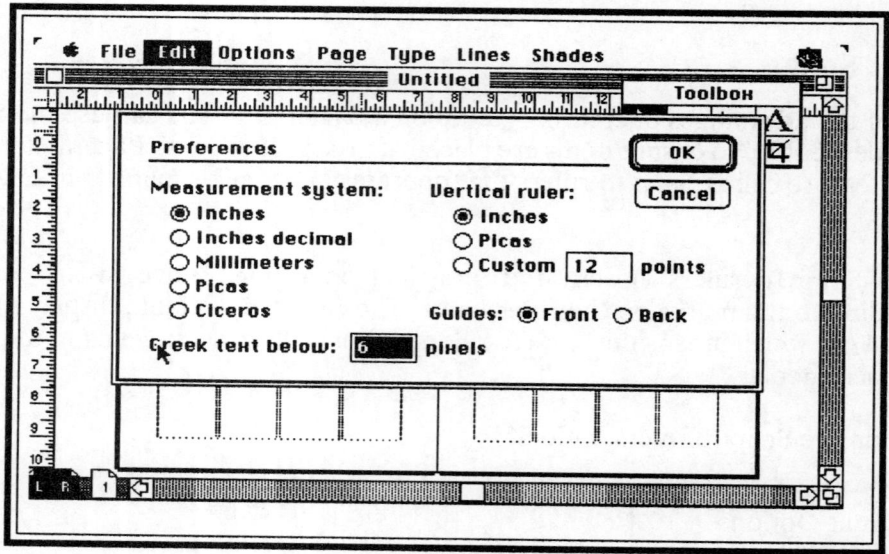

Figure 5.9   Ruler preferences dialog box.

The vertical ruler can be set for a custom increment in terms of points. For example, if you were working with large characters, 36-point for example, you might set the ruler spacing at 36-point increments. You can set both the horizontal and vertical rulers to the same measurement or set the vertical ruler to a different unit from the horizontal ruler. However, the custom increment option is available only for the vertical ruler.

You might wonder why such a useful option can be used only with the vertical ruler. The answer points out an essential difference between the significance of the horizontal and the vertical in document layouts. Because of the way text is organized, i.e., into lines of text, vertical measurements are harder to adjust than horizontal measurements. For example, if you change the width of a line, PageMaker can adjust to the change by placing a different number of characters on that line. But if you change the vertical spacing of a text block, for example, it would not be logical for PageMaker to display 1/2 a line, e.g., display the top half of the character on a line and truncate the bottom half.

When PageMaker places text vertically, it must have room for the entire line height to be displayed or else it will not display any part of the line. If a text block is drawn so that the last line cannot be displayed, then an area of blank space appears at the bottom of the block. This blank space is not significant in documents where a single text block covers the entire column. But in a newsletter layout, you would like to avoid leaving blanks at the bottom of a block.

Because the default size for text is 12 points, or 1 pica, it might be best to measure the vertical ruler in terms of picas or 12-point increments. This means each ruler increment is about the height of a typical line of text, which makes drawing blocks a bit easier than using the default increment of .125" does. Change the vertical ruler to Picas.

> **Click** on Picas under Vertical ruler:
> **Click** on OK

The vertical ruler is now divided into picas. Note that every 6 picas is equal to 1 full inch. The entire length of the text area within the page margins is 54 picas, or 6 picas times 9 inches.

5 Newsletters

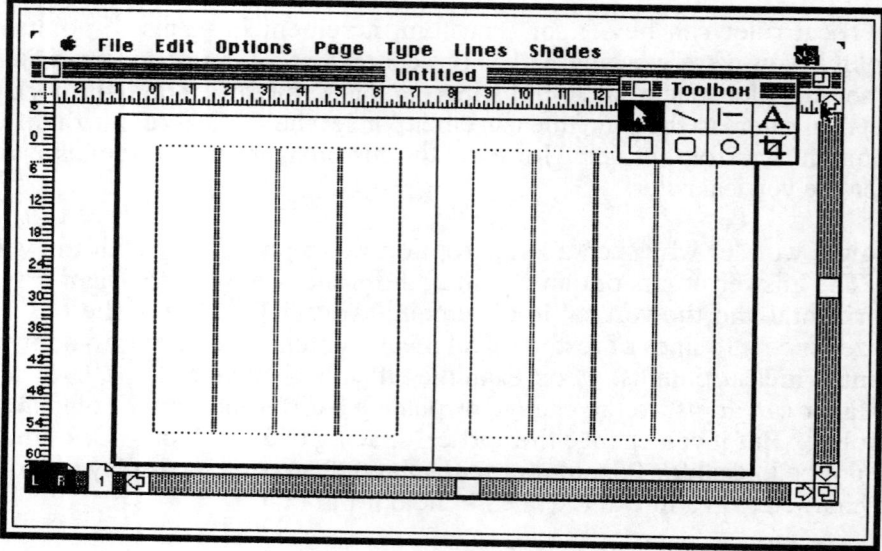

Figure 5.10   *Vertical ruler shows picas*

CUSTOM GUIDES

So far you have used two types of guides for text in PageMaker documents: margin guides and column guides. These guides have been automatically generated by PageMaker, based on the margin selections made in the Page setup dialog box and the column guides values entered in the Column guides dialog box.

PageMaker also allows you to create guide lines, horizontal and vertical, at any location on the page. For example, the column guides have divided the page into four columns. You might also want to add horizontal lines that would divide the page into sections vertically.

For example, the text area is 54 picas in length. If you divided that space into three even parts, you would put a guide line every 18 picas. Adding guide lines at 18 and 36 picas would give you guides dividing the page vertically into three equal parts.

To create a guide line, drag the ruler line. Dragging the vertical ruler will create a vertical guide, while dragging the horizontal ruler will create a horizontal guide.

Newsletters **5**

Create a custom horizontal guide line.

> **Drag** the horizontal ruler bar down

As you drag the ruler bar down, a horizontal guide line will appear, as shown in Figure 5.11.

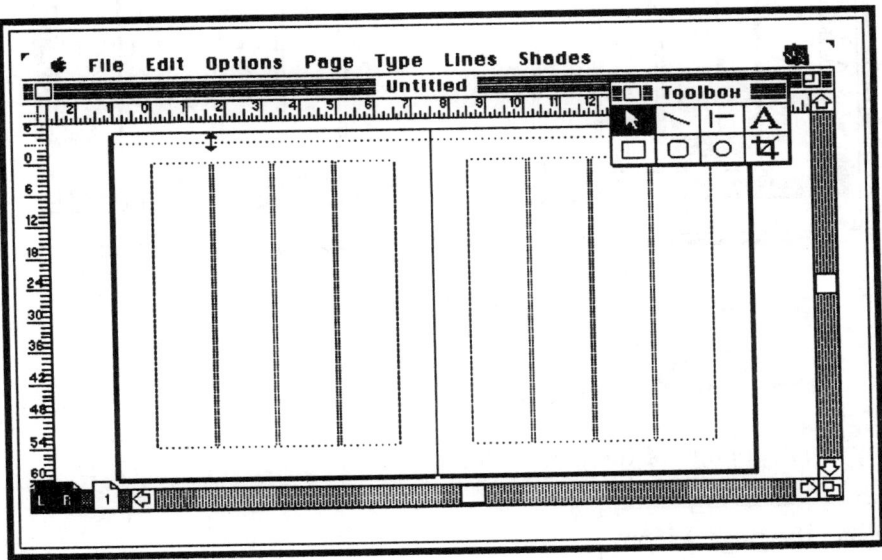

Figure 5.11   Horizontal guide appears as you drag ruler down.

Continue dragging the ruler until it is aligned at 18 picas down the page. Note that the ruler line will snap to each pica increment as it is dragged. If you release the mouse before you reach the correct position, point at the guide line and drag it again until it is correctly positioned. You can drag the line as often as necessary.

Repeat the process to create a second horizontal guide at 36 picas from the top margin.

> **Drag** the horizontal ruler bar down to 36 picas

The page is now divided vertically into four parts and horizontally in three parts.

5 Newsletters

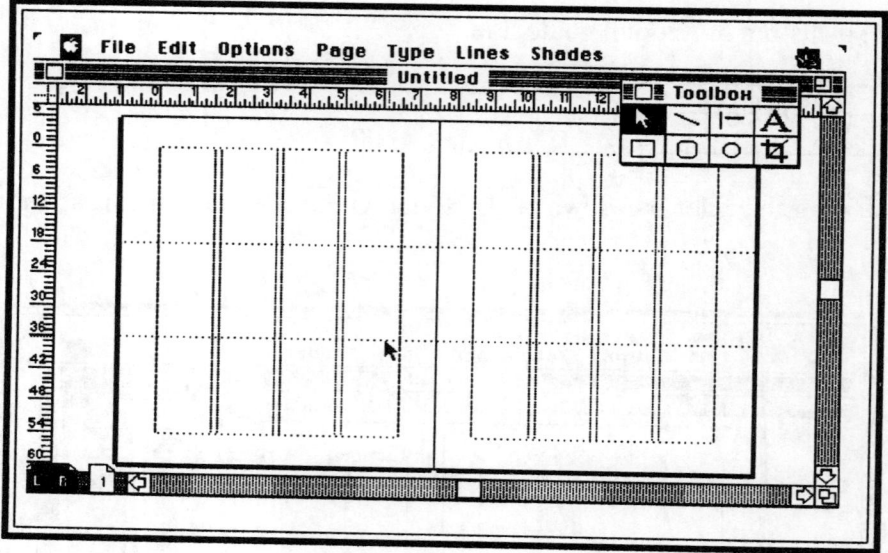

Figure 5.12   *Horizontal guides added to master pages.*

You have now set up the guides for placing the text into your newsletter.

Display the first page of the newsletter.

> **Click** on the page 1 icon

Note that even though you have selected a dual-page display, page 1 is always displayed by itself because PageMaker assumes that all documents start with a right page. Subsequent pairs of pages such as 2 and 3, 4 and 5, etc., will be displayed as dual-page pairs.

Also note that the zero point is not in the correct position to mark the beginning of the text area. The zero point was positioned when the dual pages were displayed. The first page of the publication, because it is displayed alone, throws off the ruler positioning.

You will need to position the zero point again so that it can be of use on the first page.

> **Drag** the zero point icon to the upper left corner of the page guides

CREATING A MASTHEAD

The first page of a newsletter is usually characterized by a special heading used to identify the newsletter. This heading, called a **masthead**, is usually the same on every issue of the newsletter. Before you create the masthead, it might be useful to place a horizontal guide at the top of the page to indicate the area that the masthead will occupy.

Note that the guide you are creating is not a master page guide, i.e., one that will appear on all document pages, but a guide that will appear only on the current page. This makes sense because only the first page of the newsletter will contain the masthead. Assume that the masthead should take up half of the top part of the page, i.e., the first 9 picas (about 1.5").

> **Drag** the horizontal ruler bar down to 9 picas

Note that this guide will appear only on the first page of the document. The other guides will carry over to all pages because they were created on the document's master pages.

5 Newsletters

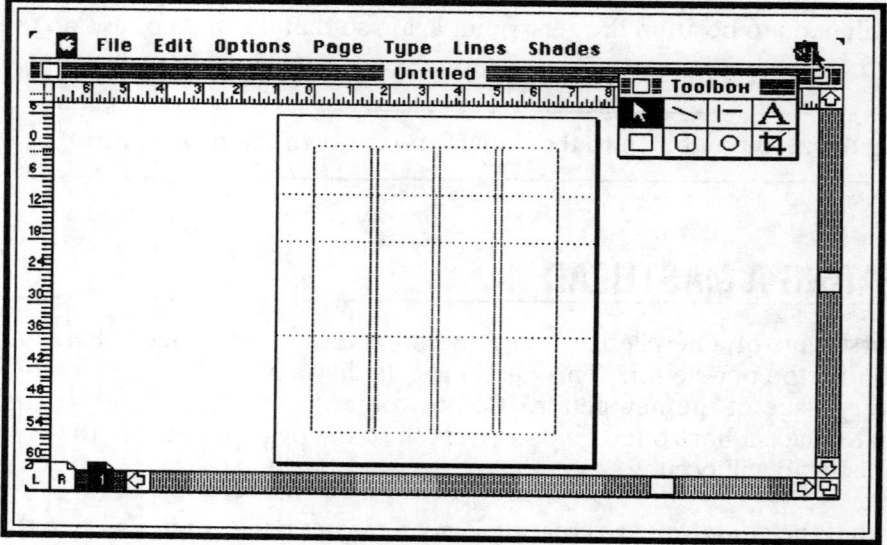

Figure 5.13   Guide line added for page 1 only.

Change to the Actual size view.

> **Point** at the center of the top margin guide
> **Option + Command + Click**

If you look at the vertical ruler line, you will notice that the precision of the ruler changes to increments of 1/4 picas. The top ruler, set to inches, changes to increments of 1/32".

You can now enter the text of the masthead. Activate the text mode.

> **Click** on the text icon
> **Click** in the upper left corner of the guides

This places a text cursor in the very top of the text area of the page. Use the Type specifications menu to select Times, 36-point, bold text. Enter

Command+t

> **Point** at Size
> **Drag** to 36
> **Click** on Bold
> **Click** on OK

Enter

The Small Business Monthly

The screen will resemble Figure 5.14. Is this what you expected?

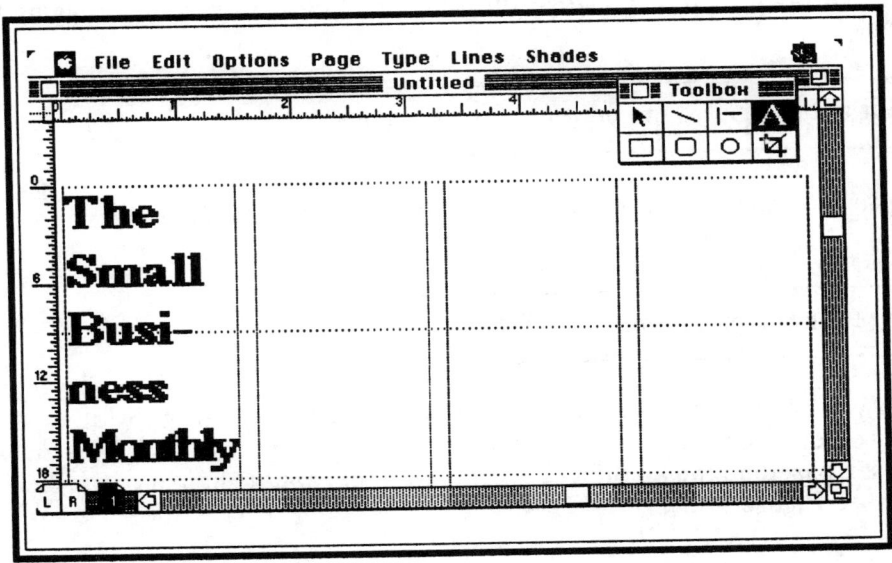

Figure 5.14   Text formatted into first column.

5 Newsletters

When you create a text block or place text into a page with column guides, PageMaker will automatically limit the width of that block to the width of the column. In this case, the text block you created was only as wide as the first column, i.e., 1/4 of the width of the entire page. The masthead text was wrapped into the first column instead of being formatted across the top of the page.

You can correct this problem by using the selection mode to stretch the text block that contains the masthead to reach across the top of the entire margin width.

Place PageMaker in the selection mode.

> **Click** on the pointer icon
> **Click** on "Small"

PageMaker selects the text block into which you have entered the masthead. If you look closely at the ends of the window shade handles that appear on the text block, you will see that each end displays a black square. These squares are the shape buttons. You can change the shape of the text block by dragging these buttons.

> **Point** at the right shape button on the top handle

Drag that button across the page to the right margin guide, as shown in Figure 5.15.

> **Drag** to the right margin guide (as in Figure 5.15).

When you release the button, the block will resize itself to the width specified when you dragged the button. Note that the height of the text block is automatically set, based on the amount of text in the block, not the height of the block you drew (see Figure 5.16).

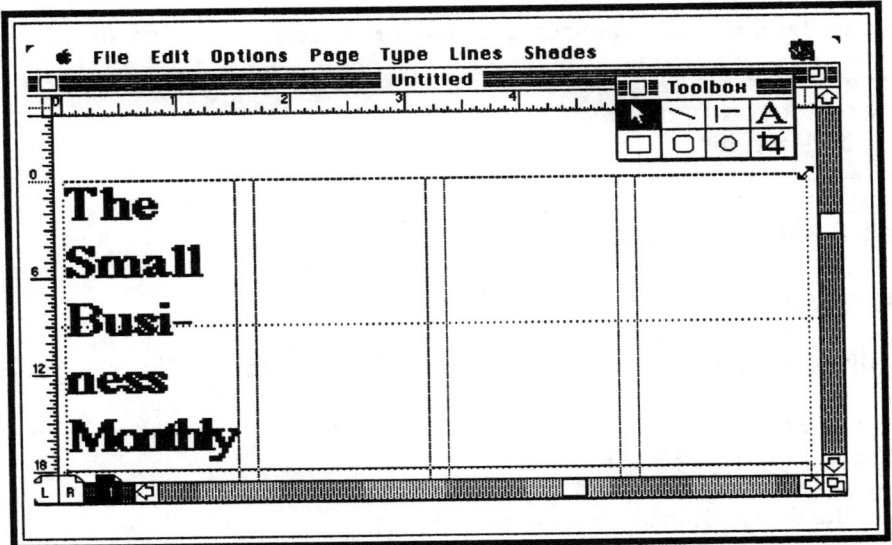

Figure 5.15   Handle button dragged to right margin guide.

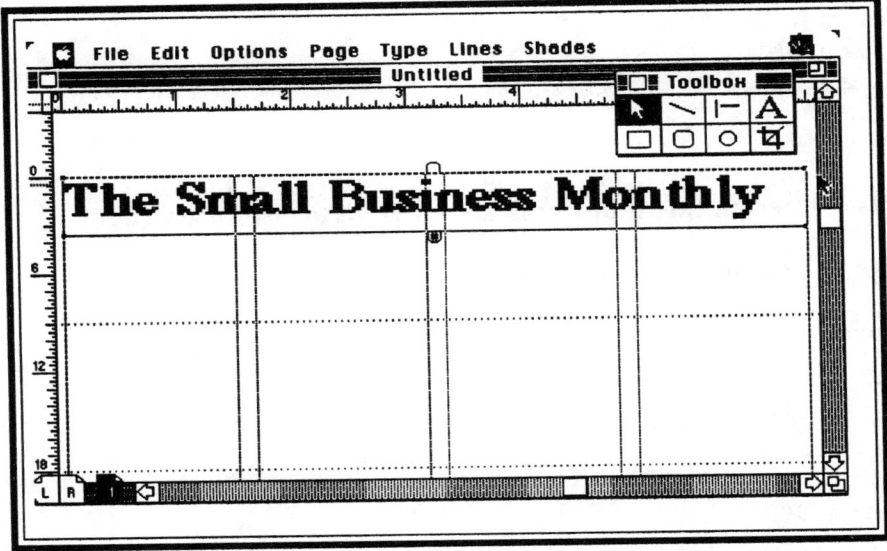

Figure 5.16   Text block set to margin width.

5 Newsletters

Return to the text mode in order to complete the entry of the masthead text.

> **Click** on the text icon
> **Click** on "Monthly"

Change the alignment to center aligned. Enter

Command + Shift + c

Move the text cursor to the end of the line and begin a second line of text. Enter

1 (numeric keypad)
[Return]

Change the text to 10-point, bold, italic. Enter

Command + t

> **Point** at Size
> **Drag** to 10
> **Click** on Italic
> **Click** on OK

Enter

The Newsletter for Small Businesses Who Want to Get Bigger [Return]

Change to 12-point, normal text. Enter

Command + t

> **Point** at Size
> **Drag** to 12
> **Click** on Normal
> **Click** on OK

Newsletters 5

Enter

Volume 6 Number 4 [Return]
March, 1989

Draw a rounded rectangle around the masthead, as shown in Figure 5.17.

> **Click** on the rounded rectangle icon
> **Drag** rectangle around masthead (as in Figure 5.17)

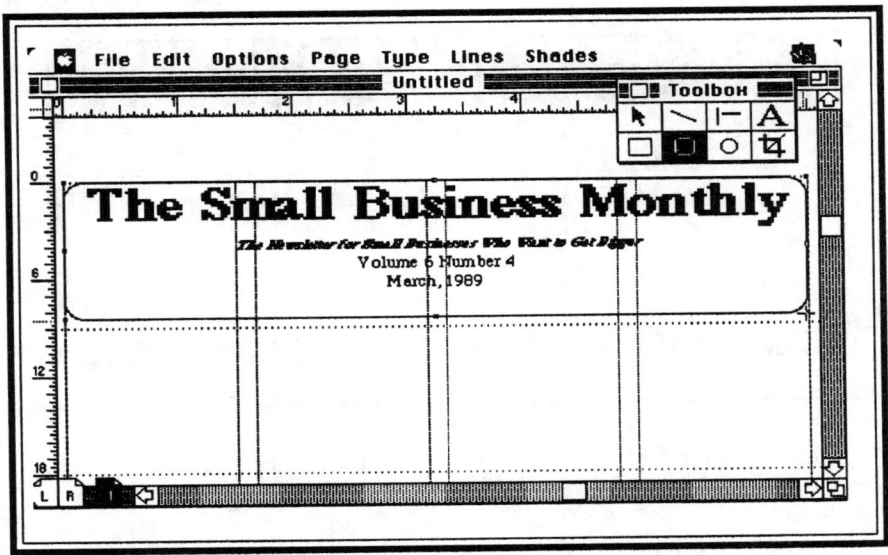

Figure 5.17   *Rectangle drawn around masthead.*

Change the rectangle's interior to a 10% shade.

> **Point** at Shade
> **Drag** to 10%

5 Newsletters

The rectangle covers the text. Move the rectangle to the bottom level of objects by entering

Command + b

The masthead is now complete.

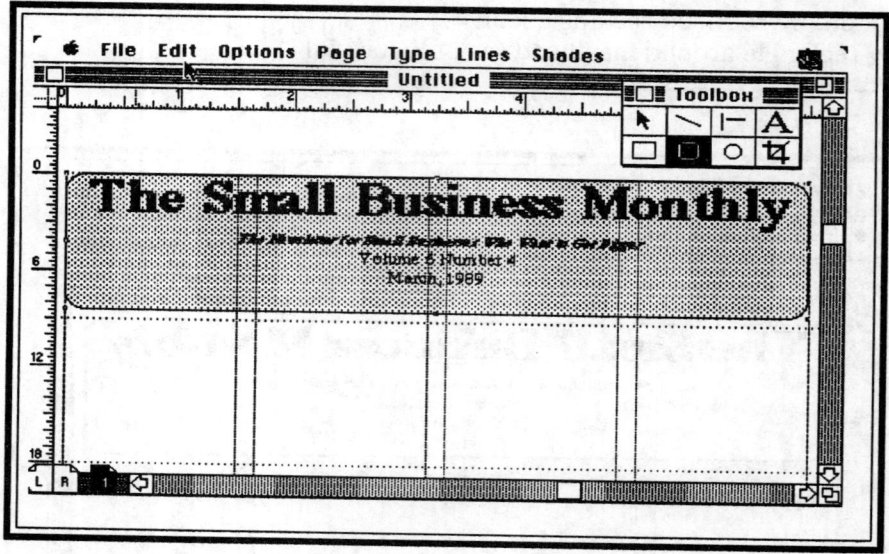

Figure 5.18   Completed masthead with shading.

Before you place any articles into the newsletter, you might want to remove the built-in styles from the style list because you already selected the style names you wanted to use when you typed the style name symbols in your text documents. Eliminating the built-in style names will shorten the list of styles so only those styles relating to the newsletter will be included.

> **Point** at Type
> **Drag** to Define styles
> **Click** on Body Text
> **Click** on Remove (5 times)
> **Click** on OK

The styles have been removed from this document.

CREATING A TEMPLATE

The steps taken so far in the production of the newsletter have created a document ready for the placement of the actual articles. The document has the proper column and vertical guide lines, plus the masthead. All the items you have created so far have in common the fact that they will be the same when you create next month's newsletters. Put another way, the document as it stands now can be used as a **template** to serve as the starting point for all future issues of the newsletter. You would save time and improve consistency if you saved a copy of the document with the steps you have taken up to this point so you could start here next month.

PageMaker anticipates the need for templates and provides a special method of saving documents as templates for future publications. PageMaker calls these documents **template files**. A PageMaker template file is a document similar in most ways to a PageMaker document. The primary difference is that files saved as templates are protected from accidental overwriting because they are given a file type different from normal PageMaker documents.

When the selection highlight is placed on the name of a template file, the setting in the Open file dialog box is automatically set to Copy instead of Original. This means when the template is loaded it is assigned the name "Untitled" instead of the original name of the file to prevent you from saving the document you create from the template in place of the template itself. This preserves the template for later use. If you do want to make changes in the actual template file, select the Original option from the Open file dialog box.

To save a file as a template, enter the save command.

Command + s

Before you enter a name and save the document, select the Template option.

> **Click** on Template

Enter the name of the template:

SBM template [Return]

Before you continue with the newsletter, close the window and load a copy of the template.

5 Newsletters

> **Point** at File
> **Drag** to Close

Open a copy of the template. Enter

Command + o

> **Scroll** the file list down
> **Click** on SBM template

The default automatically switches to Copy.

> **Click** on OK

The document loads and places you back exactly where you left off except that the window is now called "Untitled" instead of "SBM template." Next month, you could begin the newsletter in just the same way, avoiding the need to layout the guides and the masthead each time.

PLACING THE FIRST ARTICLE

You can now add the text of the document to the newsletter layout. Enter the place mode with the following command:

Command + d

Select the first text file to be inserted into the newsletter — the file called Business. You will probably need to use the folder selector box to activate the folder in which you stored the text files.

When you have displayed the folder, select the Business file, but do not click on OK.

> **Click** on Business

Selecting the Business file but not clicking on OK allows you access to a very important option you need to read the text properly. The **Read tags** option must be selected if PageMaker is to convert the text style names into PageMaker styles. Because this option is set off by default, you must remember to select it before you select OK; otherwise, the style names in the text will be treated as if they were simply part of the text, not special codes for styling.

> **Click** on Read tags
> **Click** on OK

The mouse cursor changes to the manual placement icon. In a newsletter, you want to place the text manually rather than automatically or semi-automatically because you will place parts of several articles on the same page. The automatic text flow assumes each column is filled with the same story, which is not the case in a newsletter.

To simplify text placement, switch to the Fit to window display. Enter

Command+w

Begin the text block below the first guide line, 9 picas down the page, at the left margin.

> **Point** at the left margin 9 picas down
> **Drag** two columns wide down to 36 picas (as in Figure 5.19)

The text flows into the area allocated for the first article in the newsletter.

5 Newsletters

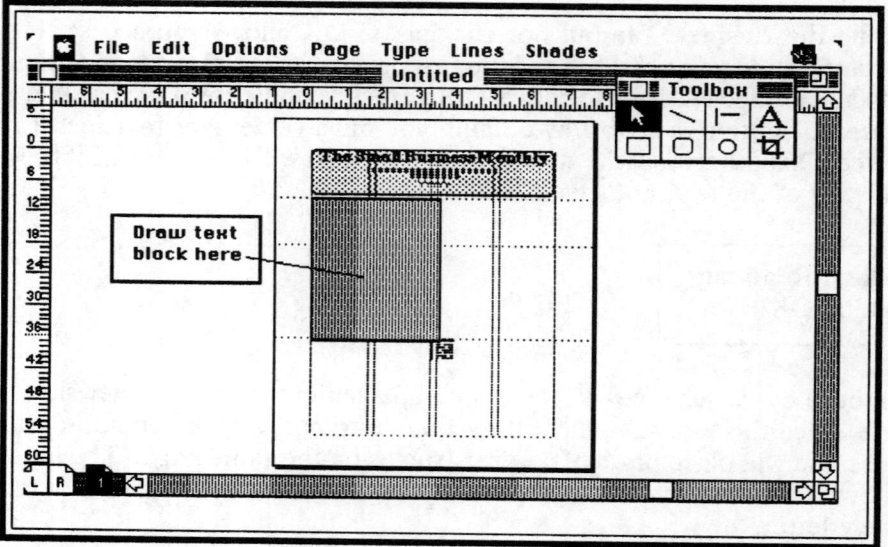

Figure 5.19 *Place first article on page.*

Setting Styles

When the text document was imported with the Read tags option active, Page-Maker automatically generated styles for each of the style names used in the text. However, styles created in this manner are all assigned the default text values of 12-point, Times, normal characters, left alignment, etc.

What is accomplished, and in the long run more important, is that each of the paragraphs in all the documents is assigned the correct style names. To format the text, including the documents not yet placed on the page, all you need to do is change the type, tabs, indents, and paragraph specifications for the styles.

If you display the Style palette, you will see that the names used in the text documents now appear as style names. Enter

Command+e

The names **1st list**, **list**, and **Normal** (if you used Microsoft Word to create the document) appear in the Style palette. If you scroll the list, you will see the rest of the style names used in the text document. You may note that you did not use the name Normal as one of your style names; however, PageMaker picked the name up because Microsoft Word always stores this as the default style for its documents. If you created the text in a different word processor that does not have a default style, you will not have a Normal style listed on the Style palette display.

Display the Define styles dialog box.

> **Point** at Type
> **Drag** to Define styles

Begin by setting the format of the standard style.

> **Click** on standard
> **Click** on Edit
> **Click** on Para

Create a .25" first-line indent, and open a 1-pica space before each paragraph. Enter

[Tab]
.25 [Tab]
[Tab]
1p [Return]
[Return]

Next, select the list style.

> **Click** on list
> **Click** on Edit
> **Click** on Type

5 Newsletters

Change the type to 10-point, bold.

> **Click** on Bold
> **Point** at Size
> **Drag** to 10
> **Click** on OK
> **Click** on OK

Next, set the format of the 1st list style.

> **Click** on 1st list
> **Click** on Edit

The 1st list style should be identical to the list style, except that the 1st list line will be preceded by 1 pica of extra space. Because list and 1st list are related styles, you can take a shortcut to formatting 1st list by filling in the Based on style option, which is currently empty. Enter

[Tab]
list

As soon as you enter the name of the base style, the specifications in the bottom of the window change to show the style as if it were based on the list style. Change the type specifications to match those of the list style.

> **Click** on Type
> **Click** on Bold
> **Point** at Size
> **Drag** to 10
> **Click** on OK
> **Click** on Para
> **Double Click** on Before

Enter

1p [Return]
[Return]

Using the Based on option does not save any steps in this case, but it links the list and 1st list styles in case further modifications are necessary. For example, if you want to change the hyphenation characteristics of both the list and 1st list styles, you can change the base style, list, and have the change flow through to 1st list.

Scroll the list in the box down to reveal the three title styles: **title, sub title,** and **topic title.** These three styles are all related. It seems useful to format all three styles with title as the base style. Select the title style.

> **Click** on title
> **Click** on Edit

Change the type to 24-point, bold.

> **Click** on Type
> **Click** on Bold
> **Point** at Size
> **Drag** to 24
> **Click** on OK

The next title will be a subtitle, which has the same settings as the title except that the point size is 18 and a 2-pica space precedes the paragraph. You did not add any space before the title style because it is used only at the beginning of an article and is never preceded by a paragraph.

> **Click** on sub title
> **Click** on Edit

Enter the base style:

[Tab]
title

5 Newsletters

Change the type and paragraph specifications.

> **Click** on Type
> **Click** on Bold
> **Point** at Size
> **Drag** to 18
> **Click** on OK
> **Click** on Para
> **Double Click** on Before:

Enter the abbreviation for 2 picas.

2p [Return]
[Return]

Next select the topic title style.

> **Scroll** the Style palette down
> **Click** on topic title
> **Click** on Edit

Enter the base style:

title

Set the specifications for this style.

> **Click** on Type
> **Click** on Bold
> **Point** at Size
> **Drag** to 14
> **Click** on OK
> **Click** on Para
> **Double Click** on Before:

Enter the abbreviation for 1.5 picas:

1.5p [Return]
[Return]

Return to the document display by entering

[Return]

PageMaker uses the style settings to format the text of the article placed into the document page. Even in the Fit to window view, the changes to the title and sub title paragraphs can be recognized.

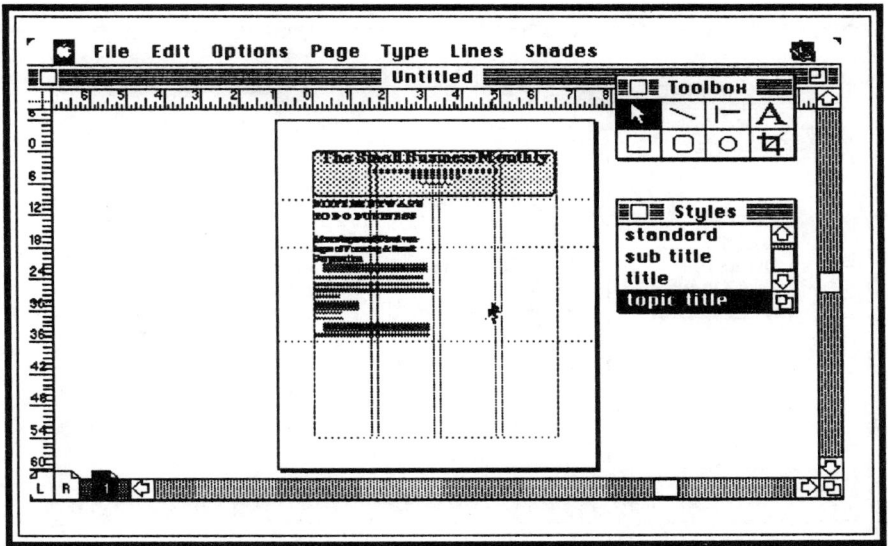

Figure 5.20   Style specifications format text.

PLACING THE SECOND ARTICLE

With the first article placed into the document, you are ready to add another story. This time add the Formalities document. Enter

Command + d

5 Newsletters

> **Click** on Formalities
> **Click** on Read tags
> **Click** on OK

Place the first part of the Formalities document next to the Business article by drawing a block for the document, starting at the 9-pica guide line in the third column and extending to 36 picas down and to the right margin, as shown in Figure 5.21.

> **Drag** text block as shown in Figure 5.21

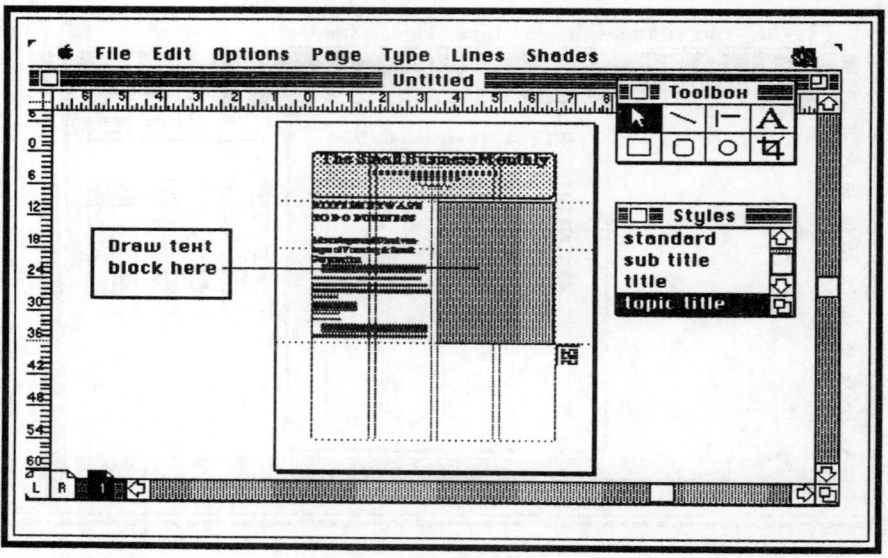

Figure 5.21   Text block for Formalities article.

When the mouse button is released, PageMaker will flow the text into the block. Note that because the styles have already been defined, the document is automatically formatted as it is placed.

Newsletters 5

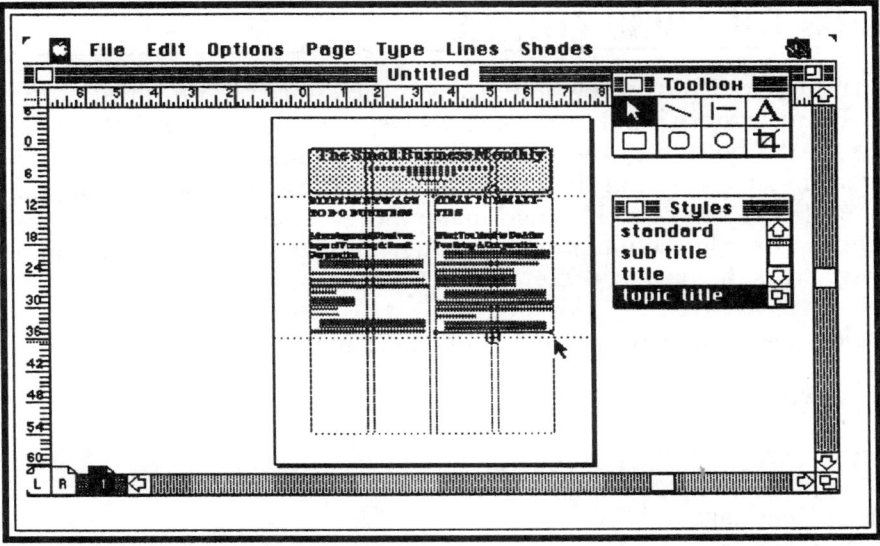

Figure 5.22   Formalities document formatted as it is placed.

The Formalities document adds a new style — hangout — to the list.

> **Point** at Type
> **Drag** to Define styles
> **Click** on hangout
> **Click** on Edit
> **Click** on Tabs

Create a hangout indent-type paragraph. Recall that the left indent icon is the bottom triangle, and the first-line indent is the top triangle.

> **Drag** the left indent icon to .25"
> **Drag** the first-line indent icon to 0"
> **Click** on .25"

Return to the document display by entering

[Return] (3 times)

PLACING THE THIRD ARTICLE

The current layout of the newsletter leaves the entire bottom third of the page empty. Because there is only one more article to add to the newsletter, you might want to fill the bottom of the page with two columns worth of that document. However, if you spread out the text in this way, the article title will appear over only one of the columns. It would make more sense to the reader if the title stretched across the columns in a manner similar to the way the masthead stretches across the page.

First, select the Setup Corp document for placement. Enter

Command + d

> **Click** on Setup Corp
> **Click** on Read tags
> **Click** on OK

Stretching a Title

Begin the placement of the article so that only the first line of the document, the article title, is displayed in the block. The point size of the characters in the title style is 24 points. Recall that each pica is 12 points and that the vertical ruler is set in increments of picas. Thus, if you use the Snap to ruler feature to draw a text block 2 picas in height, PageMaker will have room to display only the article title in this block. If the block is drawn across the page, between the left and right margins, the article title will stretch across the entire page.

> **Draw** a text block 2 picas high (as shown in Figure 5.23)

Newsletters **5**

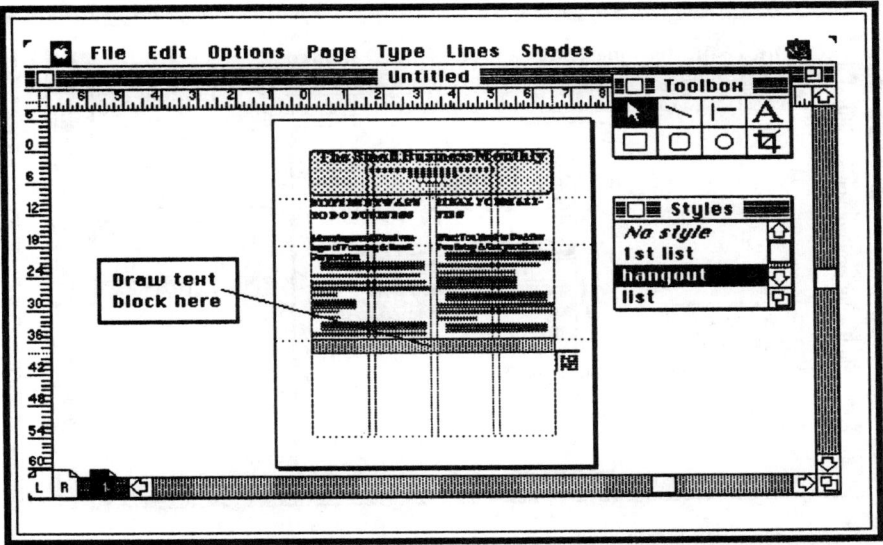

Figure 5.23   Text block for title only.

When you release the mouse button, PageMaker will flow the first line, the article's title, into the text block you just created.

To place the rest of the text into two side-by-side columns, you must select the + handle at the bottom of the title text block.

Click on the + in the handle
Draw a text block as shown in Figure 5.24

Fill the rest of the page by drawing a text block over the last empty section of the page.

Click on the + in the handle
Draw a text block in the empty corner of the page

The first page of the newsletter is complete (see Figure 5.25).

5 Newsletters

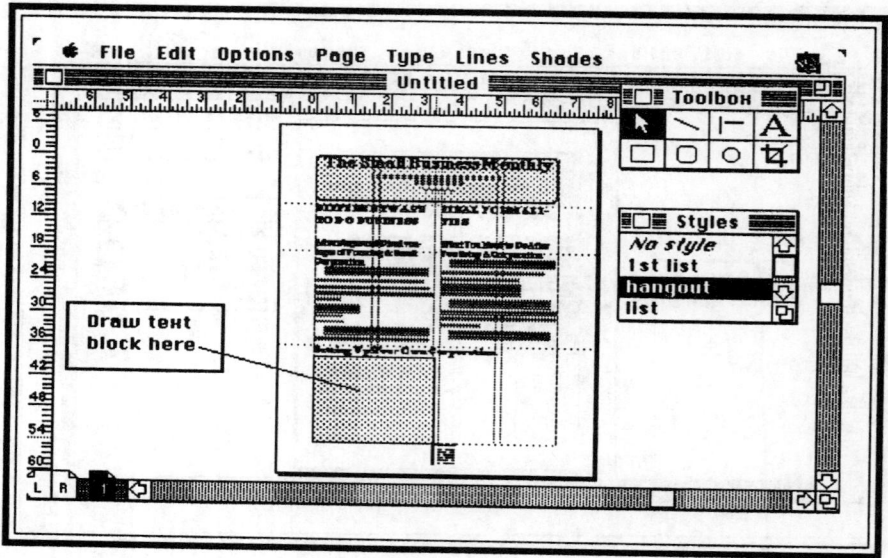

Figure 5.24   Text block to continue Setup Corp article.

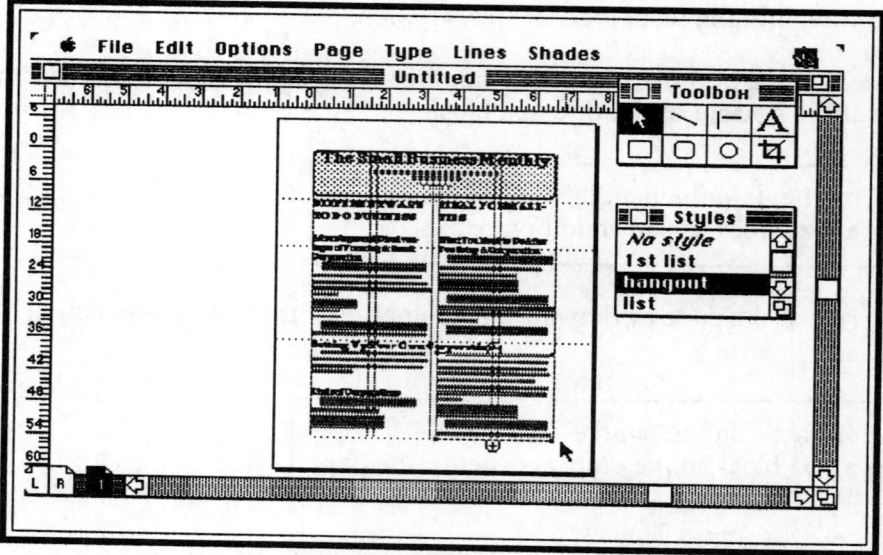

Figure 5.25   First page of Newsletter displays three separate articles.

Newsletters **5**

ADDING A NEW PAGE

You have now filled the first page with text; however, the newsletter is far from complete because there is more text for each of the three articles, plus the side bar. You will need to add pages to the newsletter in order to place the rest of the text.

Pages can be added to a document by using the Insert pages command from the Page menu.

> **Point** at Page
> **Drag** to Insert pages

The dialog box allows you to specify the number of pages to be inserted, and whether they should be placed before or after the current page. The default value for adding pages is 2 if you have selected facing pages or 1 for single-sided documents.

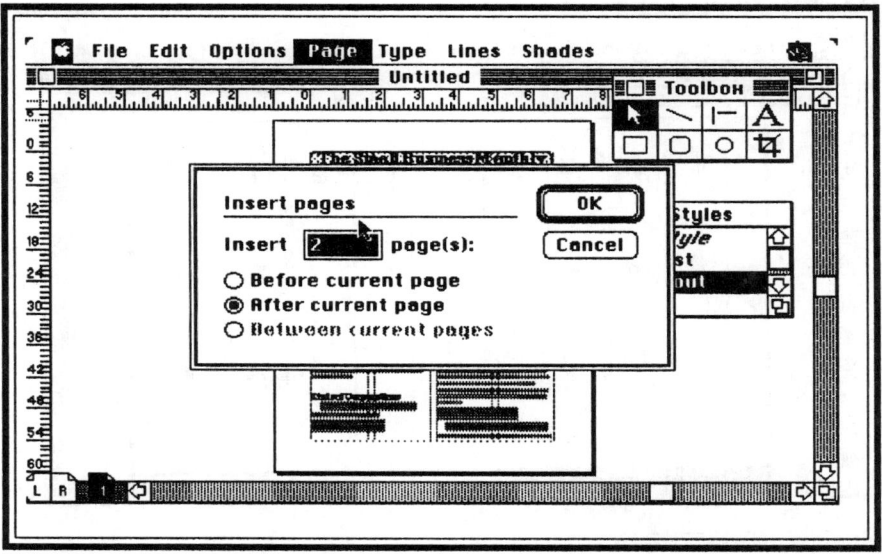

Figure 5.26   *Insert pages dialog box.*

265

5 Newsletters

Create two new pages by entering

[Return]

PageMaker displays a new set of two pages, a left page #2 and a right page #3.

CONTINUING A STORY ON ANOTHER PAGE

Now you must continue the stories started on the first page of the newsletter by placing them into text blocks on the subsequent pages.

The new pages are divided by the column guides and horizontal guides into 12 areas that can be used to place text on the page. To make it simpler to refer to locations on the pages, in Figure 5.27 numbers are assigned to each of the 12 areas on the page. Thus, when the text instructs you to draw a text block over areas 1 and 2 on a particular page, you will know which part of the page to draw the block over.

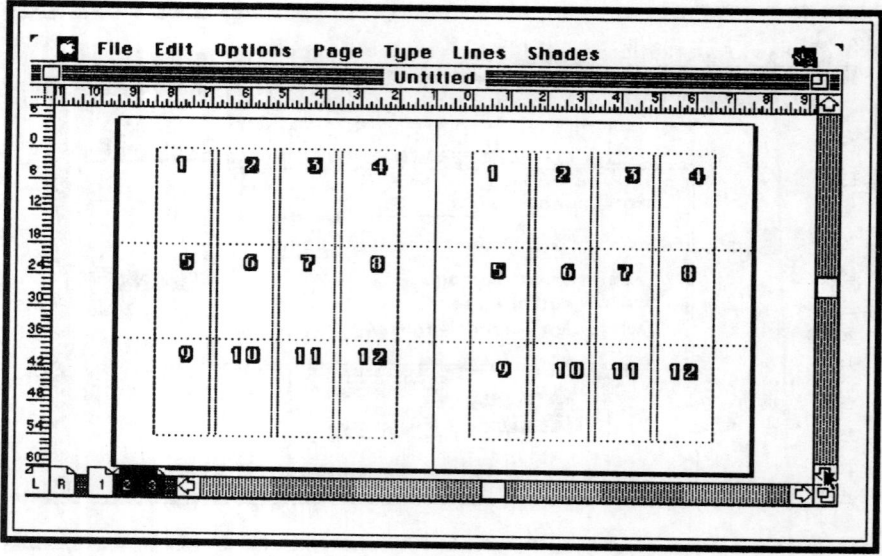

Figure 5.27   Numbers assigned to 12 areas on each page.

Newsletters 5

You can draw a text block of any size or shape. The guides help you position text blocks but do not restrict where you can draw them. In practice, you should try to use guides to maintain consistency among the pages.

To continue a story from page 1, you must activate the place mode for that article. Return to page 1.

> **Click** on page 1 icon
> **Click** on the Business article (upper left article)

Note that when you click on the text of the article, in order to select the text block you should point the cursor at an area that is not directly over a guide line. If you point at a guide line, the block will not be selected because PageMaker will think you are trying to select and move the guide line.

It may be difficult to see against the current background, but the window shade handle has appeared on the text block. Continue the story by selecting the + on the bottom handle.

> **Click** on the + in the bottom handle

The cursor icon will change to the manual placement icon, confirming that you have entered the placement mode. Change to page 2.

> **Click** on the page 2 icon

Note that the placement mode remains active when you change pages. You can now continue the story by drawing a text block into which the text can flow.

For this page, use narrower columns than those on the first page of the newsletter.

> **Drag** a text block over areas 1, 5, and 9

The text will flow into the left-most column on the page. The bottom handle will show a +, indicating there is more of the story to place.

267

5 Newsletters

Reactivate the placement mode and flow the rest of the document into the second column.

> **Click** on the + in the bottom handle
> **Drag** a text block over areas 2, 6, and 10

The handle will snap back into area 6 because that is the end of the text, as indicated by the # in the handle.

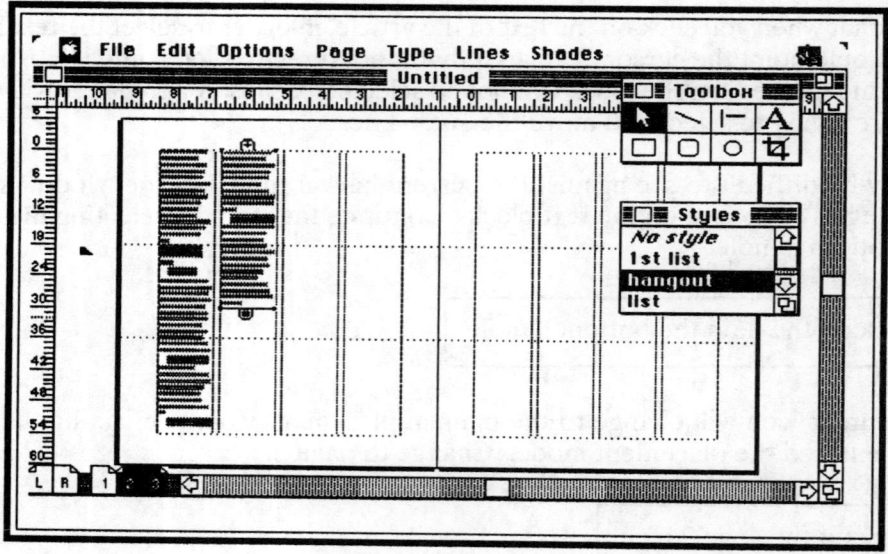

Figure 5.28   Remainder of the Business document laid out.

A "Continued From" Style

When you create a newsletter, it may be useful for your reader to be able to identify the place where an article continues from the previous page. In large newsletters, you may also want to add a block that tells where the article continues as well.

Newsletters 5

Enlarge the view so that the top of the article can be seen at the actual size.

> **Point** at the upper left corner of the guides
> **Option + Command + Click**

You will need to reduce the size of the text block to make room for the "continued from" message. Activate the text block.

> **Click** on "business"

Reduce the size of the block by two lines.

> **Drag** the top handle down two lines (as in Figure 5.29)

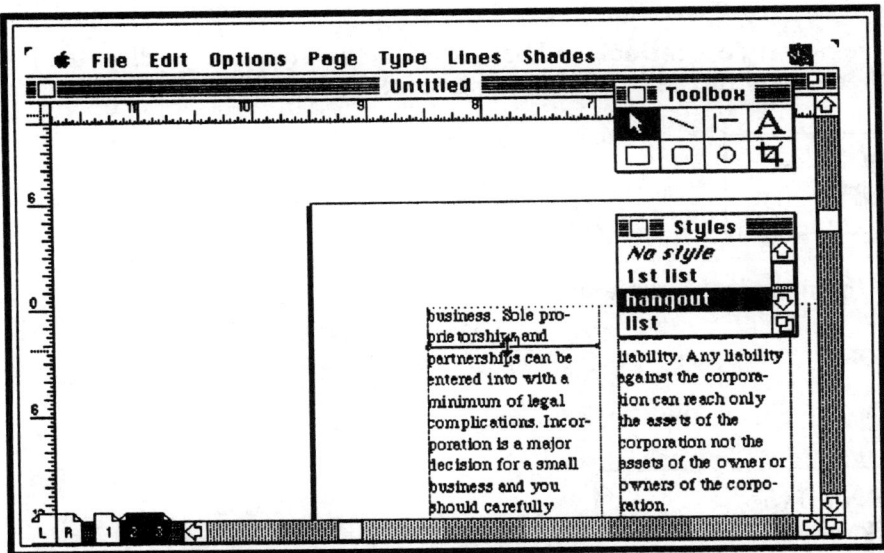

Figure 5.29   *Block reduced in size.*

269

5 Newsletters

Create a new text block in the space you have just cleared.

> **Click** on the text icon
> **Click** on the upper left corner of the guides

Enter

Doing Business from page 1 ...

The text is formatted as a hangout paragraph because hangout was the last style defined. You need to change the format to distinguish the message from the text of the article. Instead of manually formatting the text, create a new style for it because you may need to use this same style in other places in the document.

> **Point** at Type
> **Drag** to Define styles

Call the new style **Continue** and base it on the list style. First select the list style, and then create the new style based on it.

> **Click** on list
> **Click** on New

Enter the name of the new style:

Continue

Change the type to 9-point, bold, italic.

> **Click** on Type
> **Click** on Italic
> **Click** on Bold
> **Point** at Size
> **Drag** to 9
> **Click** on OK (3 times)

The message now tells readers where the article continues.

Newsletters **5**

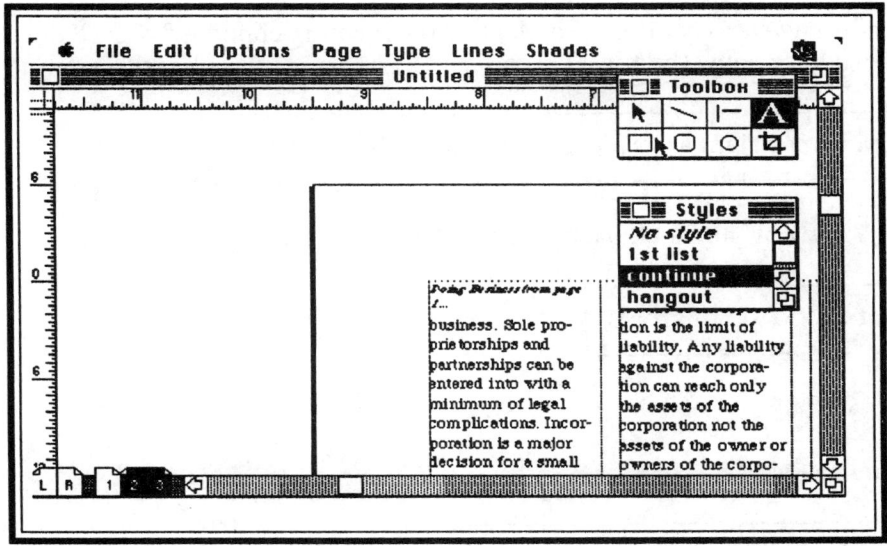

Figure 5.30   *"Continued" message placed at beginning of article.*

Continuing Another Article

Before you flow more text into the second page, you might want to create the "continued from" message first, which is faster than having to revise the text after it has been placed. Also, because there is currently a text block of that type on the page, you can simply copy the text block — block, text, and style — and place it at the beginning of the next article. You can then edit the text to use the name of the next article.

Place PageMaker into the selection mode.

> **Click** on the pointer icon
> **Click** on "Doing Business"
> **Point** at Edit
> **Drag** to Copy

271

5 Newsletters

You now have a copy of the text block in the memory clipboard. Scroll the display to the right to show the top of area 3.

> **Click** on the right arrow icon on the scroll bar (6 times)

Paste a copy of the block back into the document.

> **Point** at the top of area 3

Enter

Command + v

> **Drag** the block to the top of area 3

With the text positioned, you can change the name of the article in this "continued from" message to "Final Formalities."

> **Click** on the text mode icon
> **Double Click** on "Doing"

Enter

[Delete]

> **Double Click** on "Business"

Enter

[Delete]

Enter

Final Formalities

Newsletters 5

You have now inserted the message for the continuation of the text. Change to the Fit to window view and the selection mode.

> **Click** on the pointer icon
> **Option + Command + Click**

Return to page 1. This time you can use the keyboard shortcut for moving to the previous page — **Command + Shift + Tab**. Enter

Command + Shift + tab

Select the Final Formalities document, and activate the placement mode for that story.

> **Click** on the Final Formalities article
> **Click** on the + in its bottom handle

Return to page 2 by using the shortcut **Command + Tab** to move to the next page. Enter

Command + Tab

You can now place the text onto the page. In this case, allow PageMaker to fill the rest of the column under the text block used for the "continued from" message in area 3.

> **Point** just below the text block in column 3
> **Click**

PageMaker fills the rest of the column with text from that document.

273

5 Newsletters

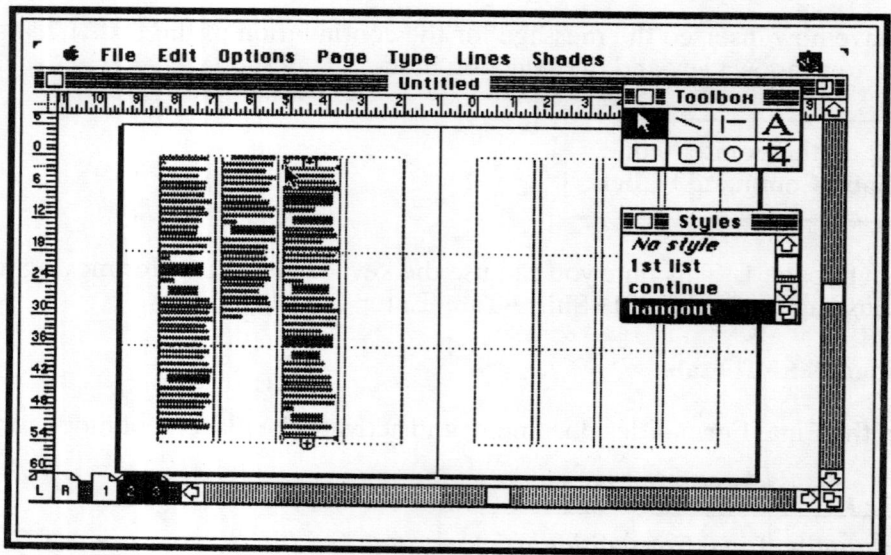

Figure 5.31   Text flowed into column.

Complete the article by flowing the text into the fourth column on the page.

> **Click** on the + in the bottom handle
> **Click** at the top of area 4

The # in the bottom handle indicates you have completed the text for this article and are ready to start placing text on page 3.

Newsletters **5**

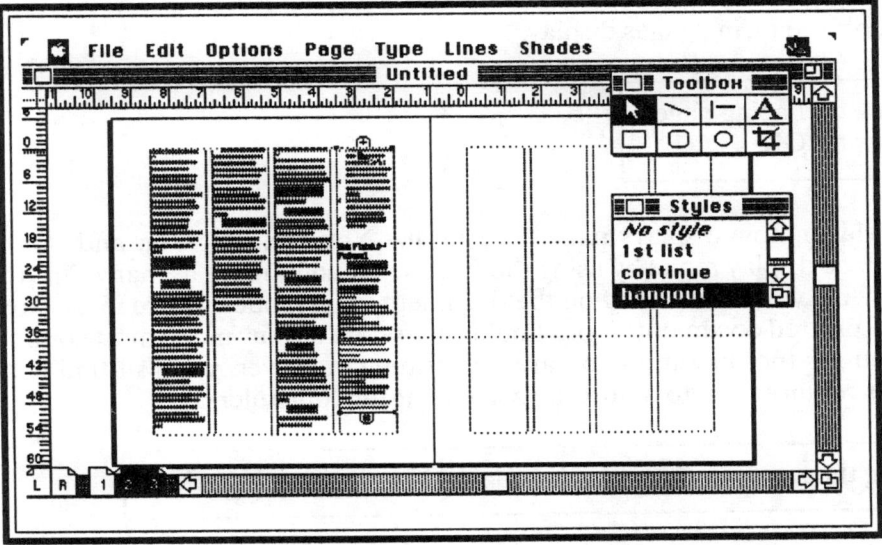

Figure 5.32   Page 2 of the newsletter is filled.

PLACING AND FORMATTING A SIDEBAR

The term "sidebar" or "insert" refers to text that is placed into a block that is not part of the articles. Sidebar text is often added by an editor to explain or expand on material related to the topics in the articles. In this case, you have a small document called "Sidebar" that contains this type of text.

Sidebar text is usually formatted to stand out from the rest of the text. It is usually enclosed in a box, often with a shaded background.

Because you do not need to refer to page 2 right now, it might be easier to work if you display only one page at a time. You can change the display method by using the Page setup dialog box.

> **Point** at File
> **Drag** to Page setup

275

Turn off the facing pages display.

> **Click** on Facing pages
> **Click** on OK

PageMaker now displays page 3 by itself. You can toggle in and out of the dual-page display mode by using the Page setup commands as many times as you want while you are working on the document. The mode you are in has no effect on the printed document. You should choose the display mode most comfortable for you for the operation you are performing; however, you will find changing modes requires you to adjust the zero point for your rulers.

> **Drag** the zero point icon to the upper left corner of the guides

Sidebars are usually placed at a prominent position on the page. This can be on the side of the page or even in the center. When the text is placed in the center it is called an "insert," but the basic idea remains the same.

Enter the place mode and select the Sidebar document for placement:

Command + d

> **Click** on Sidebar
> **Click** on Read tags
> **Click** on OK

Create a text block in the center of the page by dragging the icon over areas 6 and 7.

> **Drag** a text block over areas 6 and 7

The text is flowed into the selected areas. The + in the bottom handle tells you that the entire text does not fit into the area drawn for the text block.

Newsletters **5**

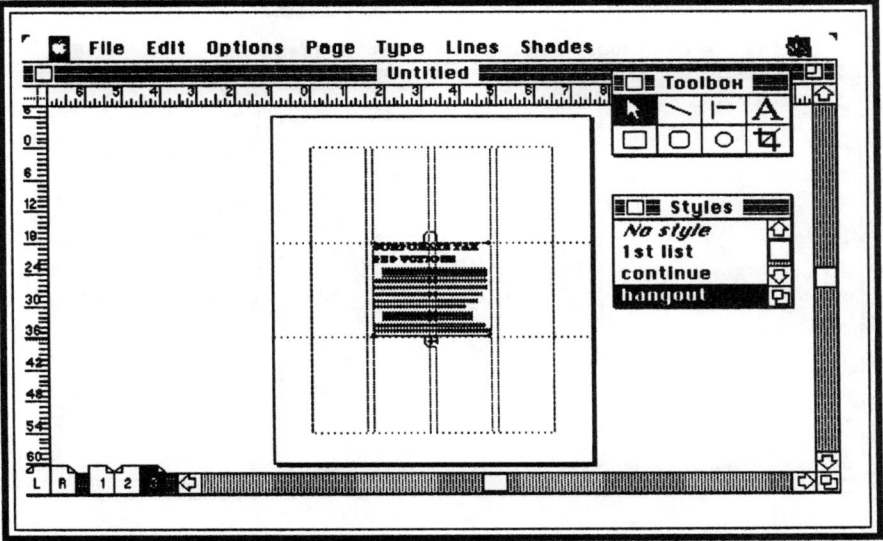

Figure 5.33   Sidebar text placed into the center of page 3.

To complete the text block layout, you need to find out the exact length that will accommodate the sidebar document. This can be done by dragging the bottom window shade handle down to the bottom margin guide.

Drag the bottom handle to the bottom margin guide

The window shade snaps back about half way to the bottom margin. The # in the handle indicates that the current block now shows the complete text of the sidebar.

To distinguish the sidebar from the other the articles, draw a rectangle around it and fill the rectangle with a 10% shade. Place PageMaker into the rectangle drawing mode.

Click on the rectangle icon
Draw a rectangle around the text (as in Figure 5.34)

5 Newsletters

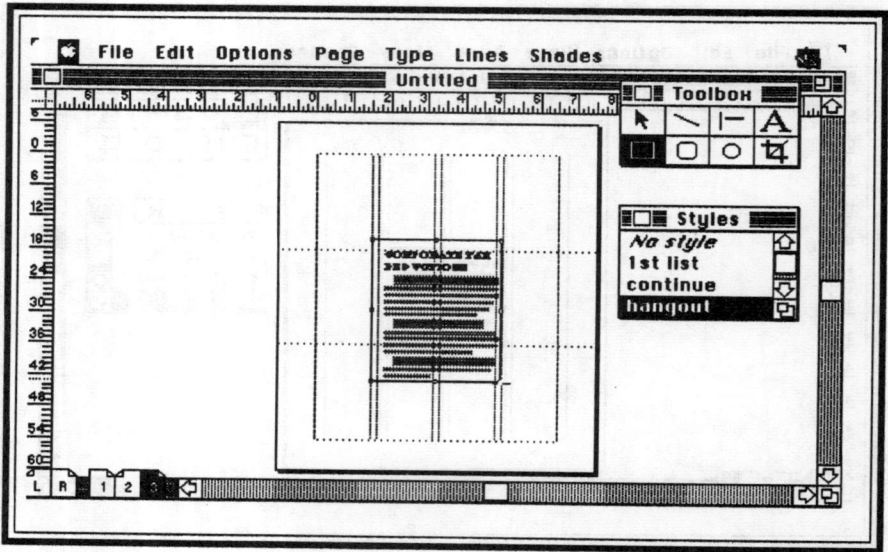

Figure 5.34   Rectangle drawn around text.

Select a 4-point line thickness for the outline of the rectangle.

> **Point** at Lines
> **Drag** to 4 pt

Select a 10% shade.

> **Point** at Shades
> **Drag** to 10%

Recall the discussion in Chapter 2 about how objects (in this case a text block and a drawn rectangle) are layered in PageMaker. Because the last item placed onto the page was the rectangle, it was placed on the top layer, covering the text. Place the rectangle on the bottom of the object stack by entering

Command + b

The rectangle now appears as a background, creating the boxed text appearance of the sidebar rectangle drawn around text.

Newsletters **5**

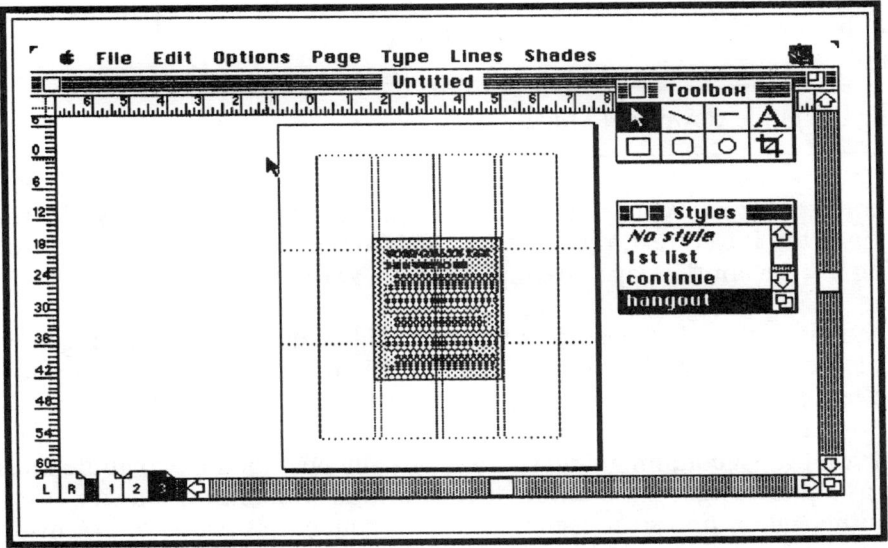

Figure 5.35   Sidebar formatted as boxed text.

Adjusting the Guides

For the most part, you have used the basic grid established on the master pages of the document to control the placement of text onto the pages of the newsletter, but on page 3, you created a text block that overflows the bounds of the standard guides.

PageMaker allows you to change the position of the guide for this page only so you can create guides to help you flow text into the remainder of the page without overlapping the boxed sidebar text placed in the center of the page. (Note that this technique is used because you placed text blocks from several different stories on a page. In Chapter 6, you will see that graphics and text can be set to automatically flow around each other.)

You can drag the guides to any position on the page. First, adjust the horizontal guides. The guide that is currently at 18 picas from the margin should be moved up to 14 picas.

> **Drag** the guide up to 14 picas

5 Newsletters

Move the other horizontal guide, currently at 36 picas, to 45 picas.

> **Drag** the guide down to 45 picas

The horizontal guides are now positioned just above and just below the top and bottom of the boxed text, respectively. This arrangement will prevent text from flowing in areas of the page already occupied by the text or the box.

You can also adjust the position of the vertical column guides by dragging them to the left or the right. In this case, the left column guide should be moved to the left so text placed into that column won't overlap the left side of the boxed text.

When you drag a column guide, you are actually positioning two guide lines that move as a pair. PageMaker automatically moves both lines when you attempt to drag either guide line so the space between columns is preserved. This makes moving column guides much easier than dragging each guide line individually. Individual manipulation would make more work, and it is unlikely you would preserve the space between columns correctly.

Drag the left column guide to the left so the left guide line is positioned at 1.25" from the left margin guide, as shown in Figure 5.36.

> **Drag** left column guides to 1.25"

Drag the two right column guide lines so that the left line of the pair is positioned at 5.25" from the left margin, as shown in Figure 5.36.

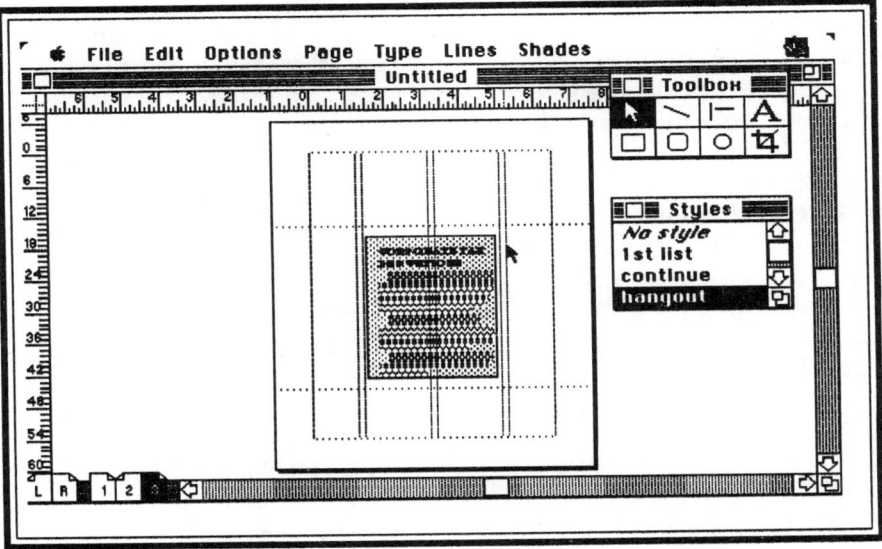

Figure 5.36   Guides repositioned on page 3.

PLACING THE REMAINING TEXT

Now that you have placed all the text except the remainder of the Setup Corp article, you can take a shortcut on page 3 by letting PageMaker automatically flow the text into the page. Because you have adjusted the column guides, you can be sure the text blocks created by the automatic flow will not overlap the boxed text placed in the center of the page.

Return to page 1 to activate the placement mode for the Setup Corp article.

> **Click** on the page 1 icon

You can see the guide line changes made on page 3 have no effect on the guide lines on the other pages. Select the Setup Corp article, the one in the bottom right corner of the page layout. Keep in mind that the text block you want to select is the last block placed from the article you want to continue.

5 Newsletters

It is important to note that in PageMaker there are no explicit signs as to which text block belongs to which story, or for that matter, which text block is the last block placed in the document for a given story. The free-form nature of Page-Maker layouts requires you to keep track of which text was placed where in the document. If you are familiar with the text of the articles, you can probably tell which blocks belong to which articles by skimming their contents. However, if you are working with unfamiliar text, you might need to make notations as to where you placed which text blocks.

One method of making such notations is to print thumbnail pages as you lay out each page and mark up the thumbnail pages to indicate where you have placed which articles.

> **Click** on the Setup Corp article (lower right corner of page)
> **Click** on the + in the bottom handle

You have now activated the placement mode for the article. Move to page 3 in order to place the text.

> **Click** on the page 3 icon

Because this is the last article that has text remaining to be placed, you can allow PageMaker to quickly complete the newsletter by automatically flowing the text into the columns as laid out on the page. You can toggle PageMaker from the manual placement mode into the automatic placement mode by using **Command + Click**, instead of **Click**.

> **Point** at the upper left corner of the guides
> **Command + Click**

PageMaker automatically fills the column on the page with text. Because there is not sufficient room for all the text on page 3, PageMaker, as part of the automatic placement process, creates a new page, page 4, and flows the last bit of text onto page 4.

Return to page 3 to see what happened.

Click on the page 3 icon

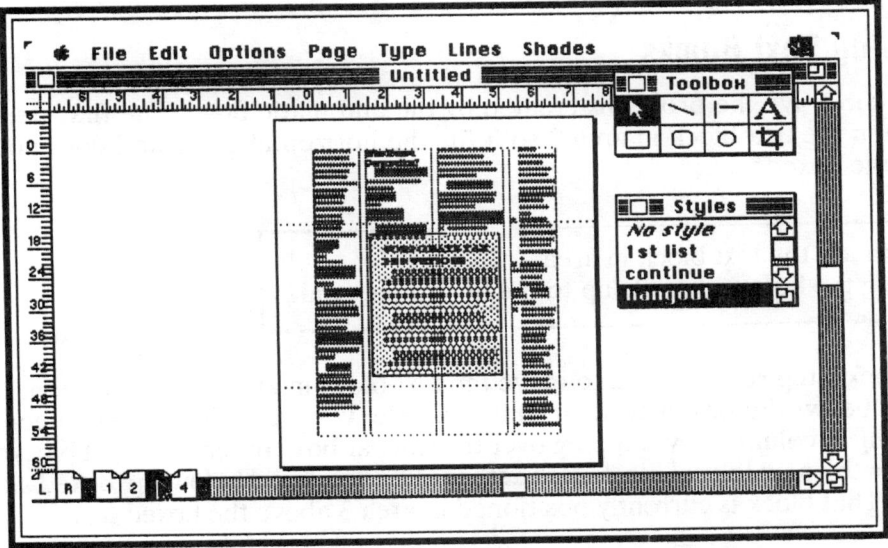

Figure 5.37   Text automatically placed on page 3.

You can see that PageMaker created four text blocks, one for each column on the page, but it would not automatically continue the columns below the box text. Instead, PageMaker began the next block at the top of the next column. The result is that two small areas below the boxed text were left blank and not filled with text.

Given the small amount of text that flowed to page 4, you might want to rearrange the text blocks to fit all the text onto page 3. (Note that if you intend to reproduce the newsletter by printing on both sides of the paper, there is little savings in creating a three-page rather than a four-page newsletter because both require the same amount of paper. If you were printing on one side of the paper, however, you would definitely want to get all the text onto three pages.)

5 Newsletters

Another problem created by the automatic text flow was that the horizontal guides positioned to prevent an overlap of the text from the article and the text did not appear to work. PageMaker automatically flowed the text until it encountered the text block for the sidebar text; it then overlapped the graphic box used to shade and enclose the side bar.

Moving Text Blocks

You can solve the problems created by the automatic flow. The first step is to shorten the text block in area 2 so it fits the horizontal guide and does not flow into the boxed text.

> **Click** on the text block in area 2
> **Drag** the bottom handle up to the horizontal guide

The next step requires you to move the text block in area 3 to the bottom of the page, below the boxed text. In this example, you want the reader to continue reading in column 2 by skipping over the sidebar box. In terms of text blocks, this means the next logical block in the story must be placed below the boxed sidebar text. That block is currently positioned in area 3 above the boxed text.

> **Click** on the text block in area 3
> **Drag** the entire text block to area 10 (as in Figure 5.38)

The block is too long for the space you have moved it to and must be shortened. Note that the bottom handle of the block may be out of the viewing area.

> **Click** on the down arrow icon on the scroll bar
> **Drag** the bottom handle up to bottom margin guide

Newsletters 5

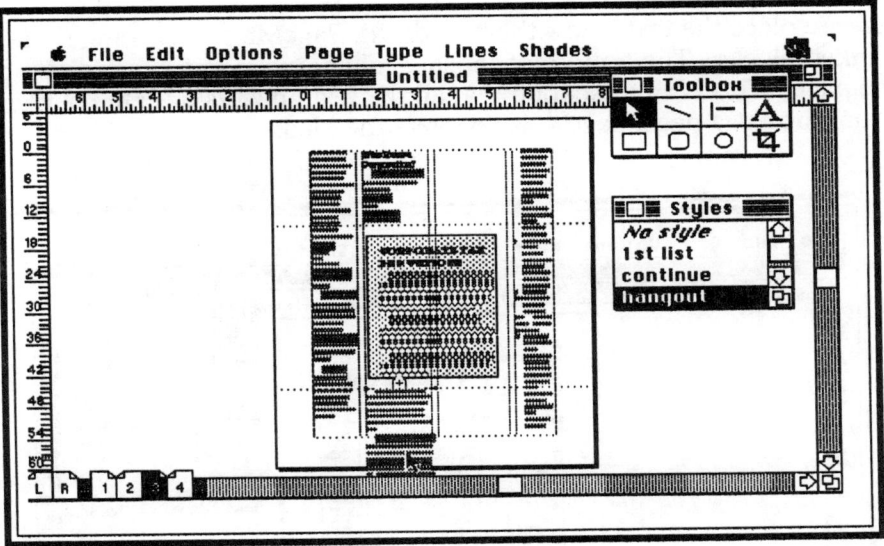

Figure 5.38   Text block moved to the bottom of the page.

Another way to keep the blocks in logical order is to insert a block between existing text blocks. This is done by selecting the + in the handle of the currently selected block. The text in the new block you create will contain the text that logically follows the text in the current text block, no matter where you place the text in the document. Note the logical order of the text blocks. In this case, you want the logical and physical order to be the same.

> **Click** on the + in the bottom handle
> **Drag** a text block over area 3

PageMaker flows the text into the area in column 3 above the boxed sidebar text. Continue the text in column 3 below the boxed text.

> **Click** on the + in the bottom handle
> **Drag** a text block over area 11

5 Newsletters

When you place the text below the boxed text, PageMaker rearranges the text in the linked blocks. The bottom of the last column no longer reaches the bottom of the page. This is an indication that all the text now fits onto the current page and that the extra page, page 4, is no longer needed.

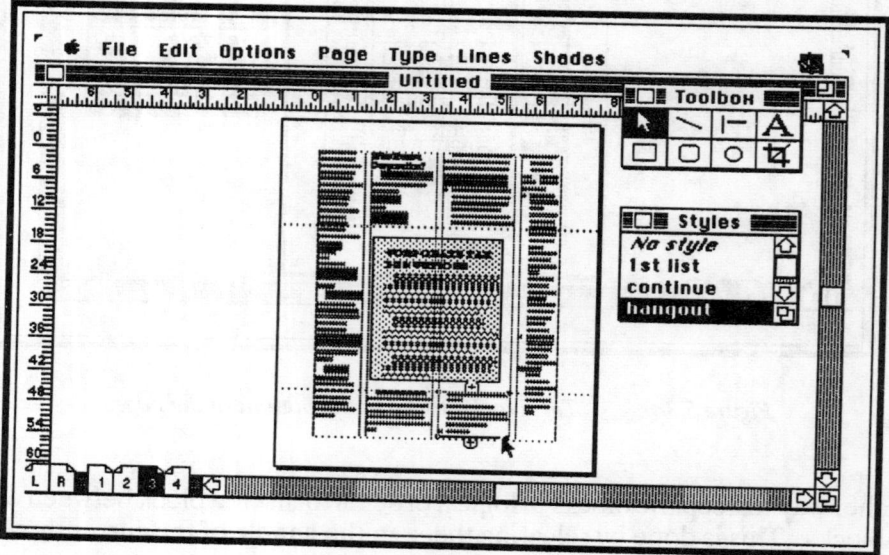

Figure 5.39   *Text now fits onto three pages.*

To make sure this is the end of the text, you can select the column.

Click on the fourth column

The bottom handle shows a #, indicating you have placed all the text from that story.

You can now print the newsletter by entering

Command + p
[Return]

If you are using an ImageWriter to print, press the Return key for the next two dialog boxes.

Pages 1, 2, and 3 of the document should resemble Figures 5.40, 5.41, and 5.42, respectively.

Save the document by entering

Command + s
SBN Mar 89 [Return]

(Figures 5.40, 5.41, and 5.42 appear on the following three pages.)

The Small Business Monthly

The Newsletter for Small Businesses Who Want to Get Bigger
Volume 6 Number 4
March, 1989

DIFFERENT WAYS TO DO BUSINESS

Advantages and Disadvantages of Forming A Small Corporation

As business owners you know that almost every business, in particular a small business, develops its own style of operating. But to the law all business operations fall into three major categories:

Sole Proprietorships
Partnerships
Corporations

This month's Small Business Newsletter is devoted to the topic of incorporation for small

Setting Up Your Own Corporation

Before you can decide whether or not you want to incorporate your business, you need to understand the advantages and disadvantages of incorporation.

Kinds of Corporations

The state of California recognizes four basic types of corporations.

Nonprofit Corporations

FINAL FORMALITIES

What You Need to Do After You Set Up A Corporation

Once you have officially set up your corporation there are still a number of important tasks that you need to carry out.

Domestic Stock Statement

You must file an Annual Domestic Stock statement with the state of California within 90 days of the date on which you filed the Articles of incorporation.

Each year you will be sent another state-

A nonprofit corporation is founded for the benefit of the public, the mutual benefit of its members or for religious purposes. The main reasons for forming this type of corporation are certain tax benefits extended to nonprofit corporations. In most cases distribution of the profits to the members of the corporation is prohibited.

Professional Corporations

Members of professions that license their members may form a professional corporation.

Figure 5.40   Page 1 of final document.

Doing Business from page 1...

business. Sole proprietorships and partnerships can be entered into with a minimum of legal complications. Incorporation is a major decision for a small business and you should carefully weigh all of the positive and negative features before you decide to take the step.

Why Incorporate?

The primary difference between a corporation and other forms of doing business is that the corporation is viewed by the law as a separate entity. The corporation is treated as a fictional person who can be taxed separately from the owners of the corporation.

When you incorporate you now become an employee of the fictional person who is the corporation. You are then eligible for tax deductible fringe benefits.

Another attractive feature of incorporation is the limit of liability. Any liability against the corporation can reach only the assets of the corporation not the assets of the owner or owners of the corporation.

On the other hand creating a corporation is not always a tax benefit. Changing corporate and personal tax rates requires that you make specific calculations to determine the tax implications of incorporation since they vary with each individual owner and business.

Final Formalities from page 1...

ment which must be filled out and sent in on or before the date indicated on the form.

Fictitious Name Statement

If your corporation will do business under any name other than the official corporation name then you must file a Fictitious Name Statement with the county in which you plan to operate.

This statement must be filed no later than 40 days following the first date upon which you carry out a transaction under the fictitious name.

Notify Creditors

If you have transferred assets from an existing business to the new corporation you are required to notify all creditors in writing of the change in ownership.

You are also required to carry out the following:

a. Obtain two copies of the Notice of Dissolution of a Partnership from a legal newspaper.
b. Fill out the notice following instructions.
c. Send the notice to a legal newspaper within 30 days.
d. Notify creditors by mail.

Tax Forms - Federal

You will need to file some or all of the following forms:

S Corporation Tax Election
Federal Employer Identification Number
Employee's Withholding Certificates
Income and Social Security Tax Withholding
Quarterly Withholding Returns and Deposits
Annual Wage and Tax Statement
Federal Unemployment Tax
Corporate Income Tax
S Corporation Income Tax Return
Corporation Employee and Shareholder Returns
Estimated Corporation Income Tax Payments

Figure 5.41   Page 2 of final document.

Note that many professions are not subject to the requirement to form a professional corporation but can form a regular profit corporation. Professions that fall into the professional corporation classification are:

Accountant
Attorney
Nurse
Veterinarian

Close Corporation

If the there are 35 or less members in the corporation it is considered a "close corporation."

Privately-Held Profit Corporation

This is the most common type of corporation and the one that most individuals would consider for their business.

Who Runs a Corporation?

Members of a corporation are classified in three ways:

Incorporator
Officer

Shareholder

A corporation needs money as well as people to operate. The value of the money or other tangible assets used to create the corporation is called "capital."

Capital can be acquired by a corporation by selling stock or borrowing money.

Debt to Equity Ratio

A. When creating a corporation out of an existing business it is a mistake to transfer all of the assets of the unincorporated business to the corporation in exchange for a note.

B. The general rule of thumb is that the debt to equity ratio should be no more than 3 to 1.

C. Example:

Book Value of Business $200,000
Debt $150,00
Equity $50,000
Dividends

A. Dividends can be paid to the members of a corporation only if the amount of earning in the corporation equals or exceeds the total amount of the dividends to be paid. In other words you cannot incur debt to pay a dividend.

B. In addition the following condition must also be met:
Corporate assets following the dividend must be 1.25 times the liabilities.

CORPORATE TAX DEDUCTIONS

Salaries paid to employees of the corporation are deductible from corporate taxes. Note that if a shareholder is paid a salary it must be a reasonable salary for services actually performed. If not, the IRS may consider these payments as nondeductible dividends.

As with salaries, payments made for employee benefits are deductible from corporate income. Medical benefits, accident, health life and disability insurance can all be paid by the corporation for their employees.

In contrast, sole proprietorships and partnerships can deduct only 25% of health and accident insurance.

Figure 5.42   Page 3 of final document.

Removing Pages

Page 4, which was created by PageMaker when it was automatically flowing text, is still part of the document even though it no longer contains information. Although a blank page 4 was not printed at the end of a document, remove it anyway. Activate page 4.

> **Click** on the page 4 icon

The Remove pages command is found on the Pages menu.

> **Point** at Pages
> **Drag** to Remove pages

The dialog box automatically defaults to removing the current page. You can override the default by entering a range of pages, or accept the default by entering

> **[Return]**

PageMaker asks you to confirm your intention to delete the page and all items on it. Here, the choice is simple because the page is clearly empty. Note that if you delete a page that contains linked text blocks you are removing that section of the text from the story. You cannot recover the text by adding a new text block after you have removed the page with the text blocks. (In such a case, to restore the text to its full form, you would use the Replace entire story option in the Place document dialog box. This replaces the abbreviated story with a new copy from the original text file.) Confirm the removal of page 4.

> **Click** on OK

5 Newsletters

Compressing a File

When you remove a page from a PageMaker document, you eliminate an unneeded page. You do not, however, reduce the amount of space occupied on the disk by the PageMaker file. If you want to reduce the size of the file and allow the space to be used by other files, you must resave the PageMaker document, using the Save as command instead of the Save command. When you use Save as, PageMaker creates a new file for the document information that uses only the space required by the current number of pages, in contrast to Save, which maintains the file size at its previous maximum size.

You can avoid actually making a duplicate file with a new name by entering the current file name as the file you want to Save as. PageMaker will prompt you to confirm your desire to overwrite the original file with the reduced copy.

> **Point** at File
> **Drag** to Save as

The name of the current document appears as the default file name.

> **Click** on OK
> **Click** on Yes

The file is now reduced to the size necessary for the current number of pages. Close the document window.

> **Drag** to Close

SUMMARY

This chapter covered the technqiues used in PageMaker for creating and organizing documents that contain more than one story.

- **Text Style Codes.** You can save time in formatting within PageMaker by inserting style codes into the text documents as you create them. Style codes are placed at the beginning of a paragraph and consist of the style name enclosed by angle brackets. The codes are read by PageMaker when you import the text into the PageMaker document. A style code applies to the paragraph it begins and all subsequent paragraphs until another style code is encountered. Note that you must select the Read tags option in the Place dialog box to prevent PageMaker form treating the codes as normal text.

- **Horizontal Guides.** In addition to setting vertical column guides, you can set horizontal guides. A guide is created by dragging the ruler line. Dragging the vertical ruler creates a vertical guide; dragging the horizontal ruler creates a horizontal guide. These guides are useful when you are dividing a page into a series of text blocks for different stories.

- **Units of measurement.** You can enter values in a unit of measurement different from the PageMaker default units by adding abbreviations to the values you enter.

- **Customized Rulers.** You can modify the ruler setup by dragging the zero point of the rulers to a specific location on the page. This feature helps you measure distances based on some point of reference that you select. You can also use the Preferences dialog box to change the unit of measurement used on the ruler. Vertical and horizontal rulers can be set to use different units of measurement.

- **Templates.** A template is a special type of PageMaker file that can be used to repeat a specific set of layout options in a new document. A template file is exactly like a normal PageMaker document except that when it is loaded, the name of the template is removed and replaced with "Untitled" to prevent accidental overwriting of the template file. Templates are used to store parts of documents, such as the column layout or master headings, that will be used again in future documents.

5 Newsletters

- **Inserting Pages.** You add more pages to a PageMaker document by using the Insert Pages command located on the Page menu. You can insert one or more pages at a time.

- **Placing Multiple Stories.** Newsletters are created by placing text from different stories in different text blocks within the same document. You can continue a text story in a block on a different page by selecting the + in that block's bottom window shade handle and moving to the page where you want to continue the document.

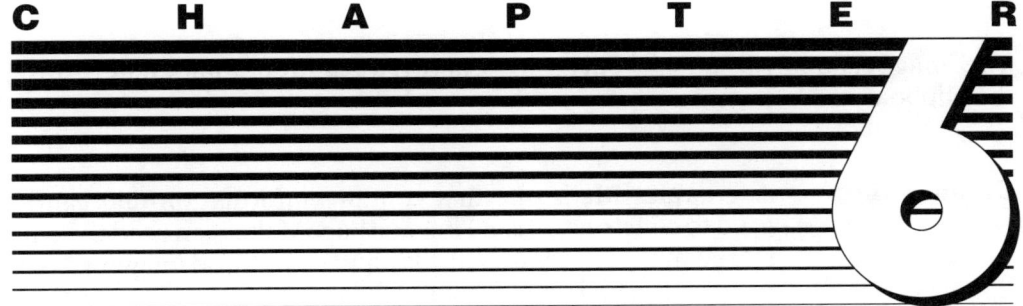

ADDING GRAPHICS TO A DOCUMENT

The term "graphic" refers to any information placed into a PageMaker document that does not consist of text characters. You have already encountered graphics in the form of lines, rectangles, and shading that you have applied to PageMaker documents. In addition to these items drawn directly onto the document pages, you can place into PageMaker graphic images created with other applications. The images can be pictures created with painting programs such as MacPaint, charts created with programs such as Excel, or images captured by scanners or links to video recorders. In this chapter, you will examine the ways in which such graphics are handled in PageMaker and how they are integrated with text.

6 Adding Graphics to a Document

The images can be placed into PageMaker in two ways: as graphics files or from the clipboard.

Graphics files   A **graphics file** is one that contains information that can be used to construct a visual image. PageMaker can read the data stored in these files and display and print these images as part of the PageMaker document. There are four different types of graphics files that PageMaker can read: paint-type, draw-type, TIFF, and EPS

Paint-type. A paint-type graphics file is also known as a **bit-mapped** graphics file. These files contain a pattern of values that have a direct correspondence to a pattern of white and black dots. Programs such as MacPaint allow you to create pictures out of arrangements of dots. The fat-bits feature found in many graphics programs allows you direct manual control over which dots are turned on or off. Because these images consist of discrete black and white bits, they are considered digital images.

Draw-type. Drawn images are usually called **vector graphics**. A vector graphic is a mathematical description of a drawing composed of lines, angles, and specific drawn objects. Programs that produce draw-type images operate much like the graphic elements within PageMaker. Each item is an object on the page that can be moved, sized, or placed in front or in back of other objects.

This type of image is usually created with CAD (computer aided design) type programs. Note that a drawn image file is different from a painted image file in that the drawn image file uses a mathematical description of the drawings, instead of a bit-mapped image.

TIFF. TIFF stands for **Tag Image File Format**. This format is used by many scanning and video interface devices to store gray-toned images. The TIFF images are capable of producing, on the printed page, continuous gray tones, in contrast to painted images created on a computer, in which shades are produced by patterns of black and white dots without gray tones.

EPS. EPS stands for **Encapsulated PostScript.** An EPS graphic is similar to a draw-type graphic in that the file does not contain the actual image but a series of instructions that can be used to create the image. An EPS contains a PostScript language program that describes how the image should be drawn. EPS files are actually composed not of images but of text because the PostScript language is composed of text commands. If you are proficient in the PostScript programming language, you can create an EPS file by entering the commands into a text file.

However, most EPS files are created by programs that allow you to draw or paint on the screen and then compile the images into PostScript commands. This is exactly what PageMaker does when it sends a document to a PostScript printer such as the LaserWriter. In Appendix A, you will find out how you can capture a page printed by PageMaker as an EPS image file.

Clipboard

Programs that create graphics files that are not compatible with PageMaker can still be the source of images moved from one application to another through the Macintosh clipboard. A good example is a chart created with Excel. When a chart is saved in Excel, the file contains a description of how the chart should be drawn by Excel, not an image of the chart. This means PageMaker would not be able to load the chart image because it lacks the ability to translate the stored data into a chart.

However, you can copy the image of the chart into the clipboard by using **Command+c**. You must then load PageMaker and paste the clipboard image into the PageMaker document by using **Command+v**. If you have sufficient memory to run both Excel and PageMaker under MultiFinder, you can avoid quitting Excel and loading PageMaker each time you want to transfer an image via the clipboard.

6 Adding Graphics to a Document

IMAGE BASICS

To work with graphics, you will need some graphics files. In this chapter you will create a graphics file directly from PageMaker so you will have something to work with even if you have no other graphics files available on your computer.

In addition to the files you will make, there are graphics files included on your PageMaker 3.0 Getting Started disk. If you installed the full PageMaker 3.0 program on your hard disk, these files are already stored in the Getting Started folder. If you did not install this folder, you can copy them from the Getting Stated disk. The files you will need are as follows:

- Tiles.eps
- Photo.tif

If you do not have access to these image files, you can perform some, but not all, of the operations discussed in this chapter.

When you begin the exercises in this chapter, make sure you have just loaded PageMaker because you want to have the PageMaker logo screen displayed so you can create the graphic image you will be working with.

When PageMaker is loaded and the logo screen is displayed, you are ready to begin.

Creating a Paint-type Image

There are many programs available for the Macintosh that provide ways to create, capture, and manipulate graphics images. When the Macintosh was first released, it was the MacPaint program that captured the interest of many people who were not used to thinking about drawing with computers.

The Macintosh system provides a simple way of creating a paint-type image file, which will serve as one of the example images used in this chapter. Pressing the combination **Command+Shift+3** (the 3 on the top row of the keyboard—not on the numeric keypad) will cause the Macintosh system to capture a paint-type image of the screen at the moment you press the combination. This can be done at any time with the exception of when you are using the mouse to display a pull down menu. The screen images displayed in this book were created by using this method.

Currently you have the Aldus corporation logo on the screen. Create an image file by entering

Command + Shift + 3

When you enter this command, the Macintosh system creates a file, Screen 0 for the first, Screen 1 for the second, and so on. The files are *always* placed in the top folder on the system disk. You can create up to 10 screen images, Screen 0 through Screen 9. If you have these 10 files in the top folder, the system will beep when you try to create another image. However, you can eliminate the problem and make more screens by either changing the names of the screen image files or placing them in a different folder.

The command you just issued created an image file that you can use as part of a PageMaker document. Create a new single-page document. Enter

Command + n
[Return]

A graphic file is placed into a PageMaker document in the same way that a text file is — through the Place command. Enter

Command + d

Use the Folder selector box to change to the top folder on the start disk. You can then scroll the file list until you locate the file named **Screen 0**, as shown in Figure 6.1. Select that file.

> **Click** on Screen 0

6 Adding Graphics to a Document

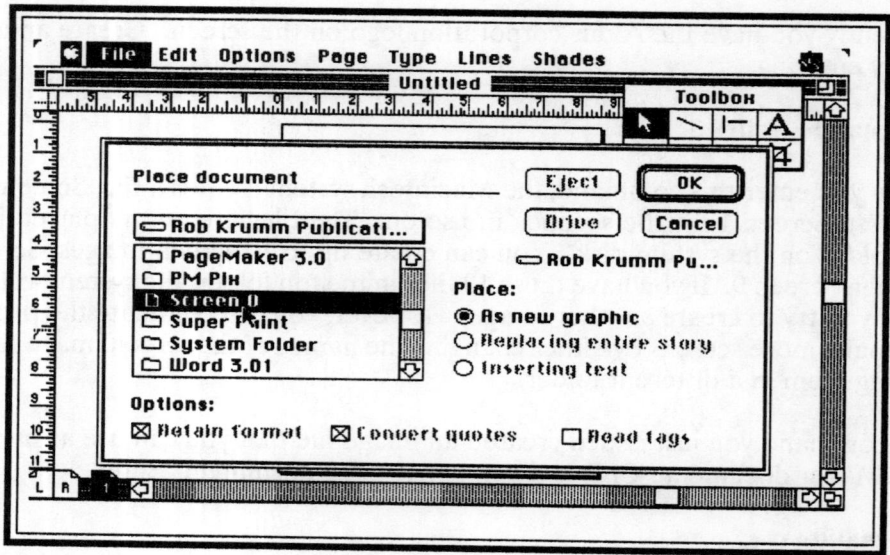

Figure 6.1   Screen 0 file selected.

Note that when you highlight a graphics file, PageMaker changes the place option to **As new graphic**. Load the image into PageMaker by entering

[Return]

PageMaker returns to the document screen. The mouse cursor icon is changed to a paint brush. The icon indicates which type of graphic is being placed. The paint brush icon appears when the file is a paint-type (bit-mapped) graphic image.

Adding Graphics to a Document **6**

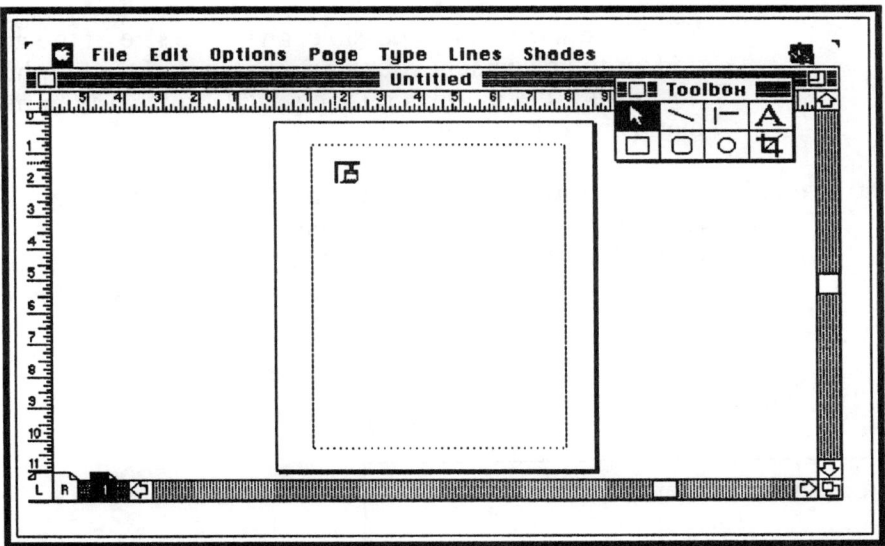

Figure 6.2   Paint brush icon indicates paint-type graphic to be placed.

Placing a graphic file into a document can be done in two ways: through automatic sizing or manual sizing.

Automatic Sizing   If you click while the paint brush icon is displayed, PageMaker will insert the image into the document, placing the upper left corner of the image at the location in which you click. The size and shape of the image are determined by the size of the image stored. The aspect ratio of the image will be the same as in the stored file. The term **aspect ratio** refers to the ratio between the length and the width of the image. Paint-type images can be distorted by changing the ratio of the length to the width. Note that a distorted image can be restored to its original aspect ratio by using the **Shift + Click** (hold) command on any of the buttons on a selected image. (The word "hold" in parentheses indicates that in order to implement this feature, you must press and hold down the mouse button longer than you would for an ordinary click of the mouse.)

301

6 Adding Graphics to a Document

Keep in mind that it is possible, given the size of the graphic and/or the placement you select, that part of the graphic may not fit into the margins on the page. You will then need to manually resize the graphic.

Manual Sizing You can directly control the size, shape, and aspect ratio of the image, as well as its placement, by dragging the mouse to draw a box to contain the image. The advantage of this method is that you know in advance what part of the page the image will occupy.

In this case, allow PageMaker to automatically size the image.

Point at the upper left corner of the guides
Click

The image is placed into the document at the top of the page. You can see, even in the reduced view, that the image shows the opening screen display of the PageMaker program.

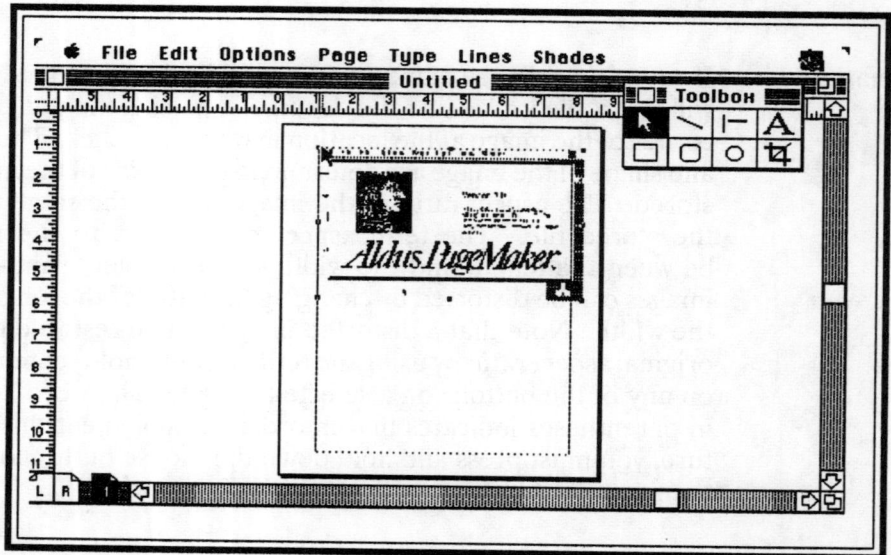

Figure 6.3   *Graphic image placed in PageMaker document.*

Adding Graphics to a Document **6**

PageMaker displays eight buttons on the image. These buttons indicate that the image is currently selected.

Sizing the Image

You can change the size and shape of the image on the page by dragging the selection buttons. For example, you could change the size and shape of the graphic so that it will fill the entire text area of the page.

> **Drag** the lower right corner button to the lower right corner of the guides

The image is expanded and distorted to fill the entire page.

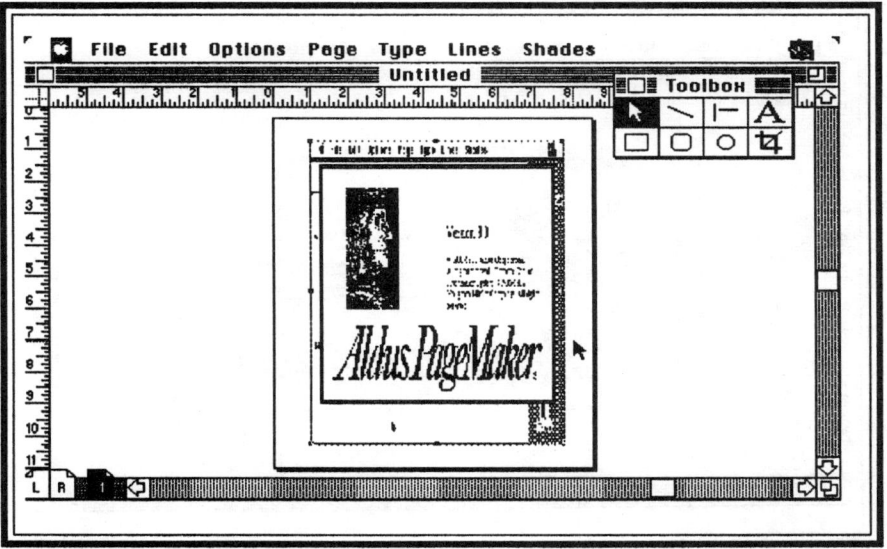

Figure 6.4   Image stretched over the entire page.

6 Adding Graphics to a Document

Forcing an image into a frame that is very different from the original frame in size and length-to-width ratio may cause a loss of resolution and clarity that renders the image unusable. PageMaker will resize the image so the aspect ratio returns to the original size if you hold down the Shift key and hold down the mouse button while pointing to any one of the selection buttons.

> **Point** at any button
> **Shift + Click** (hold)

PageMaker changes the image so it returns to the original ratio. Note that this does not mean the image will return to its original size. In this case, PageMaker enlarged the image to arrive at a frame that matched the original proportions. The result is an image much too large for the page.

Figure 6.5   Image resized to maintain original aspect ratio.

Adding Graphics to a Document 6

To change the size of the image but maintain the original proportions of length to width, you would hold down the Shift key while you drag the buttons (Shift+Drag).

> **Point** at the lower right corner button
> **Shift+Drag** the button up and to the left (as in Figure 6.6)

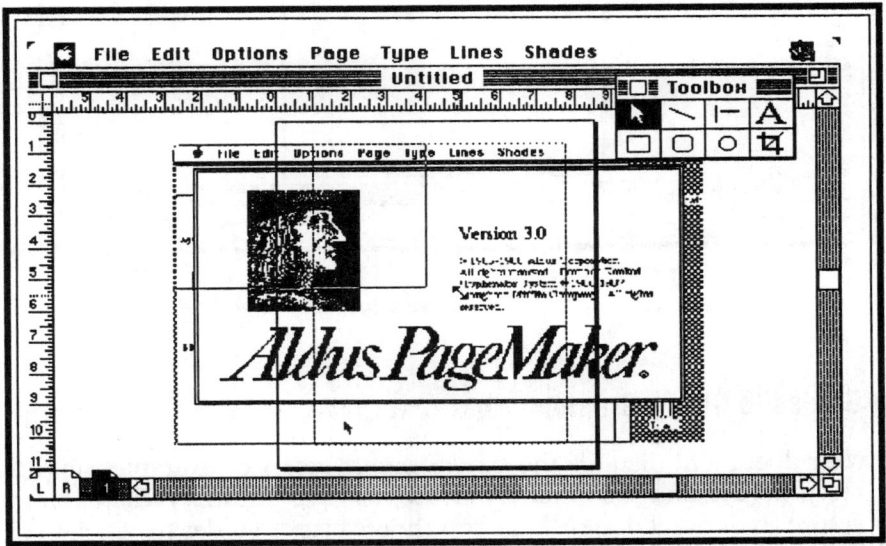

Figure 6.6   *New frame automatically maintains proportions of length to width.*

Notice as you drag the graph, the frame moves only in increments, maintaining the aspect ratio of the original image. When you release the mouse button, the figure is resized to fit the frame.

You can change the location of a graphic by pointing anywhere inside the graphic and dragging it to a new location.

> **Point** at the graphic image
> **Drag** to the top of the guides (as in Figure 6.7)

6 Adding Graphics to a Document

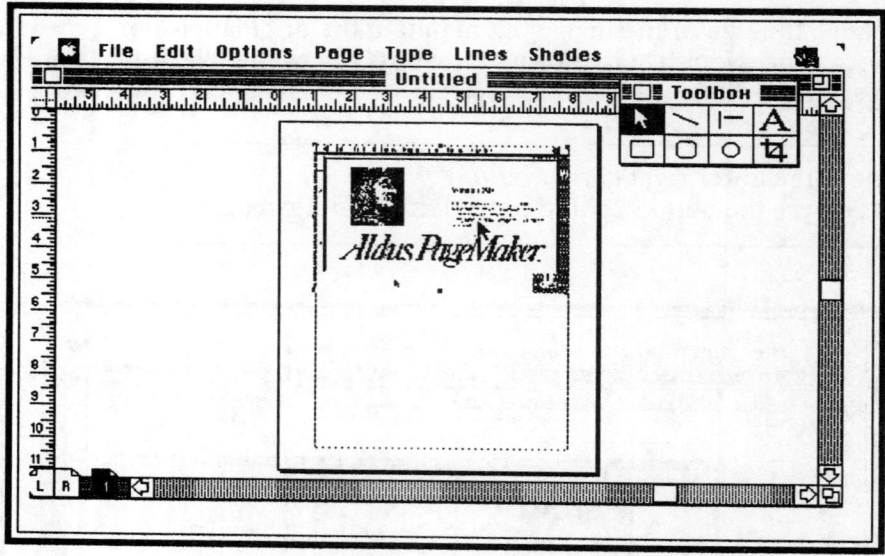

Figure 6.7   *Picture placed back into page guides.*

Using Guides to Size a Graphic

Often your document dictates the size of the image. For example, suppose you wanted to print the image so that it fits into a 3" by 5" frame. When you want to size a picture to fit exact dimensions, you should create guides to which the image can be snapped. This provides the greatest degree of accuracy in creating images of a specific size. Turn on the Snap to rulers feature by entering

Command+y

Set the zero point of the rulers to the upper left corner of the guides. Note that the upper left corner of the image should be positioned at this point as well.

> **Drag** the zero point icon to the upper left corner of the guides

Create a vertical guide at 5".

> **Drag** the vertical ruler to 5"

Create a horizontal guide at 3".

> **Drag** the horizontal ruler to 3"

Place the picture inside the frame indicated by the guides.

> **Drag** the lower right button to the lower right corner of the 3" by 5" guides

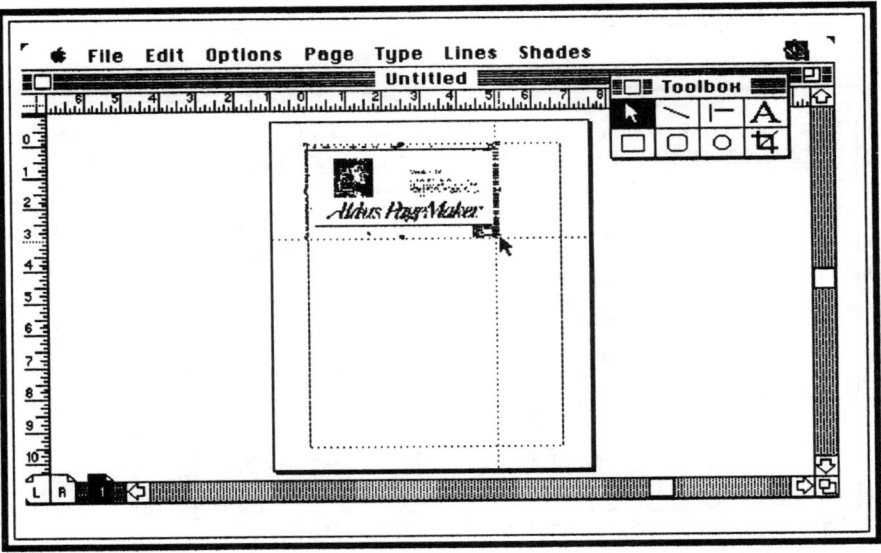

Figure 6.8   Picture sized to exact dimensions.

Note that when you drag an image to a frame of predetermined size you will probably distort the original proportions of the image. You can use the Shift+Click (hold) command to prompt PageMaker to adjust the proportions of the graphic to the original. Keep in mind this will cause a change in the size of the image. PageMaker uses the proportioned size closest to the current dimensions.

6 Adding Graphics to a Document

> **Point** at any button
> **Shift + Click** (hold)

The image is resized to the closest shape with the original proportions. In this case, that causes the image's width to be shortened.

Enlarge your view of the image.

> **Point** at the center of the image
> **Option + Command + Click**

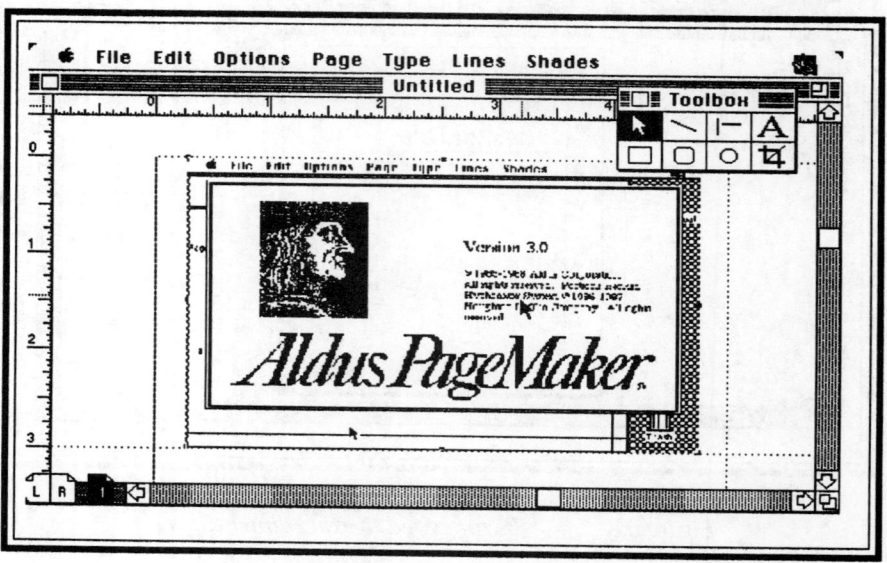

Figure 6.9   *Image sized inside 3" by 5" frame.*

Cropping

So far, your graphic operations have maintained the full contents of the original image file. PageMaker allows you to crop the image so you can display whatever part of the original image you want. Picture cropping takes place in the crop mode. The cropping icon is the one in the lower right corner of the Toolbox palette. Activate the crop mode.

> **Click** on the cropping icon

The cropping process consists of two basic operations: sizing the frame and panning the image.

Sizing the Frame	When the crop mode is active, changes in the size of the graphics frame do not affect the size or proportion of the picture. In the selection mode, PageMaker automatically adjusts the size of the image to fill the frame as the frame's size increases or decreases. In the crop mode, a change in the size of the frame simply reveals more or less of the image. In this way, you can eliminate from view parts of the image you do not want displayed.
Panning the Image	After an image has been cropped, dragging, or **panning**, the image will cause the image within the frame to move, while the frame's position on the page remains the same. The effect is that the frame of the graphic acts as a window into which you can move various parts of the graphics image.

By using the sizing and panning techniques, you can display only the part of the image you really want to display. For example, suppose you wanted to display only the human profile part of the image.

Select the image you want to crop.

> **Click** inside the image

6 Adding Graphics to a Document

The buttons appear on the outside of the image's frame. The cropping icon contains a hollow space in the center. When cropping the size of an image, you want to position the hollow space over the button you will do the cropping with. In this example, you want the lower right button.

> **Point** at the lower right button

Eliminate the unwanted portions of the image by dragging the button toward the lower right corner of the profile.

> **Drag** to the position shown in Figure 6.10

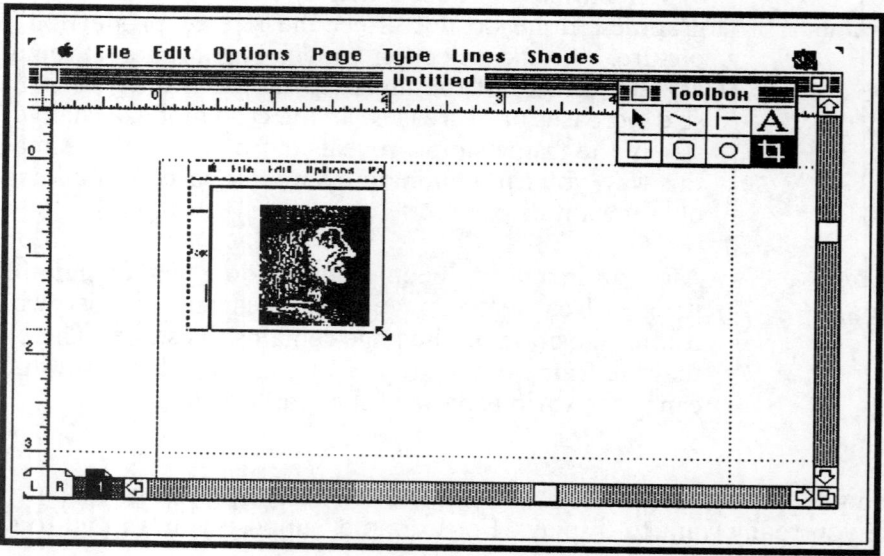

Figure 6.10   Unwanted image area cropped out of picture.

Now you need to crop the upper left section of the image.

> **Point** at the upper left button on the graphic
> **Drag** to the position shown in Figure 6.11

Adding Graphics to a Document **6**

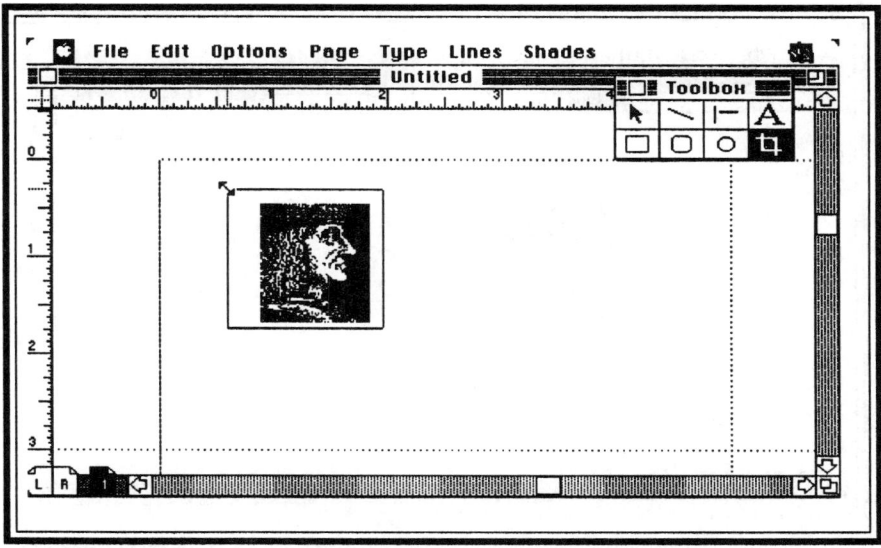

Figure 6.11   Upper left corner cropped.

Only the profile drawing remains displayed. You can adjust the position of the remaining image within the current frame by using the mouse to pan the image within the frame. If you point anywhere on the image, with the exception of the buttons, PageMaker will pan the image when you drag the mouse.

Point at the center of the image
Drag until the image is centered in the frame (Figure 6.12)

Now that you have cropped the image to show only the part of the original graphic that you want, you can manipulate the cropped image from the selection mode.

Click on the pointer icon

Now that the selection mode is active, you can change the position of the graphic on the page by dragging it.

Drag the graphic to the upper left corner of the guide (Figure 6.13)

311

6 Adding Graphics to a Document

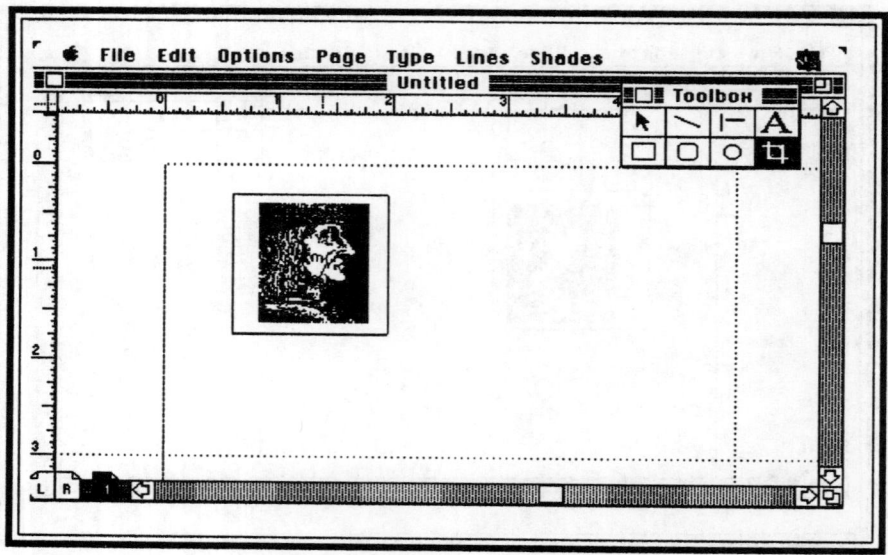

Figure 6.12   *Image panned within frame.*

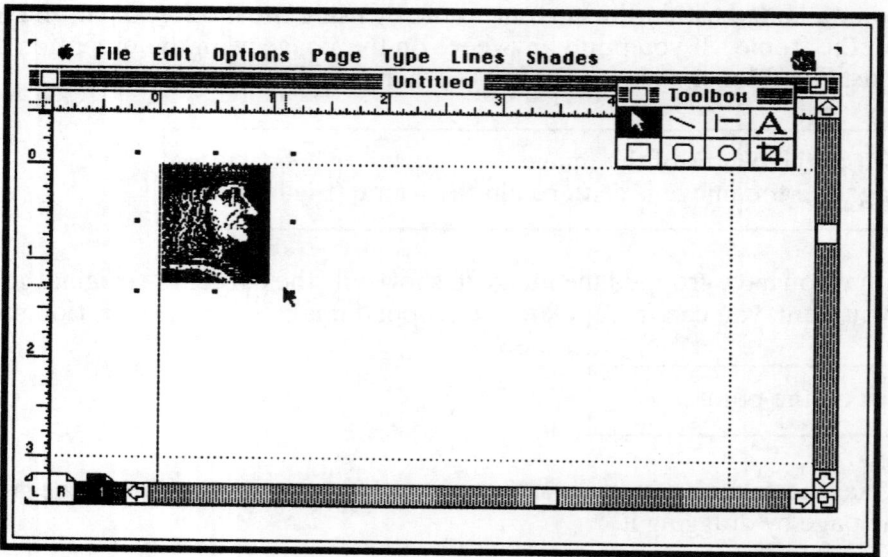

Figure 6.13   *Cropped image dragged to new position.*

Adding Graphics to a Document **6**

You can enlarge the image by dragging the buttons on the graphic. If you want to enlarge the graphic but avoid distorting the image, hold down the Shift key, while dragging (Shift+Drag).

> **Shift+Drag** the lower right button as shown in Figure 6.14

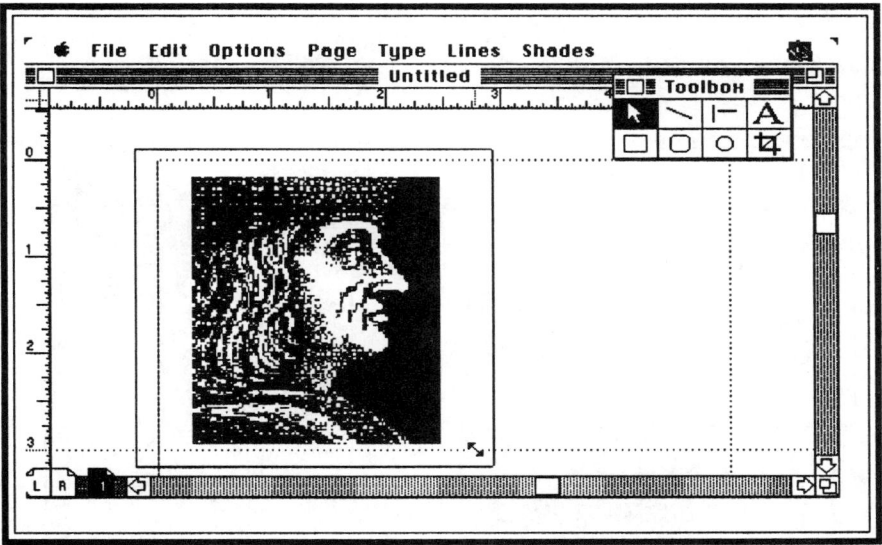

Figure 6.14   Cropped image enlarged by resizing graphic.

IMAGE CONTROL

PageMaker does not contain facilities for editing the actual images; however, if the images are bit-mapped, i.e., paint-type or TIFF files, you can alter their intensity. The image control command is found on the Options menu. Image control in PageMaker is similar to the brightness and contrast controls on a televsion or a computer monitor. This means that although you cannot change the content of the image, you can fine-tune the image to get the best printed results. Because bit-mapped images are digital images, PageMaker can manipulate the intensity and contrast within the image. EPS and draw-type images are not stored in bit-mapped format and require interpretation by the program to produce or change an image. PageMaker is equipped to display but not alter these images. As a general rule, PageMaker has more control over paint-type and TIFF images than it does over EPS or draw-type images.

6 Adding Graphics to a Document

To access the image control dialog box, you must select a paint-type or TIFF image frame. You should currently have the PageMaker logo image selected. Display the Image Control dialog box.

> **Point** at Options
> **Drag** to Image Control

PageMaker displays the Image Control dialog box. The dialog box has two main options: **Black and white** and **Screened**.

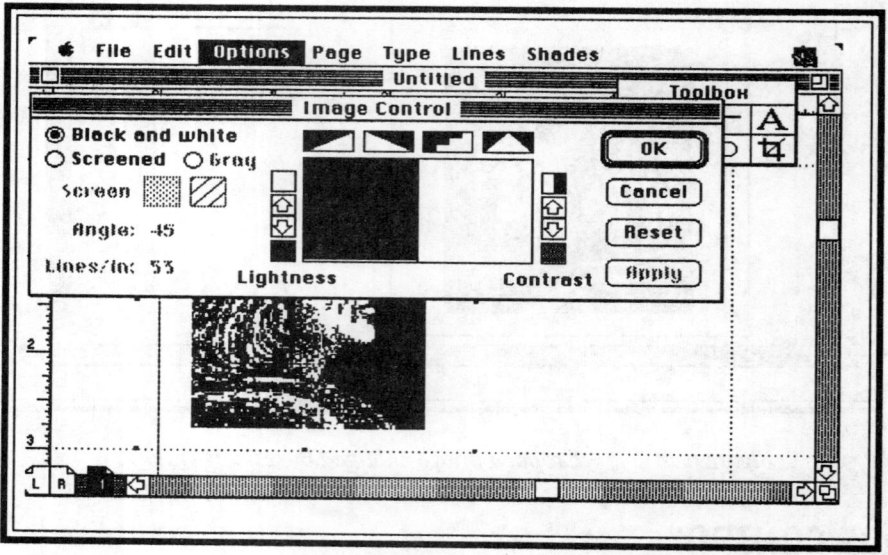

Figure 6.15   *Image Control dialog box.*

Black and white   The Black and white option treats the image as a bit-mapped picture composed of only black and white dots. This is the type of image created directly from a computer screen, such as the image captured in this example, or the type of image created by programs that store images in the paint format (referred to in some programs as the MacPaint format). When this mode is active, you are limited in the image control to one basic option — inverting the image to create an image that looks like a photographic negative. The options are limited because the contrast scale is automatically set.

Adding Graphics to a Document **6**

Screened   A screened image allows you to control the lightness (brightness) of the image and the contrast. You can slowly determine the number of lines per inch used to created screened shades and the angle at which the screen lines are ruled.

If you have a Macintosh II computer, the Gray option allows you to display a full gray-toned image on the screen.

The simplest changes in the image you can make are the ones that can be accessed by selecting one of the four special photographic effects icons: **positive**, **negative**, **posterized**, and **solarized**. These icons actually represent special combinations of lightness and contrast settings. The icons indicate how lightness and contrast icons would be set to create the special effects.

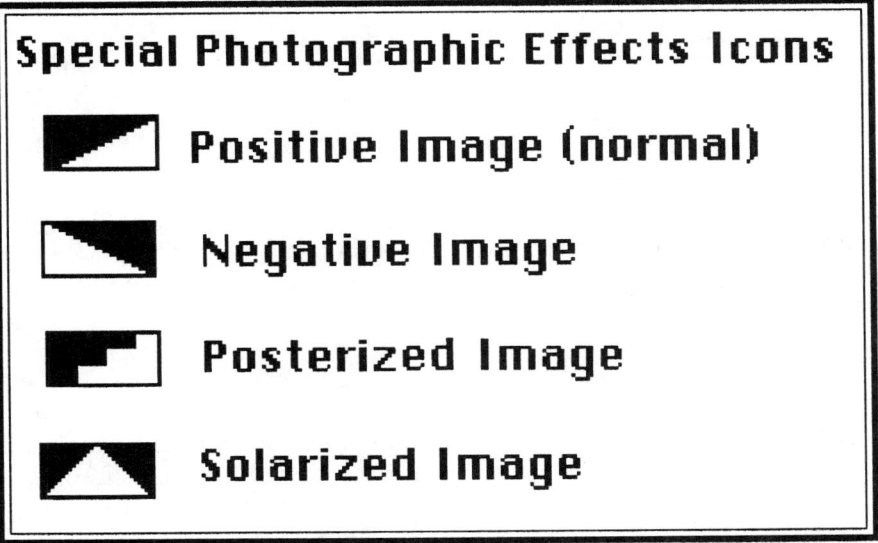

Figure 6.16   *Special photographic effect icons.*

Positive (normal) This setting prints the bit-mapped graphic exactly as it was created or captured.

Negative This option switches white for black and black for white to create an image that looks like a photographic negative of the original image.

Posterized This option affects only TIFF images. It sets the contrast between screen tones in even increments instead of smooth increments. The effect increases the overall contrast of the picture and is used when you intend to view the image from a distance, such as a wall poster — hence the term "posterize."

Solarized This is a special effect created when a photograph is exposed to a flash of light during developement — hence the name "solarized" (exposed to light). The effect is to combine characteristics of a negative with a positive image to create a special appearance. PageMaker imitates the effect of solarizing mathematically to produce an unusual image. This feature can only be used with TIFF images.

Posterized and solarized effects cannot be implemented in a paint-type image because they require more than two tones to create the effects. A paint-type image has only two tones — black and white — and cannot produce the in-between tones needed for these special effects.

For black-and-white paint-type images, the large block in the center of the Image Control dialog box is currently divided into two **tone bars**. The bar on the left controls the intensity of the black areas in the original image. The bar on the right controls the intensity of the white areas in the original image. The bars are set for solid black (on the left) and solid white (on the right) when the Black and white option is active. Select a negative image for the graphic.

> **Click** on the negative icon

Note that as soon as you select this option, PageMaker changes the display to a negative image, which you can see in the bottom half of the screen, below the dialog box, to get an idea of what effect the selection will have on the image before you print it.

Adding Graphics to a Document **6**

You will also notice that when the image is set to negative, the colors of the black and white tone bars are reversed because a negative shows black as white and white as black.

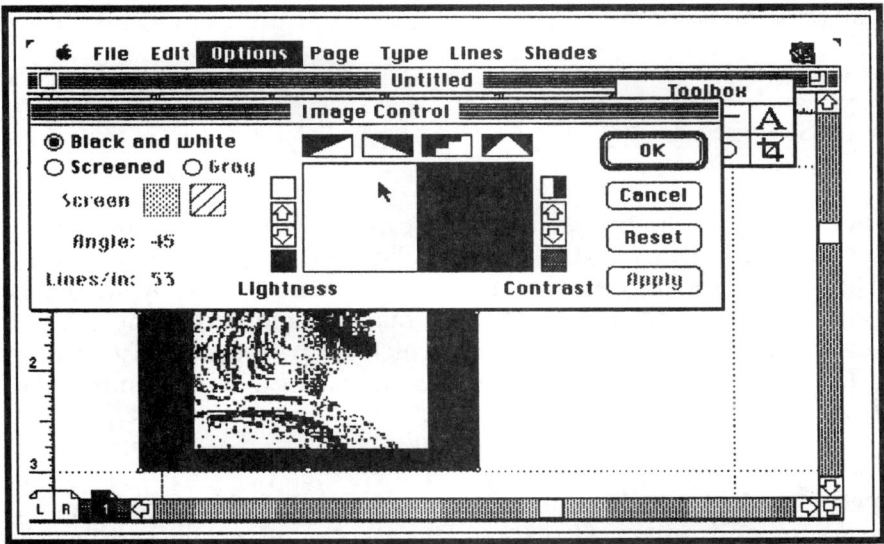

Figure 6.17   Picture changed to negative.

Change the image back to positive (normal).

Click on the positive (normal) icon

The image returns to its normal display.

6 Adding Graphics to a Document

Screened Images

You can change the image in a more subtle way by using the screened images options. **Screened** images are fine patterns of black and white dots in which the effect of gray tones is created through the density and pattern of the dots. By using the Screened options, you can soften the appearance of a stark black-and-white image. Activate the Screened options.

> **Click** on Screened

There are two aspects of the image that you can control with the Screened options, represented by two icons next to the word "Screen" in the Image Control dialog box. The icon on the left sets the image as a screened image, while the icon on the right changes the image to a patterned imaged composed of lines. A screened image is typical of a newspaper photo in which dot patterns are used to simulate tones. The line pattern is typical of television images that are composed of dots organized in horizontal lines.

Screened A black-and-white picture is composed with some areas all white and others all black. This creates an image with a very high contrast between the white and black areas. For screened images PageMaker has two controls that allow you to alter the way the white and black areas are displayed: lightness and contrast. The **Lightness** option permits you to change the intensity of the black areas by mixing in a fine pattern of white dots with the black to produce something that approximates a gray tone. This is how photos are reproduced in a newspaper. If the lightness control is used to its fullest, the black areas will appear as white. The lightness control has no effect on the white areas because they are already as light as they can be. You can change the lightness using the scroll bar labeled Lightness or by dragging the black and white tone bars (in the center of the Image Control dialog box) up or down.

Adding Graphics to a Document 6

The **Contrast** option affects both the white and the black tone bars at the same time. When an image is set to black and white, the contrast is at the maximum intensity. You can decrease the amount of contrasts by using the scroll bar labeled Contrast or by dragging the black and white tone bars up or down. A change in contrast means you are allowing PageMaker to mix some white into the black areas, and black into the white areas, softening the contrasts between black and white in the image. Note that if you set the contrast so both bars are evenly divided between white and black, the image will appear as a solid block of gray with no image visible because both white and black areas use the same pattern.

Line Pattern If you select the line pattern icon (i.e., the one with the diagonal lines), the image is changed from a screen pattern with an even distribution of the dots to a lined image in which the dots are arranged in lines of dots running at a specific angle. You can control the angle at which the lines run and the number of lines per square inch. Angles are counted clockwise, starting with 0 as a horizontal line. The default value is a 45-degree angle. The number of lines per inch sets the resolution used when the image is printed. Of course, the actual resolution is limited by the resolution of your printer.

To get a more concrete feel for what these settings mean, experiment with the current image. Begin by changing the contrast of the image.

> **Click** on the Contrast down arrow icon (3 times)

As you click the icon, white is added to the black tone bar and black is added to the white tone bar. To see the effect on the image without having to exit the dialog box, use the Apply option.

The image is changed to display mixed black and white screens in place of the solid black and white areas.

6 Adding Graphics to a Document

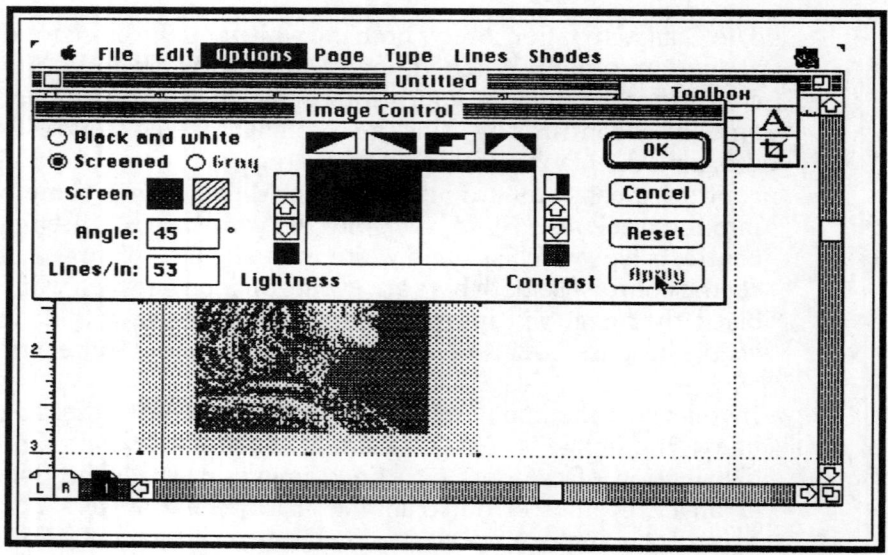

Figure 6.18   *Contrast between black and white altered.*

Change the overall lightness of the image by using the scroll bar labeled Lightness.

Click on the Contrast down arrow icon

Note that this option increases equally the amount of black in both tone bars. This will darken the overall image without changing the amount of contrast between white and black areas.

Apply the change to the image.

Click on Apply

The image darkens, but the contrast remains the same.

Change the display to a lined pattern.

Click on the line pattern icon

Adding Graphics to a Document **6**

The image does not appear to change very much; however, you can now use the line pattern options, Angle and Lines/in, to change the image. Enter

[Backspace] (2 times)
0

> **Click** on Apply

The image changes to one that is constructed of a series of horizontal lines. Enter

[Backspace]
90

> **Click** on Apply

The lines are changed to a vertical pattern. You can also change the number of lines used to print the image. The default is 53. The more lines, the finer the image; however, fine images take longer to print. Decreasing the number of lines causes the image to print faster but it will have a grainier appearance. Reduce the number of lines to 40 per inch. Enter

[Tab]
40

> **Click** on Apply

You can return to the original settings for this image by selecting the reset option.

6 Adding Graphics to a Document

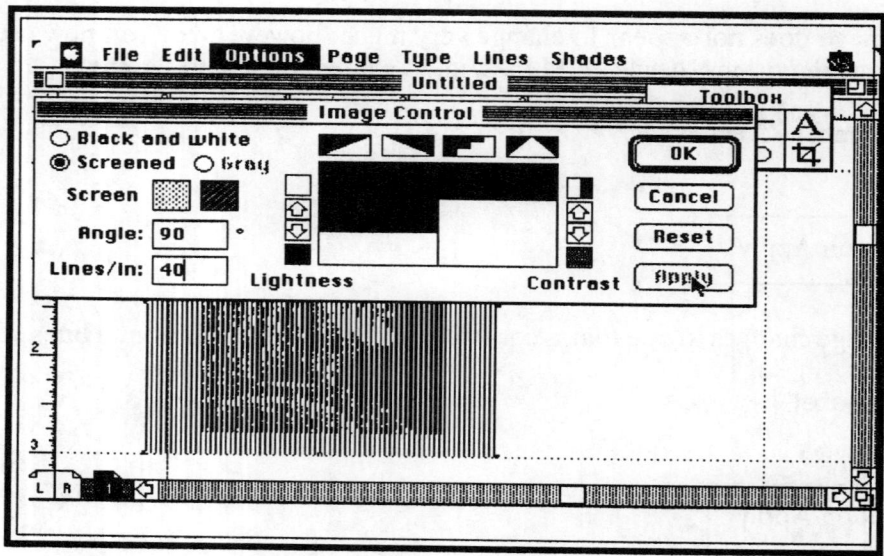

Figure 6.19   Graphic displayed as a line pattern image.

Click on Reset

The image is restored to its original appearance. Print the current image. Enter

**Command+p
[Return]**

If you are using an ImageWriter, press the Return key for the next two dialog boxes.

Click on OK

Adding Graphics to a Document **6**

TIFF Images

The TIFF image format provides PageMaker with an image that is scaled into 16 different tone areas instead of just two, as is the case with paint-type images. A 16-tone picture is closer in appearance to a photographic image than a paint-type image is because it can display 16 different patterns of black and white tones. This is not quite a complete gray scale, but it comes much closer than the black-and-white paint-type images.

Because the TIFF image can contain up to sixteen different patterns, as opposed to the paint-type pictures, which contain only two, the Image Control dialog box will show not two, but sixteen, different bars for TIFF images. These files are usually produced by scanning devices and stored in the TIFF format.

The **Photo.tif** file supplied with PageMaker on the Getting Started disk is a TIFF file and will show you how PageMaker handles TIFF images.

Create a new page in this document.

> **Point** at Pages
> **Drag** to Insert pages
> **Click** on OK

PageMaker inserts two new pages. Place a copy of the Photo.tif image onto both pages. You can leave one copy as it is when imported and then manipulate the second copy to give yourself a reference point from which to contrast the image you manipulate with PageMaker. Enter

Command + d

Select the folder that contains the Photo.tif file. If you installed the complete PageMaker setup on your hard disk, this file will probably be located in the Getting Started folder.

> **Double Click** on Getting Started

6 Adding Graphics to a Document

Scroll the file selector box until you locate Photo.tif.

> **Click** on Photo.tif
> **Click** on OK

The icon displayed is a solid gray block, indicating that the file is a TIFF format file. Place the image into the upper left corner of page 2.

> **Point** at the upper left corner of the guide on page 2
> **Click**

Repeat the process and place another copy into the top of page 3.

> **Point** at File
> **Drag** to Place
> **Double Click** on Getting Started
> **Click** on Photo.tif
> **Click** on OK

The icon displayed is a solid gray block, indicating that the file is a TIFF format file. Place the image in the upper left corner of page 3.

> **Point** at the upper left corner of the guide on page 3
> **Click**

You now have two copies of the TIFF image file.

Adding Graphics to a Document **6**

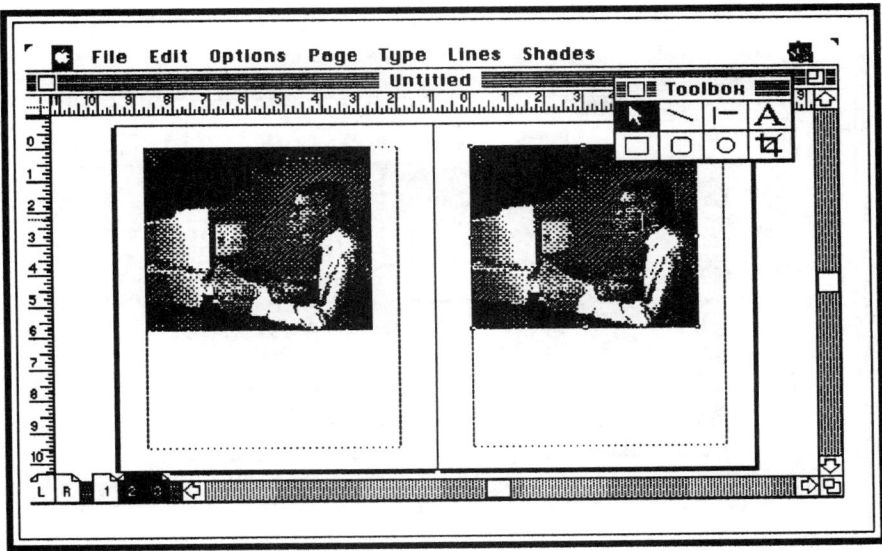

Figure 6.20   TIFF format images displayed on screen.

It is important to realize that the TIFF images will not show the smooth contrast between tones when displayed on a standard Macintosh screen. When you print the image on a PostScript printer, the printer will produce a much finer image than you see on the screen. The screen image is only a guide to the appearance of the final printed image.

To see the entire image while you are working in the Image Control dialog box, you can scroll the screen display so the images appear in the bottom section of the screen that is visible while the dialog box is displayed.

> **Click** on the up arrow icon on the vertical scroll bar (3 times)
> **Point** at Options
> **Drag** to Image Control

The Image Control dialog box appears, and the two images can still be seen in the bottom of the screen.

6 Adding Graphics to a Document

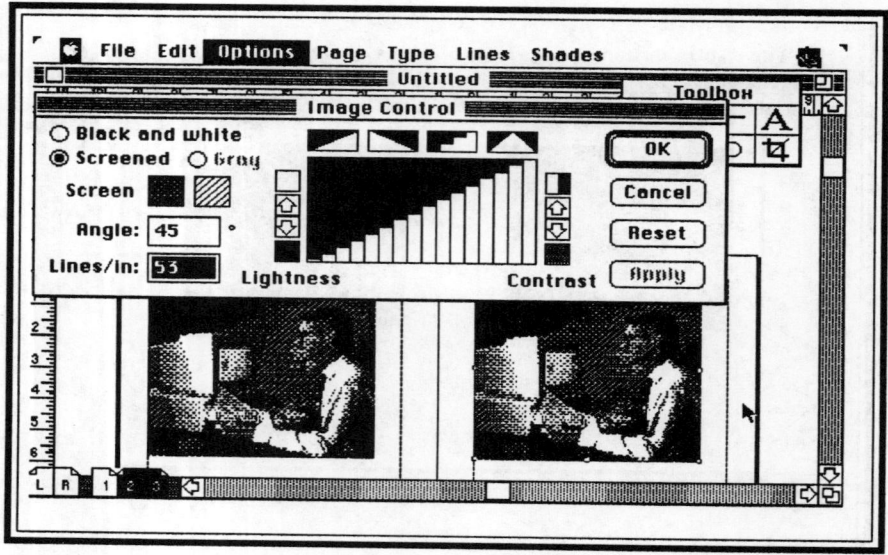

Figure 6.21   Image Control dialog box for TIFF images.

There are some significant differences between these settings and the default settings for a paint-type image. You will notice that PageMaker displays 16 tone bars inside the gray-scale box, in contrast to the two tone bars, black and white, that appear for a paint-type image.

The tone bars are arranged in an ascending order from the darkest to the lightest. The first bar on the left represents the darkest areas of the image, but even this bar is not solid black. This means that even the darkest areas in the image contain some white.

One of the options available for a TIFF file is the posterized option (the third icon from the left, above the gray-scale box). The posterized option combines several of the 16 levels so that the total number of levels is reduced to four tones, which creates a picture with stronger contrasts.

> **Click** on the posterized icon

Adding Graphics to a Document **6**

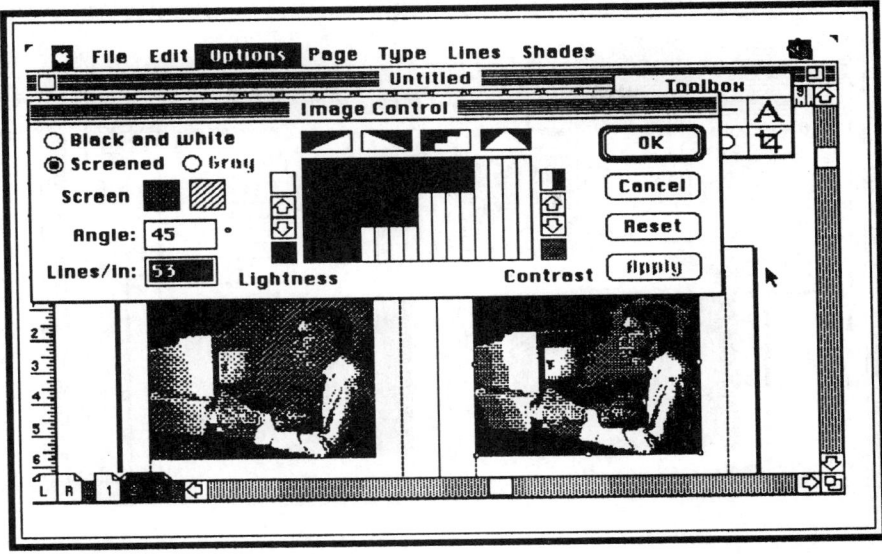

Figure 6.22   Image changed to posterized

The image on page 3 changes to show four tones instead of 16 tones. You would want to make this type of change if you were going to reproduce the printed page on a copying machine or similar device that has poorer resolution than your printer. Copiers will often muddy an image that contains many gray tones. The posterized option is a preset way of getting more contrast in the image.

Of course, you can manually override the preset posterized tone options by using the lightness and contrast scroll arrows to change overall lightness or contrast, or you can affect individual areas in the image by dragging the tone bars up or down.

For example, the four bars on the right of the scale are all set for full white. This means that the very light areas in the image will appear as all white. This will sometimes create a washed-out image. You can restore detail selectively by adding some black to the bars that are currently all white.

The same is true of the darkest areas, which are composed of all black bars. You can change the amount of white included in a tone area by dragging the white portion of the tone bar down to darken the area or up to lighten the tone.

> **Drag** the tone bars to the positions shown in Figure 6.23

6 Adding Graphics to a Document

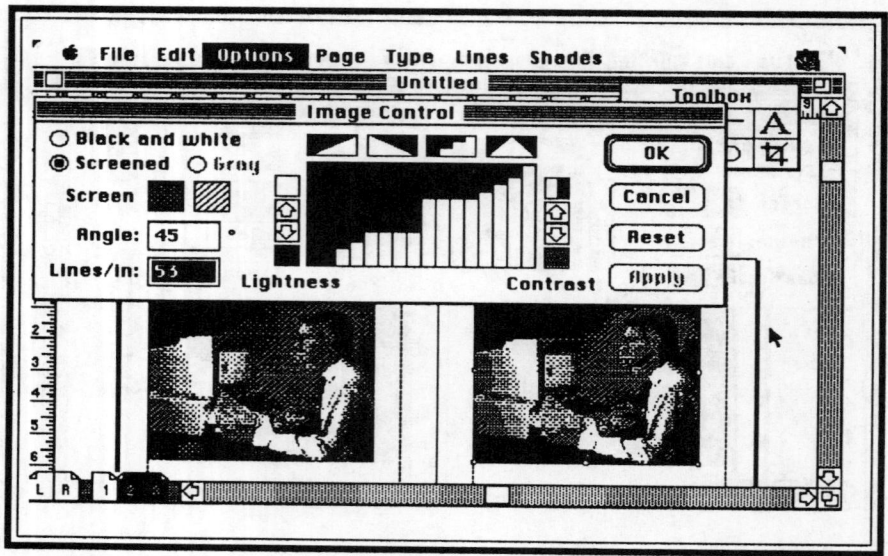

Figure 6.23   Manually setting tone contrast bars.

> **Click** on Apply

The image on page 3 now shows more contrast in the very dark and very light areas.

Return to the document and print pages 2 and 3. Enter

[Return]
Command+p

To print only pages 2 and 3,

> **Click** on From

Enter

2 [Tab]
3 [Return]

Adding Graphics to a Document **6**

The TIFF images show a greater variety of tones than the black-and-white paint-type images. In addition, the two TIFF images show a slightly different combination of tones, the result of the manipulations performed on the image on page 3.

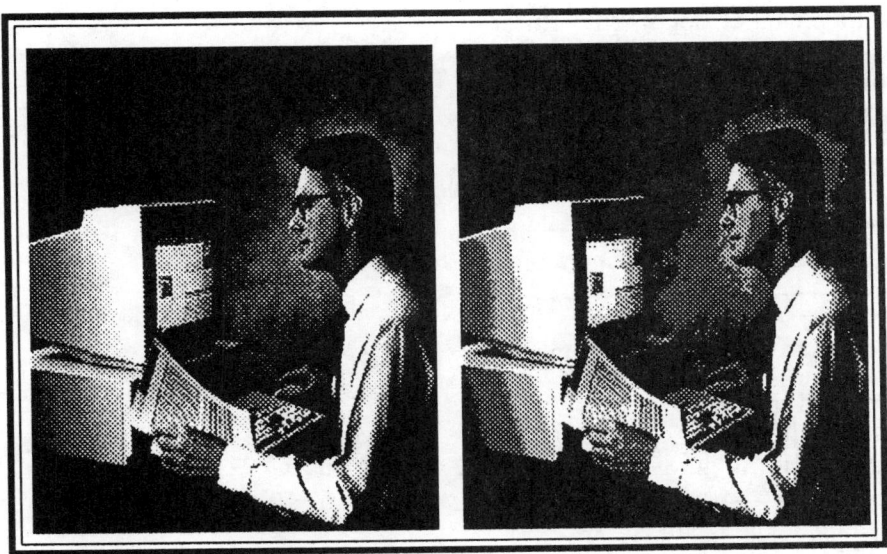

Figure 6.24   TIFF images printed.

Close the document without bothering to save these example images.

> **Point** at File
> **Drag** to Close
> **Click** on No

6 Adding Graphics to a Document

COMBINING TEXT AND GRAPHICS

The previous section explored the details of image control in PageMaker. Of course, the real goal of PageMaker is not to print isolated images but to integrate images with text to create complete documents. This section explores how you can create documents that combine picture and text elements. Begin by creating a new PageMaker document. Enter

Command+n
[Return]

Create a three-column layout for this document.

> **Click** on either master page icon

Set the format for three columns.

> **Point** at Options
> **Drag** to Column guides

Create three columns on each page. Enter

3 [Return]

You can now begin the process of adding text and graphics to the document.

A Repeating Graphic

Some documents require that a specific graphic, such as a logo or thumb tab, appear on each page. Suppose you wanted to print the profile face from the PageMaker logo at the top of each page. You could create this effect by placing the image onto the master pages. Each page would automatically display the image.

Begin by placing the image into the document. Enter

Command+d

Adding Graphics to a Document **6**

Change the folder to the top level of the start disk, which contains the Screen 0 image.

> **Double Click** on Screen 0

Place the image into the document.

> **Click** on the upper left corner of the guides

The image is placed into the document. Activate the crop mode.

> **Click** on cropping icon
> **Click** on the Screen 0 image

You can now crop the image so that only the profile is visible, as shown in Figure 6.25.

> **Drag** the lower right button to the lower right corner of the profile
> **Drag** the upper left button to the upper left corner of the profile

Now that you have cropped the image, change to the selection mode and drag it so it fits into the upper left corner of the guides on the left master page.

> **Click** on the pointer icon
> **Drag** the image to the upper left corner of the guides

6 Adding Graphics to a Document

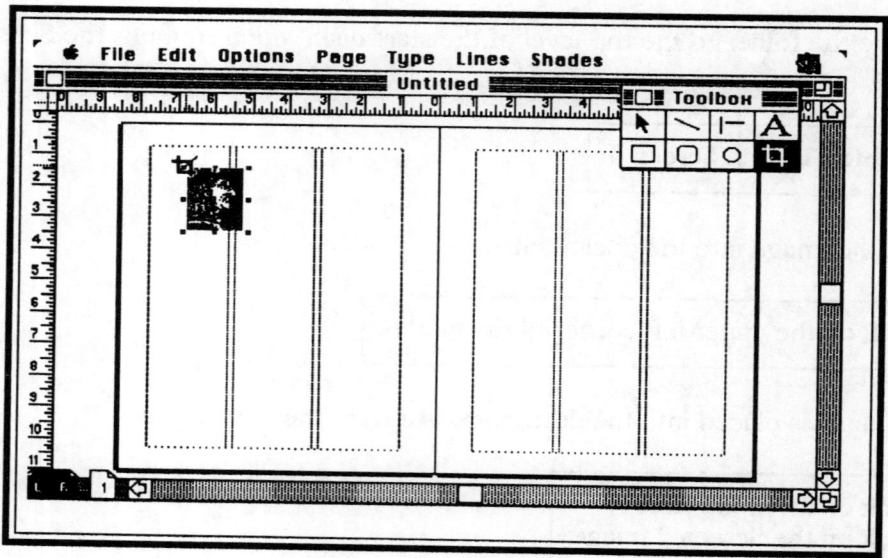

Figure 6.25   *Image cropped to show profile.*

Copying a Graphic

Along with the image positioned in the upper left corner of the left master page, you want to place the same image in the upper right corner of the right master page. You could place another copy of the original graphic into the document, but if you did that you would need to crop the full-sized image until you isolated the profile again. A simpler method would be to make a copy of the currently selected image and paste it back into the document. Copy the profile image into the clipboard. Enter

Command + c

Paste a copy of the image back into the document by entering

Command + v

PageMaker places a copy of the profile image back into the document. Images pasted back into a document are always placed in the center of the work area.

Adding Graphics to a Document **6**

You will want to place this image in the upper right corner of the guides in the right master page; however, the Toolbox palette probably covers that corner of the display. You can remove the Toolbox palette from the screen temporarily by using the Toolbox command on the Edit menu.

> **Point** at Edit
> **Drag** to Toolbox

With the palette removed, drag the image to the upper right corner of the guides on the right master page.

> **Drag** the image to the upper right corner of the guides

The master pages should now resemble Figure 6.26.

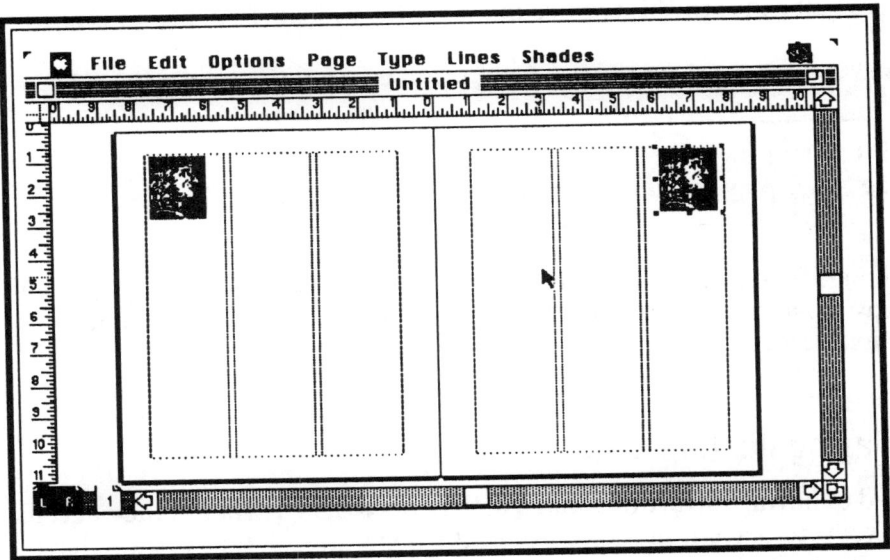

Figure 6.26   *Image copied onto right master page.*

6 Adding Graphics to a Document

Suppressing Master Page Items

You are now ready to move to the actual pages of the document. Enter

Command + Tab

PageMaker displays the first page in the document, including the graphic image that you added to the master pages. Frequently you will want the first page to have a different format from the other pages of the document. For example, you probably don't want the graphic image displayed in the upper right corner of page 1.

PageMaker solves this problem by allowing you to suppress text or graphics added to the master pages on any page of the document by using the Display master items command found on the Pages menu. The default setting for this command is on, meaning that master page items will appear. If you deselect this option, the master page items will not appear on the current page unless you specifically reset the Display master items command for this page. Keep in mind that the Display master items settings for each page or dual-page display are independent of each other. You can turn this feature on or off for whichever pages you want.

Here, you want to suppress the graphic image from the right master page.

> **Point** at Pages
> **Drag** to Display master items

The image is removed from this page. The column guides are not affected by the Display master items command—only text and graphics from the master pages are suppressed.

Displaying the Clipboard

Instead of having the profile image in the upper right corner of the page, for page 1 you want to place it in the center of the page. Recall that you still have a copy of the image in the clipboard. You can confirm this by displaying a window that shows the current contents of the clipboard.

Adding Graphics to a Document 6

> **Point** at Edit
> **Drag** to Show clipboard

The clipboard window shows that the profile is still stored in memory.

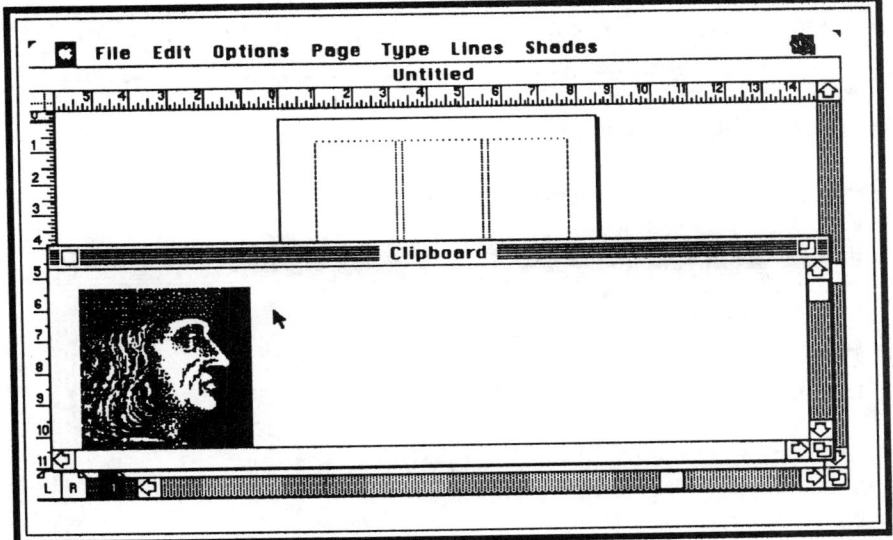

Figure 6.27   Clipboard windows reveal image is still in memory.

Return to the document window.

> **Click** on the document window

Paste a copy of the graphic back into the document.

Command + v

6 Adding Graphics to a Document

PageMaker places a copy of the graphic into the center of this page. Note that the graphic is a bit smaller than the column width. Fill the column width by dragging the lower right button on the graphic to the right column guide of the center column. To make sure that you do not distort the aspect ratio of the image, use the **Shift+Drag** technique, which means that PageMaker will limit the dragging to image sizes that maintain the correct proportions.

> **Shift+Drag** the lower right button to the center column's right guide

The image is centered in the page.

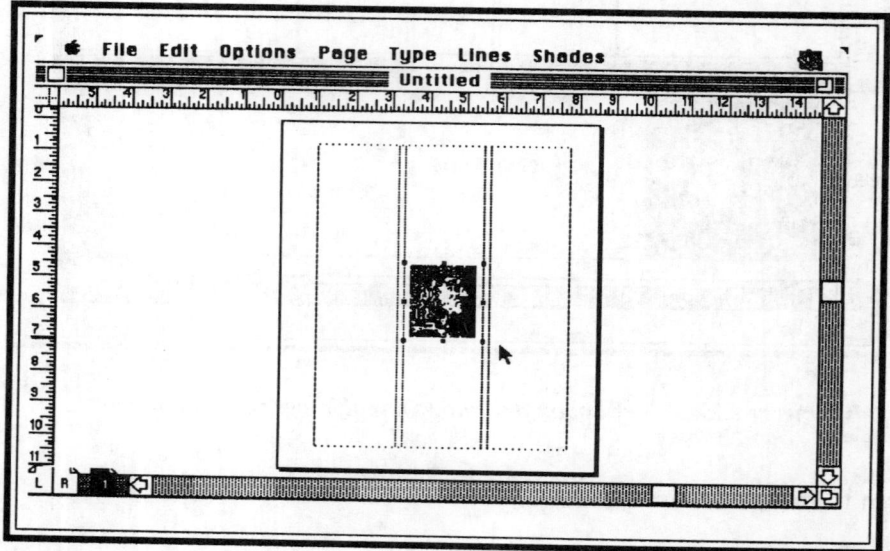

Figure 6.28   *Image placed in the center of the page*

Flowing Text Around a Graphic

With the image properly placed onto the page, you can now place text into the document. In this case, you will use the text from the Setup Corp document. You can also format the text by copying the styles used in the SBN Mar 89 newsletter document.

First copy the styles.

> **Point** at Type
> **Drag** to Define styles
> **Click** on Copy

Activate the folder in which you placed the SBN Mar 89 newsletter document. Copy the styles.

> **Click** on SBN Mar 89
> **Click** on OK
> **Click** on OK

Next, place the text of the Setup Corp document into the current document. Use the automatic flow method to place all the text in a single operation.

> **Point** at File
> **Drag** to Place
> **Click** on Setup Corp
> **Click** on Read tags
> **Click** on OK
> **Point** at the upper left corner of the guides
> **Command + Click**

PageMaker automatically flows all the text into the document; however, the text flows right over the graphic image placed in the center of the middle column.

6 Adding Graphics to a Document

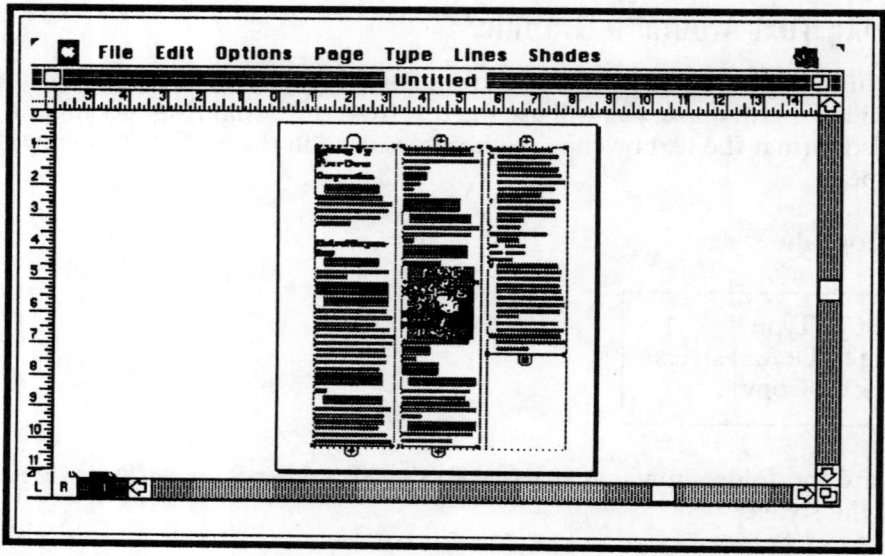

Figure 6.29   Text covers graphic image.

Each graphic carries a text wrap setting. This setting controls the relationship between text blocks and graphic images placed on pages. By default, graphic images are assigned the none option for text wrap, which means that when a text block conflicts with a graphic image, PageMaker simply overlays one with the other. Whichever item was on the page first is covered by the newly placed item. In this example, the graphic is covered by the text.

PageMaker allows you to automatically resolve these placement conflicts by assigning the graphic a different text wrap option. To do this, you must select the item and then choose an option from the Text wrap dialog box.

Select the graphic.

> **Click** on the profile image

PageMaker didn't select the item that you clicked on. Recall that when you flowed the text onto the page, PageMaker automatically placed the the text on top of the graphic. When you try to select the graphic, PageMaker doesn't react because you are actually pointing at the text block that is positioned on top of the graphic that is already selected.

Adding Graphics to a Document 6

There are two ways to solve this dilemma. One is to use **Command+b** to place the currently selected item, the text block, on the bottom of the object stack. Then you could select the graphic normally because it would be on top of the text. However, it is not necessary to actually change the order of the stacked items to select the graphic. PageMaker allows you to move through a stack of items by using **Command+Click** to select. Command+Click will select the next level item each time it is used on an area of a page that contains stacked items. Select the graphic, but this time use Command+Click.

> **Command+Click** on the profile image

This time, PageMaker moves the window shade handles off the text blocks and on to the graphic image. With the image selected, you can now use the Text wrap dialog box to separate the text from the graphic.

> **Point** at Options
> **Drag** to Text wrap

PageMaker displays the Text wrap dialog box.

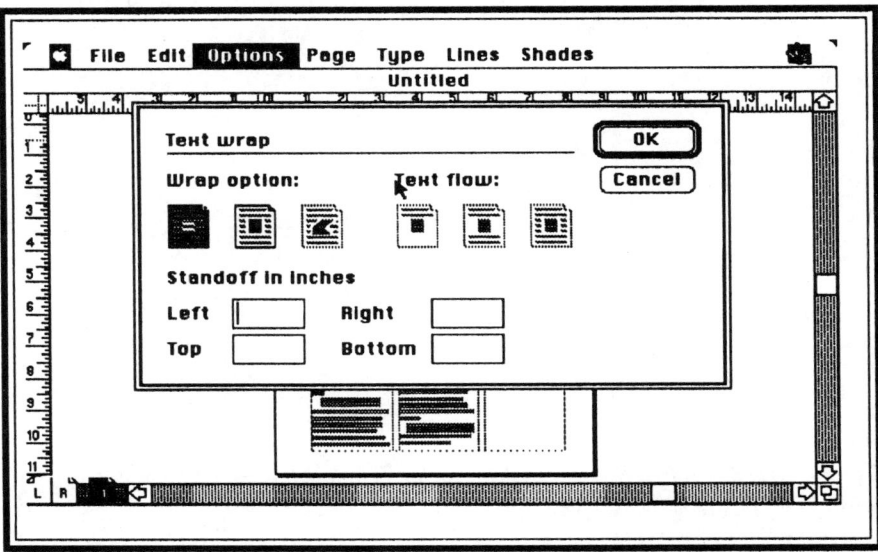

Figure 6.30   *Text wrap dialog box*

6 Adding Graphics to a Document

There are two major options in this dialog box — Wrap option and Text flow — each represented by three icons.

Wrap option   The Wrap option selection determines what happens when text and graphics encounter each other. The default action is **none** (i.e., the items are layered over one another) and is represented by the left-most icon under the Wrap option. The middle icon represents the **wrap around graphic frame** option, which causes text to flow around the graphic, keeping the two separate. The third icon is the **wrap around custom adjusted graphic frame** option. This option cannot be directly selected from the menu but can be created by manipulating the graphic itself.

Text flow   When the wrap around frame option is selected, the Text flow option determines where the text will resume following the graphic. The left-most icon under this option represents a **column break** option, which means that the text flow will resume at the top of the next column or page. The middle icon is the **jump over** option. With this option, the text flow resumes in the same column following the object. The last icon is the **all sides** option. This option allows text to flow around the sides of a graphic if the graphic is narrower than the column width.

Adding Graphics to a Document 6

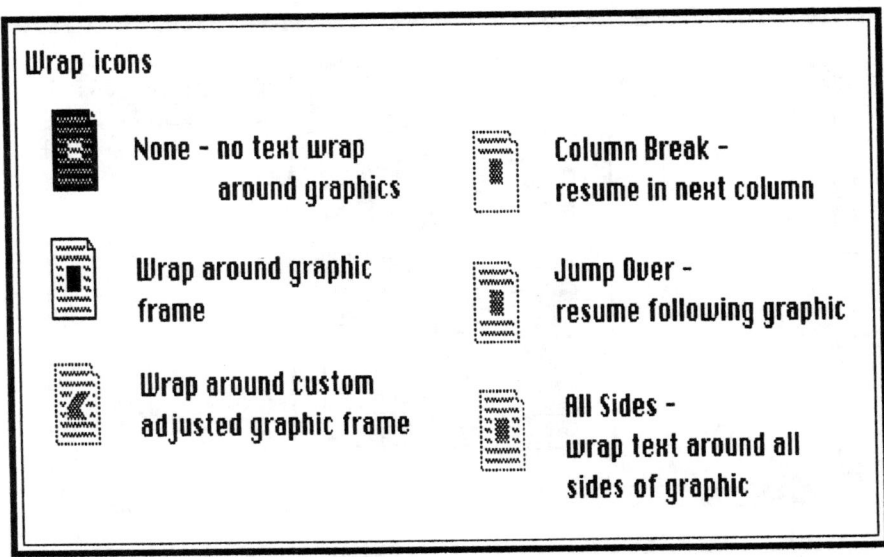

Figure 6.31   *Closeup of text wrap icons.*

> **Click** on the wrap around frame icon

When you select this icon, PageMaker automatically fills in the value for the Standoff in inches option. The **standoff** is an area of blank space surrounding the graphic that is added when the wrap around graphic frame option is selected. The default value is .167", about 12 points, on all sides of the graphic. In this case, increase the values to .25" on each side. Enter

.25 [Tab]
.25 [Tab]
.25 [Tab]
.25 [Return]

PageMaker rearranges the text blocks so none of the text overlaps the graphic. PageMaker uses the standoff values to add a border of blank space between the text and the graphic. Note that when wrap around graphic frame option is active, the graphic object has two sets of guides and buttons around it.

6 Adding Graphics to a Document

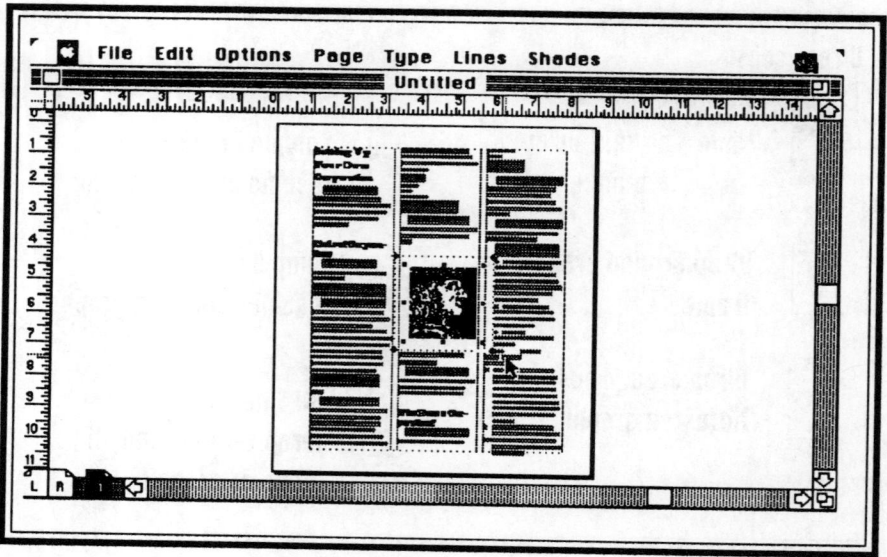

Figure 6.32   *Text wrapped around a graphic.*

The inner buttons are the graphic buttons that you have been using to size, move, and crop the graphic items. These buttons control the image.

The outer set of buttons is used to control the size and shape of the frame, including the standoff space. If you drag these buttons, you can change the size and even the shape of the frame used to flow text around the graphic. If you increase the size of the frame, the standoff space is increased and the text automatically flows around the frame, leaving more space between the text and the graphic.

Note that it is possible, but not the usual practice, to drag or reduce the size of the frame so that the frame does not cover all of the graphic. If you do this, the text block will flow over the part of the graphic that is no longer protected by the frame. If you display the text wrap dialog box in this situation, you will see a negative value entered for the standoff space.

Adding Graphics to a Document 6

Flow Around Master Page Items

To continue the document, insert a pair of new pages.

> **Point** at Page
> **Drag** to Insert pages
> **Click** on OK

Place another copy of the Setup Corp document onto page 2. Enter

Command + d

> **Click** on Setup Corp
> **Click** on Read tags
> **Click** on OK
> **Point** at the upper left corner of the page guides on page 2
> **Command + Click**

Again, the text flows over the graphic, but to correct this problem by setting the text flow around the graphic, you must select the graphic item first. In this case, that means going back to the master pages in which the graphic that appears in the corners of these pages is actually placed.

> **Click** on the master page icons

You can select graphics and set the text wrap specifications for the left and right page at the same time.

> **Point** at the image on the left page
> **Click**
> **Point** at the image on the right page
> **Shift + Click**
> **Point** at Options
> **Drag** to Text wrap

Select text flow around.

343

6 Adding Graphics to a Document

> **Click** on the text wrap around graphic frame icon
> **Click** on OK
> **Click** on the page 2 icon

The text is still placed over the graphic. As it turns out, settings for master page graphics do not affect text wrap on pages other than the master pages. In this case, you must manually move the text block so it does not to overlap the graphic.

> **Click** on the first column on page 2
> **Drag** the top window shade handle below the image

You have now manually prevented the overlap of text on a master page graphic.

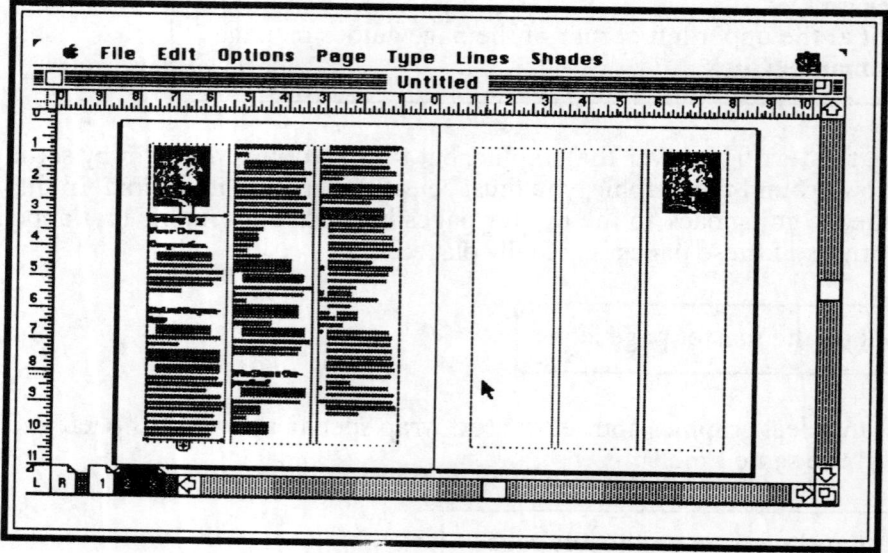

Figure 6.33   Master page graphic exposed on page 2.

Spreading a Graphic Across Pages

One of the advantages of a two-page layout is that you can place a graphic that extends across the left and right pages. This type of layout is frequently used in magazines.

Load the Photo.tif file into the document. Enter

Command + d

Change to the folder that contains the Photo.tif file, usually the Getting Started folder. Scroll the list until Photo.tif is displayed.

> **Double Click** on Photo.tif

If you want to place a graphic in the center of the current layout, you can have PageMaker locate the center for you. Remember, once a graphic is placed into the clipboard, it will automatically be placed in the exact center of the layout once it is pasted back into the document. You can take advantage of this by placing the graphic anywhere on either page. Then use **Command + x** to cut it from the document and place it in the clipboard. If you follow that command with **Command + v**, the graphic will automatically be placed in the center of the two-page layout.

> **Click** anywhere on either page

Enter

Command + x
Command + v

The image is placed in the exact center of the two-page layout. Set the graphic for text wrap around.

> **Point** at Options
> **Drag** to Text wrap
> **Click** on the wrap around graphic frame icon
> **Click** on OK

345

6 Adding Graphics to a Document

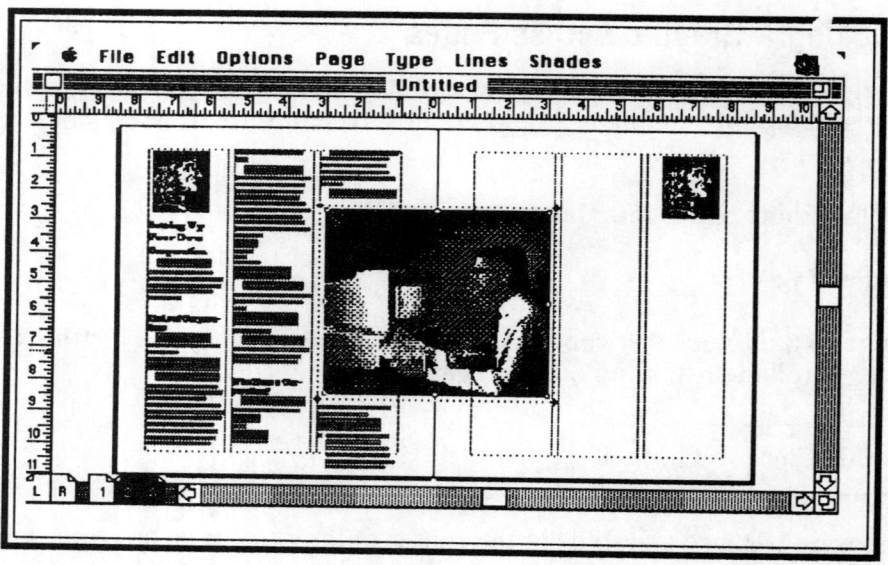

Figure 6.34   Text flows around graphic in the center of a two-page layout.

The revised text flow causes the last column on page 2 to extend past the bottom margin. Correct this by reflowing the text.

> **Click** on the third column text block
> **Drag** the bottom handle up to the bottom margin
> **Click** on the + in the bottom handle
> **Point** at the upper left corner of the guides on page 3
> **Command + Click**

The text flow continues around the graphic until the entire story is displayed.

Adding Graphics to a Document **6**

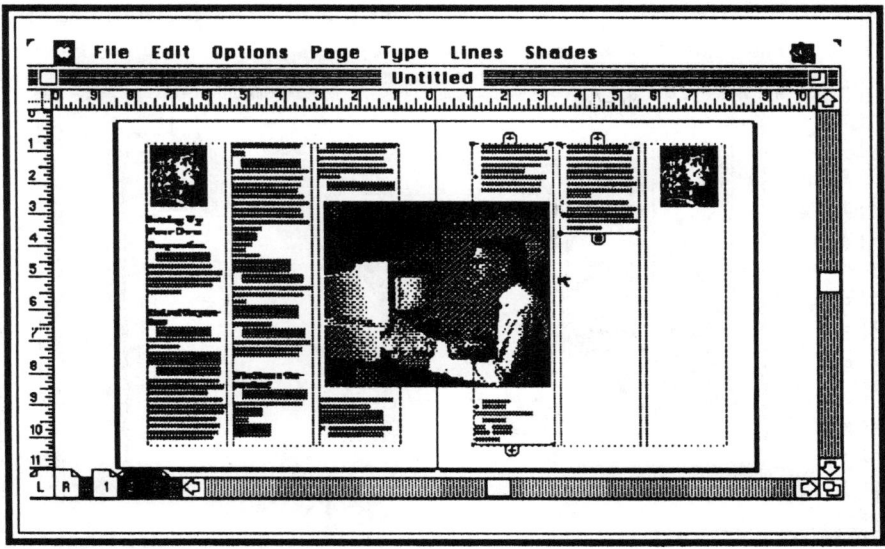

Figure 6.35   *Text flow completed around graphic.*

Framing a Graphic

Often you will want to surround a graphic with a frame in order to clearly mark off the graphic from the text. Suppose you wanted to draw a rectangular frame around the image in the center of the page.

Display the Toolbox palette.

> **Point** at Options
> **Drag** to Toolbox

Select the rounded rectangle drawing tool.

> **Click** on the rounded rectangle icon

Draw a rectangle around the center graphic, as shown in Figure 6.36.

> **Draw** rectangle around graphic (as in Figure 6.36)

6 Adding Graphics to a Document

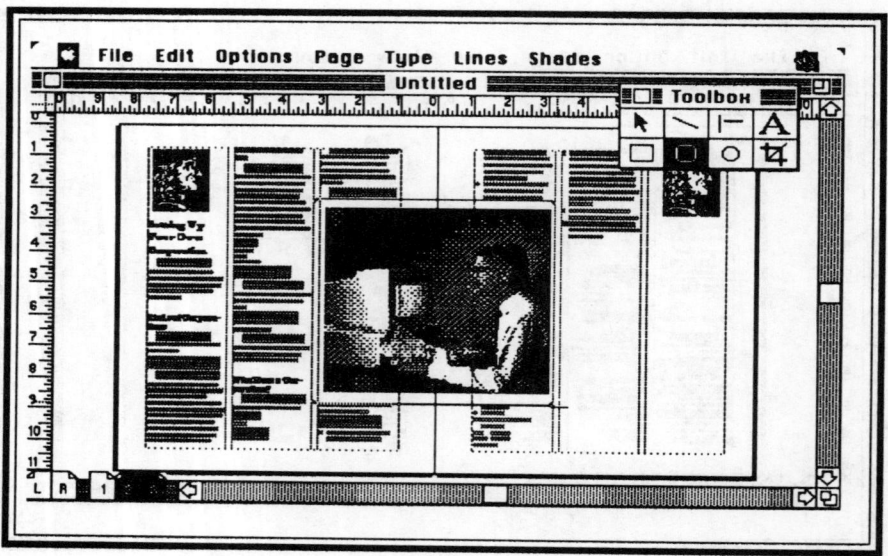

Figure 6.36   Rectangle drawn around graphic.

Set the line thickness to 8 points.

> **Point** at Lines
> **Drag** to 8 pt

The last step is to increase the standoff space to include the rectangle within the wrap text frame of the graphic.

> **Click** on the pointer icon
> **Click** on the graphic
> **Point** at Options
> **Drag** to Text wrap

Enter a standoff space value of .5" all around the image:

.5 [Tab]
.5 [Tab]
.5 [Tab]
.5 [Return]

The additional standoff space creates a text wrap that provides sufficient space for the graphic and its rectangular frame.

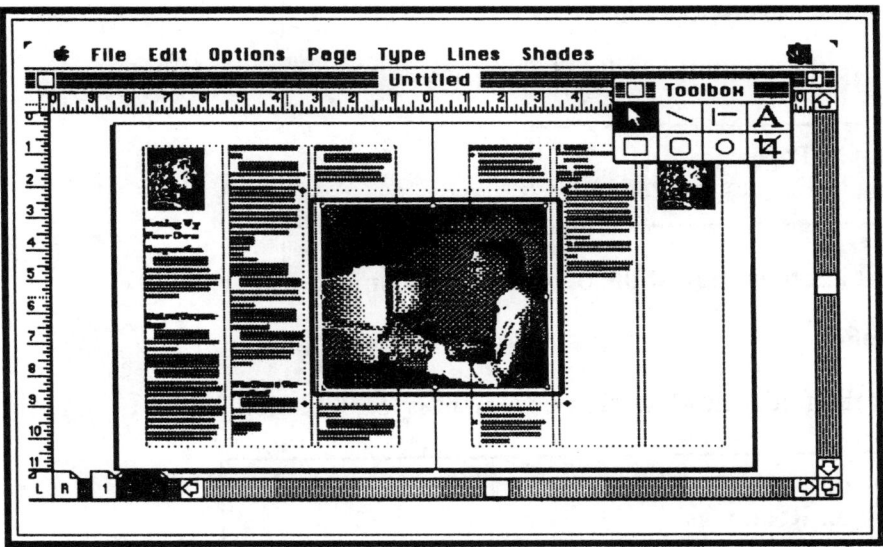

Figure 6.37   *Graphic frame increased to include rectangle.*

TEXT FLOW AROUND IRREGULAR SHAPES

Up to this point, all the graphics you have been working with have been rectangular in shape. PageMaker automatically creates a rectangular text wrap frame for each graphic. However, sometimes the graphic image is not rectangular, and you need to alter the shape of the frame to allow text to wrap around the irregularly shaped object.

The Tiles.eps file contains a graphic image that is not a rectangle. This image will illustrate how you can wrap text around objects that are not rectangular. Tiles.eps is an Encapsulated PostScript (EPS) image file.

Insert a new pair of pages.

6 Adding Graphics to a Document

> **Point** at Pages
> **Drag** to Insert pages
> **Click** on OK

Remove the master page items from these pages.

> **Point** at Pages
> **Drag** to Display master items

Import another copy of the Setup Corp document. Enter

Command + d

Select the folder in which that document is located.

> **Click** on Setup Corp
> **Click** on Read tags
> **Click** on OK
> **Point** at the upper left corner of the guides on page 4
> **Command + Click**

Next, import the Tiles.eps image file. Enter

Command + d

Change to the folder that contains the Tiles.eps file.

> **Click** on Tiles.eps
> **Click** on OK

In positioning the graphic, you will use a variation on the technique used before to place the item in the center of the layout. Before you perform the placement, change to a single-page display. This will prompt PageMaker to place the graphic in the center of page 4.

Adding Graphics to a Document 6

> **Point** at File
> **Drag** to Page setup
> **Click** on Facing pages
> **Click** on page 4 icon
> **Click** anywhere on the page

Cut and paste the image. Enter

Command + x
Command + v

Note that when you changed page setups, the master page graphic returned.

> **Point** at Page
> **Drag** to Display master items

Finally, change the text wrap attributes of the graphic.

> **Point** at Options
> **Drag** to Text wrap
> **Click** on the wrap around frame icon
> **Click** on OK

6 Adding Graphics to a Document

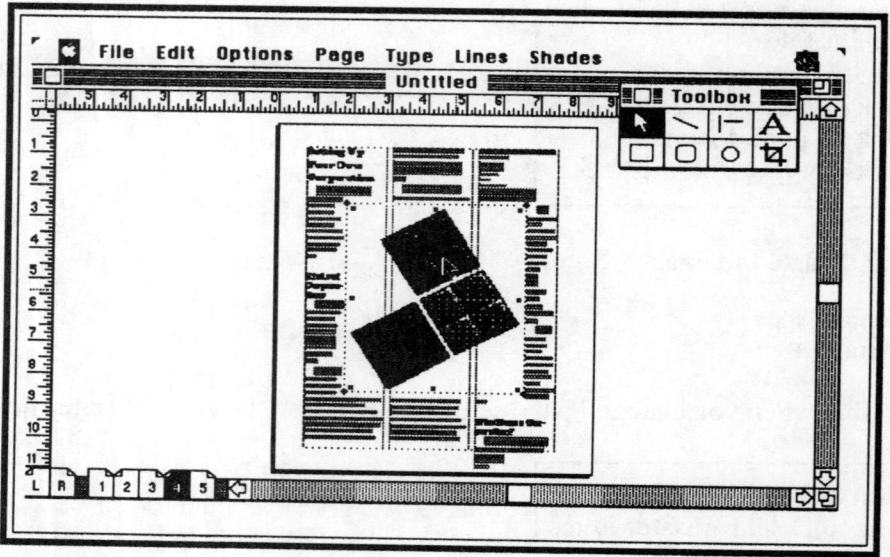

Figure 6.38   *Non-rectangular object placed in document.*

Manual Adjustment of Graphic Frame

Images imported into PageMaker are always treated as rectangular objects. This is logical if you think about how the graphics were originally created because when you create images with computer software you are working in a rectangular window. When you save a graphics file, the program saves the image and the frame of reference on which it was created. Thus, when a graphic whose shape is not a rectangle is imported, you also import a rectangular frame of reference along with it, which is what you see in Figure 6.38.

As noted previously, PageMaker allows you to alter the size of the text wrap frame around a graphic, independent of the graphic itself. This alteration includes reducing the frame size so the text wrap frame is smaller than the graphic. When the image is rectangular, this feature causes the text to flow over some portion of the image and should thus be avoided. But for images with a non-rectangular shape, you can make use of this feature because part of the image is simply blank space.

Adding Graphics to a Document **6**

You can allow text to wrap into these blank areas by manually altering the shape of the text wrap frame to more closely conform to the shape of the graphic. This can be done by dragging the diamond-shaped buttons that appear in the corners of the text wrap frame. Remember that these buttons are distinct from the square buttons that appear on the graphic image itself.

The diamond-shaped buttons do not affect the size or shape of the graphic; they only affect the text wrap frame around the graphic.

Begin with the diamond in the lower right corner of the text wrap frame.

Drag the lower right corner diamond to the bottom of the image (as in Figure 6.39)

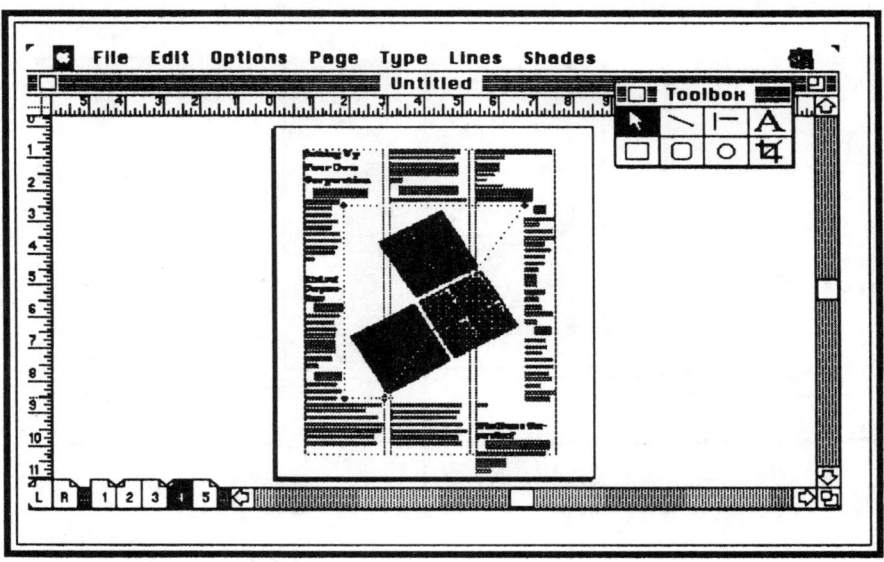

Figure 6.39   Frame changed by dragging diamond

6 Adding Graphics to a Document

You have reduced the area of the text frame, but the text does not seem to flow into the reduced area because of the order in which the items are stacked. Recall that the graphic was placed after the text, so the graphic image is on top of the text. When you changed the text wrap frame, the white portions of the graphic hid the text that had flowed into that area. To solve the problem, place the graphic at the bottom of the item stack. Enter

Command + b

You can now see that the text has flowed into the area that was opened when you reduced the text wrap frame.

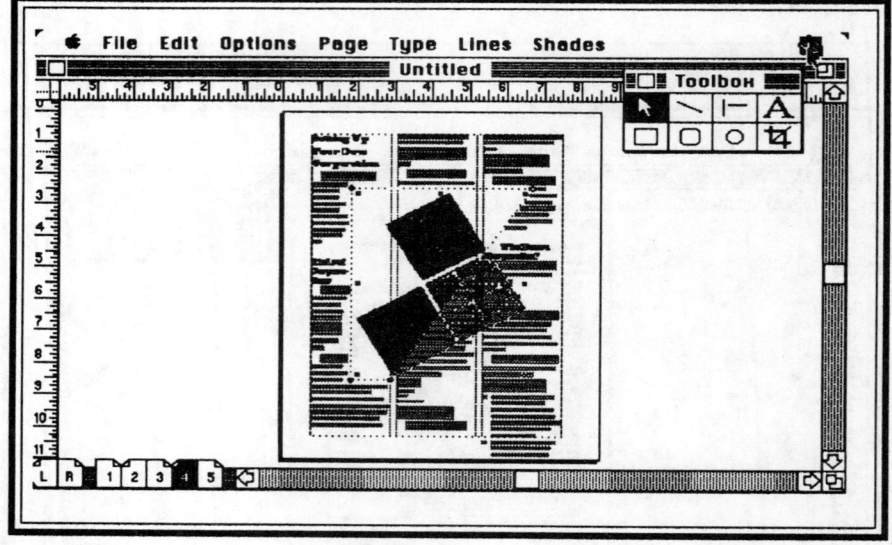

Figure 6.40   Text flows over graphic.

Adding More Buttons

The shape of the graphic makes it clear that the four corner diamond-shaped buttons cannot alter the shape of the text wrap frame sufficiently to fit the shape of the object. You can add as many additional buttons as you need to shape the frame the way you want.

Adding Graphics to a Document **6**

A new button is added by clicking the mouse at any point on the text wrap frame border. The current example requires you to add a button about midway on the diagonal line. You can then drag the new button to the corner of the graphic to align the text wrap frame with the side of the image.

> **Click** on the text frame line (as in Figure 6.41 — left side)
> **Drag** the new diamond to the corner of the image (as in Figure 6.41 — right side)

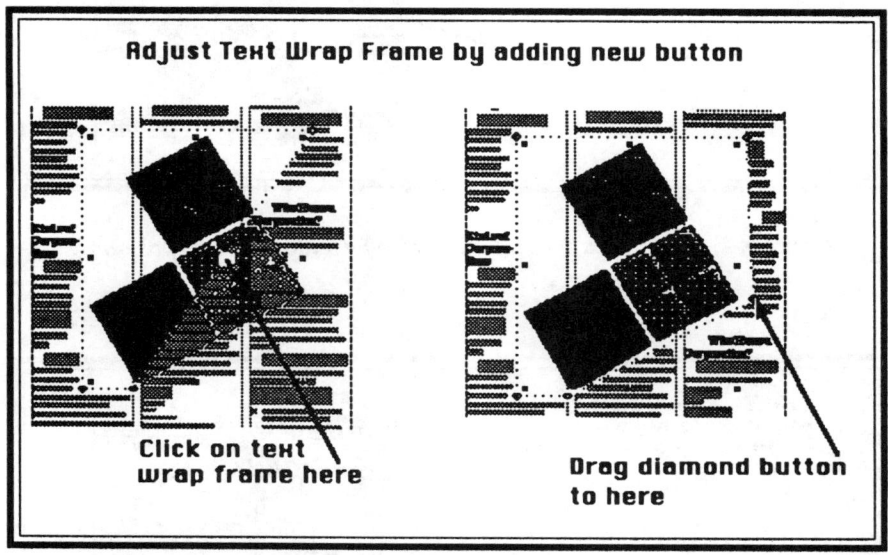

Figure 6.41   *Adding a new button and adjusting the text wrap frame.*

The next series of illustrations shows how the frame can be changed to exactly fit the shape of the graphic. Follow the five steps outlined in Figures 6.42-6.44.

355

6 Adding Graphics to a Document

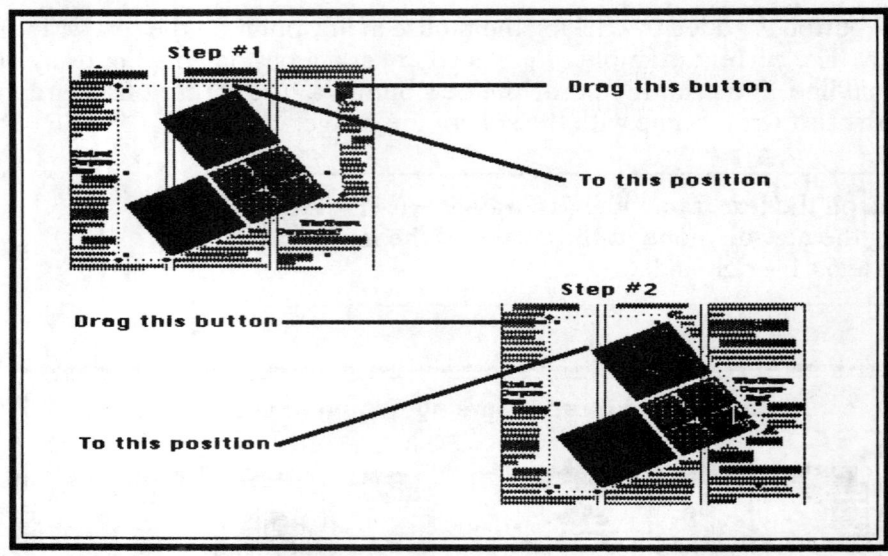

Figure 6.42   Steps #1 and #2: dragging buttons to new positions.

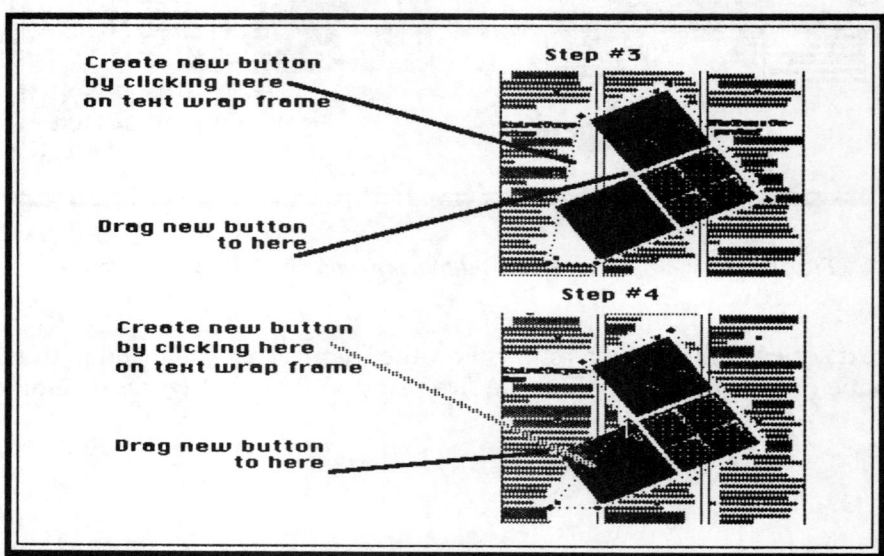

Figure 6.43   Steps #3 and #4: creating and dragging two new buttons.

Adding Graphics to a Document **6**

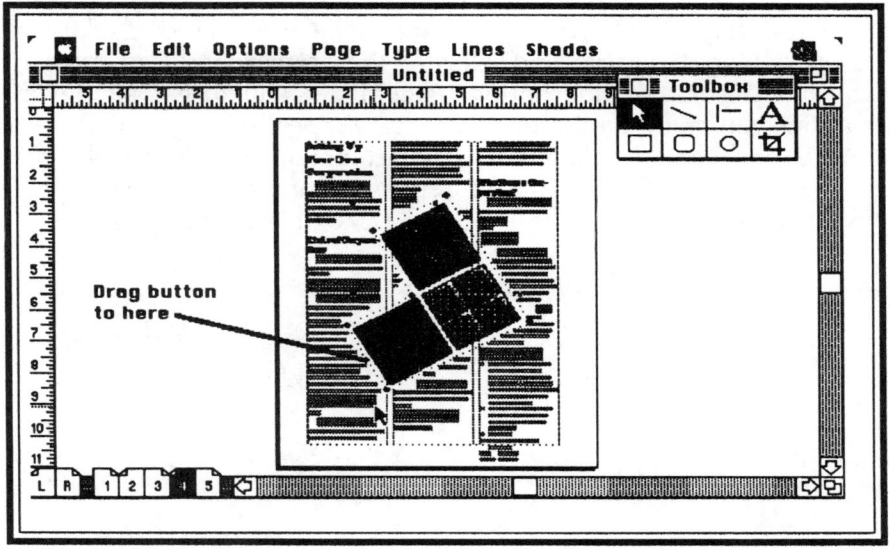

Figure 6.44   Step #5: dragging button to new position.

Print the document to see the results of these graphic operations. Before printing, you need to change the page setup back to facing pages because the graphic on pages 2 and 3 is spread over two pages. (If you are not in the facing pages setup when you print, only the half of the image that appears on page 2 will print.)

Point at File
Drag to Page setup
Click on Facing pages
Click on OK

Enter

Command + p
[Return]

6 Adding Graphics to a Document

You can restore the graphics text wrap frame to the original rectangular shape by using the Text wrap dialog box and selecting the wrap around frame icon. Note, however, that if you use this option, PageMaker will forget all the manual manipulations you made on the text wrap frame for the image. This operation cannot be undone with the Edit menu's Undo command, so it is probably best that you save the document first so you can return to the manually shaped text wrap frame by reloading the document if you don't like the rectangular shape.

Save the document and close the window.

Command+s
images [Return]

> **Point** at File
> **Drag** to Close

SUMMARY

In this chapter you learned how PageMaker deals with different types of graphic images.

- **Graphic Images**. Graphic images are images stored in files created by applications other than PageMaker. PageMaker can load four types of image files:

    Paint-Type. Paint-type images are also called **bit-mapped** graphics. They are the most common type of graphic image produced by applications such as MacPaint. These images consist of patterns of black and white dots.

    Draw-Type. Draw-type images are files that contain **vector graphics**, mathematical descriptions of graphic objects. This type of image is often called **line art**.

    TIFF. Tag Image Format File is a special form of bit-mapped graphic, in which 16 different levels of gray are recorded for the image.

    EPS. Encapsulated PostScript files are text files containing PostScript language instructions that can be translated into a visual image.

- **Sizing**. You can change the size and shape of the graphics imported into PageMaker by dragging the buttons that appear on each selected graphic. If you use the **Shift + Drag** combination, the size changes will maintain the original aspect ratio, i.e., the proportion of width to height in the original images. Normal dragging permits you to distort the proportions of the image.

- **Moving**. If you point at and drag any part of the image, with the exception of the buttons, PageMaker changes the position of the image on the page.

- **Cropping**. PageMaker provides a cropping mode. In the cropping mode, dragging a graphic's buttons does not change the size of the image but reduces the amount of the image displayed on the page. If you drag the image, the image remains in its current position on the page; however, the portion of the image that is displayed within the graphic frame is **panned** as you drag the image. The cropping mode operations allow you to display an isolated part of a larger image. Once an image has been cropped, it can be moved and sized in the selection mode.

- **Image Control**. Bit-mapped images — either paint-type or TIFF images — can be manipulated by the Image Control options in PageMaker. The image control options allow you to alter the black/white balance of each gray level used in an image — two levels in paint-type or 16 levels in TIFF images. You can also convert screen images into line-pattern images and choose the direction of the line pattern and the number of lines per inch to print the pattern. The Image Control dialog box also provides special gray level combinations that produce negative, posterized, or solarized images. Note that posterized and solarized images can be made for TIFF images only.

- **Text Wrap Around Graphics**. When graphics are placed into a document, you can use the Text wrap dialog box to create a text wrap around the graphic. You can select standoff width values, which create white space between the text and the graphic image. You can continue the text in the next column or page, continue it following the image, or have it flow around the image on all sides.

- **Text Wrap Frame**. Images that are not rectangular can have their text wrap frames adjusted to allow text to flow as closely as possible around the image.

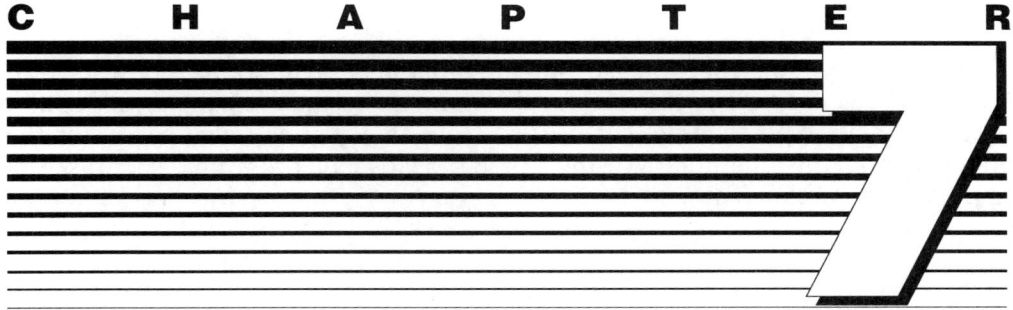

SPREADSHEETS AND CHARTS

U_p to this point in the book, you have been working with documents organized in text paragraphs with one or more columns on a page. Some documents are not organized in paragraphs but in rows and columns, such as spreadsheets (also called "worksheets," e.g., those created with applications such as Microsoft Excel.) Microsoft Excel can produce charts that provide a graphic illustration of data in a spreadsheet.

Although Microsoft Excel can create charts and tables such as spreadsheets, it cannot combine both text and graphics into a single printed page; however, that is exactly what PageMaker is designed for. In this chapter, you will learn how to take Microsoft Excel spreadsheet data and charts and combine them into a single PageMaker document.

7 Spreadsheets and Charts

This chapter assumes that you are familiar with the basic operations of Microsoft Excel. Microsoft Excel was chosen for this example because it is the most popular program of its type for the Macintosh. Note that you can also carry out the operations in this chapter by using other spreadsheet programs, such as Full Impact from Ashton-Tate.

CONVERTING A SPREADSHEET TO TEXT

Microsoft Excel stores spreadsheet data in its own special file format; however, you can save the spreadsheet as a text file. (Note that Microsoft Excel menus and dialog boxes refer to a spreadsheet as a "worksheet." For the purposes of this chapter, the two terms are identical.) PageMaker can read the text file version, which enables you to import the spreadsheet information into PageMaker.

Figure 7.1 shows a simple Microsoft Excel spreadsheet that consists of four columns and 13 rows of data. Create the spreadsheet shown or use an existing one of similar dimensions.

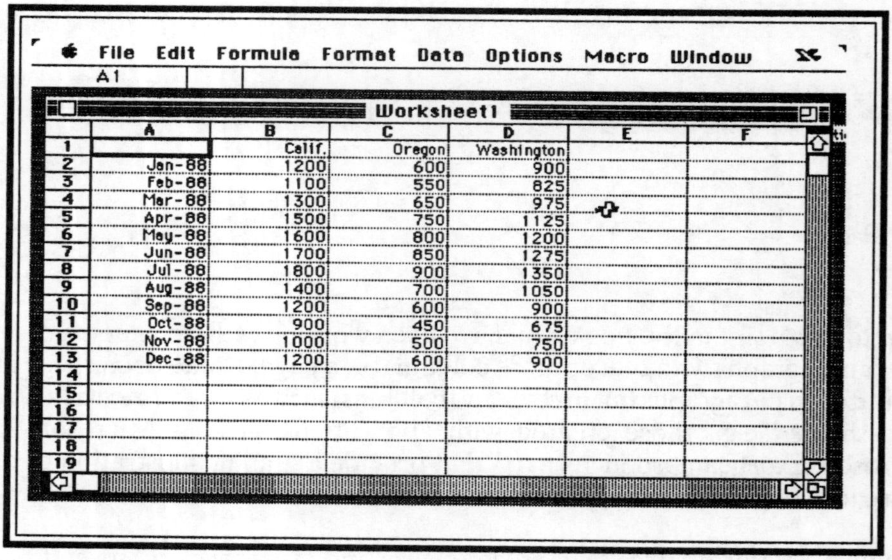

Figure 7.1   *Microsoft Excel spreadsheet table.*

Note that in using Microsoft Excel it is not necessary to enter all of the information manually. The dates in column A were generated by entering the first date, **1/1/88**, and then using the **Data Series** command to fill in the next 11 months. An **MMM-YY** format was used to format the dates. The values in column B were entered; however, columns C and D can be calculated using the formula **=B2/2** in C2 and the formula **=C2*1.5** in D2. You can use the **Edit Fill Down** command to copy the formula down the columns. Note that these instructions are not an attempt to fully describe how to work with Microsoft Excel; they are only notes about how this particular spreadsheet was prepared.

Save the spreadsheet as a text file that can be imported into PageMaker.

> **Point** at File
> **Drag** to Save as

Microsoft Excel displays the Save Worksheet as dialog box. At the bottom of the box are six options for the format of the file. The default option is Normal, which is the normal Microsoft Excel format.

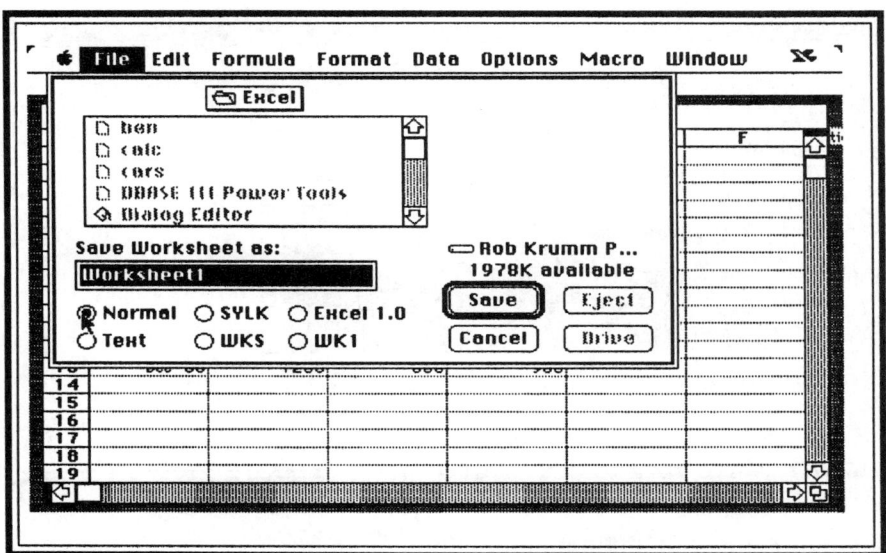

Figure 7.2   Microsoft Excel Save Worksheet as dialog box.

7 Spreadsheets and Charts

To create a file that can be accessed by PageMaker, select the Text format.

> **Click** on Text

Save the file under the name **worksheet text** by entering

worksheet text [Return]

CHARTS

Microsoft Excel can also create charts based on the data in the worksheet table. Figure 7.3 shows a typical chart that you can create with Microsoft Excel. Create a chart based on your Microsoft Excel worksheet. The exact appearance of the chart does not matter. An example chart is shown in Figure 7.3

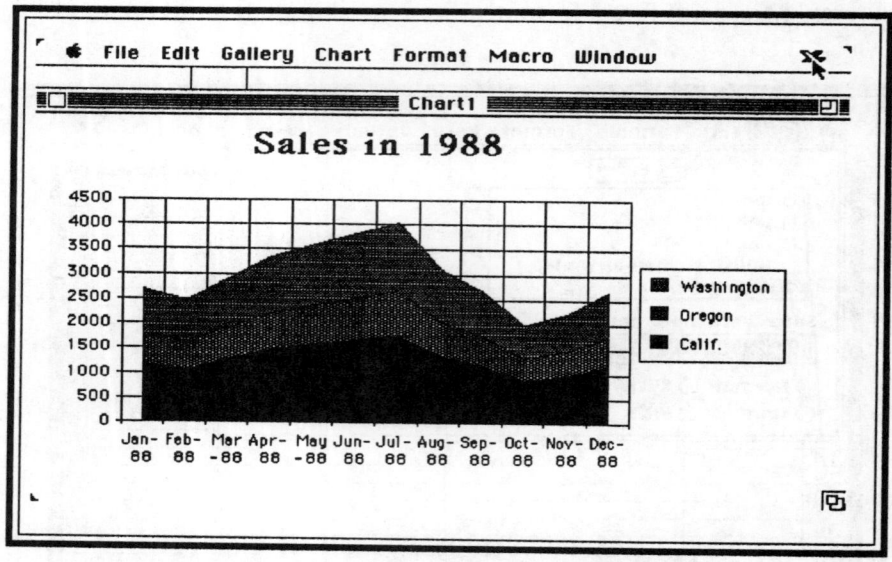

Figure 7.3   *Microsoft Excel chart.*

Spreadsheets and Charts 7

When the chart has been created, you can copy the chart into the Macintosh clipboard by using the Copy Chart command.

> **Point** at Edit
> **Drag** to Copy Chart

The command has two options: As Shown on Screen and As Shown when Printed.

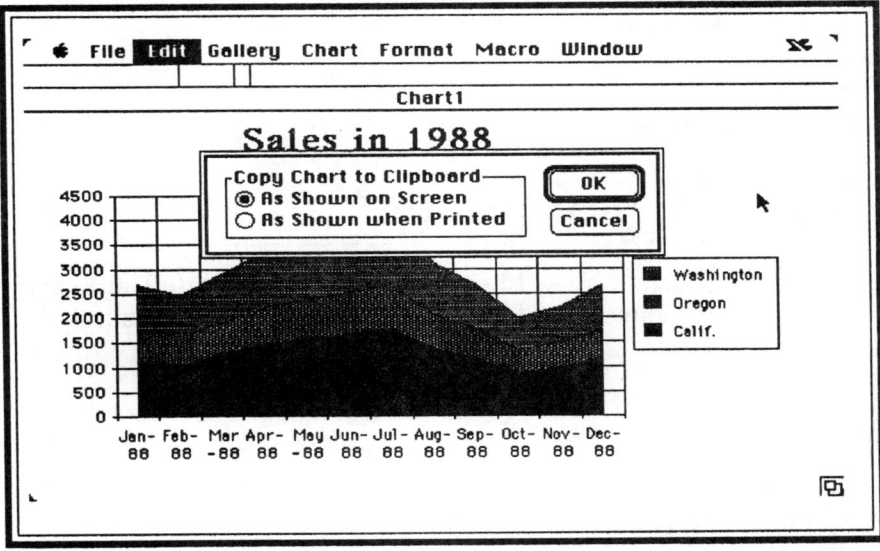

Figure 7.4   *Copy Chart to Clipboard options.*

As Shown on Screen copies the image of the chart as it currently appears on screen. As Shown when Printed copies the chart the way it will appear when it is printed. Because the shape and size of the window in which the chart is displayed affects the screen image, the As Shown when Printed option is a more consistent way to capture images.

> **Point** at As Shown when Printed
> **Click** on OK

365

7 Spreadsheets and Charts

The image of the chart as it appears when printed is copied into the Macintosh clipboard. Keep in mind that to transfer this image to PageMaker, you must refrain from copying or cutting other items into the clipboard until you have pasted the chart into the PageMaker document.

Exit Microsoft Excel and load PageMaker.

Create a new single-sided document. Enter

Command + n

> **Click** on Double-sided
> **Click** on OK

IMPORTING SPREADSHEET TEXT

The information saved as a spreadsheet text file can be imported into PageMaker in the same manner as any other text file — by using the Place command. Enter

Command + d

Change the folder select to the folder in which you saved the spreadsheet text file.

> **Click** on the worksheet text file
> **Click** on OK

Place the text into the document.

> **Point** at the upper left corner of the page guides
> **Click**
> **Point** at the top window shade handle
> **Option + Command + Click**

Spreadsheets and Charts 7

Enter

Command + 7

The spreadsheet text is placed into PageMaker as a block.

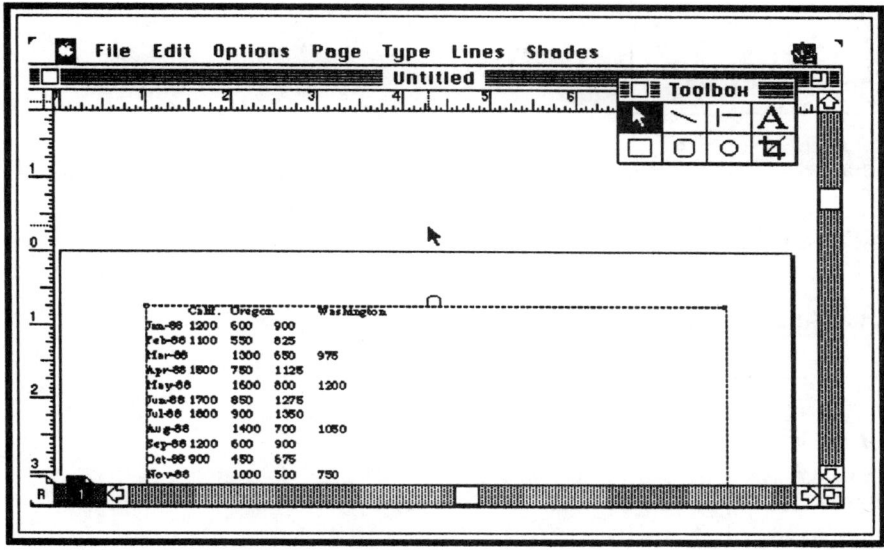

Figure 7.5   Spreadsheet data placed into PageMaker document.

The text that was imported appears as a series of lines and does not appear to align in columns because each item is separated from the others on the same line by a tab. Recall that PageMaker automatically sets the tabs stops at 5" apart. The default tab settings will not correctly align these columns. You must create a style that will format the text correctly.

Place PageMaker into the text mode.

> **Click** on the text icon
> **Click** on "Washington"

7 Spreadsheets and Charts

Select all of the text for formatting.

Command + a

Display the Define styles dialog box.

> **Point** at Type
> **Drag** to Define styles
> **Click** on New

Create a new style called worksheet based on the Body text style. Enter

worksheet [Tab]
Body text

Begin by selecting the type specifications

> **Click** on Type
> **Point** at Size
> **Drag** to 14
> **Click** on OK

Next set the tab stops.

> **Click** on Tabs

Clear all of the existing tab stops.

> **Click** on Clear

Set the tab types to decimal tabs.

> **Click** on Decimal

Set tabs at 3", 4.5", and 6".

> **Click** on 3"
> **Click** on 4.5"
> **Click** on 6"

Indent the left margin 1".

> **Drag** the left margin icon to 1"

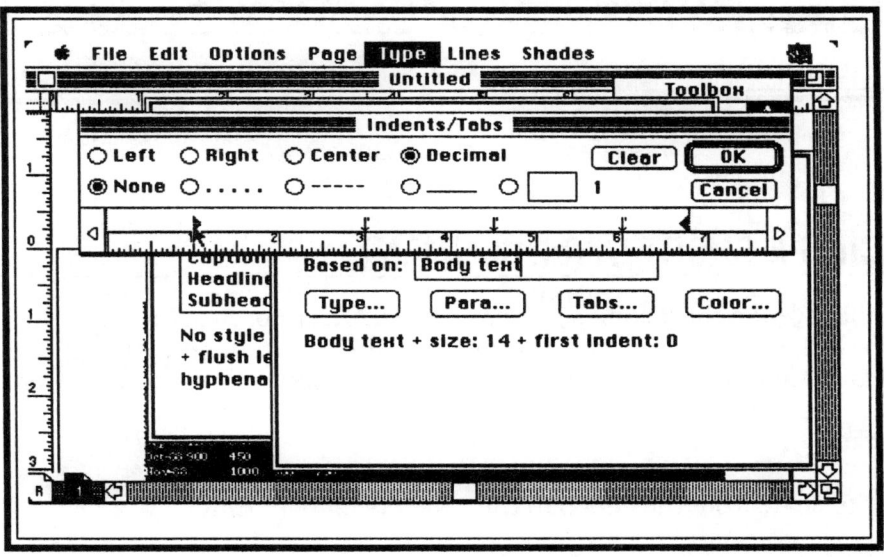

Figure 7.6   Tabs set for alignment of text in columns.

Return to the document window by entering

[Return] (3 times)

The text is aligned in columns similar to the alignment of the information in the original spreadsheet.

7 Spreadsheets and Charts

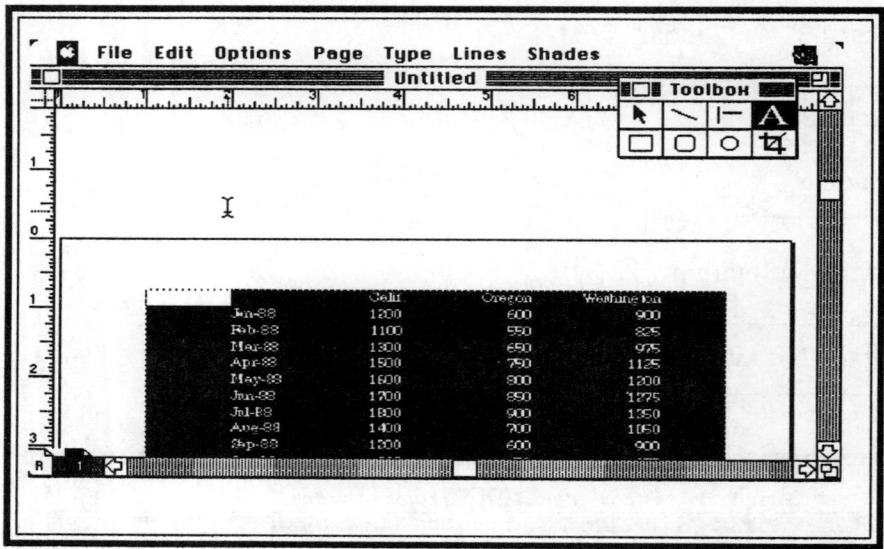

Figure 7.7   Text aligned in columns.

PLACING A CHART IN A DOCUMENT

You still have the chart copied from Microsoft Excel stored in the clipboard. You can place that chart onto the current page of the document by using the paste command, **Command+v**. Change to the Fit to window display mode by entering

Command+w

Paste the chart from the clipboard into the document. Enter

Command+v

The chart from the clipboard is placed into the document.

Spreadsheets and Charts 7

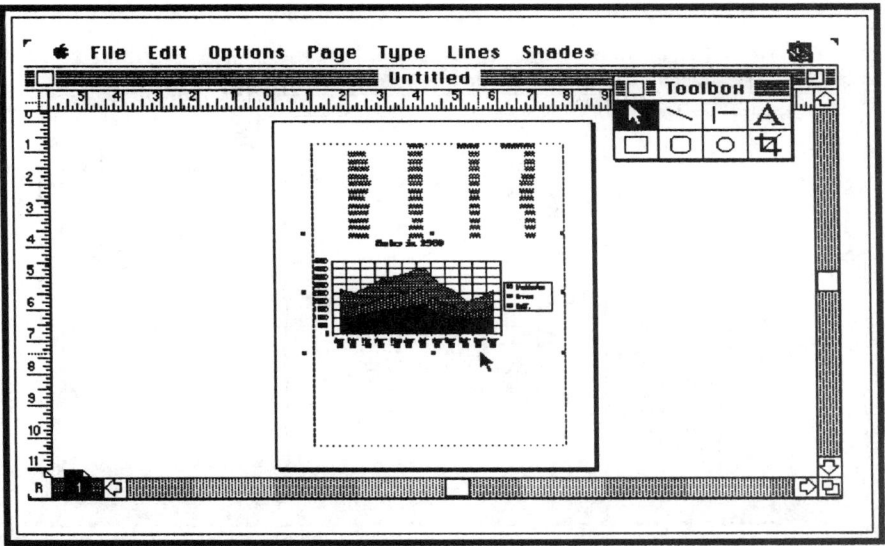

Figure 7.8   Chart copied into document.

You can position the image just as you would any other graphic image in PageMaker.

> **Drag** the chart to the position shown in Figure 7.9

Print the document. Enter

Command+p
[Return]

If your printer is an ImageWriter, press the Return key for the additional dialog boxes. Save the document and close the window. Enter

Command+s
worksheet [Return]

> **Point** at File
> **Drag** to Close

7 Spreadsheets and Charts

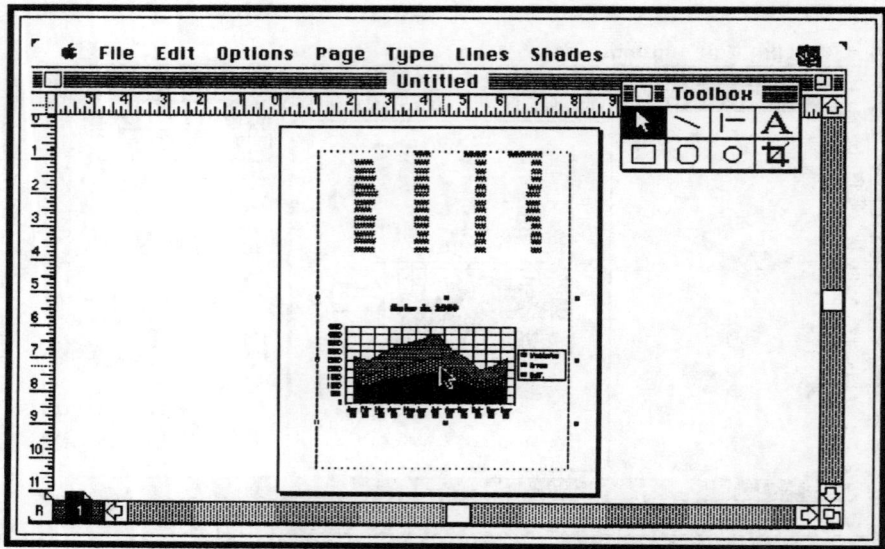

Figure 7.9   Chart repositioned on page.

SUMMARY

Information such as data and charts can be imported from spreadsheet programs such as Microsoft Excel into PageMaker.

- **Text**. The Microsoft Excel **Save as** command allows you to store the information from a spreadsheet in a text format that can be placed into PageMaker.

- **Charts**. Microsoft Excel does not save charts in a format that can be read by PageMaker; however, charts can be imported by copying them into the clipboard using the **Copy Chart** command. Note that this means that you can import only one chart at a time.

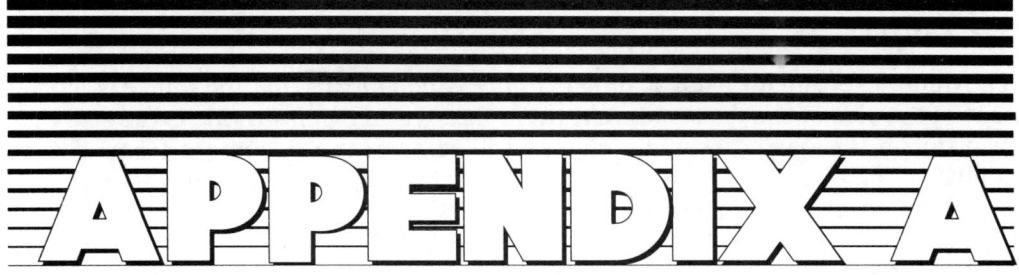

ADDITIONAL PRINTING OPTIONS

This appendix contains some additional information about printing options available in PageMaker. Note that this appendix does not contain a full lesson on each item discussed. It is meant to serve as reference material on the subject of printing.

Appendix A: Additional Printing Options

SCALING

The default setting for print scaling is 100%, which means that the image will print so that the size of the characters shown in the Actual display mode is the size they print at on the page. You can change the scale of the document from 25% to 1000%. The effect is similar to reducing or enlarging a photograph, except that there will be no loss of resolution.

Keep in mind that when using values greater than 100%, it is possible to exceed the image area of the printer, thereby losing part of the printed image.

Scaling is useful when you need to reduce or enlarge a document without changing the actual layout. When a document is scaled, all of the elements in the document maintain their proportions to one another.

SUBSTITUTE FONTS

You may have noticed that not all of the font selections you make with PageMaker result in the same quality of print. For example, text that is printed in the Times font has a smooth, more well-formed appearance than text printed in the Geneva font. This is because the fonts that are listed actually fall into two different categories: downloaded bit-mapped fonts and PostScript-resident fonts.

Downloaded bit-mapped fonts These fonts are supplied with the Macintosh system. They are designed to print on any of the printers available for the Macintosh. When you choose to print one of these fonts, the Macintosh sends a description of the characters in that font to the printer. This process is called **downloading**. Downloading is a process very much like copying a file. Instead being copied onto another disk, the information is placed into the memory of the printer. What is significant for PageMaker users who have laser printers is that the type of font description that is downloaded is a bit-mapped graphic image similar to the paint-type graphic images discussed in Chapter 6. The resolution of these fonts is usually less than that of the PostScript-resident fonts.

PostScript-resident fonts

PostScript printers are supplied with a number of fonts, typically 35 or more, that are resident in the printer. Note that in this usage the term "font" refers to a combination of type style and font. For example, Times, Times Italic, Times Bold, and Times Bold Italic would be considered four different resident fonts. Resident fonts have two advantages. First, because they are built into the printer, they avoid any delays caused by downloading fonts from the Macintosh system. Second, the fonts print at a higher resolution than the fonts that are downloaded from the Macintosh system.

While the Macintosh system has great flexibility when it comes to fonts, these two types of fonts can be a bit confusing because the font menus do not make a distinction between them. In addition, not all of the resident fonts available from the printer appear in the font list. You must use the Font/DA Mover program to add the names of fonts available in your printer to the font lists that appear in your applications such as PageMaker.

The Substitute fonts option, if selected, will cause PageMaker to automatically substitute resident fonts for downloaded fonts when the document is printed. PageMaker will normally make the following substitutions.

Font	Substitute
New York	Times
Monaco	Helvetica
Geneva	Courier

Note that PostScript-compatible downloadable fonts can be purchased from vendors such as Adobe or Bitstream. Although these fonts are downloaded, they are compatible with the PostScript language and produce fonts with the same resolution as the built-in fonts.

Appendix A: Additional Printing Options

POSTSCRIPT PRINT OPTIONS

A special series of options is available if you are using a PostScript printer. The options are listed on a special dialog box that appears if you **Option + Click** on OK in the normal Print dialog box.

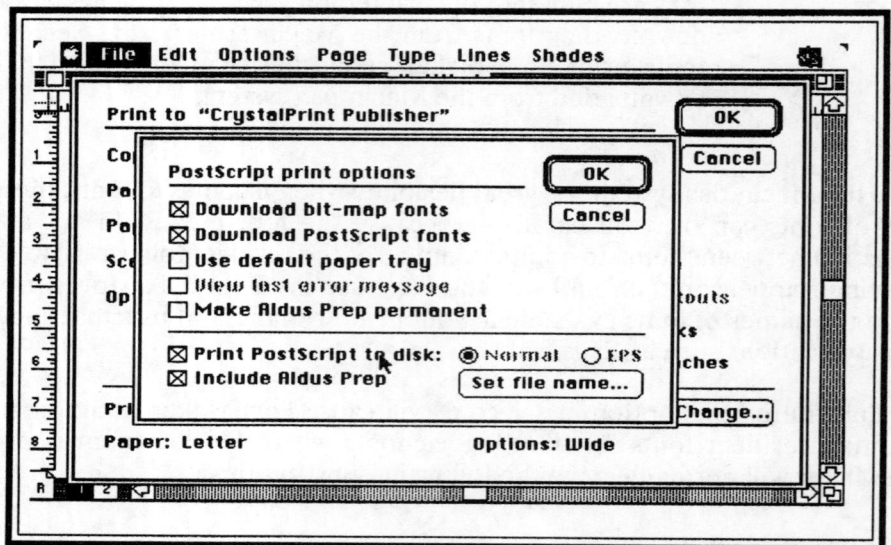

Figure A.1   *PostScript print options dialog box.*

The options in the top part of the menu control aspects of the PostScript printing process. The two most significant options are the first two options, which control the downloading process. These options determine whether fonts will be downloaded during the print process.

You can set the downloading option separately for bit-mapped fonts and PostScript fonts.

PostScript Printer Files

The bottom section of the PostScript options menu is used to create **PostScript Printer Files**. These files are important for two reasons. PostScript files are a handy means for providing professional printers with an electronic version of your document, which can the be printed at high resolution on phototypesetting equipment such as Linotronic 100 or 300 typesetting machines.

You can also use PostScript files to create graphic images (Encapsulated PostScript format) of your PageMaker document pages.

PREPARING FILES FOR PHOTO TYPESETTING

PageMaker uses the PostScript system for printing. If you are using a laser printer with PageMaker, the printer uses the PostScript page description language to print your documents. This means that when you send a document to the printer (e.g., the LaserWriter), PageMaker translates all of the items placed on each page — text and graphics — into a computer program written in the PostScript page description language. The program consists of text sentences that the printer is able to read and understand. Printers that work with PostScript actually contain a small computer that reads and executes these commands and in so doing creates the actual printed document.

It is important to understand a bit about PostScript in order to take advantage of one of its most important features — **printer independence**. Printer independence refers to the fact that once you have created a PostScript-compatible file based on a document, that file can be printed on any PostScript printer or typesetter. The printer can adjust the PostScript operations to produce printing at the highest resolution possible with that printer. This means that even if you create a document using a LaserWriter at 300-dots-per-inch resolution, the same document can be printed on a Linotronic 100 that has a resolution of 1200 dots per inch.

Appendix A: Additional Printing Options

To create a PostScript file, select the Print PostScript to disk option. The Include Aldus Prep option is related to whether or not the file will be printed on a printer that has the Aldus Prep information already loaded into it or not. Aldus Prep is a dictionary of operations that prepares a PostScript printer to print a PageMaker document. Including Aldus Prep in your disk files will cause them to be larger than if you choose not to include that information. On the other hand, if you are not sure that the printer on which you will eventually have the files printed will have the Aldus Prep present, you should include it in the file. The default setting is to include the Aldus Prep.

When creating a printer file, you should make sure that the Normal button is selected.

PageMaker will automatically generate a file name, e.g., PostScript01, PostScript02, etc. If you want to enter a file name of your own, click on the Set file name option. You can also select a folder for the print file.

Once the files have been created, they can be copied to floppy (removable) disks or transmitted via modem to a typesetter for processing. Keep in mind that the typesetter does not need to have PageMaker in order to print the printer files. Also note that you cannot load these files back into PageMaker. You can only load regular PageMaker documents into PageMaker for editing or revision.

ENCAPSULATED POSTSCRIPT (EPS) GRAPHICS

You can convert any single page of a PageMaker document into an Encapsulated PostScript (EPS) graphics image file by using the PostScript options menu.

First, you must choose to print a single page by selecting the From option on the normal print menu and specifying a single page, e.g., From 12 to 12. If you include more than a single page, the file will not have the proper format to be loaded as a graphic.

Once you have selected the page to capture, activate the PostScript options menu by using **Option+Click** on OK in the Print dialog box.

Select the Print PostScript to disk option. Then select EPS to designate that you want to create an EPS graphics file.

In most cases, you should eliminate the downloading of bit-mapped and PostScript fonts. Downloading Macintosh bit-mapped fonts such as Geneva or New York will cause an error when you attempt to load the graphic into PageMaker.

You can use the Set file name option to select a file name for the graphic, or you can allow PageMaker to automatically generate the file name for you.

The resulting file can be loaded into PageMaker as a graphic, using the Place command just as you would with any other EPS graphic file.

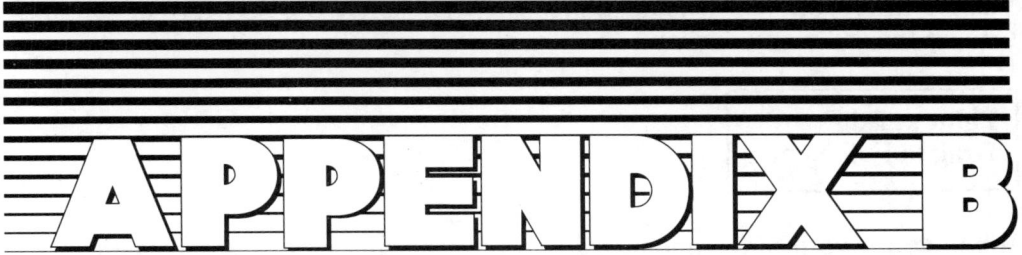

NOTES FOR MICROSOFT WORD VERSION 4 USERS

If you are using Microsoft Word version 4, released in the spring of 1989, you need to save your text as a Microsoft Word 3.01 document because PageMaker 3.0 cannot read the newer Microsoft Word text file format. This appendix shows you how to do just that.

Appendix B: Notes for Microsoft Word Version 4 Users

To save Microsoft Word 4.0 documents in Microsoft Word 3.01 format you must turn on the full menu display.

> **Point** at Edit
> **Drag** to Full menus

When you save the document, use the Save as command instead of the Save command.

> **Point** at File
> **Drag** to Save as

In the bottom left corner of the Save as dialog box, you will see the File Format button. This button allows you to change the file format.

> **Click** on File format

Select the format option labeled 3.0/ Microsoft Write.

> **Click** on 3.0/ Microsoft Write

Also, select the Default format for file option so that each time you save the file it will be saved in this format.

> **Click** on Default format for file

Return to the previous dialog box.

> **Click** on OK

Appendix B: Notes for Microsoft Word Version 4 Users

Enter the name of the file and Click on OK to complete the saving process. Selecting Default format for file means that you do not need to go through this procedure if you change and resave this file. It will always be saved in the Microsoft Word 3.01 format unless specifically changed through the File format dialog box.

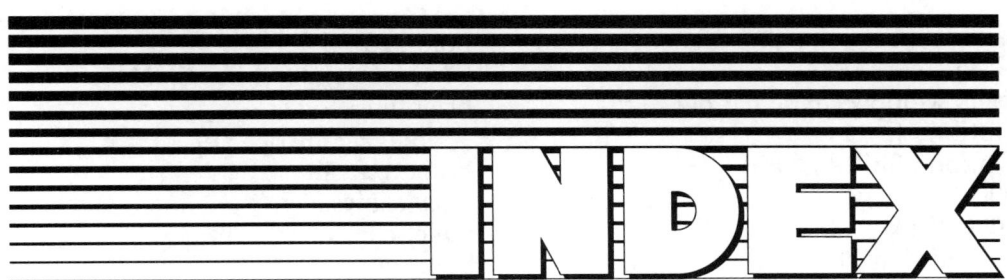

\+
    in styles, 122
    in window shade handle, 116
Option+[, 114
Option+Shift+[, 114
200% display, 8
50% display, 8
75% display, 8

A

abbreviations
    measurement, 234
actual size, 9
    screen display, 7
adding text blocks, 200
add new page, 265
alignment
    center, 27
    general, 27
    justified, 27
    left, 27
    right, 27
    tabs, 74
apply styles, 134
    multiple-line selections, 142
aspect ratio, 301
auto leading, 59
autoflow command, 181 - 182
automatic flow, 180

B

bars
    scroll screen, 12
base style, 137 - 138
big first letter, 213 - 218
black and white
    image control, 314 - 315
blocks
    text, 29

bold, 20
    Command+Shift+b, 22
brightness
    image control, 319
bring to front
    graphics, 97
bullet character, 108
bullet symbol, 32
bullets, 33, 141

C

case, 58
change display
    Command+Option+Click, 8
clipboard, 297
    copy graphics, 364
    show, 334 - 335
codes
    style symbols, 225
columns
    general, 173 - 176
    hyphenation, 189
    layout, 231
    spread text, 196
    text flow, 185
combining text and graphics, 330
Command+1
    actual size, 10
    tabs, 76
Command+2
    200% size, 10
Command+5
    50% size, 10
Command+7
    75% size, 10
Command+a
    select all, 28
Command+b
    send to back, 98, 278
Command+c

copy, 36
Command+d
   place text, 111
Command+Delete
   delete space, 65
Command+e
   style palette, 121
Command+m
   paragraph attributes, 60
Command+Option+Click
   change display, 8
Command+Option+p
   page number, 162
Command+p
   print, 42
Command+period
   stop print, 44
Command+s
   save, 47
Command+Shift+/
   strike through, 22
Command+Shift+3
   screen capture, 299
Command+Shift+arrow, 20
Command+Shift+b
   bold, 22
Command+Shift+c
   center, 27
Command+Shift+d
   outline, 22
Command+Shift+Delete
   add space, 65
Command+Shift+i
   italic, 22
Command+Shift+j
   justified, 27
Command+Shift+L
   left, 27
Command+Shift+r
   right, 27

Command+Shift+space
   normal, 22
Command+Shift+u
   underline, 22
Command+Shift+w
   shadow, 22
Command+t
   type specifications, 57
Command+u
   snap to guides, 204
Command+v
   paste, 36
Command+w
   fit to window, 10
Command+x
   cut, 36
Command+y
   snap to rulers, 237
compress file, 292
continue story, 266 - 268,
   271 - 273, 275
   text blocks, 149
contrast
   image control, 319
copy
   styles, 125, 177 - 178
   text blocks, 68
copy style dialog box, 179
copy text, 36
copyright symbol, 32
create
   document, 3
crop mode, 309 - 312
cropping
   graphics, 309 - 312
   panning image, 309 - 312
   sizing frame, 309 - 312
   toolbox, 17
customized styles, 124
cut and paste, 36

D

DA Mover
    fonts, 22
define styles, 124
define styles dialog box, 125
delete tabs, 81
diagonal line
    toolbox, 16
dialog box
    copy style, 179
    define styles, 125
    edit styles, 127
    image control, 317
    insert pages, 265
    laser printer, 46
    place, 112
    PostScript options, 376
    preferences, 238
    tabs, 76
    tabs/indents, 157
    text wrap, 339
direct entry of text, 14
display
    200%, 8
    50%, 8
    75%, 8
    actual size, 7
    basics, 7
    dual-page, 232
    facing pages, 232
    fit to window, 8
    greeked text, 40
    mode, 7
document
    create new, 3
draw mode, 84
drawing
    bring to front, 97
    enclosed area, 95
    frame around graphics, 347

line styles, 85
lines, 84
outlines, 95
perpendicular lines, 94
points, 85
rectangle, 88
select graphics, 89
send to back, 97
shading, 95
shading 10%, 97
text blocks, 203
drop shadows
    graphics, 99 - 101
dual-page display, 232

E

edit
    styles, 128 - 129
    text, 14
ending a page, 145 - 146
entry of text, 14
EPS files, 378
Excel
    charts, 364
    graphics, 297
    import into PageMaker, 366
    paste chart, 370
    save as text, 363
Excel spreadsheets, 361 - 362

F

facing pages display, 232
file
    compress, 292
    graphic, 300
    new, 3
    save, 47
files
    copy, 251

printer format, 377
read tags, 253
template, 251
tiles.eps, 298
first letter 213 - 218
fit to window display, 8
fixed leading, 59
flow
   text, 180
   text and graphics, 337
   text automatic, 180 - 182
   text semi-automatic, 183
font
   text, 19
fonts
   Font/DA Mover, 22
   scaled, 22
   screen, 22
footer
   master pages, 163
format
   override styles, 122
formatting
   change styles, 135 - 136
   first line, 143 - 144
   manual, 118
   paragraph indents, 139
   settings, 119
   with styles, 117

G

graphics
   add buttons to frame, 354
   adjust graphics frame, 352 - 353
   black and white, 314 - 315
   bring to front, 97
   buttons, 89
   combine with text, 330
   cropping of, 309 - 312
   draw frame, 347
   drop shadows, 99 - 101
   enclosed area, 95
   graphics frame, 352
   image control, 313
   image files, 295
   move, 90
   multiple objects, 92
   newsletter, 250
   perpendicular lines, 94
   screened, 315
   selection of, 89
   send to back, 97, 278
   shading, 95
      10%, 97
   size image, 303 - 306
   spread across pages, 345
   text flow around, 337
graphics files
   bit mapped, 296
   draw-type, 296
   EPS, 297
   paint-type, 296
   TIFF, 296
greeked text, 40
guides
   adjusting of, 279 - 280
   column guides, 173 - 176
   custom, 240 - 242
   horizontal, 240 - 242
   master columns, 174 - 176
   master pages, 231
   page-by-page, 174 - 176
   rulers, 240 - 242
   snap to, 204

H

handles
   # handle, 116
   + handle, 116
   blank handle, 116

window shade handle, 40 - 41
header
   master pages, 163
hyphenation
   auto, 191
   general, 189
   paragraph, 61
   prompted, 191

I

icons
   master page, 160
image control
   16 levels, 326
   black and white, 314 - 315
   brightness, 319
   contrast, 319
   dialog box, 317
   general, 313
   icons, 315
   line-pattern images, 319
   manual contrast, 328
   negative image, 316
   positive image, 316
      posterized image, 316, 326
   screened, 315
   screened images, 318
   solarized image, 316
   TIFF images, 323
   tone bars, 316, 328
import
   spreadsheet data, 361 - 362
   styles, 125, 177 - 178, 253
   text from spreadsheets, 363, 366
import text, 111
importing text, 14
inches
   rulers, 233
indents
   first line, 143 - 144
   hanging, 152
   negative indents, 153
   paragraph, 61, 139
   positive indents, 153
insert
   page, 265
   text block, 205 - 212
   text blocks, 200
insert pages
   dialog box, 265
irregular shapes
   text wrap, 349, 353 - 354
italic, 20
   Command+Shift+i, 22

K

kerning
   add space, 65
   delete space, 65
   paragraph, 61, 64
keyboard
   selection, 20

L

laser printer dialog box, 46
laser printers, 45
leaders
   tabs, 79
leading
   type, 58
letterhead
   example of, 55
lift effect, 205 - 212
line-pattern images
   image control, 319
lines
   drawing, 84

ruling lines, 84
linking styles, 137 - 138
linked blocks, 205

M

manual flow, 180
manual page numbering, 159
margins
    change default, 110
    changing default, 6
    default, 6
    inside, 5
    of page, 5
    outside, 5
    set, 5
master page
    text wrap, 343
master pages
    columns, 173 - 176
    footer, 163
    general, 160
    guides, 231
    header, 163
    icons, 160
    page numbers, 160
    repeating text, 163
    suppress items, 334
masthead
    newsletter, 243 - 250
measurement
    abbreviations, 234
    preferences, 238
    rulers, 233
    table of units, 234
mode icons
    toolbox, 16
move
    text blocks, 199
move image within frame, 309, 312

multiple objects
    graphics, 92
multiple selection
    text blocks, 197

N

negative image
    image control, 316
new page, 145 - 146
newsletter
    boxed insert, 275 - 277
    continue story, 266 - 268, 271 - 273, 275
    graphics, 250
    masthead, 243 - 250
    place, 252, 259 - 263
    place story, 252, 259 - 263
    sidebar, 275 - 277
newsletters
    general, 223
normal
    Command+Shift+space, 22
numbers
    pages, 159

O

objects, 39
    bring to front, 97
    move, 39
    position, 39
    send to back, 97, 278
    text blocks, 54
Option+8
    bullet, 32, 108
Option+Drag
    scroll screen, 12
Option+g
    copyright symbol, 164
Options, 4

organization, 2
orientation 4
outline
    Command+Shift+d, 22
outlines
    drawing, 95
oval
    toolbox, 17
override
    styles, 122

P

page
    add new, 265
    double sided, 55
    end, 145 - 146
    graphics spread across, 345
    insert, 265
    insert page number, 162
    manual numbering, 159
    margins, 5
    master items, 334
    master pages, 160
    numbers, 159
    page number symbol, 162
    remove page, 291
    repeating numbers, 159
    start new page, 145 - 146
    suppress master items, 334
    threading, 146
    thumbnails, 165
page numbers
    master pages, 160
page setup, 3 - 4
page size, 4
PageMaker logo, 2
pages, 4
palette
    styles, 121
    toolbox, 16
paper size, 4
paragraph
    big first letter, 213 - 218
    first line, 143 - 144
    general, 60
    hanging indents, 152
    hyphenation, 61, 189
    indents, 61, 139
    kerning, 61, 64
    negative indents, 153
    positive indents, 153
    space before, 129
    spacing, 61
    tabs, 155
    tabs/indents, 156
paragraphs
    change style format, 135 - 136
    settings, 119
paste
    clipboard graphics, 370
paste text, 36
pasteboard, 13
perpendicular line
    toolbox, 17
perpendicular lines
    drawing, 94
photo.tif, 298
    image control, 323
picas
    rulers, 233
picture control, 313
place
    as new story, 113
    automatic sizing, 301
    convert quotes, 114
    dialog box, 112
    graphic image, 300
    import text, 111
    insert text, 113

manual placement, 115
manual sizing of graphics, 302
newsletter, 252, 259 - 263
read tags, 114, 253
replace story, 113
retain format, 114
size graphics, 301
spreadsheet text, 366
TIFF image, 323
with text tags, 224
place command, 111
point size, 19
pointer mode
   text blocks, 67
   toolbox, 16
points, 19
   rulers, 233
position
   type, 59
positive image
   image control, 316
posterized image
   image control, 316
PostScript options
   dialog box, 376
   printing, 374
PostScript printer files, 377
PostScript-resident fonts
   printing, 374
preferences
   dialog box, 238
   measurement, 238
   rulers, 238
prepare text documents
   word processing, 108
print
   document, 42
   stop print, 44
printer
   laser printers, 45
   ImageWriter, 43 - 44
printing
   document, 42
   download bit-mapped fonts, 373
   files, 377
   lasers, 45
   PostScript options, 374
   PostScript-resident fonts, 374
   reduced, 165
   scaled fonts, 373
   stop, 44
   substitute fonts, 373
   thumbnails, 165
printing to EPS files, 378
proportion
   graphic image, 301

Q

quotes
   convert, 114

R

ratio
   aspect, 301
read tags, 114
rectangle
   drawing, 88
remove
   styles, 131
   page 291
repeating
   text, 163
repeating items
   suppress on page, 334
repeating numbers
page, 159
repeating text
   footer, 163

    header, 163
    master pages, 163
rounded rectangle
    toolbox, 17
rulers
    cicero, 234
    guides, 240 - 242
    inches, 233
    measurement, 233
    picas, 233
    points, 233
    preferences, 238
    set, 235
    snap to, 237
    zero point, 235
ruling lines, 84

S

save
    document, 47
    file, 47
scaled fonts
    printing, 373
screen dump, 299
screen fonts, 22
screen image, 299
screen layout, 7
screened
    image control, 315
screened images
    image control, 318
scroll bars 12
scroll screen, 12
select graphics
    drawing, 89
selection
    add to selection, 197
    all text, 28
    apply styles, 142
    keyboard, 20

    multiple-line selections, 142
    multiple selection, 197
    Shift + Click, 197
    text blocks, 67
semi-automatic flow, 180
semi-automatic flow icon, 184
send to back
    graphics, 97, 278
set tabs, 80
shading
    drawing, 95, 97
shadow
    Command + Shift + w, 22
shape
    text blocks, 203
Shift + Click
    multiple selection, 197
Shift + Left arrow, 20
Shift + Right arrow, 20
show clipboard, 334 - 335
sidebar
    place in document, 275 - 277
size graphics
    place, 301
size image
    graphics, 303 - 306
snap
    to rulers, 237
    to guides, 204
solarized image
    image control, 316
spacing
    before paragraph, 129
    paragraph, 61
specifications
    type, 57
spreadsheets, 361 - 362
standoff
    text wrap, 341
stop printing, 44

story
    add text block, 200
    automatic flow, 180 - 182
    continue, 149, 266 - 268,
        271 - 273, 275
    general, 149
    in newsletter, 252, 259 - 263
    insert text block, 200
    interrupt, 205 - 212
    manual flow, 180
    semi-automatic flow, 180, 183
strike through
    Command+Shift+/, 22
style
    text, 20
styles
    + sign, 122
    apply, 134
    base style, 137 - 138
    body text, 120
    built-in, 120
    bullets, 141
    caption, 120
    change formats, 135 - 136
    copy, 177 - 178
    copy style, 125
    create, 120, 126
    customized, 124
    define styles, 124
    define styles dialog box, 125
    edit, 128 - 129, 138
    edit style, 125
    edit style dialog box, 127
    first-line exception, 143 - 144
    general, 117
    hanging indents, 152
    headline, 120
    import, 120, 177 - 178, 253
    indents, 139
    links, 137 - 138
    multiple-line selections, 142
    negative indents, 153
    new, 126
    new style, 124
    override, 122
    palette, 121, 134
    positive indents, 153
    read tags, 253
    remove, 131
    remove style, 125
    settings, 119
    style name, 124
    subhead 1, 120
    subhead 2, 120
    tabs, 155
    text tags, 224
    user-defined, 124
subscript
    type, 59
substitute fonts
    printing, 373
superscript
    type, 59
symbols
    text entry of, 31

T

tab, 34 - 35
tab stops, 74
tables
    tabs, 155
tabs
    alignment, 74, 78
    center, 78
    decimal, 78
    delete, 81
    dialog box, 76
    in text blocks, 74
    leaders, 79

    left, 78
    right, 78
    set stops, 80
    styles, 155
tabs/indents, 156
tabs/indents dialog box, 157
tags
    place story with, 253
    place text, 114
templates, 251
temporary automatic flow, 185
text, 19
    automatic flow, 180 - 182
    combine with graphics, 330
    copy, 36
    cut, 36
    flow, 180
    flow around, 337
    font, 19
    greeked, 40
    hyphenation, 189
    manual flow, 180
    paste, 36
    place command, 111
    repeating, 163
    semi-automatic flow, 180, 183
    size, 19
    special symbols, 31
    style, 20
    style symbols, 225
    temporary automatic flow, 185
    text blocks, 29
    toolbox, 17
    weights, 20
text attributes, 19
text block
    # handle, 116
    + handle, 116
    add, 200
    as objects, 54
    big first letter, 213 - 218
    blank handle, 116
    change shape, 203
    continue story, 149, 266 - 268, 271 - 273, 275
    copy, 68
    flow around graphics, 337
    general, 29
    insert, 29, 200, 205 - 212
    interrupt story, 205 - 212
    linked, 205
    logical order, 200
    move, 39, 66, 199, 284
    multiple, 53
    multiple selection, 197
    non-linked, 205
    physical order, 200
    place command, 115
    position, 39
    select, 67
    send to back, 278
    snap to guides, 204
    spread across columns, 196
    tabs, 74
    threading, 146, 149
    window shade handles, 40 - 41
text document
    Business, 228
    CORPORATIONS, 109
    Formalities, 227
    Setup Corp, 230
    Side Bar, 229
text entry, 14
text wrap
 dialog box, 339
    general, 337
    icons, 341
    irregular shapes, 349
    master page, 343
    standoff, 341

text flow, 340
wrap options, 340
text
   size, 19
   font, 19
   style, 20
threading
   text blocks, 146, 149
thumbnails
   printing, 165
TIFF image
   place, 323
TIFF images, 323, 329
tone bars
   image control, 316
toolbox, 16
   cropping, 17
   diagonal line, 16
   draw lines, 84
   oval, 17
   perpendicular line, 17
   rounded rectangle, 17
   selection mode, 16
   text, 17
trademark symbol, 32
transfer graphics, 297
transfer to photo typsetter, 377
type
   auto leading, 59
   case, 58
   fixed leading, 59
   leading, 58
   position, 59
   subscript, 59
   superscript, 59
type specifications, 57
typing text, 14

U

underline
   Command+Shift+u, 22

W

weights
   text, 20
window shade handles, 40 - 41
   # handle, 116
   + handle, 116
   blank handle, 116
word processing
   prepare text documents, 108
   prepared with tags, 224
   text entry, 14
word processor
   read tags, 253
work area
   pasteboard, 13

Z

zero point
   rulers, 235

RELATED TITLES FROM MIS:PRESS

WordPerfect for the Macintosh
For the user who wants to take full advantage of the power of WordPerfect for the Macintosh, this book documents, in step-by-step fashion, all the major features included in the Macintosh version of this best-selling word processor. It also includes an introductory section for PC and WordPerfect users coming to the Macintosh for the first time.
Rob Krumm   0-943518-91-1 $19.95

WordPerfect 5.0 for IBM PCs and Compatibles
First-time users and WordPerfect veterans will find this comprehensive, step-by-step guide a streetwise sourcebook to the best-selling word processor for IBM PCs and compatibles. Contains everything you need to know, including 5.0's new desktop publishing features.
Rob Krumm   0-943518-97-0 $19.95

Ventura 2.0
This book is a sure cure to desktop publishing headaches with Ventura Publisher version 2.0 for the IBM. Krumm delivers a clearly written, comprehensive guide that quickly teaches users how to make the most of this powerful software. Includes basic editing, graphics, fonts, page layout, format and document creation, as well as 2.0's new table generation and color separation features.
Rob Krumm   1-55828-006-5 $22.95

Running HyperCard with HyperTalk
This book teaches you how to build applications with HyperTalk inside HyperCard. Includes a complete HyperTalk reference guide covering the basics of HyperTalk's object-oriented programming principles. Brief examples of HyperTalk scripts are used to demonstrate key points.
Barry Shell   0-943518-79-2 $19.95   w/disk $39.95

Concise Guide to HyperTalk
This book, based on Apple's HyperTalk language syntax, serves as a quick reference guide for users who want to create custom HyperCard applications. Information in each chapter is organized alphabetically for easy referencing. Brief examples of HyperTalk are used throughout the book to demonstrate key points.
BarryShell   0-943518-84-9 $9.95

XCMDs for HyperCard
Pascal and C programmers who want to develop new programming skills using HyperCard should grab this guide. This definitive step-by-step reference shows how to create and use HyperCard's external commands (XCMD's) and functions (XFCN's), create new commands, and extend and customize commands to specific programming needs. It defines XCMD's and XFCN's and tells you how to call them from HyperTalk, fit them into the inheritance path, and much more.
Gary Bond   0-943518-85-7 $24.95 w/disk $49.95

Teach Yourself C
From concepts to cutting code, there's no better introduction to C programming for the IBM. Readers learn skills they'll use for a lifetime—program structure, numbers and arrays, variables, input/output, strings, menu creation, data storage, and more. You will begin writing simple programs and then progress gradually to more extenisve programs—like those professional programmers create. Also includes special help getting started with TurboC and QuickC.
Charles Siegel   0-943518-99-7 $19.95

MANAGEMENT INFORMATION SOURCE, INC.
P.O. Box 5277 • Portland, OR 97208-5277
(503) 222-2399

*A*vailable where fine books are sold.

*C*all free
1-800-MANUALS

M A N A G E M E N T   I N F O R M A T I O N   S O U R C E ,   I N C .